CIM
STUDY TEXT

Advanced Certificate

Effective Management for Marketing

New in this July 2001 edition

- Updated in response to review commissioned on behalf of CIM
- New section on continuous assessment
- Updated Marketing at Work examples

BPP Publishing
July 2001

First edition June 1999
Third edition July 2001

ISBN 0 7517 4118 3 (previous edition 07517 4106 X)

British Library Cataloguing-in-Publication Data
A catalogue record for this book
is available from the British Library

Published by

BPP Publishing Limited
Aldine House, Aldine Place
London W12 8AW

www.bpp.com

Printed in Great Britain by Universal Progressive

All our rights reserved. No part of this publication may be reproduced, stored in a retrieval system or transmitted, in any form or by any means, electronic, mechanical, photocopying, recording or otherwise, without the prior written permission of BPP Publishing Limited.

We are grateful to the Chartered Institute of Marketing for permission to reproduce in this text the syllabus, tutor's guidance notes, personal development plans and past examination questions. We are also grateful to Karen Beamish of Stone Consulting for preparing continuous assessment material.

BPP Publishing Limited
2001

Contents

	Page
HOW TO USE THIS STUDY TEXT	(v)
SYLLABUS	(x)
TUTOR'S GUIDANCE NOTES AND WEBSITE LINKS	(xii)
THE EXAM PAPER	(xiv)
STUDY CHECKLIST	(xvii)
CONTINUOUS ASSESSMENT	(xviii)

- Aims and objectives • Structure and process • Preparing for assignments
- Presentation of the assignment • Time management for assignments • Tips for writing assignments • Writing reports • Assignment 1 : Personal Development Portfolio for Effective Management for Marketing • Core and optional assignments (examples: internal marketing; team management)

PART A: THE NATURE OF MANAGEMENT AND ORGANISATION ISSUES
1	Managing the examination	3
2	What is management?	15

PART B: PERSONAL EFFECTIVENESS
3	What makes a good manager?	45
4	Time management	66
5	The manager as a communicator	88

PART C: MANAGING PEOPLE
6	Managing the team	137
7	Recruitment and selection	160
8	Improving team performance	186
9	Managing change	223
10	Managing client relations	240

PART D: INTERNATIONAL INFLUENCES ON MANAGEMENT STYLE
11	International influences on management	265

PART E: REVIEWING YOUR PROGRESS
12	Reviewing your progress	291

ILLUSTRATIVE QUESTIONS	305
SUGGESTED ANSWERS	311
LIST OF KEY CONCEPTS	345

Contents

	Marks
INDEX	346
ORDER FORM	
REVIEW FORM & FREE PRIZE DRAW	

HOW TO USE THIS STUDY TEXT

Aims of this Study Text

To provide you with the knowledge and understanding, skills and applied techniques required for passing the exam

The Study Text has been written around the new CIM Syllabus and the CIM's Tutor's Guidance notes (reproduced below, and cross-referenced to where in the text each topic is covered).

- It is **comprehensive**. We do not omit sections of the syllabus as the examiner is liable to examine any angle of any part of the syllabus - and you do not want to be left high and dry.
- It is **on-target** - we do not include any material which is not examinable. You can therefore rely on the BPP Study Text as the stand-alone source of all your information for the exam, without worrying that any of the material is irrelevant.

To allow you to study in the way that best suits your learning style and the time you have available, by following your personal Study Plan (see below)

You may be studying at home on your own until the date of the exam, or you may be attending a full-time course. You may like to (and have time to) read every word, or you may prefer to (or only have time to) skim-read and devote the remainder of your time to question practice. Wherever you fall in the spectrum, you will find the BPP Study Text meets your needs in designing and following your personal Study Plan.

To tie in with the other components of the BPP Effective Study Package to ensure you have the best possible chance of passing the exam

Recommended period of use	Elements of BPP Effective Study Package
3-12 months before exam	**Study Text** Acquisition of knowledge, understanding, skills and applied techniques
1-6 months before exam	**Practice and Revision Kit (9/2001)** Tutorial questions and helpful checklists of the key points lead you into each area. There are then numerous Examination questions to try, graded by topic area, along with realistic suggested solutions prepared by marketing professionals in the light of the Examiner's Reports.
1–6 months before exam	**Success Tapes** Audio cassettes covering the vital elements of your syllabus in less than 90 minutes per subject. Each tape also contains exam hints to help you fine tune your strategy.

How to use this Study Text

Settling down to study

By this stage in your career you may be a very experienced learner and taker of exams. But have you ever thought about *how* you learn? Let's have a quick look at the key elements required for effective learning. You can then identify your learning style and go on to design your own approach to how you are going to study this text - your personal Study Plan.

Key element of learning	Using the BPP Study Text
Motivation	You can rely on the comprehensiveness and technical quality of BPP. You've chosen the right Study Text - so you're in pole position to pass your exam!
Clear objectives and standards	Do you want to be a prizewinner or simply achieve a moderate pass? Decide.
Feedback	Follow through the examples in this text and do the Action Programme and the Quick quizzes. Evaluate your efforts critically - how are you doing?
Study Plan	You need to be honest about your progress to yourself - do not be over-confident, but don't be negative either. Make your Study Plan (see below) and try to stick to it. Focus on the short-term objectives – completing two chapters a night, say - but beware of losing sight of your study objectives
Practice	Use the Quick quizzes and Chapter roundups to refresh your memory regularly after you have completed your initial study of each chapter

These introductory pages let you see exactly what you are up against. However you study, you should:

- **Read through the syllabus and teaching guide** - this will help you to identify areas you have already covered, perhaps at a lower level of detail, and areas that are totally new to you

- **Study the examination paper section,** where we show you the format of the exam (how many and what kind of questions and so on)

Key study steps

The following steps are, in our experience, the ideal way to study for professional exams. You can of course adapt it for your particular learning style (see below).

Tackle the chapters in the order you find them in the Study Text. Taking into account your individual learning style, follow these key study steps for each chapter.

Key study steps	Activity
Step 1 *Chapter topic list*	Study the list. Each numbered topic denotes a **numbered section** in the chapter.
Step 2 *Setting the scene*	Read it through. It is designed to show you **why the topics in the chapter need to be studied** - how they lead on from previous topics, and how they lead into subsequent ones.
Step 3 *Explanations*	Proceed **methodically** through the chapter, reading each section thoroughly and making sure you understand.
Step 4 *Key concepts*	**Key concepts** can often earn you **easy marks** if you state them clearly and correctly in an appropriate exam.
Step 5 *Exam tips*	These give you a good idea of how the examiner tends to examine certain topics – pinpointing **easy marks** and highlighting **pitfalls**.
Step 6 *Note taking*	Take **brief notes** if you wish, avoiding the temptation to copy out too much.
Step 7 *Marketing at Work*	Study each one, and try if you can to add flesh to them from your **own experience** - they are designed to show how the topics you are studying come alive (and often come unstuck) in the **real world**.
Step 8 *Action Programme*	Make a very good attempt at each one in each chapter. These are designed to put your **knowledge into practice** in much the same way as you will be required to do in the exam. Check the answer at the end of the chapter in the **Action Programme review**, and make sure you understand the reasons why yours may be different.
Step 9 *Chapter roundup*	Check through it very carefully, to make sure you have grasped the **major points** it is highlighting.
Step 10 *Quick quiz*	When you are happy that you have covered the chapter, use the **Quick quiz** to check your recall of the topics covered. The answers are in the paragraphs in the chapter that we refer you to.
Step 11 *Illustrative questions*	Either at this point, or later when you are thinking about revising, make a full attempt at the **illustrative questions**. You can find these at the end of the Study Text, along with the **Answers** so you can see how you did.

How to use this Study Text

Developing your personal Study Plan

Preparing a Study Plan (and sticking closely to it) is one of the key elements in learning success.

First you need to be aware of your style of learning. There are four typical learning styles. Consider yourself in the light of the following descriptions. and work out which you fit most closely. You can then plan to follow the key study steps in the sequence suggested.

Learning styles	Characteristics	Sequence of key study steps in the BPP Study Text
Theorist	Seeks to understand principles before applying them in practice	1, 2, 3, 7, 4, 5, 8, 9, 10, 11 (6 continuous)
Reflector	Seeks to observe phenomena, thinks about them and then chooses to act	
Activist	Prefers to deal with practical, active problems; does not have much patience with theory	1, 2, 8 (read through), 7, 4, 5, 9, 3, 8 (full attempt), 10, 11 (6 continuous)
Pragmatist	Prefers to study only if a direct link to practical problems can be seen; not interested in theory for its own sake	8 (read through), 2, 4, 5, 7, 9, 1, 3, 8 (full attempt), 10, 11 (6 continuous)

Next you should complete the following checklist.

Am I motivated? (a)

Do I have an objective and a standard that I want to achieve? (b)

Am I a theorist, a reflector, an activist or a pragmatist? (c)

How much time do I have available per week, given: (d)

- the standard I have set myself
- the time I need to set aside later for work on the Practice and Revision Kit and Passcards
- the other exam(s) I am sitting, and (of course)
- practical matters such as work, travel, exercise, sleep and social life?

Now:

- take the time you have available per week for this Study Text (d), and multiply it by the number of weeks available to give (e). (e)
- divide (e) by the number of chapters to give (f) (f)
- set about studying each chapter in the time represented by (f), following the key study steps in the order suggested by your particular learning style.

This is your personal **Study Plan**.

Short of time?

Whatever your objectives, standards or style, you may find you simply do not have the time available to follow all the key study steps for each chapter, however you adapt them for your particular learning style. If this is the case, follow the Skim Study technique below (the icons in the Study Text will help you to do this).

Skim Study technique

Study the chapters in the order you find them in the Study Text. For each chapter, follow the key study steps 1-2, and then skim-read through step 3. Jump to step 9, and then go back to steps 4-5. Follow through step 7, and prepare outline Answers to the Action Programme (step 8). Try the Quick quiz (step 10), following up any items you can't answer, then do a plan for the Examination question (step 11), comparing it against our answers. You should probably still follow step 6 (note-taking), although you may decide simply to rely on the BPP Passcards for this.

Moving on...

However you study, when you are ready to embark on the practice and revision phase of the BPP Effective Study Package, you should still refer back to this Study Text:

- as a source of **reference** (you should find the list of key concepts and the index particularly helpful for this)

- as a **refresher** (the Chapter roundups and Quick quizzes help you here).

A note on pronouns

On occasions in this Study Text, 'he' is used for 'he or she', 'him' for 'him or her' and so forth. Whilst we try to avoid this practice it is sometimes necessary for reasons of style. No prejudice or stereotyping according to sex is intended or assumed.

Syllabus

SYLLABUS

Aims and objectives

- To examine organisational theory and its impact on marketing management practice

- To introduce the concepts of management theory and examine their effectiveness in practice

- To relate management theory and practice to the role of marketing and how marketing activities can be improved

- To introduce the concepts and consequences of change management and marketing's role in managing change

- To introduce international influences on current management practice

- To develop and enhance personal effectiveness and the key skills required within a marketing management context

Learning outcomes

Students will be able to:

- Describe the organisation cultures and their positive and negative impact on marketing management

- Explain the theory underpinning effective management of self, other people, resources and client relationships

- Describe the principles of managing change that minimises resistance and maximises successful outcomes and the role of marketing in the management of change and achieving a marketing orientation

- Determine communications problems typically faced by managers and describe strategies for improving and solving these problems

- Explain the principles and techniques of successful negotiation with internal colleagues and external customers, suppliers, distributors etc with a view to mutually successful outcomes

- Undertake a personal skills audit, using mechanisms introduced on courses, with the intention of identifying personal strengths and weaknesses and planning and implementing improvements. Students will be encouraged to identify continuous professional development opportunities

- Describe the role of human resource management planning and its contribution to ensuring effective levels of marketing staffing and skills

- Devise training and development plans for marketing personnel to improve individual and team effectiveness

- Devise methods for motivating marketing staff to improve individual and team effectiveness

- Explain concepts of building and managing effective teams and the role of leadership

- Describe international influences on management practice and their uses and abuses

Syllabus

Covered in chapter

1	**The nature of management and organisation issues (15%)**	
1.1	Changing nature of business.	1
1.2	Organisation cultures and their impact on marketing management practice	1
1.3	The role and functions of the manager	1
2	**Personal effectiveness (30%)**	
2.1	The responsibilities and activities of the marketing manager and leadership styles	2, 6
2.2	Personal skills audits and improving management performance	3
2.3	Improving time management, delegation, managing meetings, problem solving and decision making	2, 4, 5
2.4	Interpersonal communications effectiveness (verbal, non verbal, listening skills, negotiating, internal marketing, handling discipline and grievances)	5, 8, 9
2.5	HRM planning for marketing jobs, tasks and marketing personnel	7
3	**Managing people (40%)**	
3.1	Managing and improving effectiveness of individuals	3, 4, 8
3.2	Managing and building effective teams	3, 6, 8
3.3	Motivation and improving marketing job satisfaction	8
3.4	The role of marketing personnel appraisals	8
3.5	Improving marketing personnel performance - training and development	8
3.6	Managing client relationships, customer service and conducting negotiations	10
3.7	Managing change effectively through individuals and teams	9
3.8	Knowledge management	5
4	**International influences on management style (15%)**	
4.1	Different management perspectives and their values	11
4.2	Problems encountered by global organisations	11
4.3	Managing across borders	11

Tutor's guidance notes

TUTOR'S GUIDANCE NOTES

The following is BPP's summary of the Tutor Manual produced by the CIM for this subject.

The aim of this subject is to equip marketers with the knowledge and skills needed to bridge a perceived gap in marketing management capability. The emphasis is on providing inputs into other organisational functions to promote a high standard of customer service.

Students should be aware that business success in the future will depend upon effective management of people. The subject emphasises:

- Leadership, motivation and team building
- All forms of management communication
- Internal and external negotiation
- Human resource aspects including appraisal and development
- Understanding organisation structure and culture and managing change.

International influences on management has been introduced to the syllabus to form an introduction to International Marketing Strategy at Diploma level.

Students should aim to develop a critical awareness of the management practices they encounter in the workplace, keeping appropriate notes and records.

The first section of the syllabus, Nature of Management and Organisation Issues, is intended to provide an overview of management and the business environment. Students should understand that management roles vary from company to company and that culture is rarely as simple in practice as in theory.

The Personal Effectiveness part of the syllabus should be approached with a clear marketing orientation to management. Clear analysis is needed so that realistic objectives can be set and improvement opportunities identified. 'Leadership styles, time management techniques and communication styles ...must be adapted to suit the circumstances within which they are practised. Human resource planning can only be effective if the organisation is actively involved in effective strategic planning.'

A similar clear marketing orientation is needed for the Managing People part of the syllabus. Motivation is a key management activity. Training should address clear objectives and should be evaluated. Organisational change should be accepted as a reality and managed rationally. Current activities and performance should be evaluated and the people who will have to implement change must be included in the planning process.

The International Influences on Management Style section should emphasise the need to understand the impact of management style in different cultural environments and bear it in mind as management practice evolves.

Websources

As indicated above, you need to read a variety of sources to do well in this paper, including Internet sites. With this in mind, the CIM has listed a number of relevant websites for each part of the syllabus.

Tutor's guidance notes

These web addresses have been extracted from the CIM's on-line tutor support.

Syllabus Section	Web Address	Description
The Nature of Management and Organisation Issues	www.employ.co.uk	Provides useful information on employment law for employers and employees.
	www.dti.gov.uk/ir.index.htrm	Useful information on employment relations, latest legislation, research on labour markets and employment practices such as minimum wage and parental leave.
	www.inst.mgt.org.uk	Excellent website of the Institute of Management, with extensive libraries, events, case studies and links.
Personal Effectiveness	www.human-resources.org	Human Resource Learning Centre. Site contains free executive summaries of articles on change management, interpersonal skills, leadership skills, benchmarking etc.
	www.srg.co.uk	The Self Renewal Group - provides useful tips on managing your time, leading others, managing human resources, motivating others etc.
	www.balancetime.com	The Productivity Institute provides free articles, a time management email newsletter, and other resources to improve personal productivity.
	www.lifelonglearning.co.uk	Encourages and promotes Lifelong Learning through press releases, free articles, useful links and progress reports on the development of the University for Industry (UFI).
Managing People	www.greatplacetowork.gov.uk	Contains HRM case studies of staff development, motivation and training.
	www.ipd.co.uk	The Professional Practice section of the Institute for Personnel Development site provides access to papers on best practice, key facts and survey reports.
	www.iipuk.co.uk	The public body responsible for the Investors in People Standard.
International Management	www.mckinseyquarterly.com (see 'economic performance' section)	Free full text articles on globalisation, economic development and cultural issues from one of the world's premier business journals
	www.eiu.com	The Organisation for Economic Cooperation and Development site links to articles, policy documents and other extensive resources on global trading issues, labour market deregulation and social policies.
		The Economist Intelligence Unit provides detailed reports and other information about establishing and managing operations across national borders.

The exam paper

THE EXAM PAPER

Assessment methods and format of the paper

	Number of marks
Section A: one compulsory case study, with related questions	40
Section B: three questions from six (20 marks each)	60
	100

Time allowed: 3 hours

Analysis of past papers

June 2001

Part A (compulsory case study: 40 marks)

1   An article about teleworking in the context of a computer company
    (a) Problems and implications of teleworking
    (b) Managing the teleworking workforce

Part B (three from six: 20 marks each)

2   Winning back a client
3   Managing international differences
4   Personal improvement plan
5   Marketing research managers
6   Outsourcing marketing skills
7   Launching a new product range

December 2000

Part A (compulsory case study: 40 marks)

1   A publicly-funded theatre company is implementing a change programme and seeking to enhance the brand
    (a) Auditing internal communications
    (b) Induction programme to improve newly recruited actors' perceptions of the company
    (c) Internal communications plan to improve motivation and its value to the brand

Part B (three from six: 20 marks each)

2   Appraisal system to improve service performance in a travel agency
3   Recruiting business-to-business marketers
4   Improving customer service in response to complaints
5   Leadership and its role in turning round poor performance
6   Managing change
7   Improving customer focus in a 'technical skills' orientated culture

The exam paper

June 2000

Part A (compulsory case study: 40 marks)

1. Multi-unit managers in the hospitality industry now manage a number of units within a single brand, rather than being responsible for all the brands within an area. They must deploy a wide range of managerial skills including those relating to people management and marketing.
   (a) Describe the skills, experience and special attributes needed by a multi-unit manager
   (b) Produce a plan for a 6 month induction programme for multi-unit managers without prior experience of the hospitality industry
   (c) Produce a training and development programme to cover the two years following induction

Part B (three from six: 20 marks each)

2. Personal skills audit
3. Gaining commitment to change
4. Dealing with a grievance interview
5. Internal negotiation
6. Improving efficiency and time management
7. National cultural differences and marketing management

December 1999 (first new syllabus sitting)

Part A (compulsory case study: 40 marks)

1. A medium sized manufacturing company has undergone change over the last 6 years with mixed results. Internal and external surveys have revealed low morale and reduced customer satisfaction. A report is required by the Chief Executive
   (a) Outline the findings of the surveys
   (b) Recommend how to achieve marketing orientation
   (c) Address the shortage of marketing skills

Part B (three from six: 20 marks each)

2. Time management action plan
3. Building teams in an individual-focussed culture
4. Negotiation between production and sales
5. Purpose, process and benefits of appraisals
6. Management style for a flexible and responsive organisation
7. Role of human resource planning

Old syllabus

June 1999

Part A (compulsory case study: 40 marks)

1. A train operating company addresses working relationships within the UK railway system, with a view to improving customer service.
   (a) Improving relationships
   (b) Reasons for improvement
   (c) Implications for marketing management
   (d) Controls for ensuring success

The exam paper

Part B (three from six: 20 marks each)

2 Personal skills audit (report)
3 Induction programme for new recruits (plan)
4 Conflict resolution in a field sales team (action plan)
5 Increasing the efficiency and effectiveness of meetings
6 Improving motivation in a charitable organisation (report)
7 Managing change and fostering customer focus (report)

December 1998

Part A (compulsory case study: 40 marks)

Banks are dealing with a major increase in their use of temporary staff.

1 (a) Communications
  (b) Team management
  (c) Customer service

Part B (three from six: 20 marks each)

2 Sales teams and customer groups
3 Appraisal scheme introduction and benefits
4 Management development for enhanced corporate effectiveness
5 Dealing with customers: staff development
6 Motivation and change management
7 Customer relations: improving customer care

June 1998

Part A (compulsory case study: 40 marks)

A computer company is expanding.

1 (a) Implications of growing workforce: recruitment and induction
  (b) Imposing consistent company culture
  (c) Development of internal communications

Part B (three from six: 20 marks each)

2 Improving customer service and satisfaction
3 Problems with performance of team member
4 Implications of changes in organisational structure
5 Performance of new product development team
6 Appointment of a charity's marketing manager
7 Reorganisation of sales and marketing team

STUDY CHECKLIST

This page is designed to help you chart your progress through the Study Text, including the Action Programme and illustrative questions. You can tick off each topic as you study and try questions on it. Insert the dates you complete the chapter's Action Programme and questions in the relevant boxes. You will thus ensure that you are on track to complete your study before the exam.

	Text chapters Date completed	Action programme Number	Action programme Date completed	Illustrative questions Number	Illustrative questions Date Completed

PART A: THE NATURE OF MANAGEMENT AND ORGANISATION ISSUES

1 Managing the examination				1	
2 What is management?				2	

PART B: PERSONAL EFFECTIVENESS

3 What makes a good manager?				3	
4 Time management				4	
5 The manager as a communicator				5, 6, 7	

PART C: MANAGING PEOPLE

6 Managing the team				8, 9	
7 Recruitment and selection				10	
8 Improving team performance				11, 12, 13, 14	
9 Managing change				15	
10 Managing client relations				16, 17	

PART D: INTERNATIONAL INFLUENCES ON MANAGEMENT STYLE

11 International influences on management				24	

PART E: REVIEWING YOUR PROGRESS

12 Reviewing your progress					

Continuous assessment

GUIDE TO CONTINUOUS ASSESSMENTS: EFFECTIVE MANAGEMENT FOR MARKETING

- Aims and objectives of this guide
- Introduction
- Continuous assessment structure and process
- Preparing for assignments: general guide
- Presentation
- Time management
- Tips for writing assignments
- Writing reports

Aims and objectives of this *Guide to Continuous Assessments*

- To understand the scope and structure of the Continuous Assessment process
- To consider the benefits of learning through continuous assessment
- To assist students in preparation of their assignments
- To consider the range of communication options available to students
- To provide assistance in the development of the Personal Development Portfolio (PDP)
- To look at the range of potential assessment areas that assignments may challenge
- To assist with time-management within the assessment process

Introduction

It is now over five years since the Chartered Institute of Marketing (CIM) introduced continuous assessment (ie assignment based assessment) as an alternative to the examination process.

At time of writing, there are over 80 CIM Approved Study Centres that offer the Continuous Assessment option as an alternative to examinations. This change in direction and flexibility in assessment was externally driven by industry, students and tutors alike, all of whom wanted a test of practical skills as well as a knowledge-based approach to learning.

At the Advanced Certificate level, both *Effective Management for Marketing,* the basis of this particular module, and *Marketing Operations* can be assessed through an assignment route as opposed to the examination due to the practical nature of both syllabuses, which cover marketing in practice as well as marketing theory.

Clearly, both of these subject areas lend themselves to assignment-based learning, due to their practical nature. The assignments that you will undertake provide you with an opportunity to be **creative in approach and in presentation.** They enable you to give a true demonstration of your marketing ability in a way that perhaps might be inhibited in a traditional examination situation.

Continuous assessment offers you considerable scope to produce work that provides existing and future **employers** with **evidence** of your **ability.** It offers you a **portfolio** of evidence which demonstrates your abilities and your willingness to develop continually your knowledge and skills. It will also, ultimately, help you frame your continuing professional development in the future.

It does not matter what type of organisation you are from, large or small, as you will find substantial benefit in this approach to learning. In some cases, students have made their own organisation central to their assessment and produced work to support their organisation's activities, resulting in subsequent recognition and promotion: a success story for this approach.

So, using your own organisation can be beneficial (especially if your employer sponsors you). However, it is equally valid to use a different organisation, as long as you are familiar enough with it to base your assignments on it. This is particularly useful if you are between jobs, taking time out, returning to employment or studying at university or college.

To take the Continuous Assessment option, you are required to register with a CIM Accredited Study Centre (ie a college, university, or distance learning provider). **Currently you would be unable to take the Continuous Assessment option as an independent learner.** If in doubt you should contact the CIM Education Division who will provide you with a list of local Accredited Centres offering Continuous Assessment.

Structure and process

The **assignments** that you will undertake during your studies are set **by CIM centrally** and not by the study centre. This standardised approach to assessment enables external organisations to interpret the results on a consistent basis.

There are three assignments per module.

- Assignment 1: Personal Development Portfolio Assignment
- Assignment 2: Core assignment
- Assignment 3: Optional Assignment

The purpose of each assignment is to enable you to demonstrate your ability to research, analyse and problem-solve in a range of different situations. You will be expected to approach your assignment work from a professional marketer's perspective, addressing the assignment brief directly, and undertaking the tasks required. Each assignment will relate directly to the syllabus module and will be applied against the content of the syllabus.

Assignment 1

The Personal Development Portfolio will run for the duration of your module, maximising your potential to show your own personal development through your learning. This assignment is singularly about **you** and how, through a range of activities, you **develop your strengths** and start to **address your weaknesses**. We will be looking at your overall approach to this assignment later in this unit.

Assignment 2

Assignment 2 is a core assignment. It is mandatory, so all students will be taking this assignment.

Assignment 3

However, Assignment 3 enables students to choose from four assignment options. In doing this, students will be able to select the assignment most appropriate to their individual needs, of a greatest personal benefit.

You will typically have six weeks to complete Assignments 2 and 3, from the time the assignment brief is issued until the submission date. This is a national standard set by CIM, and is a maximum period for the assessment work to be undertaken. Clearly, time management will be an issue with these two assignments in particular. Again, we will be looking at this issue shortly.

Whilst we can focus clearly upon the Personal Development Portfolio in Assignment 1, the bases of **Assignments 2 and 3 are not known in advance** (like an examination situation). This has been established as good practice so that no one student or study centre is advantaged over another. Therefore, all students will receive the assignments 2 and 3 as 'unseens'. Although we do not know

Continuous assessment

what the themes for the Assignments 2 and 3 will be, we can look at **potential** themes in order to focus your minds on typical approaches that you might take.

All of the Assignments clearly indicate the links with the syllabus and the assignment weighting (ie the contribution each assignment makes to your overall marks).

Once your Assignments have been completed, they will be marked by your accredited centre, and then **moderated** by a CIM External Moderator. When all the assignments have been marked, they are sent to CIM for further moderation. After this, all marks are forwarded to you by CIM (not your centre) in the form of an examination result. Your **centre** will be able to you provide you with some written feedback on overall performance, but **will not** provide you with any detailed mark breakdown.

Preparing for Assignments: a guide

Before looking at the Personal Development Portfolio and potential assignment themes and approaches, it might be helpful to consider how best to present your assignment. Here you should consider issues of detail, protocol and the range of communications that could be called upon within the assignment.

Presentation of the Assignment

You should always ensure that you prepare two copies of your Assignment, keeping a soft copy on disc. On occasions assignments go missing, or second copies are required by CIM.

- Each Assignment should be clearly marked up with your name, your study centre, your CIM Student registration number and ultimately at the end of the assignment a word count. The assignment should also be word-processed.

- The assignment presentation format should directly meet the requirements of the assignment brief, (ie reports and presentations are the most called for communication formats). You **must** ensure that you assignment does not appear to be an extended essay. If it does, you will lose marks. In many of the assignments, marks are awarded for presentation and coherence.

- The word limit may not always be included in the assignment brief. However, you should not exceed 3000 words unless otherwise specified. For the Personal Development Portfolio, more than 2000 words is unnecessary.

- **Appendices** should clearly link to the assignment and can be attached as supporting documentation at the end of the report. However failure to reference them by number (eg Appendix 1) within the report and also marked up on the Appendix itself will lose you marks. Only use an Appendix if it is **essential** and clearly adds value to the overall Assignment. The Appendix is not a waste bin for all the materials you have come across in your research, or a way of making your assignment seem somewhat heavier and more impressive than it is.

Time management for Assignments

One of the biggest challenges we all seem to face day-to-day is that of managing time. When studying, that challenge seems to grow increasingly difficult, requiring a balance between work, home, family, social life and study life. It is therefore of pivotal importance to your own success for you to plan wisely the limited amount of time you have available.

Step 1: Find out how much time you have

Ensure that you are fully aware of how long your module lasts, and the final deadline (eg 10 weeks, 12 weeks, 14 weeks etc). If you are studying a module from September to December, it is likely

that you will have only 10-12 weeks in which to complete your assignments. In other words, one assignment spans the **duration** of the course, and **two** assignments, to be completed within six weeks to complete, also run through the course. This might sound challenging, but it is manageable.

Step 2: Plan your time

Essentially you need to **work backwards** from the final deadline, submission date, and schedule your work around the possible time lines. Clearly if you have only 10-12 weeks available to complete three assignments, you will need to allocate a block of hours in the final stages of the module to ensure that all of your assignments are in on time. *Failure to submit your assignments on the due date could mean that your marks are capped at 50%.*

Step 3: Set priorities

You should set priorities on a daily and weekly basis (not just for study, but for your life). There is no doubt that this mode of study needs commitment (and some sacrifices in the short term). When your achievements are recognised by colleagues, peers, friends and family, it will all feel worthwhile.

Step 4: Analyse activities and allocate time to them

Consider the **range** of activities that you will need to undertake in order to complete the assignment and the **time** each might take. Remember, too, there will be a delay in asking for information and receiving it.

- Preparing terms of reference for the assignment, to include the following.

1	A short title
2	A brief outline of the assignment purpose and outcome
3	Methodology – what methods you intend to use to carry out the required tasks
4	Indication of any difficulties that have arisen in the duration of the assignment
5	Time schedule
6	Confidentiality – if the assignment includes confidential information ensure that this is clearly marked up and indicated on the assignment
7	Literature and desk research undertaken

  This should be achieved in one side of A4

- A literature search in order to undertake the necessary background reading and underpinning information that might support your assignment
- Writing letters and memos asking for information either internally or externally
- Designing questionnaires
- Undertaking surveys
- Analysis of data from questionnaires
- Secondary data search
- Preparation of first draft report

Always build in time to spare, to deal with the unexpected. This may reduce the pressure that you are faced in meeting significant deadlines.

Continuous assessment

Warning!

The same principles apply to a student with 30 weeks to do the work. However, a word of warning is needed. Do not fall into the trap of leaving all of the work on your Portfolio assignment to the last minute. If you miss out important information or fail to reflect upon your work adequately or successfully you will be penalised for both. Therefore, time management is important whatever the duration of the course.

Tips for writing Assignments

Everybody has a personal style, flair and tone when it comes to writing. However, no matter what your approach, you must ensure your assignment meets the **requirements of the brief** and so is comprehensible, coherent and cohesive in approach.

Think of preparing an assignment as preparing for an examination. Ultimately, the work you are undertaking results in an examination grade. Successful achievement of all four modules in a level results in a qualification.

There are a number of positive steps that you can undertake in order to ensure that you make the best of your assignment presentation in order to maximise the marks available.

Step 1 – Work to the Brief

Ensure that you identify **exactly what the assignment asks you to do**.

- If it asks you to be a marketing manager, then immediately assume that role.
- If it asks you to prepare a report, then present a report, not an essay or a letter.
- Furthermore, if it asks for 3,000 words, then do not present 1,000 or 5,000 unless in both instances it is clearly justified, agreed with your tutor and a valid piece of work.

Identify if the report should be **formal or informal**, who it should be **addressed to**, its **overall purpose** and its **potential use** and outcome. Understanding this will ensure that your assignment meets fully the requirements of the brief and addresses the key issues included within it.

Step 2 – Addressing the Tasks

It is of pivotal importance that you address **each** of the tasks within the assignment. **Many students fail to do this** and often overlook one of the tasks or indeed part of the tasks.

Many of the assignments will have two or three tasks, some will have even more. You should establish quite early on, which of the tasks:

- Requires you to collect information
- Provides you with the framework of the assignment, ie the communication method.

Possible tasks will include the following.

- *Compare and contrast.* Take two different organisations and compare them side by side and consider the differences ie the **contrasts** between the two.

- *Carry out primary or secondary research.* Collect information to support your assignment and your subsequent decisions

- *Prepare a plan.* Some assignments will ask you to prepare a plan for an event or for a marketing activity – if so provide a step by step approach, a rationale, a time-line, make sure it is measurable and achievable. Make sure your actions are very specific and clearly explained. (Make sure your plan is SMART.)

- *Analyse a situation.* This will require you to collect information, consider its content and present an overall understanding of the actual situation that exists. This might include looking at internal and external factors and how the current situation evolved.

- *Make recommendations.* The more advanced your get in your studies, the more likely it is that you will be required to make recommendations. Firstly **considering and evaluating your options** and then making justifiable **recommendations**, based on them.

- *Justify decisions.* You may be required to justify your decision or recommendations. This will require you to explain fully how you have arrived at this decision and to show why, supported by relevant information, this is the right way forward. In other words, you should not make decisions in a vacuum; as a marketer your decisions should always be informed by context.

- *Prepare a presentation.* This speaks for itself. If you are required to prepare a presentation, ensure that you do so, preparing clearly defined PowerPoint or overhead slides that are not too crowded and that clearly express the points you are required to make.

- *Evaluate performance.* It is very likely that you will be asked to evaluate a campaign, a plan or even an event. You will therefore need to consider its strengths and weaknesses, why it succeeded or failed, the issues that have affected it, what can you learn from it and, importantly, how can you improve performance or sustain it in the future.

All of these points are likely requests included within a task. Ensure that you identify them clearly and address them as required.

Step 3 – Information Search

Many students fail to realise the importance of collecting information to **support** and **underpin** their assignment work. However, it is vital that you demonstrate to your centre and to the CIM your ability to **establish information needs**, obtain **relevant information** and **utilise it sensibly** in order to arrive at appropriate decisions.

You should establish the nature of the information required, follow up possible sources, time involved in obtaining the information, gaps in information and the need for information.

Consider these factors very carefully. CIM are very keen that students are **seen** to collect information, **expand** their mind and consider the **breadth** and **depth** of the situation. In your *Personal Development Portfolio*, you have the opportunity to complete a **Resource Log**, to illustrate how you have expanded your knowledge to aid your personal development. You can record your additional reading and research in that log, and show how it has helped you with your portfolio and assignment work.

Step 4 – Develop an Assignment Plan

Your **assignment** needs to be structured and coherent, addressing the brief and presenting the facts as required by the tasks. The only way you can successfully achieve this is by **planning the structure** your Assignment in advance.

Earlier on in this unit, we looked at identifying your tasks and, working backwards from the release date, in order to manage time successfully. The structure and coherence of your assignment needs to be planned with similar signs.

In planning out the Assignment, you should plan to include **all the relevant information as requested** and also you should plan for the use of models, diagrams and appendices where necessary.

Continuous assessment

Your plan should cover your:

- Introduction
- Content
- Main body of the assignment and then
- Summary
- Conclusions and recommendations where appropriate

Step 5 – Prepare Draft Assignment

It is good practice to always produce a **first draft** of a report. You should use it to ensure that you have met the aims and objectives, assignment brief and tasks related to the actual assignment. A draft document provides you with scope for improvements, and enables you to check for accuracy, spelling, punctuation and use of English.

Step 6 – Prepare Final Document

In the section headed 'Presentation of the Assignment' in this unit, there are a number of components that should always be in place at the beginning of the assignment documentation, including **labelling** of the assignment, **word counts**, **appendices** numbering and presentation method. Ensure that you **adhere to the guidelines presented**, or alternatively those suggested by your study centre.

Writing reports

Students often ask 'what do they mean by a report?' or 'what should the report format include?'

There are a number of approaches to reports, formal or informal: some report formats are company specific and designed for internal use, rather than external reporting.

For Continuous Assessment process, you should stay with traditional formats.

Below is a suggested layout of a Management Report Document, as recommended by the CIM Training Division. Prepared by the Senior Moderator and Delegate Mentor, it is presented to for delegates on a broad range of sales and marketing programmes.

- **A Title Page** – includes the title of the report, the author of the report and the receiver of the report
- **Acknowledgements** – this should highlight any help, support, or external information received and any extraordinary co-operation of individuals or organisations
- **Contents Page** – providing a clearly structured pathway of the contents of the report – page by page
- **Executive Summary** – a brief insight into purpose, nature and outcome of the report, in order that the outcome of the report can be quickly established
- ***Main body of the report divided into sections, which are clearly labelled***. Suggested labelling would be on a numbered basis eg:
    - 1.0   Introduction
    - 1.1   Situation Analysis
    - 1.1.1 External Analysis
    - 1.1.2 Internal Analysis
- **Conclusions** – draw the report to a conclusion, highlighting key points of importance, that will impact upon any recommendations that might be made
- **Recommendations** – clearly outline potential options and then recommendations. Where appropriate justify recommendations in order to substantiate your decision
- **Appendices** – ensure that you only use appendices that add value to the report. Ensure that they are numbered and referenced on a numbered basis within the text. If you are not going to reference it within the text, then it should not be there
- **Bibliography** – whilst in a business environment a bibliography might not be necessary, for an **assignment-based report it is vital**. It provides an indication of the level of research, reading and collecting of relevant information that has taken place in order to fulfil the requirements of the assignment task. Where possible, and where relevant, you could provide academic references within the text, which should of course then provide the basis of your bibliography and your Resource Log for the PDP. References should realistically be listed alphabetically and in the following sequence
    - Author's name and edition of the text
    - Date of publication
    - Title and sub-title (where relevant)
    - Edition 1st, 2nd etc
    - Place of publication
    - Publisher
    - Series and individual volume number where appropriate.

Assignment One – the Personal Development Portfolio

On the following three pages you will find your Personal Development Portfolio for Effective Management for Marketing.

The **six** tasks that you will undertake will highlight the scope of your existing skills and your future continuing professional development.

Firstly read the assignment through and look at each of the tasks. Then we will discuss at how you can best approach it.

The resources you will need for this assignment are: a lever arch file, folder dividers and plastic wallets.

Continuous assessment

Continuous Assessment Assignment

Academic Session 2001 – 2002

Effective Management for Marketing

Assignment No. 1 - Personal Development Plan (PDP)

This assignment is the Personal Development Plan, which is compulsory.

Candidates must complete this assignment in order to complete their portfolio which will also include the core assignment and an optional choice assignment.

July 2001

Continuous assessment

ASSIGNMENT 1 – PERSONAL DEVELOPMENT PLAN (PDP)

Assignment Brief

The purpose of this assignment is to enable and encourage you to reflect upon how applicable the learning on your CIM Advanced Certificate has been within your professional development process. Furthermore it aims to illustrate how the learning process has allowed you to develop different attitudes and styles of working, over your period of study.

The format that the PDP will take is entirely up to the individual, as long as the main headings shown below are covered. It is recommended that you commence the PDP approximately three weeks into your module, and you should continue to evaluate your learning up to the end of your CIM Certificate.

The purpose of the PDP is for you to evaluate how the CIM Advanced Certificate course has benefited you, perhaps with reference to certain specific situations, rather than great detail on one particular aspect of your learning.

Part of your learning on any CIM course\module is reading around the subject or accessing other information sources. The CIM workbook is just a basis on which to develop. Evaluation of other resources should be part of your personal development.

It is suggested you work to a maximum of 2,500 words; supporting evidence must be kept to a minimum. This assignment is designed to be reflective, and perhaps less structured, than the others you will be completing for this module.

There are proformas attached if you wish to use them to complete the tasks, (for example keeping a resource log), but nothing is compulsory and it maybe best for you to develop your own individual style.

A skills analysis sheet for Effective Management for Marketing is attached and should be completed as a start point to enable you to focus on the skills you may wish to evaluate.

Continuous assessment

Assignment tasks:
Tasks to be covered within this assignment are:

Task 1

- A personal assessment of your strengths and weaknesses. This could take the form of a personal SWOT. Someone else completing a SWOT analysis showing his or her views of you could also be included.

- Examine and evaluate any other forms of personal assessments you may have undergone, such as work-based appraisals, Belbin or other personal profiling.

- From this analysis, select areas that you feel would personally benefit from developing from new, or, existing skills to be developed further.

Task 2

- Write a Career Development plan, which includes
    - A description of your present role and attach a recent job description.
    - A brief Career History showing how you arrived at this point.
    - How you see your career developing over the next five years.

Task 3

- Refer back at your analysis for Task One and Task Two. Select one recognised strength and one weakness, which you think is key to you achieving your career plan. Give reasons for your choice.

Task 4

For each of the two skills selected show:

- Your evaluation of your present skills in this area.

- How you believe you could develop \ develop further within that area. What actions would be required? What time scale \ costs would be involved.

- How often would you need to review your progress?

- A learning diary detailing specific learning occasions, which occur during the module, relevant to developing these skills. This should be contained in a maximum of 5 A4 sheets.

Task 5

- A reflective statement on your experience of the learning process. How does this compare with your expectations? Evaluate how your CIM Advanced Certificate studies have helped you to develop, and how you could plan your next stage of development.

Task 6

- What resources have you accessed as part of your CIM Advanced Certificate, and how helpful were they.

- Which would you recommend to others, give reasons for your recommendations?

This Assignment carries 30% of the marks for your final assessment

Continuous assessment

Role of the PDP

The Personal Development Portfolio (PDP) assignment is designed to develop your own personal and individual skills. Each Continuous Assessment module available from CIM has the same assignment, but requires you to look at the **context of the module that you are studying for**. For example, this particular module focuses on Effective Management for Marketing. However, you might also be studying for Management Information for Marketing Decisions at this time. If this is the case, you will see that **both assignments are identical in terms of the tasks that should be undertaken, but the differences come in terms of the skills audit that you undertake, as the skills audit** frames the basis of your assignment.

The PDP has in the past been described as a 'powerful learning vehicle'. The process of developing the log is developmental and allows for dialog and self-reflection to take place.

The activities involved in the PDP process have been designed to enable you to evaluate your progress in meeting the learning outcomes of the syllabus and using them as your own development objectives. To reflect the important nature of this, the PDP assignment equates to almost one third of your examination grade, ie 30%.

Self-reflection is deemed an important part of the process, whereby you are given the opportunity to reflect on your current abilities, and then on the various development activities undertaken. You will reflect on how you approach the work, how the work turned out and perhaps what you could improve in the future. Essentially you should look at the self-reflection process as one that could ultimately improve your future performance.

Task 1 – The SWOT analysis and skills audit

In the table on the page after next you will see a skills audit. You will find this document very helpful in managing Task One of this PDP Assignment. The assignment asks you to undertake an **analysis** of your **strengths** and **weaknesses**, and also a consideration of the **opportunities** and **threats** that face you in your everyday environment.

A good starting point for this is to look at the skills audit below and assess your ability in each of the areas listed. You will see that you can grade the areas in terms of importance. Clearly if you skills level is **below 2**, then this can be categorised as a **weakness** and could potentially be subject to further development. If it is above 2 then either there is room for improvement, or indeed your could find that you are actually quite confident in this area. In addition to this, you are asked about the importance of this area to your role currently and **in future**. This is where **strengths** and **opportunities** come into play. Where you establish that you are currently doing something successfully, this could be determined as an overall strength. This could then present opportunities for you in the future, as your strengths enable you to develop your role and move towards a promotion or a new role altogether.

From this skills audit, you are to select key areas that you feel would be personally beneficial to you. You will see that, within the grid, there are some areas that have been **filled** in to provide you with an insight as to what this means. The comments in this instance show that the person completing the PDP has a number of areas that need development in connection with a new role, that of a marketing assistant.

When undertaking the skills audit you should think carefully about your existing role and your future potential roles: not just about improving yourself in the immediate future, but also about the potential scope of a five-year career plan, which you will be developing in task 2.

You may have undertaken a range of similar assessments within your own organisation, or your may have recently been through a performance appraisal with your employer. If so, use these processes to assist you in considering your existing position in relation to the skills audit; the

Continuous assessment

comments in your appraisal feedback will help you determine your performance to date, and areas of future training and development.

From your personal perspective, you should consider using your appraisals and skills audit as part of your learning process. As well as meeting your learning objectives for your CIM qualifications, you could be going some way towards meeting your work based objectives. This approach presents an opportunity for you to involve your line manager in your self assessment and the project, thereby showing how PDP process might move you closer towards meeting your appraisal objectives.

Continuous assessment

INSERT INTO PORTFOLIO	Syllabus Ref	Current Skill Level		Importance to Current Role		Likely Future Importance		YOUR COMMENTS
		None	High	Low	Vital	Low	Vital	
PERSONAL COMPETENCIES	EM							
1.1 Showing concern for excellence	2.1	0 - 1 - **2** - 3		[ ] [ ] [ ] [X]		[ ] [ ] [ ] [X]		Showing concern for excellence is imperative to my role as a marketing manager in a financial services company, however, I am relatively new to this role and need to grasp the concepts associated with achieving service excellence in my company.
1.2 Setting and prioritising objectives	2.1	0 - 1 - 2 - 3		[ ] [ ] [ ] [ ]		[ ] [ ] [ ] [ ]		
1.3 Monitoring actual vs planned activities	2.1	0 - 1 - 2 - 3		[ ] [ ] [ ] [ ]		[ ] [ ] [ ] [ ]		
2.1 Sensitivity to the needs of others	2.1	0 - 1 - 2 - 3		[ ] [ ] [ ] [ ]		[ ] [ ] [ ] [ ]		
2.2 Relating to others	2.1	0 - 1 - 2 - 3		[ ] [ ] [ ] [ ]		[ ] [ ] [ ] [ ]		
2.3 Obtaining others' commitment	2.1	0 - **1** - 2 - 3		[ ] [ ] [ ] [X]		[ ] [ ] [ ] [X]		As I am relatively new to my role, managing people is something I am learning about constantly, as is trying to gain the commitment of my team. My environment is subject to considerable change, which means continuous change in role, in service offering, which makes it increasingly difficult for staff to remain committed. Gaining an insight into commitment, motivations behind commitment would be highly relevant both now and in the future.
2.4 Presenting oneself positively	2.1	0 - 1 - 2 - 3		[ ] [ ] [ ] [ ]		[ ] [ ] [ ] [ ]		
3.1 Showing self confidence and drive	2.1	0 - 1 - 2 - 3		[ ] [ ] [ ] [ ]		[ ] [ ] [ ] [ ]		
3.2 Managing own emotions and stress	2.1	0 - 1 - 2 - 3		[ ] [ ] [ ] [ ]		[ ] [ ] [ ] [ ]		
4.1 Collecting and organising information	2.1	0 - 1 - 2 - 3		[ ] [ ] [ ] [ ]		[ ] [ ] [ ] [ ]		
4.2 Identifying and applying concepts	2.1	0 - 1 - 2 - 3		[ ] [ ] [ ] [ ]		[ ] [ ] [ ] [ ]		
4.3 Taking decisions	2.1	0 - 1 - 2 - 3		[ ] [ ] [ ] [ ]		[ ] [ ] [ ] [ ]		
OTHER SKILLS & ATTRIBUTES								
Time management and work prioritisation	2.5	0 - 1 - **2** - 3		[ ] [ ] [ ] [X]		[ ] [ ] [ ] [X]		Time management is a nightmare. My organisation is driven by customer service standards that require set response times along with varying service procedures, some of which had times attached to them. The volume of work and continuous change and my involvement in this stretches my time to the limit. Any hints and tips that could be learned in relation to time management are a must to my continuing success.
Plan projects	2.8	0 - 1 - 2 - **3**		[ ] [ ] [ ] [X]		[ ] [ ] [ ] [X]		My company is very focused on project management and I have therefore had a lot of project management experience. We are provided with software, procedures etc that support the project management planning, however, encouraging my team to adhere to the requirements and timing involved can sometimes prove difficult.
Written comms: letters and memos	2.7	0 - 1 - 2 - 3		[ ] [ ] [ ] [ ]		[ ] [ ] [ ] [ ]		

Continuous assessment

Written comms: reports and briefings	2.7	0 - 1 - 2 - 3	[ ] [ ] [ ] [ ]	[ ] [ ] [ ] [ ]
Written comms: project specs/proposals	2.7	0 - 1 - 2 - 3	[ ] [ ] [ ] [ ]	[ ] [ ] [ ] [ ]
Oral comms: talks and presentations	2.7	0 - 1 - 2 - 3	[ ] [ ] [ ] [ ]	[ ] [ ] [ ] [ ]
Plan and manage team activities	3.3/4	0 - 1 - 2 - 3	[ ] [ ] [ ] [ ]	[ ] [ ] [ ] [ ]
Delegate tasks and responsibility	2.6	0 - 1 - 2 - 3	[ ] [ ] [ ] [ ]	[ ] [ ] [ ] [ ]
Plan and manage meetings	2.8	0 - 1 - 2 - 3	[ ] [ ] [ ] [ ]	[ ] [ ] [ ] [ ]
Analyse job/team roles to prepare job specs	3.1	0 - 1 - 2 - 3	[ ] [ ] [ ] [ ]	[ ] [ ] [ ] [ ]
Recruit, select and induct staff	3.1/2	0 - 1 - 2 - 3	[ ] [ ] [ ] [ ]	[ ] [ ] [ ] [ ]
Counsel, advise or mentor staff	3.2	0 - 1 - 2 - 3	[ ] [ ] [ ] [ ]	[ ] [ ] [ ] [ ]
Appraise staff performance	3.4	0 - 1 - 2 - 3	[ ] [ ] [ ] [ ]	[ ] [ ] [ ] [ ]
Plan and manage staff development	3.7	0 - 1 - 2 - 3	[ ] [ ] [ ] [ ]	[ ] [ ] [ ] [ ]
Plan and manage interviews (job or other)	3.1/2	0 - 1 - 2 - 3	[ ] [ ] [ ] [ ]	[ ] [ ] [ ] [ ]
Plan and manage a change programme	3.8/9	0 - 1 - 2 - 3	[ ] [ ] [ ] [ ]	[ ] [ ] [ ] [ ]
Lead client/customer meetings/negotiations	3.7	0 - 1 - 2 - 3	[ ] [ ] [ ] [ ]	[ ] [ ] [ ] [ ]
Build and maintain professional networks	2.7	0 - 1 - **2** - 3	[ ] [ ] [ ] [X]	[ ] [ ] [ ] [X]	Networking is an absolute must, particularly in my industry. Whilst it is something I am relatively good at, I perhaps need to take a more planned approach to it, building up records, databases of my network, giving it some focus and purpose.
YOUR OWN CHOICE (discuss with tutor)				Please ensure that you note the syllabus reference.
		0 - 1 - 2 - 3	[ ] [ ] [ ] [ ]	[ ] [ ] [ ] [ ]
		0 - 1 - 2 - 3	[ ] [ ] [ ] [ ]	[ ] [ ] [ ] [ ]

Continuous assessment

When you have completed your skills audit, put it in your lever arch file at the front, as it will be a constant source of reference and reminder to you whilst you are progressing through the course.

Task 2 – Career Development Plan

This task requires you to write a Career Development Plan. This is quite an interesting concept and might for many provide the first real opportunity for you to sit down and really consider where do you go from here. It is quite often an interesting activity for students to undertake. Think along the following lines:

- Where am I now?
- Where do I want to go in the future?
- How am I going to get there?

These three questions will form the basis of your career development plan.

Step 1 Firstly, in order for you to analyse where you are now, it is helpful to open a section within your PDP file titled **Career Development**. In this particular section, insert your Curriculum Vitae, existing job description and a brief career history. Think about where you started off, your first job, where you are now (ie your existing job), how many job changes you have had and career changes. You should also think about any promotions you have encountered in your career history. What was the nature of the promotion? What strengths assisted you in achieving the promotion? What opportunities did it provide you with?

Step 2 Secondly, consider where you want to go in the future. Why are you taking the CIM qualifications, what are you expecting them to achieve for you? Are you moving into new business areas, new business sectors or using these qualifications as a tool to assist you promotion prospects within your own organisation? Whatever the reason, start to analyse them, and map out potential stages you might embark upon in the next five years, both in terms of career and training and education to aid your prospects of career progression.

You will probably find this quite a challenging task. You may find that you cannot complete it early on in the course, and you may wish to take time to think it over. Your PDP assignment should be ongoing throughout the duration of your module, which gives you time to sit back and think about the future, areas of interest that have arisen as a result of the course, or areas of interest that you know the course can develop for you. However, you should establish some framework of career development by the time you are a third of the way through your module.

Task 3 – Selection of Key Development Points

This task is very brief and requires you to review your skills audit and career plan, and select the areas of development most appropriate to you. The task requires you to select **one** particular **strength** from the skills audit and SWOT analysis, which you can further develop and enhance in order to exploit career opportunities, and one **weakness**, that reduces effectiveness in your existing role. Dealing with this could aid future roles and promotion prospects.

If you look back at the grid in figure 1.2, you might select *showing concern for excellence*. This particular point was registered as a weakness, something that is not so important now, but will be vital to a new role. As a new manager you know that the demands on service excellence are increasing and this form of development will be invaluable to your role now and in future.

For the strength, it is likely that you might select the area relating *planning projects*. Currently this appears to be an overall strength in your current role, important to your current role, and vital to the future marketing management role. Therefore you would, in this instance, think about how

(xxxiii)

Continuous assessment

you might develop this further and exploit your abilities to gain recognition for your skills in this area, with a view to personal promotion. However the big challenge to you here is engaging your team in this process, gaining their commitment and getting them to manage their time. As your core and optional assignments look at pertinent issues relating to these subject areas, you will find them invaluable in developing your ability to manage people and projects successfully.

Whichever point you select, you must be able to **justify your choice**, explaining why it is important to you to address these two key areas and how they might help you achieve your career development plan. This essentially acts as your rationale for development.

Task 4 – Action Plan and Learning Diary

This task sees you starting to prepare for action. Now that you have identified your **key development points** and justified your selection, you need to define some sense of direction, action and outcome.

In order to do this, you should consider what your development pathway is going to consist of.

Continuing with the example we have used so far, to develop your budgeting skills, which you have highlighted as a weakness, you could:

Reflecting on the scope of planning, managing projects, leading teams, team and individual co-ordination and communications, project reviews and project closure. You might decide to take a more reflective approach here, in order than you can identify strengths and weaknesses with your current procedures and consider how you might develop them effectively in the future.

You now need to plan your approach, for example:

- Develop an action plan on a **week-by-week basis**, which predetermines how you are going to develop your activities throughout the duration of the module.

- The action plan should include **date** of action, **description** of the action, proposed **outcome** and **proposed date** of outcome. Action plans, like objectives should be SMART (Specific, measurable, achievable, realistic and timed), provide direction directive and should propose clear outcomes. Give the actions a **reference** number so that your tutor can cross-reference your actions with the learning diary.

- Your action plan should include **key review points.** (When are you going to review your development? Reviews will take place at the end of each activity or indeed activities will be reviewed half way through and at the end.) Ensure that you put in **progression measurement points** to ensure that you remain on target. This action plan should provide the basis of a development strategy.

- Develop a **'success criterion' for each action.** Analyse your current position, undertake an internal situation analysis, looking at your team singularly and across the organisation as a whole at project planning, team co-ordination and effective communications. Use the analysis as the basis of a review.

- This success criterion provides you with an **opportunity to consider what you have done**, how it could be improved, and then develop the work further for more successful project management. This approach shows progression, development and improvement.

    Regular **feedback** from your tutor and employer, if you have involved them in the process, is essential to give you a clear insight into your progression.

- **Keep a learning diary**. This learning diary should be a record of your activities, including how the activity went, how successful it was, the benefit of the activity and proposing further action. Clearly divide your pages so that your tutor, when marking your assignment, can see how the learning diary records your actions in line with your action plan. Ensure

that you cross-reference your actions, so that it is clear how the actions and the learning diary interlink. (This should be no longer than 5 pages of A4 – remember the word limit is 2000 words.)

When you do decide the basis of the development points, and are considering how to formulate your action plan and what activities you should undertake, please be aware that you can use elements of your other assignment work to support your development. Should you do this, it should be by negotiation with your tutor and your work should be cross-referenced in order to provide evidence.

Whilst previously a standard approach to recording this information was provided by CIM, it is now entirely up to you and your tutor to decide the best way of presenting this information. However, we recommend develop key headings for each activity (ie your action plan and learning diary) so that the two are compatible. (You will note that this is stated in the introductory part of the assignment.)

Task 5 – Reflective Statements

You are required to **reflect upon your activities** and your personal development in the selected areas for the duration of your course. Students often underestimate this part of the assignment, and fail to address it effectively. It is this part of the assignment that actually brings all of your work together, gives it purpose and future direction.

Here are the key components that you should always include:

- Where did you start of (ie why did you choose the particular elements of the key skills unit as your development points?)

- What activities have you undertaken?

- How do you think that they might help you in your career plan?

- How effective were you in improving your performance and behaviour in respect of your selected development points?

- How have you improved and why?

- How will you continue to develop this area in the future, how do you anticipate you might use it?

- The reflective statement is not just reflecting on what has been, but is developmental considering what is to come!

Task 6 – Resource Log

The CIM are very keen that you **read broadly** to support your learning and personal development. Reading, surfing the Internet, working through journals and newspapers is a critical aspect of your professional, vocational and academic development. In order to **prove** that you have looked at each of these areas, and that you have **applied** the theory in the context of your learning and personal development **you are required to make a record of your resources**.

Here you should look at the following:

- Provide a list of books and journals you have read – this could of course include this BPP Effective Management for Marketing in Study Text, but should also include others (for example as suggested in the CIM's reading list).

- Explain the basis of your reading in summary format and how it helped you in progression your action plan and the key development points within it.

Continuous assessment

- Would you recommend this text to others? If so, why? Justify your recommendations overall.

For the purpose of Effective Management for Marketing, therefore, we will look at **Internal Marketing** and **Managing Teams**. These are two key areas in relation to this module.

You may need to assume an operational management stance in your response to the assignment. **However, it is likely that the assignment will give you a role.** You must look at your assignments from a management context. You are after all, through these studies, being prepared for marketing management at an operational level.

Internal marketing

Internal marketing is a very hot subject in today's business environment. Organisations seems to becoming more tuned in to communication with staff, hosting consultations, using various exchanges to involve staff in the future direction of the organisation. However, whilst they might be more tuned in the concepts of internal marketing, it would appear that there is still along way to go.

The stages that you should do to complete your assessment will require you to demonstrate an understanding of internal marketing, internal customers and planning and developing internal marketing plans. Your role will be that of the Marketing Manager. This scenario is based upon the concept of a previous CIM assignment and *is not an actual assignment.*

Do not forget to read your Study Text in respect of internal marketing and project planning. These will be critical components to this assignment. This is an all round assignment in many respects, you will find your workbook a useful resource.

Taking into consideration issues relating to preparing for assignments and writing reports, start to develop a **report** taking into account the following issues.

You are to prepare a report outlining the basis of a future internal marketing project plan, providing an overview of the current situation, clearly defined internal marketing objectives, and an insight into the utilisation of appropriate elements of the marketing mix.

You will have a limited **budget**, which you can set in context of your own organisation and relevant to the sales turnover. This should be broken down and illustrated and justified.

You should provide a timeline of how you will implement your new ideas and new activities. Your work should be fully justified and all statements clearly qualified in terms of content and context.

- The previous CIM assignment for this particular area focused upon change within a set scenario, however for the purpose of this exercise, you are going to focus upon your own organisation. To get your assignment off the ground, focus on a situation analysis, describing the situation of your organisation in respect of morale, motivation, level of change, and the positive and negative outcomes of change. This provides you with a backdrop to introduce your own organisation, what they are and their current position.
- Clearly define theoretically the basis of internal marketing and internal customers, Then compare the theory with your organisation to date, building upon the situation analysis you have previously prepared.
- How seriously is internal marketing taken?
- Does internal marketing exist within your organisation?
- What do people think of the current level of activity You could, for example, the influence of Information Communication Technology. Are there flexible working arrangements, are quality procedures in place? Do they add value, if so how?

- The next stage is to take your analysis and look at the **strengths** and **weaknesses** of the organisation as a way of establishing a route forward that will impact positively upon the business. You are to prepare a **project plan**, that will clearly **illustrate how your recommendations for improvement should come into play and be implemented**. The project plan should include a clearly illustrated time line with a parallel **budget** illustration, showing how the budget will be allocated and when.

- You must, in making your recommendations, **use the analysis** you have provided to form the basis of your **justification** of your actions. **Each aspect of the project plan must be based upon a key objective relating back to internal marketing**. You should introduce frequent measurement points and evaluation techniques that will monitor the effectiveness of your plan. These should be fully described and their outcome explained.

- You should look at this from a management perspective. You are a marketing manager, and you must take a professional management approach to this. Whilst you recommendations will relate to tactical activities in nature, your analysis, project management and recommendations must be from an operational management perspective, (ie a project plan that others can work to and implement). So you should ensure that your work is transparent, clear, representative of the situation and meaningful.

- Remember the basis of this assignment is the 'effective management of marketing'.

As always remember to bring your assignment to a conclusion, culminating in your analysis, recommendations and proposed outcomes.

Ensure that your timeline and budget allocations are included as appendix if you have not put them in the main body of the report.

NB. This is based upon a CIM assignment, not an actual CIM Assignment, as it is likely that future assignments may be aligned to the **actual assignment** in this subject area. However, this does provide a detailed approach to an assignment of this nature.

Team Management

Managing teams has been central to much of your learning in respect of **Effective Management for Marketing**. The focus of the syllabus is to enable marketing managers to manage their teams, change and customer relationships effectively.

As a marketing **manager** you will be expected to take a planned and proactive approach to developing teams to that they are committed, focused, effective, efficient and able to deliver an outcome in the desired time.

For you to develop this ability, you review and reflect on the nature of your team, the roles of teams, and how teams can be developed, managed, trained and motivated to achieve the **clearly defined** marketing objectives that your organisation has set. Your role in this assignment is that of Marketing Manager.

To approach this assignment you have been asked to produce a **report to your Senior Manager on the effectiveness of teams within the marketing function**. You will be asked to take into account team communication, team motivation and team development. Unusually, you have also being asked to look at some written theory about how teams work in order to justify your thinking on how teams can be developed to underpin your suggestions.

Ultimately you are to make **recommendations** on how team performance can be improved in order to ensure that teams assist the achievement of corporate goals and marketing objectives.

Do not forget to read your BPP Study Text and the associated chapters on Teams, you will find it very useful. However, you will need to read more broadly for this assignment, as there is some emphasis on the importance of management theory in respect of teams. Refer to your CIM recommended reading list for guidance.

Taking into account the outline brief above, prepare a report to your senior manager.

Continuous assessment

With consideration of the following key points, and others that you might feel are relevant or valid to your own organisation.

- As with the previous assignment, commence with a situation analysis. Considering the following points
  - How does the organisation value teams and how important are they?
  - What are the benefits of teams generally and to your organisation?
  - Do the teams in your organisation affect the bottom line of the business and are they effective and efficient?
  - What is the structure of your team, or one with which you are familiar in your organisation?
  - Describe their roles and responsibilities, including your team
  - How do teams interact with one another?
  - Is there a structured approach to team formation?
  - What are the channels of communication like?
  - How well does the team communicate?
- These are just some of the questions you should ask yourself in arriving at an overall situation analysis.
- The next stage of the task is to look at **motivation** factors affecting teams – look at this from a theoretical perspective and then apply it to your situation.
- How do you think motivation within the team could be improved?
- The next step asks you to address team development – what are the components of team development that currently exist, and how could team development and performance be enhanced. Therefore you should consider the following:
  - The basic concepts of management
  - Recruitment of team members – how efficient is it?
  - Is there an effective selection process?
  - How are team members monitored, both corporately as a team and individually as a valued individual?
  - What training and development is undertaken?
  - What is the appraisal system – does it work?
- Answering these questions and examining closely the remainder of your analysis, will give you an indication of where your organisation is in relation to teams, where the marketing department is in relation to teams, and how you might improve overall team performance, particularly in the marketing function.

From this you should then provide the following.

- A range of recommendations based upon your analysis
- Your recommendations should be clearly justified, all statements qualified and you should clearly demonstrate why your suggested improvements would make a difference overall.

The difficulty with this assignment will be to know **where to stop**. It could be a significant project, but extremely valuable to your overall learning and experience in the work place. As we have already suggested, this is not an actual CIM assignment, but is a variation on a theme. **The CIM assignment is likely to be much more focused, but will involve you in consideration of many of the above issues.**

This approach has posed many **questions** in relation to your teams, rather than handing your solutions on a plate. As a marketing manager these questions will help you structure your report in the context of your **own organisation**. They will provide a context for effective team building.

A word of advice and a reminder of previous advice. Take care to watch that you do not exceed your word limited. You could quite easily write a huge amount. The questions are to focus your mind. Your challenge will be to present meaningful analysis that actually builds on those questions in a succinct, meaningful and professional way.

Unit Summary: Effective Management for Marketing

You may have come to the end of the unit feeling that this is going to be hard work. Well you would be right in thinking this. But, as we suggested in the early part of this unit, it is likely to be one of the most beneficial learning processes you will embark upon, as you take your CIM qualifications.

The process of development prepares you to be a marketing professional in the future. It provides you with practical experience and an opportunity to apply the theory in a practical situation. You will demonstrate to your existing or future employer that you have the ability to learn, develop, grow, progress and contribute significantly to the marketing activity within the organisation.

You have been provided with a range of hints and tips in presentation of assignments, development of your PDP and approaches to your core and optional assignments.

Continuous assessment, like examinations, is a serious business, and you should consider the level of ongoing commitment that this process requires. The more you put in the more you are likely to get out. It will not be enough to leave all of your PDP work to the end of the course as it destroys the ethos and benefit of the assignment. Use it as a continuous development tool for the duration of the course. A structured approach to the learning process will maximise its benefits to you.

We have tried to give you some insight into how to approach the core and optional assignments that you will embark upon. However, these are only examples and do not reflect the real ones. What they do show you is the level of detail you should enter into in order to produce an effective and professional piece of work.

The CIM qualifications are professional qualifications and therefore, to be successful you must take a professional approach to your work.

Part A
The nature of management and organisation issues

1 Managing the Examination

Chapter Topic List

1	The need for skill development and practice
2	The importance of exam technique and practice
3	Preparing for Section A questions
4	Preparing for Section B questions
5	Preparing for effective study

Part A: The nature of management and organisation issues

1 THE NEED FOR SKILL DEVELOPMENT AND PRACTICE

1.1 This subject was introduced in 1994 to fill a perceived gap in the CIM examinations. It can be assessed on a continual basis internally at a suitable UK centre, though the option of assessment by examination is always going to be available. The intention of the Institute is to provide a syllabus which will encourage students to develop a wide range of management skills which will be of direct and immediate value to them as practising marketers.

1.2 How this study text will help you

- It provides you with the knowledge and understanding of management tools.

- It identifies the frameworks which will help you to work through a variety of management situations, such as problem solving and decision making.

- It offers hints, tips and checklists which will be of practical help when you are faced with these situations.

- It suggests activities and exercises which will give you the chance to develop and practise the skills needed by the successful marketing manager.

1.3 Practising these skills will be critical to your success in the examination. Theory alone will be unlikely to equip you adequately to tackle the practical questions and scenarios which this examination will feature.

> **Action Programme 1**
>
> Take some time now to identify the opportunities and support which will be available to help you gain the necessary experience and practice.
>
> Take 15 minutes to brainstorm a list of **possible** options available to you. Think widely - not just in the context of work, but include your social life, family and friends as well as college and colleagues who you are studying with.
>
> If you are not currently employed, try and identify a local voluntary group who could do with some help and offer to manage the summer fete or some other fund raising project.

1.4 This CIM subject is a real opportunity for you to take stock of your personal skills and add real value to your CV through improved competences across a range of management activities. Open a workbook or section of your file which you can utilise as a **personal log book**. Add your refined list of development opportunities to this for reference.

1.5 In the examination you will need to comment on the processes you recommend, anticipate problems of implementation and so on. Keeping a record of the various activities and development exercises you undertake will help you to provide these from your own personal experience and observations. This should also be incorporated in your log book.

2 THE IMPORTANCE OF EXAM TECHNIQUE AND PRACTICE

2.1 Just as it is necessary to practice and develop management skills if you wish to be a successful manager, so you need to **practise examination technique** if you want to be a successful student.

2.2 A review of the examiner's comments from *any* CIM paper (or probably any examination centre for any professional body) will reveal the same weakness and cause of failure: exam technique. You would not consider entering a marathon without practising your running: you should not enter for exams without the same gradual build up, designed to develop your technique and stamina.

2.3 Throughout your study you should be preparing written answers to questions, getting used to working under the time constraints typical of an examination, and having your work critically assessed by a tutor, colleague or a tutorial service.

2.4 There are techniques for preparing for examinations and one of the main requirements is to attempt questions **as they are set**. You will find questions and exercises throughout the Study Text: use them. Review your work against the solutions we offer. Notice the differences. Do not simply assume that if your approach is different it must be wrong. There is seldom a single best method. We offer only a suggested model, but do review yours again carefully and **be sure that you answered the questions which were set**.

2.5 **Typical mistakes highlighted by the examiner**

(a) **Not answering the question as set**. This may mean using FMCG examples when the question was set in the context of a business-to-business sector; only putting the benefits when the question asked for a discussion. In particular the examiner has highlighted candidate failure to distinguish between how a problem should be **analysed** and what should be done to **solve** the problem.

Rule: Read the question with great care. Read it again and refer to it whilst you are preparing your answer.

(b) **Putting into the answer everything you know about a subject**. This saturation bombing approach means the answer is in there, somewhere **but the examiner has to sort it out**.

Rule: be selective. Think about what is asked and provide only relevant information.

(c) **Lack of commercial credibility**. Think about your recommendations: are they realistic? It takes time to attract, recruit and induct new staff, so do not be seen to try and achieve this in three weeks. Recommendations for a week-long in-company training course may be fine for a larger manufacturer but the small supplier with only ten people would have to close the business down.

(d) **A failure to work in the format specified and present work clearly**. You will find most of the questions at Advanced Certificate level ask you to prepare an outline presentation, report, memo or training checklist. **You must work in the format specified**. Where none is indicated, a normal report format is acceptable. The examiner has highlighted the following presentational points as being of particular importance.

- Use headings and sub headings.
- Leave 25% white space per page.
- Models, charts and diagrams should be clearly labelled and cover between $1/3$ and $1/2$ a page.
- New questions should begin on a new page.
- Colour (not red) can be used to highlight key points.
- Lines should be drawn with a ruler.
- Students should not use their own names in reports and memos.

Part A: The nature of management and organisation issues

3 PREPARING FOR SECTION A QUESTIONS

3.1 The paper consists of two parts. Section A is worth 40% of the marks and will therefore take 64 minutes of the examination time. It will consist of a mini-case study about 1,000 words in length.

3.2 This section will require you to analyse a situation, consider the information or data provided, identify a solution and make recommendations. This is the basic process of planning and problem solving.

3.3 **Steps in a planning decision**

(a) Recognise an opportunity to be exploited or a problem to be dealt with.

(b) Relate problems to **relevant theories and concepts**.

(c) **Establish goals or objectives** as the end result of exploiting the opportunity or solving the problem.

(d) **Forecast relevant information** (for example, about products, markets, competition, prices, wage rates, technology and so on). Some planning assumptions should be established which are agreed and used by managers throughout the organisation. An accepted set of assumptions about the environment in which the organisation will operate, and the resources it will have at its disposal, will provide guidelines for planning decisions.

(e) Consider **possible realistic courses of action** for the achievement of the objectives.

(f) Compare the various courses of action and **select the best course.**

(g) Formulate **detailed plans** for carrying out the chosen course of action.

- Supporting plans for the provision of the required resources such as materials, equipment, trained labour and finance

- Standards of performance required such as quality and time-scale; and measurement criteria

- Numerical plans or budgets indicating targets for achievement, sales prices, budgeted sales and production quantities and expenditure budgets

(h) Decide how the plan will be monitored when implemented, and what needs monitoring may identify (exam resources, further research and so on).

3.4 These steps in planning apply to one-off as well as routine plans or projects as well as to planning at senior management, middle management and junior management levels.

They will be the key stages in tackling Section A mini-cases.

3.5 Tackling a mini-case

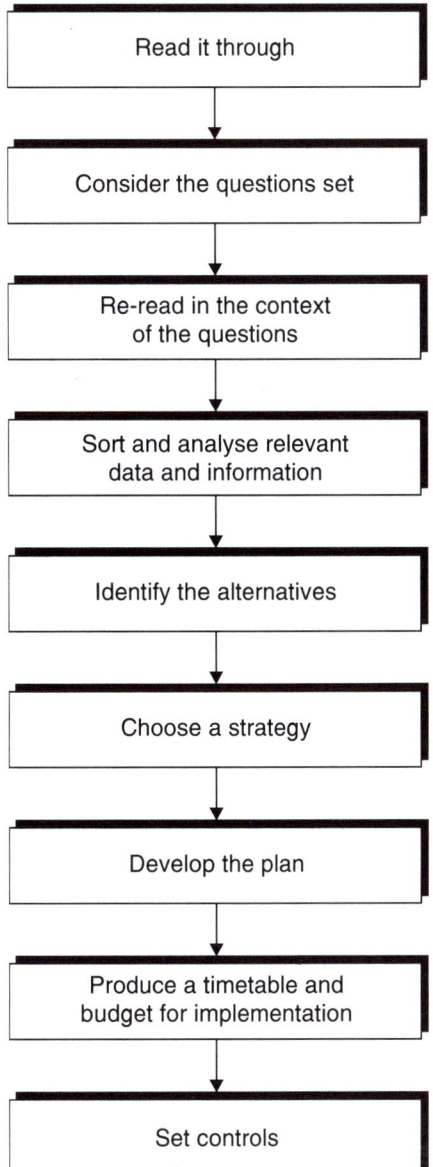

As you work through this Study Text you will find cases and scenarios which will give you the opportunity to practise these skills. Look at the following extract from a typical mini-case for this paper.

3.6 EXAMPLE

Leisurestop is a nationwide chain of 75 stores specialising in hobbies and sports equipment. They have doubled the number of outlets over the last five years, and expect to open their hundredth store within 36 months. In the early days of the business, staff were well trained, had extensive product knowledge and were very loyal to the business. High standards of customer care were essential to the positioning of the stores. As the newly appointed marketing manager of Leisurestop, you are concerned by the findings of a 'small customer' survey which compares your service with that of a leading competitor and the features and services the customers perceive as important.

Part A: The nature of management and organisation issues

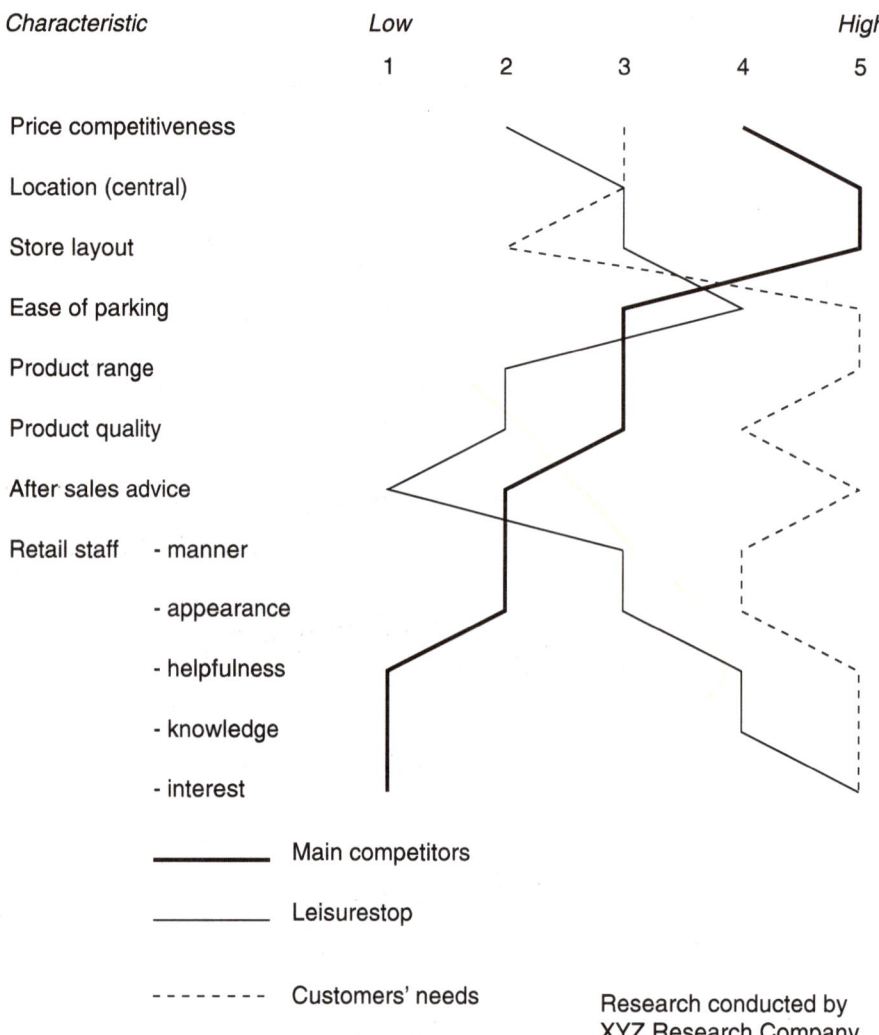

Further investigations undertaken by you have identified the following.

(a) 25% of new employees do not get induction training. (This includes all part-time and weekend staff.)

(b) Staff turnover is rising.

This year (forecast)	Last year	Previous year
20%	18%	15%

(c) There are at least 20 unfilled vacancies at any one time and store managers have been unable to resolve problems of staff levels at peak times.

3.7 Now you have read through the Leisurestop scenario, consider the following questions.

- What do you think are the **main problems** faced by the company?
- What might the **causes** of these problems be?
- Use this framework to list the strengths and weaknesses of leisureship.

Strengths	Weaknesses

- What actions would you consider taking if you were the marketing manager?

3.8 SOLUTION

As you work through this Study Text, you will develop more knowledge of skills to help you to tackle cases like this with confidence. The objective here is to give you an indication of the **level** and **style of work** you can expect so that you work through the course with the outcome needed in mind.

3.9 You might have identified that Leisurestop have a problem with customer care. Staff are failing to live up to the expectations of the customers and the competitors are doing better in this aspect of the business.

3.10 The cause could be too rapid growth and inadequate training. Staff turnover is increasing, indicating that morale may be a problem. Staff shortages may be causing remaining staff to work under pressure and the failure of managers to solve staffing level problems indicates some training may be needed here.

Strengths	Weaknesses
Growing business	Poor parking
Good product range and quality	Poor customer care
Central locations	Rising staff turnover
Well merchandised outlets	Weak managers?
Undertaking research?	Lack of effective staff training

3.11 There are a number of further steps you might take as the marketing manager.

- A further analysis of a competitor's staff training approach
- A detailed audit of customer care issues
- A programme of customer care training
- Development of induction training for **all** staff
- The introduction of a bonus scheme based on customer care targets

4 PREPARING FOR SECTION B QUESTIONS

4.1 The second part of the examination paper offers you a choice of three questions from six. Each is worth 20 marks.

4.2 Although shorter in length, these also may be in the form of a mini scenario which you will need to consider in order to recommend a course of action. You will have 32 minutes for each of these questions, so they will need to be treated in some depth.

4.3 **Approach**

(a) Read the question through carefully.

- What is it about?
- What are you asked to do?
- What role have you been given?
- What are the constraints (eg time, budget)?

(b) Take time **to plan your answer**. It will need to take into account the style and tone indicated by the role which you have been allocated. You might find the **content/context** framework helpful as a basis for your plan.

4.4 **Question.** As the newly appointed marketing manager of Leisurestop you have been asked to produce a report to management giving recommendations for improving the standards of customer care.

Content	*Context*
Strategies for improving customer care.	In the context of a rapidly expanding retailer whose current customer care levels are poor and deteriorating.
Training	
Motivation	Service sector - operational level staff are key.
Attitude changing	
Organisation?	

A self-assessment checklist

4.5 When reviewing your work, you might care to try the self-assessment checklist below to assess your answers.

Content

1. Is the answer relevant to the **specific question asked**?
2. Are key points and recommendations supported and justified?
3. Is relevant knowledge and theory indicated where appropriate?
4. Is the approach logical and thorough?
5. Are recommendations credible in terms of the scale of the business and its problems and the time available?
6. Have I provided budgets, timetables and control criteria to help in implementation?
7. Have I adopted the role and demonstrated my **own** management skills?
   - Internal marketing of plans?
   - Communication?
   - Problem solving?
   - Decision making?
   - Time keeping?

Layout

8. Does the answer use the specified layout?
9. Have diagrams and flow charts been used to make the work easier to follow?
10. Does the work demonstrate my skills as a professional communicator?
    - Is the tone appropriate?
    - Is there lots of white space?
    - Are the headings clear?
    - Does the use of colour enhance the content?
    - Is it easy to read?

5 PREPARING FOR EFFECTIVE STUDY

5.1 Finding time to undertake the exercises and activities as well as practising examination answers is important to your exam success. As this course is essentially about planning, planning your study is a good practical opportunity to think about time management and project planning.

1: Managing the examination

5.2 Ask yourself these questions.

- Where are you now?
- How long do you have before the examination?
- How many hours a week can you study?
- How many other exams are you preparing for?

5.3 Use this weekly planner to identify study times and try to stick to them.

Day	Time					
	6 - 9 am	9 - 12 noon	12 - 3 pm	3 - 6 pm	6 - 9 pm	9 - 12 midn't
Monday						
Tuesday						
Wednesday						
Thursday						
Friday						
Saturday						
Sunday						

5.4 A checklist for study time is offered below.

1	A number of shorter study periods are more effective than one long marathon session.
2	Break large tasks up into smaller units. The sections within each chapter of these study texts cover a specific aspect of a topic. Each could be the focus for a short study session.
3	Allow time for review and reflection and to complete your own notes after each chapter. This will make revision much easier.
4	Early in the day is usually more effective study time than late in the day. Can you get up 40 minutes earlier?
5	Look for opportunities to study which will make better use of your time. Can you read on the journey to work? Do half an hour's work during a lunch break? If you have your work planned, you should always have short exercises or reading available when you have a spare minute.
6	Allow plenty of time for revision at the end of the course.

Part A: The nature of management and organisation issues

5.5 When you have identified what has to be done and how much time you have to do it you can produce a week-by-week planner and set yourself objectives (eg to have completed Chapter 3 by the end of next month). If you are working at a college use the tutor's lecture plan to guide the topics for completion each week. These may be in a different order to our Study Text, but you can use the index to sort out a reading and work plan which matches it.

Week	Objective	Hours spent	Achieved
1	Chapter 2	6	
2	Chapter 3	4	
3	Chapter 4	7	X outstanding (section 4)
4	Chapter 5	2	Completed 4.4

5.6 You will want to add to this plan work-based activities which you are advised to undertake. You can add these as you work towards them in the Study Text, but allow yourself plenty of time to implement them and take care to include your progress on these activities as part of a regular review.

5.7 You can make early preparation for a number of activities within the course by collecting the following in advance.

(a) Examples of customer communications, such as letters, reports, presentations and brochures. These can be those received from your bank etc or your organisation.

(b) Obtain examples of house style from those areas of the organisation dealing with customers such as finance, dispatch and marketing.

(c) Obtain four annual reports, including if possible, one from a not-for-profit organisation.

(d) Paperwork associated with recruitment and selection

- Job advertisements and descriptions (send off for three or four)
- Internal paperwork used by your company
- Your own job description and any appraisal documents you have

(e) The paperwork associated with a meeting, within work or outside it, from the notice to agenda and minutes.

(f) A system set up for you to build your personal development log as discussed earlier in this unit.

(g) One or two of the **general interest** management books which will provide you with more general background and illustrations. There are many of these around but they are not written as study texts. Visit your library or bookstore; a few of the titles you may want to look for include:

- *When Giants Learn to Dance* (RM Kanter)
- *Making it Happen* (John Harvey-Jones)
- *In Search of Excellence* (Peters and Waterman)

Furthermore, the broadsheet newspapers often have articles about management issues, particularly the *Financial Times*.

As far as the marketing trade press is concerned, the CIM's own journal, *Marketing Business*, regularly has articles that are relevant to this paper.

Revision and exam practice

5.8 To revise successfully, you need the help of your notes. Revision should be revision, not new learning and it should be **active**, not just reading through. It might help you to summarise your notes as you revise.

5.9 It can also help if you practise your exam technique. Exams are about time management as much as anything else. You should learn to allocate your time according to the marks available. The question bank at the back of this Study Text can be used for exam practice. Suggested time allocations are offered. You might also choose to get more exam practice from the BPP *Practice & Revision Kit* for this subject which contains a large bank of questions and suggested solutions, both tutorial questions to warm you up, and exam-style questions. An order form can be found at the end of this Study Text.

5.10 Take time to organise and plan your study before moving on. Good luck with the course.

Chapter Roundup

- The *Effective Management for Marketing* paper emphasises the importance of skill development. Knowledge alone will not be adequate for you to pass the examination - you will need to demonstrate your ability to use that knowledge in practical situations.

- At the earliest opportunity observe or participate in activities such as interviewing, timetabling, negotiation or budgeting.

- Most students fail exams because of a failure of examination technique. This can only be developed through practice and evaluation.

- Make a point now of promising yourself to undertake the exercises and cases included and to review your answers with any solutions suggested.

- The examiners highlight some common exam mistakes. These include not answering the questions asked and not being selective in offering what you know to the examiner.

- The question paper contains two sections. You will need to develop experience at handling both parts.

- Careful planning of your time and the scheduling of activities related to the course will help you get the most out of it, with the minimum of stress.

Part A: The nature of management and organisation issues

> **Quick Quiz**
>
> 1 Why is it important to practise skills in this subject? (see para 1.3)
> 2 List the mistakes examiners typically find in answers from students with poor exam technique. (2.5)
> 3 How long will you have to spend on Section A? (3.1); one question in Section B? (4.2)
> 4 List the steps in a planning decision. (3.3)
> 5 List the steps outlined for helping you tackle a Section A mini-case. (3.5)
> 6 What steps would you follow when tackling a Section B question? (4.3)
> 7 What is the significance of content and context when planning an exam answer? (4.3)
> 8 What factors would you use to evaluate the quality of layout of a candidate's exam paper? (4.5)
> 9 What are the rules for making the most effective use of your study time? (5.4)
> 10 What is the purpose of maintaining a week-by-week planner? (5.5)

Action Programme Review

1 Once you have established your list of possibilities, follow up the most likely ones or those that are potentially most valuable. Talk to the Training Manager or your boss at work and see what support they can provide. You would ideally like the opportunity to sit in and observe or manage meetings and be given opportunities to develop skills in communication, project planning and negotiation. You may be surprised by the amount of help you can get. Find out about public meetings which you can observe, and go along to public presentations and talks to observe the techniques of public speaking and presentations.

You will not be short of opportunities, but you will need to make the most of them; even routine opportunities at work should not be taken for granted. No matter how experienced a planner, presenter or negotiator you are, there will be room for personal improvement.

Now try illustrative question 1 at the end of the Study Text

2 What is Management?

Chapter Topic List	Syllabus reference
1 Setting the scene	
2 The management task: its functions and value	1.1, 1.2
3 Organisational culture	1.2
4 The activities of the manager	1.3
5 An historical overview of the changing roles and philosophies of management	1.1
6 Forecasting the future role of managers	1.1
7 The responsibilities of the marketing manager	1.1, 1.3

Learning Outcomes

- Students will be able to explain the theory underpinning effective management of self, other people, resources and client relationships.
- Students will be able to describe organisation cultures and their positive and negative impact on marketing management.

Key Concepts Introduced

- Formal organisation
- The functions of the manager
- Culture
- Control

Examples of Marketing at Work

- Regional electricity
- Corporate downsizing
- Executive style at Granada

Part A: The nature of management and organisation issues

1 SETTING THE SCENE

1.1 This chapter introduces you to some of the main ideas of management theory, to give you an overview of its context within the organisation, and to put the personal skills and development discussed in the later chapters in a suitable context.

1.2 A manager works in an **organisation,** which is a group of people who are directed to achieving goals. The best way of getting people to achieve organisational goals has been much disputed. Traditional theories of management are described in Section 2 and are contrasted with more recent theories of what managers' roles should be: a manager should be able to plan and control the activities of the organisation - but a manager's own job can appear completely chaotic, with interruptions and many demands. (In Section 5 we describe how the old certainties about management are being undermined by events.)

1.3 In Section 3, we discuss **planning and decision making.** As a marketing manager you will inevitably be involved in planning marketing activities - indeed, as we shall see in Chapter 4, your own time must be planned and controlled as well. We also give you a brief model to apply when you are making decisions - another aspect of the management task.

1.4 In Sections 4 and 5 we offer you an overview of how the management role has changed. In Section 4 we relate these changes to the marketing orientation, with which you must by now be familiar. The sort of stresses managers and workers are under are discussed in Section 5, as firms react to new technology and global competition to reduce the number of management layers and decentralise power.

1.5 Finally we discuss the specific role of the marketing manager, who is the customer's champion within the organisation, as well as the organisation's main communicator with customers. The role of looking after customers and the necessary skills involved in this are discussed in detail in Chapter 10.

Links with other papers

1.6 Issued raised in the Effective Management for Marketing paper are relevant to other Advanced Certificate paper. Customer service – and the human resource implications of this – is an important feature of the Marketing / Customer Interface paper: improving customer service requires firm attention to the 'people' aspects of management.

2 THE MANAGEMENT TASK: ITS FUNCTIONS AND VALUE

The manager and the organisation

2.1 Any business is an example of an **organisation,** that is, a **social system created and maintained in order to achieve predetermined objectives.**

2.2 Organisations exist to get results which individuals cannot achieve alone, because of limitations imposed on them by the environment and their own physical, or biological limitations.

2.3 **Management** is needed in organisation so that individuals work effectively towards the common goal. It involves:

- Vision and a sense of direction to pursue the goals and objectives
- A plan to achieve the objectives
- Organisation of the productive resources

2: What is management?

- Co-ordination of activities
- Control, to ensure that scarce resources are used efficiently and that the organisation is on track to achieve the set objectives

2.4 There have been a number of different approaches to a theory of management over the years.

(a) The **classical school**, exemplified by a 19th-century French industrialist, *Henri Fayol*, tried to lay down universal principles for the structure and organisation of a business. They took a logical, prescriptive approach to such things as the organisation of work, the management structure and channels of communication.

(b) **Scientific management** was based on the work of *FW Taylor*, an American engineer and manager working at the end of the 19th century. Taylor suggested that organisations would be more efficient if their knowledge, experience and practices were analysed, and the best methods established by management. Workers would be selected and trained in the proper methods and motivated by the improved earnings that would result.

(c) The **human relations** school shifted attention towards the people in organisations, and how they could be motivated to make the organisation more efficient. The early writers like *Mayo* thought that the most important factor for people at work was their relationships with other people, and **that teamwork was therefore the way to success.** Later writers, such as *Herzberg*, considered that people have many different reasons for working, or for working well, and suggested that management would have to pay attention to their **needs for challenge, interest, recognition and self development.**

(d) The **systems approach** is based on the idea that a work organisation is a system; it takes in inputs from its environment (eg people, money and materials), processes them and sends outputs back to the environment (eg goods and information). The organisation is in fact a complex system, because it is made up of sub-systems such as technology and methods of working; information systems; social systems; personnel systems and control systems. The systems approach suggests that organisations can only be efficient and effective if they adapt to the demands of the sub-systems within them and to the influences and demands from the environment.

(e) The **contingency approach** grew out of the systems approach, and is widely accepted today. It says that organisations have to adapt to different influences and demands; there is no single best way to design or run an organisation. What is right for one organisation is not necessarily right for another, and managers will have to analyse and respond to their own business circumstances.

As can be seen from this brief review, managers not only undertake day-to-day roles but they are supposed to identify the most effective way of organising the available resources to achieve the desired objectives and to ensure that all the **stakeholders** of the organisation have their needs satisfied.

Stakeholders

2.5 **Stakeholders** are all those individuals or institutions who have a legitimate interest in the organisation's activities. They include **shareholders, employees, suppliers and customers**. Less directly involved are the local community; special interest groups such as environmentalists; unions and the government. The manager must be cognisant of all these groups and bear their needs in mind when making decisions.

Part A: The nature of management and organisation issues

Organisation structure

> **Key Concept**
> **Formal organisation** means the official, management-approved system of relationships between individuals in an organisation. It includes such things as policies, rules, procedures and the structure of departments and management responsibilities.

2.6 Functions of the formal organisation structure

- **Links individuals in an established network of relationships** so that authority, responsibility and communications can be controlled

- **Groups together the tasks** required to fulfil the objectives of the organisation, and **allocates** them to suitable individuals or group

- **Gives the authority required** to perform the allocated functions, while **controlling behaviour** and resources in the interests of the organisation as a whole

- **Co-ordinates the objectives and activities** of separate units, so that overall aims are achieved without gaps or overlaps in the flow of work required

- **Facilitates the flow of work**, information and other resources, through planning, control and other systems

2.7 A formal organisation structure promotes a number of **desirable outcomes**.

- Unity or **congruence** of objectives and effort

- **Clarity** in expressing objectives

- **Control over interpersonal relationships**, the exercise of authority, use of resources, communication and other systems, thus offering predictability and stability for planning and decision making

- **Controlled information flow** throughout the structure which aids co-ordination and improves employee satisfaction

- The establishment of **precedents, procedures, rules and norms** to facilitate decision making

Functions of management

> **Key Concept**
> **The functions of the manager** define the nature of the manager's job. Unlike professionals, such as lawyers and accountants, the manager's role is not primarily the deployment of **knowledge** but consists mostly of the **performance of certain roles within an organisation. It is practical and driven by performance.**

2.8 Many writers have sought to analyse the manager's operational functions The weighting of the various responsibilities will change according to the seniority of the manager, his/her specialist function, and the structure and culture of the organisation.

Henri Fayol

2.9 Henri Fayol undertook one of the first systematic approaches to analysing and defining the manager's job.

He described five functions with which most practising managers are still able to identify.

(a) **Planning.** Selecting the objectives and methods for achieving them, either for the organisation as a whole or for a part of it. Planning might be done exclusively by **line managers** who will later be responsible for performance; however, **advice** on **planning** decisions might also be provided by **staff managers** who do not have line authority for putting the plans into practice.

(b) **Organising.** Establishing the structure of tasks to be performed to achieve the goals of the organisation; grouping these tasks into jobs for an individual; creating groups of jobs within departments; delegating authority to carry out the jobs, providing systems of information and communication and co-ordinating activities within the organisation.

(c) **Commanding.** Giving instructions to subordinates to carry out tasks over which the manager has authority for decisions and responsibility for performance.

(d) **Co-ordinating.** Harmonising the activities of individuals and groups within the organisation. Management must reconcile differences in approach, effort, interest and timing.

(e) **Controlling.** Measuring and correcting activities to ensure that performance is in accordance with **plans**. Plans will not be achieved unless activities are monitored, and deviations identified and corrected as soon as they become apparent.

2.10 Several writers followed Fayol with broadly similar analyses of management functions. Other functions which might be identified, for example, are **staffing** (filling positions in the organisation with people), **leading** (unlike commanding, 'leading' is concerned with the interpersonal nature of management) and acting as the **organisation's representative** in dealing with other organisations (an ambassadorial or public relations role, particularly important to marketing manager's work).

2.11 Note the changing emphasis from classical to human relations ideas: many theorists now reject Fayol's concept of 'commanders', arguing instead that managers should approach the same function by being **communicators, persuaders** and **motivators**.

Managerial roles: Mintzberg

2.12 Another way of looking at the manager's job is to observe what managers **actually do**, and from this to draw conclusions about what **roles** they play or act out. *Henry Mintzberg* identified **ten managerial roles,** which managers take on as appropriate to their personalities and the nature of the task in hand.

2.13 **Interpersonal roles**

- Figurehead — Performing ceremonial and social duties as the organisation's representative, for instance at conferences
- Leader — Uniting and inspiring the team to achieve objectives
- Liaison — Communication with people outside the manager's work group or the organisation

2.14 **Informational roles**

- Monitor — Receiving information about the organisation's performance and comparing it with objectives

19

Part A: The nature of management and organisation issues

- (5) • Disseminator — Passing on information, mainly to subordinates
- (6) • Spokesman — Transmitting information outside the unit or organisation, on behalf of the unit or organisation

2.15 **Decisional roles**

- (7) • Entrepreneur — Mobilising resources to get things done and to seize opportunities
- (8) • Disturbance-handler — Rectifying mistakes and getting operations, and relationships, back on course
- (9) • Resource allocator — Distributing resources in the way that will most efficiently achieve defined objectives
- (10) • Negotiator — Bargaining for required resources and influence

2.16 Most managers will discharge the majority of these roles. Different 'hats' will be worn more frequently according to the seniority and situation of the manager. **Brand managers** are likely to be very involved in liaison, monitoring and disturbance handling, whilst the **marketing director** has an important role as a leader, perhaps figurehead, negotiator and entrepreneur.

Action Programme 1

Consider your own role as a manager, or that of a manager you know.

1. What functions and roles are performed routinely?
2. What weightings would you allocate in terms of Mintzberg's role analysis?
3. If possible, compare your analysis with the job description for the post. How accurate do you think the description is? How would you recommend changing it if there was the need to appoint someone new to the post?
4. Now consider the role and functions of a more senior manager in the organisation. How do they differ? Can you identify the kind of new skills a manager might need to develop in order to be prepared for promotion within the organisation?

2.17 Probably you identified a further dimension to the work of the manager when completing this exercise: the operational or specialist functional responsibilities of being a sales manager (financial or production specialist).

The value of management

2.18 Management is essential for converting the inputs of the operation into valued outputs and for satisfying stakeholders' needs. Managers are the element which economists call **enterprise**, without which the other factors (land, labour and capital) cannot function. They are the custodians of the organisation's resources and are responsible for making the best use of them.

Management development

2.19 Whilst it is widely accepted that investment can improve the productivity of land, labour and capital, the concept of investing to improve the quality of 'management' is less widely recognised. It is only recently that writers such as *Charles Handy* have highlighted the lack of structured management development characteristic of the UK.

2.20 The analysis of roles undertaken by the manager might suggest the manager has to be a Jack or Jill of all trades, but master of none. This breadth of remit means that managers must be aware of their own strengths and weaknesses, taking responsibility for their own development and aware of how the requirements made of them are likely to change with promotion and career progression.

3 ORGANISATIONAL CULTURE

3.1 Organisations often have their own distinctive culture. In wider society, culture is defined by such things as shared history, attitudes and opinions, aesthetic activities and accepted patterns of behaviour. An organisation's distinctive culture is established in the same way. However, unlike a society, an organisation is defined largely by its purpose, and this is a further influence on its culture.

> **Key concept**
> The word, **culture** is used by sociologists and anthropologists to encompass 'the sum total of the beliefs, knowledge, attitudes of mind and customs to which people are exposed in their social conditioning.'

3.2 Knowledge of the culture of a society is clearly of value to businesses in a number of ways.

(a) **Marketers** can adapt their products accordingly, and be fairly sure of a sizeable market. This is particularly important in export markets.

(b) **Human resource managers** may need to tackle cultural differences in recruitment. For example, some ethnic minorities have a different body language from the majority, which may be hard for some interviewers to interpret.

> **Key concept**
> **Culture** in an organisation is the sum total of the beliefs, knowledge, attitudes of mind and customs to which people are exposed during their interaction with the organisation.

3.3 Culture is both internal to an organisation and external to it. The culture of an organisation is embedded in the culture of the wider society.

3.4 *Peters and Waterman*, in their book *In Search of Excellence*, found that the 'dominance and coherence of culture' was an essential feature of the 'excellent' companies they observed. A 'handful of guiding values' was more powerful than manuals, rule books, norms and controls formally imposed (and resisted). They commented: 'If companies do not have strong notions of themselves, as reflected in their values, stories, myths and legends, people's only security comes from where they live on the organisation chart.'

3.5 All organisations will generate their own cultures, whether spontaneously or under the guidance of positive managerial strategy. The culture will exist in three main areas.

(a) **Basic, underlying assumptions** which guide the behaviour of the individuals and groups in the organisation. These may include customer orientation, or belief in quality, trust in the organisation to provide rewards, freedom to make decisions, freedom to make mistakes and the value of innovation and initiative at all levels.

(b) **Overt beliefs** expressed by the organisation and its members, which can be used to condition the assumptions mentioned above. These beliefs and values may emerge as

sayings, slogans and mottoes, such as *IBM's* motto, 'think'. They may emerge in a rich mythology of jokes and stories about past successes and heroic failures.

(c) **Visible artefacts** - the style of the offices or other premises, dress rules, display of trophies, the degree of informality between superiors and subordinates etc.

Management can encourage this by selling a sense of the corporate mission, or by promoting the corporate image. It can reward the right attitudes and punish (or simply not employ) those who are not prepared to commit themselves to the culture.

3.6 An organisation's culture is influenced by many factors.

(a) **The organisation's founder.** A strong set of values and assumptions is set up by the organisation's founder, and even after he or she has retired, these values have their own momentum. Or, to put it another way, an organisation might find it hard to shake off its original culture. Peters and Waterman believed that 'excellent' companies began with strong leaders.

(b) **The organisation's history.** *Johnson and Scholes* state that the way an organisation works reflects the era when it was founded. Farming, for example, sometimes has a craft element to it. The effect of history can be determined by stories, rituals and symbolic behaviour. They legitimise behaviour and promote priorities. (In some organisations certain positions are regarded as intrinsically more 'heroic' than others.)

(c) **Leadership and management style.** An organisation with a strong culture recruits managers who naturally conform to it.

(d) **Structure and systems** affect culture as well as strategy. Handy's description of an Apollonian role culture (bureaucracy) is an example (among others) where **organisational form** has **cultural consequences**.

Culture and structure

3.7 Writing in 1972, *Roger Harrison* suggested that organisations could be classified into four types. His work was later popularised by Charles Handy in his book 'Gods of Management'. The four types are differentiated by their structures, processes and management methods. The differences are so significant as to create distinctive cultures, to each of which Handy gives the name of a Greek God.

3.8 **Zeus** is the god representing the **power culture** or **club culture**. Zeus is a dynamic entrepreneur who rules with snap decisions. Power and influence stem from a central source, perhaps the owner-directors or the founder of the business. The degree of formalisation is limited, and there are few rules and procedures. Such a firm is likely to be organised on a **functional** basis.

eg. ADVANTAGE

(a) The organisation is capable of adapting quickly to meet change.

(b) Personal influence decreases as the size of an organisation gets bigger. **The power culture is therefore best suited to smaller entrepreneurial organisations, where the leaders have direct communication with all employees.**

(c) Personnel have to get on well with each other for this culture to work. These organisations are clubs of 'like-minded people introduced by the like-minded people, working on empathetic initiative with personal contact rather than formal liaison.'

3.9 **Apollo** is the god of the **role culture** or **bureaucracy. There is a presumption of logic and rationality.**

(a) These organisations have a **formal structure**, and operate by well-established **rules and procedures**. Individuals are required to perform their job to the full, but not to overstep the boundaries of their authority. Individuals who work for such organisations tend to learn an expertise without experiencing risk; many do their job adequately, but are not over-ambitious.

(b) **The bureaucratic style can be very efficient** in a stable environment, when the organisation is large and when the work is predictable.

3.10 **Athena** is the goddess of the **task culture. Management is seen as completing a succession of projects or solving problems**.

- The task culture is reflected in project teams and task forces. In such organisations, **there is no dominant or clear leader. The principal concern in a task culture is to get the job done**. Therefore the individuals who are important are the **experts** with the ability to accomplish a particular aspect of the task.

- Performance is judged by **results**.

- Task cultures are expensive, as experts demand a market price.

- Task cultures also depend on variety, and to tap creativity requires a tolerance of perhaps costly mistakes.

3.11 **Dionysus** is the god of the **existential culture**. In the three other cultures, the individual is subordinate to the organisation or task. **An existential culture is found in an organisation whose purpose is to serve the interests of the individuals within it**. These organisations are rare, although an example might be a partnership of a few individuals who do all the work of the organisation themselves (with perhaps a little secretarial or clerical assistance).

- Barristers (in the UK) work through chambers. The clerk co-ordinates their work and hands out briefs, but does not control them.

- Management in these organisations are often lower in status than the professionals and are labelled secretaries, administrators, bursars, registrars and chief clerk.

- The organisation depends on the **talent of the individuals;** management is derived from the consent of the managed, rather than the delegated authority of the owners.

3.12 The descriptions above interrelate four different strands.

- The individual
- The type of the work the organisation does
- The culture of the organisation
- The environment

Organisational effectiveness perhaps depends on an appropriate fit of all of them.

Culture and strategy

3.13 Culture is an important filter of information and an interpreter of it, as suggested in the diagrams below.

- Ignoring culture

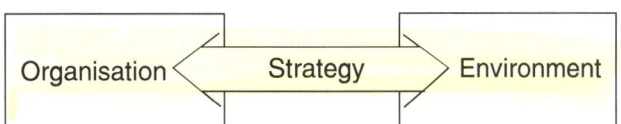

- Including culture

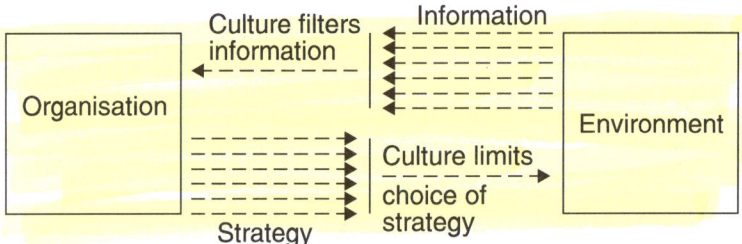

Culture filters and reconfigures environmental information. At the same time culture filters out a number of strategic choices. For example, a firm might have a cultural predisposition against embarking on risky ventures. Another culture might have an ingrained 'Buy British' approach. Finally, **if culture is embodied in *behaviour*, existing behaviour may make a strategy incompatible with the culture and so impossible to implement**.

3.14 A model of culture which focuses specifically on a firm's approach to strategy was suggested by *Miles and Snow*, who outlined three strategic cultures, and a fourth 'non-strategic' culture.

(a) **Defenders like low risks, secure niche markets, and tried and trusted solutions**. These companies have cultures whose stories and rituals reflect historical continuity and consensus. Decision-taking is relatively formalised. (There is a stress on 'doing things right' ie efficiency.) Personnel are drawn from within the industry.

(b) **Prospectors are organisations where the dominant beliefs are more to do with results** (doing the right things ie effectiveness). They seek to expand and increase market presence, and move into new areas.

(c) **Analysers try to balance risk and profits**. They use a core of stable products and markets as a source of earnings, like defenders, but move into areas that prospectors have already opened up. Analysers follow change, but do not initiate it.

(d) **Reactors**, unlike the three above, **do not have viable strategies**, other than living from hand to mouth.

 **Marketing at work**

Miles and Snow's analysis was applied to the responses by the regional electricity companies (RECs) to takeover bids. (The RECs are responsible for supplying and distributing electricity.)

At privatisation they 'shared a common heritage and hence ... greater similarities than would be found in more well-established private sector market places'.

- The largest REC, Eastern Group, 'embraced' the possibility of an alliance with Hanson. Eastern exhibits the characteristics of a 'prospector'. Its chief executive is 'non-REC' 'with a North American corporate pedigree and a greater interest in activities outside the traditional REC field'.
- Norweb and Midlands were 'cautious prospectors' which allow significant degrees of decentralisation, and a 'willingness to bring in executives with experience external to the industry'. They countenance 'strategic alliances'.
- Many of the RECs 'have demonstrated classical defender strategies'. They have specific features.
  - hierarchical company structures
  - board membership drawn from within the industry
  - incremental growth, rather than more rapid growth by entering new business areas; little enthusiasm for diversification

Financial Times

3.15 *Deal and Kennedy* (*Corporate Cultures*) consider cultures to be a function of the willingness of employees to take **risks**, and how quickly they get **feedback** on whether they got it right or wrong.

High risk

	BET YOUR COMPANY CULTURE ('Slow and steady wins the race') Long decision-cycles: stamina and nerve required eg oil companies, aircraft companies, architects	**HARD 'MACHO' CULTURE** ('Find a mountain and climb it') eg entertainment, management consultancy, advertising
Slow feedback			*Fast feedback*
	PROCESS CULTURE ('It's not what you do, it's the way that you do it') Values centred on attention to excellence of technical detail, risk management, procedures, status symbols eg banks, financial services, government	**WORK HARD/PLAY HARD CULTURE** ('Find a need and fill it') All action - and fun: team spirit eg sales and retail, computer companies, life assurance companies

Low risk

Culture and management

3.16 Matters such as the dress code, etiquette and forms of address are superficial aspects of organisational culture. More important are the prevailing **style of management** and the **attitude of the organisation to its market and other stakeholders.**

Managerial styles

3.17 **Managerial style** is discussed further in Chapter 6. For now, it can be regarded as defined by the extent to which subordinates participate in the decision-making process. It can be assessed against a scale ranging from autocratic to democratic. It is important to take a contingency approach to managerial style; there is no single style which is appropriate for all circumstances. A manager dealing with a sudden crisis would probably be brisk and incisive. The same person considering arrangements for an office party in 6 months' time would probably consult widely among the staff.

3.18 Managerial style often reflects organisational structure. A very hierarchical organisation with very clearly defined internal boundaries will encourage an autocratic style. A more fluid structure needs a more participative style.

Attitude to the market and stakeholders

3.19 Many organisations have a formal **mission statement** which defines their approach to their market and their stakeholders. Whether or not explicitly stated, the organisation's attitudes form part of its culture. An important aspect is the extent to which the organisation exploits its customers and other stakeholders, and the extent to which it co-operates with them. For example, the mis-selling of personal pensions by the UK insurance industry is a clear example of a culture of exploitation of customers. Exploitation of small suppliers by taking extended credit is very common among larger firms but **Just in Time purchasing** in the motor industry has led to a much more co-operative approach to suppliers. Similarly, a company which emphasises quality must secure the commitment of the workforce to the goals of the organisation.

Action Programme 2

Return to the ten managerial roles and analyse your own experience and expertise in each area. Turn this into a strengths and weaknesses analysis. Whilst doing this, try to identify opportunities for developing areas of weaknesses. Here are some examples.

- Internal training programmes
- Job shadowing with colleagues
- Observation, secondments or work with community or social groups

4 THE ACTIVITIES OF THE MANAGER

4.1 The manager has many functions and must take responsibility for a range of business activities. In this section, we provide you with an overview of these activities to give a context for the development of the management skills covered in detail in this course.

Planning

4.2 Planning enables the organisation to cope with the uncertainty of the future in a way that will allow its objectives to be achieved. There are three important steps to planning.

- **Objective-Setting**. Deciding what the organisation, and units within it, should achieve

- **Forecasting**. Anticipating, as far as possible, what opportunities and threats are likely to be offered by the future

- **Detailed planning**. Making decisions about what to do, how and when to do it and who should be responsible for it

Even the best plans may go wrong, but plans give direction and predictability to the work of the organisation, and enable it to adapt to environmental changes without crisis.

4.3 Planning affects all levels of management from the determination of overall direction, down to the detail of day-to-day operational tasks. There is a **hierarchical structure** of plans in which broad, long-term strategies lead to medium-term policies which are supported by short-term operational decisions.

An approach to planning

4.4 A systematic approach to planning, based on results and objectives involves:

Step 1. **aims;** which dictate
Step 2. **priorities,** or '**key result areas**'; for which there should be
Step 3. **standards;** and
Step 4. **detailed targets;** so that
Step 5. **action plans;** can be formulated and implemented, subject to
Step 6. **monitoring;** and
Step 7. **control** action where required.

4.5 Through your studies at Advanced Certificate and Diploma Level and your work as a practising marketer you will be called upon to produce specific and often detailed plans. The above framework can be used as a basis for section headings within a report or plan.

> **Key Concept**
> **Control** is the process of monitoring the activities of individuals and units, and taking whatever actions may be necessary to bring performance into line with plans, by adjusting performance or, possibly, the plans themselves.

Control

4.6 **Control is required because unpredictable events occur and actual performance deviates from what was expected and planned.** For example, a powerful new competitor may enter the market, or there may be an unexpected rise in labour costs. Control systems allow managers to identify deviations from plan and to do something about them before they have adverse consequences.

4.7 **Planning and control are intimately linked.**

(a) It is necessary to verify whether or not the plan has worked or is working, and whether the objectives of the plan have been/are being achieved. This is where control becomes part of the planning process.

(b) Actual results and performance are therefore compared to the plan. If there are deviations, weaknesses or errors, control measures will be taken - which involves adjusting or setting further plans for ongoing action. Thus planning becomes part of the control process.

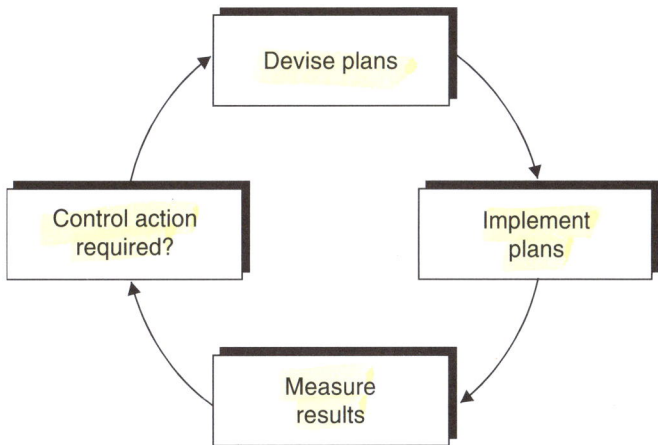

Budgets

4.8 An important aspect of both planning and control activity is the **budget** and you may be asked to make budget recommendations in the examination. Do not worry about the actual costs of various activities; the examiners are more interested in the fact you have been through the process of **identifying the key cost areas**.

4.9 A budget, since it has different purposes, might mean different things to different people.

(a) As a **forecast** of the expected performance of the organisation, it helps managers to look into the future. Given conditions of rapid change and uncertainty, however, this function will only be helpful over short periods of time. Budgets will often be updated or superseded.

(b) As a **means of allocating resources,** it can be used to decide what resources are needed and how much should be given to each area of the organisation's activities. Resource allocation is particularly important when some resources (usually finance and qualified staff) are in short supply. Budgets often set ceilings on spending by administrative and service departments - or project teams.

(c) As a **yardstick** against which to compare **actual performance,** the budget provides a means of indicating where and when **control action** may be necessary (and possibly where some managers or employees are open to censure for achieving poor results).

(d) As a **target** for achievement, a budget might be a means of **motivating the workforce** to greater personal accomplishment.

Action Programme 3

So what do things cost?

Over the next few weeks do some comparative shopping, ask questions or do some research to find out some basic costs. These will be useful when you need to select **financial budgets**.

Cost £

- 1 day's management consultancy
- 1 day's training (in house)
- 1 week's training course per person
- ½ page of advertising in a newspaper:
    local paper
    national paper
- 1 direct mail shot per 1,000
- Recruiting 1 new salesperson

Decision making and problem solving

4.10 In a business, a **decision** is usually the result of choosing between available or anticipated options and is often taken on the grounds of future projections. **The decision-making process thus involves value judgements and risk taking.** The earlier management authors highlighted decision-making as one of the key differences between management and workers.

4.11 How systematic should decision-making be? It has been suggested that too much time is spent thinking about decisions; and that the essence of good decisions is to make them firmly and quickly, and then get on with the work. However, risky or important decisions do need to be taken with care.

4.12 There are two approaches, which are applicable to different types of decision.

(a) **Scientific decision making** depends on the quantitative techniques of management, which measure and express all viable alternatives. It assumes that full and complete information will lead to the ideal solution. This approach ignores individual flair and fails to recognise that many management decisions have to be taken without the luxury of time in which to evaluate alternatives. Events will continue to evolve and may enforce a decision.

(b) **Reaction decision** theory assumes that once policies and corporate plans are established, decisions that are required follow as a natural result of those plans. In this way, decision making is regarded as an extension of the process of implementing corporate plans. Decisions are therefore partly predetermined by the detail of the plans.

2: What is management?

The decision sequence

4.13 There is a generally accepted rational model of decision making and problem solving.

We have a problem	Identify and define the problem
	Analyse the problem
What solution can we find?	Appraise available resources
	List and compare alternative solutions
	Select the optimum solution
Now implement the solution	Draw up action plan to implement solution
	Carry out plan
	Monitor progress/effectiveness of plan

4.14 You cannot find an answer unless you are asking the right question. Careful **definition of the problem** and examination of its causes frequently produce a definition of the solution. For example, a manager concerned with declining sales volume might concentrate on improving sales staff performance because there appears to be a direct link, while ignoring more subtle effects like product obsolescence and changes in fashion.

4.15 Decisions should be based on as many facts about the situation as it is possible to obtain with reasonable effort and at reasonable cost. However, most decisions are based on incomplete information, because all the information is not available or because, beyond a certain point, the gathering of **more** information would not be worth the extra time and cost involved. A good decision can be made without all the facts, but a manager must know what information is missing in order to evaluate the degree of risk involved in the decision.

4.16 There is rarely only one solution to a problem and much of a manager's skill will be exercised in framing, comparing and finally choosing between alternative solutions. Especially where creativity or innovation is required, it is advisable to generate as many options as possible. **Brainstorming** is a technique usually involving a group, where ideas are generated without immediate evaluation or comment so that creativity is not stifled.

4.17 An **action plan** to implement the chosen decision should be drawn up by the supervisor responsible in consultation with the subordinates who must put it into action. If a manager has to sell a decision to subordinates, it probably means that they have not been consulted properly in the evaluation of alternatives. We will discuss consensus decision making, and gaining acceptance of decisions later.

Action Programme 4

You have been given the opportunity from your employer to attend a two-week marketing manager's course at the CIM's training centre at Moor Hall, or to work on secondment for six weeks helping in the launch of a national charity appeal.

Summarise the process which you would go through to evaluate these options and make a decision between them.

Part A: The nature of management and organisation issues

4.18 Managers get decisions wrong, perhaps up to half the time. It helps if these are not decisions critical to the success of the business, but what is more important is that managers recognise and review their poor decisions, both to take corrective action and to learn from the decision and improve their decision making generally.

Action Programme 5

Make a list of five significant decisions which you have made over the last month or so, either at home or work. Can you remember the steps you went through to come to the decision?

How would you assess those decisions in retrospect? Was the decision right? Was it the best? If not what actions did you take to put it right?

4.19 To be effective as decision makers, managers need a framework that can be used as a reference point throughout their work. This diagram illustrates the decision sequence.

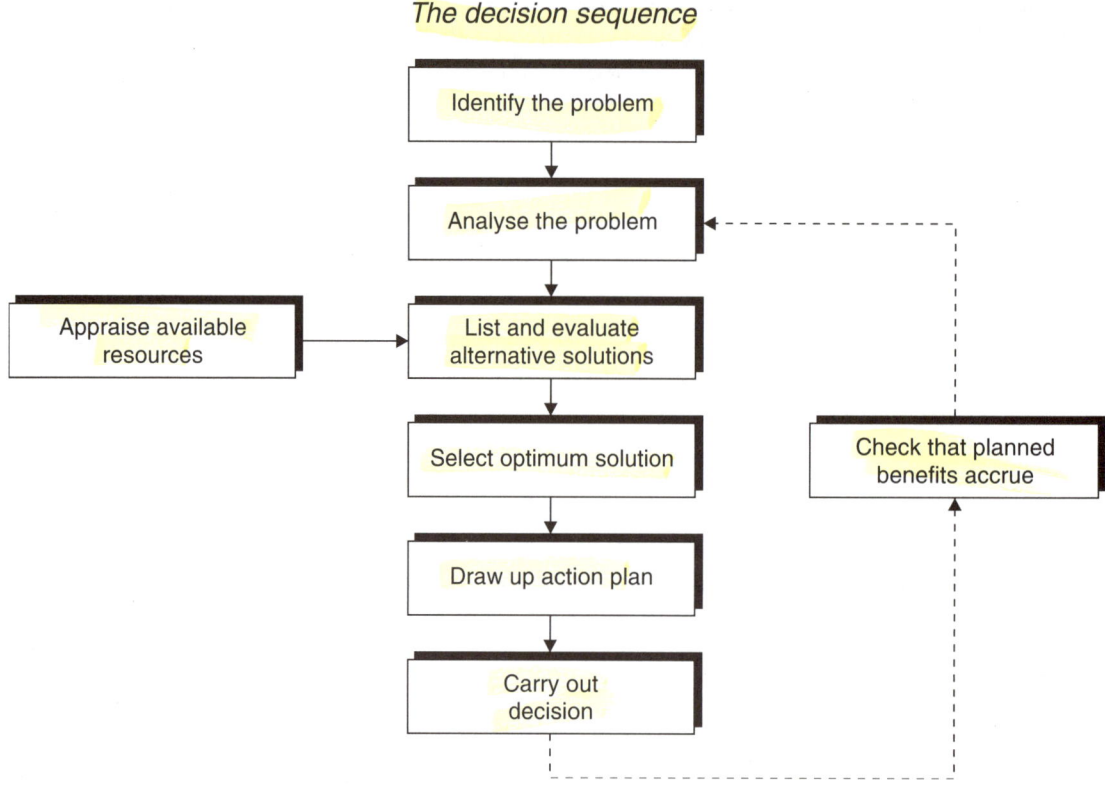

The decision sequence

5 AN HISTORICAL OVERVIEW OF THE CHANGING ROLES AND PHILOSOPHIES OF MANAGEMENT

Fashions in management

5.1 It is perhaps not surprising when you review the range of roles and activities taken on by managers to find also that over time there have been fashions in management style. The paternalism of a Victorian operation and the commanding and hierarchical style associated with the large organisations of the 1950s and 1960s, have gradually given way to the notion of managers as **leaders** and **facilitators**, increasingly seen as a central part of the team, rather than apart from it. Such changes are the result of a number of factors but, most importantly, they occur because managers are constantly seeking better ways of combining the resources in their charge in order to achieve competitive effectiveness.

2: What is management?

The changing worker

5.2 Many of a manager's resources are **people**, who are unpredictable and have changing expectations and attitudes to both work and the organisations which employ them. No-one in the UK now expects to have a job for life, especially one with the same employer. There tends therefore to be less loyalty to the company than there was in the past. Declining loyalty is the price paid for greater flexibility. Similar trends are evident across the world, so that even in Japan where lifetime employment was very common, there are no longer the guarantees there were.

5.3 Just as the **marketer** has to be aware of the changing needs of the customer, and appreciate that the age, educational background, aspirations and income of the target segment are constantly changing, so too the **manager** must recognise similar developments in employees. Mutually profitable exchange lies at the heart of both the buyer/seller and the employer/employee relationships. The employee offers skills, energy and effort, but has **expectations** and **needs** which must be met. They include a clean, safe work place and reasonable conditions; their absence certainly causes dissatisfaction, but other positive **motivators** are needed to promote high performance. Job satisfaction, prospects for promotion and peer recognition are amongst the key motivators. We will be returning to the issues of **motivation** later in this Study Text.

The changing environment

5.4 The external environment contains both challenges and opportunities for the manager. New technology and operational methods have increased output whilst free trade has increased competition. Economic fluctuations, government policy and legal changes have all influenced the business environment over time. An obvious change is the change in the balance of power between manufacturer and customer, forcing managers to change their views or **philosophy of business**. A developing business may well pass through the following stages.

Stage 1	Philosophy	Emphasis
Demand exceeds supply: a seller's market	Managers are centred on needs of operation: **production orientated**.	The organisation could grow be more successful by producing more, so managers concentrate on processes, operations, seeking ways to make more effective use of inputs: an inward looking focus.
Stage 2		
Output and new competitors increase. Demand and supply become more equal.	Managers seek to ensure their output is taken up by available customers. A **sales orientation**.	Production is now fine - but there are no longer queues of unsatisfied customers. Managers now turn their attention to advertising and selling to 'push' finished goods at customers
Stage 3		
Output continues to grow. Supply exceeds demand - a buyer's market exists	To survive, managers must be sure they satisfy customer needs. A **market orientation**.	Emphasis on market research to identify and anticipate customer needs before putting scarce resources into production. The customer now comes before the production process. Managers are externally focused.

Part A: The nature of management and organisation issues

Stage 4

| Legal and consumer pressures on environmental and quality issues | Firms consider the long-run interest of customers and society not just short-term mutually profitable exchange. Kotler's *Human Orientation*, or the **societal marketing concept**. | Emphasis becomes broader, encompassing environmental issues, the ethics of business activities and the wider interests of society not just satisfaction of the individual. Now managers have needs of both society *and* the customer to satisfy. |

Action Programme 6

How would you go about identifying the management philosophy of a particular organisation? Produce yourself a checklist and use it to evaluate the development stage of managers in the organisations below.

(a) Your organisation
(b) Your local doctor's surgery
(c) Your bank
(d) Your sports club/leisure centre
(e) The suppliers/intermediaries of your company

5.5 Managers have been forced to change their approaches and attitudes, as the external environment has changed. This process of change is ongoing and frequently painful. Managers are the ones who knock down the old ways or systems and build the new.

5.6 Responding to changes, or staying adaptable enough to be **able** to respond to changes, is not easy for organisations. Their formal organisation structures and practices may not be flexible enough to allow for unexpected events or quick changes of direction. They have to make long-term plans which cannot quickly be altered.

5.7 Perhaps the trickiest problem with managing organisational change is the fact that people dislike it. They frequently resist changes to their jobs.

(a) **Any** change makes people feel insecure and uncertain

(b) They fear a threat to their competence or success in their jobs

(c) Change disrupts the social structure and relationships they are used to, for example, if there is relocation or redundancies.

5.8 The implementation of change is seldom easy. Changes in crisis situations are often resisted less than routine changes, however, because people understand that there is an urgent **need** for change and that change is in their own interests. Managers should address and try to overcome resistance rather than simply pushing change on people.

6 FORECASTING THE FUTURE ROLE OF MANAGERS 6/01

Pressures for change

6.1 Traditionally structured organisations tend to have certain characteristics in common.

(a) Belief in **universal laws** like the **span of control** principle (a small number of subordinates for each manager)

(b) Very **tall structures** (ie lots of different management levels) with **close supervision** at every level

(c) **Hierarchical control** through a rigid chain of command (as in an army)

(d) **Problem-solving** of a fragmented, directive, mechanistic kind, solely devoted to putting things right once they had gone wrong (instead of making sure they did not go wrong in the first place)

(e) **Single function specialisms** like 'production' and 'sales', with departmental barriers and careers concentrated in one activity

(f) **Individualism** reflected in incentive systems and the encouragement of competitive behaviour

(g) **Focus on tasks and responsibilities** in job descriptions rather than the concept of adding value and using initiative for the organisation as a whole and for its customers

(h) **Systems** which were reactive and procedure-bound with opportunity being seen as a very positive employee asset

6.2 In the past, also, managers have been able to impose change on other people. Nowadays, **change has a dramatic impact on managers themselves**. The impetus for these changes has come from a number of external forces, most importantly the following.

(a) **New technology**. Improved information systems have meant that many middle managers previously involved in passing information have effectively been made redundant. Senior managers no longer need them to access or transmit information. New technologies have also increased the proportion of **knowledge workers** in the organisation. These people need less supervision as they plan and control their own work.

(b) **Recession.** The economic downturn, experienced across the world in the late 1980s and early 1990s effectively reduced demand, forcing many mature organisations into buyer's markets. In an attempt to get closer to customers and cut costs, senior management has **delayered** the organisational structure. Organisations are **flatter**, with senior management closer to the market. There are thousands fewer managers employed today in giant organisations such as *IBM* and *British Telecom*.

(c) The problems associated with the management of large bureaucratic organisations have been recognised. Many, such as the former *ICI*, have given up on the strategy of decades based on building competitive advantage through scale and cost economies and instead are looking for flexibility and responsiveness from smaller autonomous and de-centralised units. ICI demerged into two new companies, the 'new ICI' and the pharmaceuticals firm, *Zeneca*.

(d) Similarly the flexible manager encourages communication across the organisation with **cross-functional teams**. These are **task-centred**, replacing the vertical communication of functionally orientated tall structures.

6.3 Reasons for the gradual but perceptible shift away from the traditional organisation and management approaches include the following:

(a) **Everything global**: we now live in what has been described as a global village, with a global economy, a global marketplace, battered by global forces (political, economic, social, technological and religious).

(b) **Everything new**: organisations have come to appreciate that they are unlikely to survive unless they are responsive to the expectations of their customers; for some,

there is a very new perspective if they previously operated in a monopolistic (or quasi-monopolistic) environment and did not regard their clients as customers at all.

(c) **Everything faster**: with techniques of **mass customisation**, it is now possible to order a tailor-made Toyota from a Tokyo car showroom and have the car delivered 24 hours later.

(d) **Everything different**: it is no longer sufficient to keep doing the same things, it is now necessary to progressively do them better. The world of work has entered a major paradigm shift towards entirely different expectations about performance, challenging the conventional assumptions of old.

(e) **Everything turbulent**: there is no going back to the peace and quiet of organisational stability in a world of slow social and technological change - instead, organisations must continue to cope with messy, paradoxical, ambiguous scenarios.

6.4 The essential features for the new world of work have been eloquently discussed by *Hammer and Champy* in *Re-Engineering the Corporation: A Manifesto for Business Revolution* (1993). Hammer and Champy envisage the following trends.

(a) **Work units**: from functional departments to process teams

(b) **Jobs**: from simple tasks to multi-dimensional work. The old model offered simple tasks for simple people, whereas the new approach reflects complex jobs for smart people

(c) **Roles**: from 'controlled' to '**empowered**'. In a team environment, people have the chance to learn more about the work process as a complete entity; performing the role becomes more satisfying, with a greater sense of completion and accomplishment, and more learning and growth built in. The corollary is that jobs are more challenging and difficult. **Empowerment** reduces the planning and controlling responsibilities of managers

(d) **Values**: from protective to productive. People in organisations have to believe that they work for their customers, not for their bosses

(e) **Managers**: from supervisors to coaches

(f) **Executives**: from scorekeepers to leaders

(g) **Structures**: from **hierarchical** to **flat** (see below)

Action Programme 7

What have been the recent changes in your organisation or one with which you are familiar. Take time to talk to the managers involved - find out how those changes have affected them and their roles. What do they think the job will be like in 10 years time?

How structures have changed

6.5 A hierarchical structure is illustrated in the organisation chart below.

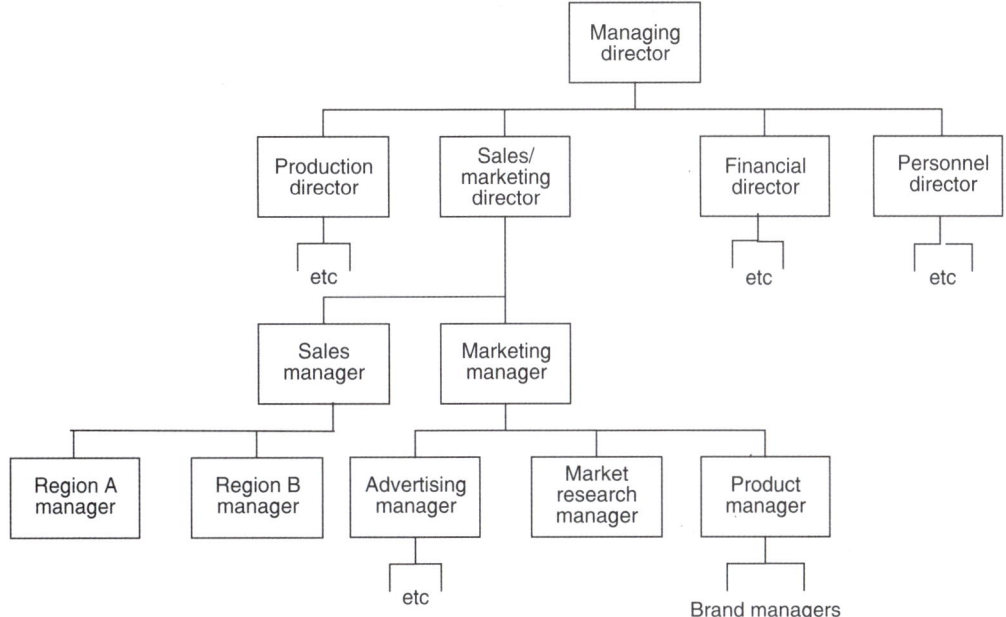

This type of structure gives clear lines of authority and responsibility.

6.6 A *matrix structure* may be used when lines of authority and responsibility are more complex.

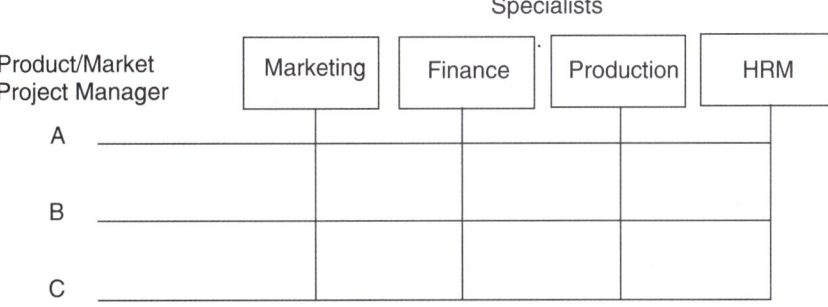

(a) Horizontal lines of authority and responsibility are superimposed on the normal vertical departmental lines. Thus allows manager A, B, and C to improve efficiency by providing tight coordination across departments. Some employees report to two managers. This idea can also be used temporarily when a multi-department project is to be managed.

(b) Whilst flexible and easing cross-company communication, this suggests that managers need even more effective communication and team building skills than hitherto.

6.7 The traditional **tall** hierarchical structure supporting senior management has been stood on its head.

Part A: The nature of management and organisation issues

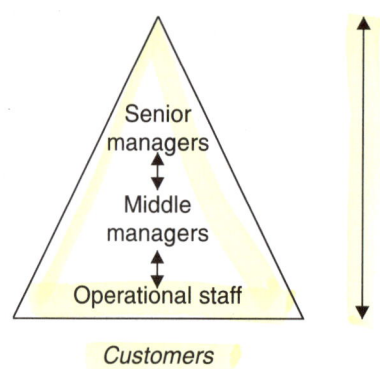

- Managers were a long way from customers
- Only the lowest grade of staff had customer contact!!
- Expensive structure of middle managers to support the organisation and its systems

Changes have been dramatic.

- The organisation is **flatter**
- Senior management now perceive their role as facilitating and supporting the operational staff in direct customer contact

The implications

6.8 There have been changes in roles and in attitudes. The manager of the future must possess certain vital qualities.

- Flexibility
- The ability to promote change and cope with it
- Obsession with quality and customer care
- Effective communication skills
- Leadership
- The ability to look at the organisation as a whole ('helicopter vision')

He or she will be a member of a smaller team, will be expected to take on more responsibility and will be more accountable than previously. Finally, the reduction in management layers means that there will be fewer managers.

6.9 Some writers have been very pessimistic, especially about the future for middle managers.

(a) *Rosabeth Moss Kanter* suggests that middle managers 'are squeezed between the demands of strategies they do not influence and the ambitions of increasingly independent-minded employees'.

(b) *Peter Drucker* notes: 'Whole layers of management neither make decisions nor lead ... instead their main, if only function, is to service as relays, human boosters for the faint, unfocused signals that pass for communication in the traditional, pre-information organisations'.

6.10 **Grounds for optimism about management**

(a) **Managerial roles are now more generalist,** with increased responsibilities and more tasks.

(b) **Managers are managing larger teams** or groups of people, with a wider mix of staff.

(c) **The new manager is more accountable:** this greater focus on performance means attempts to measure added-value more carefully and, hence, redesigned performance review (appraisal) systems.

2: *What is management?*

(d) Because of the explosion in IT, **managers have better information** on which to base their decisions.

(e) Moreover, because IT has taken much of the drudgery out of the manager's administrative activities, **the manager has more time** for the people aspects, for strategic thinking, for 'customer' service, and for dealing with routine tasks more efficiently.

(f) **Managers are learning new skills,** concerned with managing change, financial know-how, marketing, strategic planning and the motivation of multi-function teams.

6.11 In some research studies, the majority of participating managers are positive about the changes and how these changes are influencing their roles. Indeed, many argue that previous frustrations have been removed.

(a) **Flatter hierarchies** mean that most managers are closer to top management in the strategic and policy-making areas. Further, most managers have clear domains of responsibility, plus more control over the resources needed to achieve results.

(b) **'Empowerment'** is generating the opportunity to take on new challenges, to broaden expertise, to innovate and to take risks.

(c) Managerial careers may be more problematic, but it is a mistake to assume that all managers are continually striving for advancement.

Marketing at Work

In the 1990s, there was a decimation of middle managers at a number of large companies.

- BP. A new chairman announced 1,000 job losses of which 160 were head office managers - a 30% cut at head office.
- BT. Project Sovereign involved a change in structure. Of a total cut in jobs of 19,000, 6,000 came from management ranks. Recently, BT has announced it also wanted to cut senior management jobs.
- Harley Davidson, in the US, cut the number of production controllers at one of its plants from 27 to 1.

The reasons for this trend are as follows.

- Information technology makes the information-processing work of middle managers redundant.
- The trend towards team-working, whereby responsibility is devolved to groups of workers, renders redundant the directing and controlling role of middle managers.

On the other hand, there has been criticism at the increase in the number of managers in the UK's National Health Service, which was felt in some quarters, however, to be under-managed.

7 THE RESPONSIBILITIES OF THE MARKETING MANAGER

General management and specialist managers

7.1 So far we have been considering the general role of management but now we need to turn our attention specifically to **the role of the marketing managers.**

7.2 All managers wear two hats.

- They are leaders and organisers
- They deploy specialist skills

7.3 **However, the marketing manager also acts as the bridge between the company and its external audiences,** particularly customers.

Part A: The nature of management and organisation issues

(a) The marketing manager represents the customer's needs and interests *within* the organisation. The marketing manager is the customer's champion.

(b) Marketing managers often have the ambassadorial or figurehead role in the organisation; many of their teams also share this responsibility. Moreover, the marketing department generally creates relationships with customers, and controls the firm's communications with them.

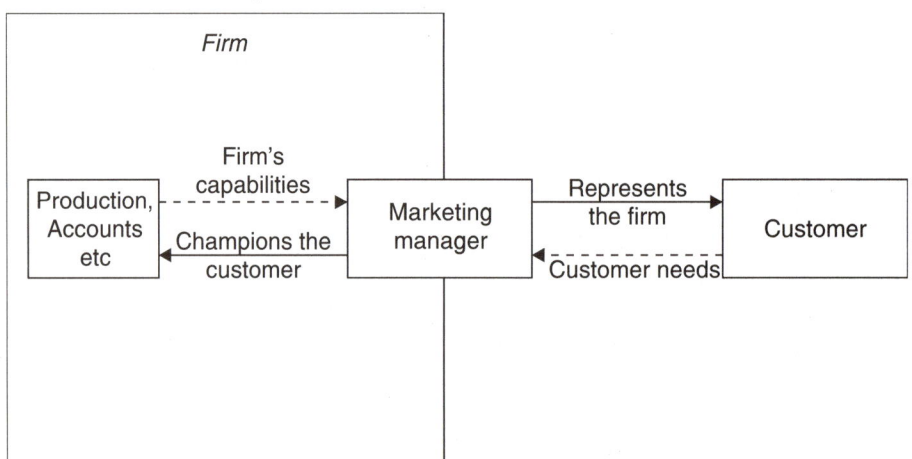

Embedding the market orientated culture

7.4 Marketing managers have not been very effective at spreading the gospel of customer orientation. Too many of their colleagues perceive marketing as being the same as advertising, selling or promotion and have **operational**, but no **strategic**, expectations of the marketing expert.

7.5 In many sectors, marketers have even reinforced the product focus of the business with their system of brand management in which managers are given responsibility for individual brands, **rather than the needs of customers**. It is only now that a number of FMCG manufacturers are re-assessing the value of the traditional brand manager, replacing them with the more market-orientated manager.

7.6 Much of the marketing philosophy has, however, been picked up by the *Total Quality Management* (TQM) movement, with the concepts of **internal customers, relationship marketing** and quantification of value added at each stage of the production process. Whether these developments are called marketing or something else is relatively unimportant, as long as the philosophy of customer satisfaction is effected within the business. An important role will remain for the managers responsible for external liaison, and for identifying and anticipating the changing needs of their customer base. We refer to these issues later in this Study Text.

Influencing the mix

7.7 The degree of freedom the marketing department has to determine the mix elements varies, because of required financial targets, existing production equipment and distribution systems. The marketing department probably has most control over promotion.

(a) The **product** element will be affected by the degree to which the marketing department has an influence over production and R&D.

(b) The **place** element will be affected by the degree to which the marketing department can influence distribution.

(c) The type of **price** demanded for a product will reflect the cost to a degree, and the finance department will have an inevitable influence. This also includes credit offered and payment terms each of which has an impact.

(d) The **promotion** element is under the direct control of the marketing department, even though many activities will be subcontracted.

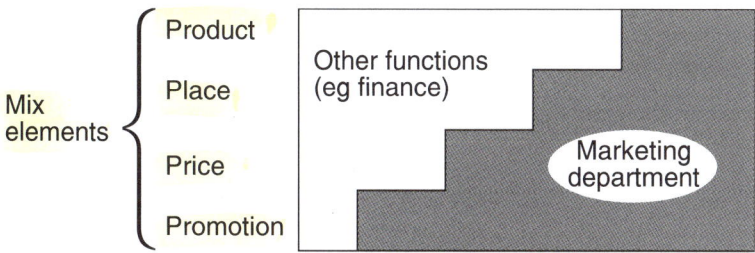

Degree of influence

Arguably although the personnel in the **marketing department** may have limited influence in some cases, the **marketing orientation should have been adopted by all** in the organisation.

7.8 Embedding the marketing orientation means convincing other departments that for long-term success they should place the customer at the focus of their decision-making, and use their specialist expertise with this in mind.

Marketing at work

Marketing Business for December 1997/January 1998 included a profile of Charles Allen, chief executive of the UK television and hotels group, Granada. His tactics for what is a diverse group are to challenge received wisdom partly by moving executives around, and by a three-year planning process supported by elaborate monthly reviews. The formal reviews take place in the office, but other than that Charles Allen spends a lot of time seeing managers and staff locally. He believes that tough targets should be set. 'Management may want to move a business by five or ten per cent (but) my challenge would be to donate it in three years. By looking at it that way you're not just talking about the numbers, you're looking at how to do things completely differently'.

Allen sees aggressive selling as key to business success. 'If you don't sell, you don't exist. That basic fact often gets lost among profit structures and strategies and so on.' Marketing directors set out a plan and are reviewed six months later on the progress they have made. Charles Allen is not impressed by 'backside-covering', people saying that although planned sales have not been achieved, awareness has been raised for example. He also believes that marketing directors have not convinced chief executives of the importance of marketing. Partly this is due to over-complication, using advertising terminology which chief executives do not understand. In addition, Allen is concerned that marketing directors last an average of eighteen months in any one job, arguing that to make serious impact on most brands, marketing directors need to be in the job for three to five years.

Some staff find Charles Allen's approach invigorating. Others find him autocratic and de-motivating to deal with if you disagree with him or do not fit into the team the way he wants. Even if marketing staff do deliver in the way he wants, the group faces other problems because of what is seen as its excessive diversity and low growth potential of certain areas.

7.9 You will learn at Diploma level that marketing managers can play a significant role in the overall strategy of a business. This is one way of embedding a marketing orientation - but not all firms have got there yet!

Part A: The nature of management and organisation issues

Exam Tip

While the principles of management have been examined in the past, most exam questions will be more practically based. You are unlikely to come across purely theoretical questions.

Even so, the theory is fundamental to your studies for this exam, but when you tackle questions, you must always attempt to apply it to the practical problems given. A good approach is to put yourself in the shoes of a marketing manager taking a marketing approach to using the theory you have learned. In June 2001, there was a general question about changes to the workplace.

Chapter Roundup

- Managers play a critical role in the organisation. They act as catalysts, responsible for the transformation of resource inputs into desired and valued outputs.

- Managers are responsible for the **scarce resources** entrusted to them, which must be used efficiently if value is to be added to the organisation, and if its objectives are to be achieved.

- **Culture** is important both in organisations and in the wider world. It is the knowledge, beliefs, customs and attitudes which people adhere to.

- Harrison's four-fold classification of organisations, popularised by Handy, is a useful analysis of some common aspects of culture.

- Culture colours organisation's view of its environment and hence influences its strategy. **Defenders** like low risk solutions and niche markets **Prospectors** are more adventurous and concerned with results. **Analysers** try to balance risk and profits. **Reactors** do not have viable strategies. Deal and Kennedy analyse culture in terms of inherent risk in the industry and the speed with which feedback is available on strategic decisions.

- In undertaking these responsibilities, the manager can be asked to carry out a number of activities (such as planning, control and decision-making) and to play a variety of roles (eg interpersonal, informational, decisional). These roles will themselves change with seniority and circumstance.

- The **role of the manager** has changed over time, influenced by changes in the **environment** and the prevalent business **culture**.

- Pressures on the role of management include the speed of change, customer power and global competition.

- Today's view is more humanistic than scientific - emphasising an art rather than a science of management.

- Recent changes in ideas as to what makes the best **organisation structure** have led to a flattening and inversion of the old tall pyramid. There are resulting changes for the manager of today who needs to be more flexible and take on more responsibilities.

- The marketing manager has a role to play in bringing the organisation and customers together, but it is just as important for the marketing manager to **embed the marketing concept** in the organisation.

2: What is management?

Quick Quiz

1. What are the typical responsibilities of the manager? (see para 2.3)
2. What does the 'human relations' school of management suggest are the important responsibilities of managers? (2.4)
3. Who are stakeholders and why are they important to the manager? (2.5)
4. What were the five management functions identified by Fayol? (2.9)
5. Mintzberg identified ten roles of managers and sub-divided these into three broad categories: what are they? (2.13 – 2.15)
6. What is the main value of managers? (2.18)
7. Describe Harrison's analysis of organisations. (3.7 – 3.11)
8. How did Miles and Snow analyse strategic culture? (3.14)
9. Describe Deal and Kennedy's analysis of culture. (3.15)
10. What steps are involved in a systematic approach to planning? (4.4)
11. What is control? (4.6, Key concept)
12. What are the different roles of budgets? (4.8)
13. Distinguish between scientific and reaction decision-making. (4.12)
14. Draw up a rational model for making decisions. (4.13)
15. What characterises product orientated management philosophies, sales orientated management philosophies, and customer orientated management philosophies. (5.4)
16. What are the recent changes which have stimulated changes in the role of managers? (6.2 – 6.4)
17. What is a matrix structure and how does it work? (6.6)
18. Suggest a possible change in the senior management role as a result of flatter organisations. (6.7)
19. What is the role of the marketing manager? (7.3)
20. What is the link between *Total Quality Management* and marketing? (7.6)
21. What departments does the marketing manager often deal with? (7.7)

Action Programme Review

1. The differences between levels of management will normally reflect breadth of scope and responsibility. Authority over spending is usually carefully controlled. Did you find any anomalies, especially with regard to job descriptions and what is actually done? It is not uncommon for job descriptions to lag behind what is actually done.

4. **Problem definition** is crucial to this decision. Before you can assess the options you must establish **decision criteria**. What do you want to get out of the activity you choose? Something prestigious for your CV? Specific career relevant experience? General personal development? Wider benefits such as social interaction and knowledge of the wider world? The two, theoretically distinct, stages of problem definition and appraisal of potential solutions may interact, since you may not be aware of all the possible benefits you could derive without considering what the solutions offer.

6. You might consider the points below.

   - Stated aims of values
   - Status of sales and marketing people
   - Any listing of customer complaints or other feedback
   - Behaviour of management in relation to products and markets
   - Perceived quality of products and service

Now try illustrative question 2 at the end of the Study Text

Part B
Personal effectiveness

3 What Makes a Good Manager?

Chapter Topic List	Syllabus reference
1 Setting the scene	
2 What are the characteristics of an effective manager?	2.1
3 Assessing management skills	2.2, 3.2
4 Techniques for developing management skills.	2.2, 3.1

Learning Outcomes

- Students will be able to undertake a personal skills audit with the intention of identifying personal strengths and weaknesses and planning and implementing improvements.
- Students will be able to devise training and development plans for marketing personnel to improve individual and team effectiveness.

Key Concepts Introduced

- Personality
- Dualism in human nature
- Personal development plans
- Learning contract
- Learning styles

Example of Marketing at Work

- Allied Domeq's middle management workshop

Part B: Personal effectiveness

1 SETTING THE SCENE

1.1 In the last chapter, we examined the many and varied dimensions which make up the role of the manager. These activities range from planning and resource allocation, to the skills of problem solving, decision making and communication. The person who can take on such a range of tasks and responsibilities clearly needs to have certain aptitudes and characteristics. Throughout this chapter the Action Programmes concentrate on your own **personal development plan,** commencing with a **personal skills audit.**

1.2 In Section 2 we explore some of the aspects of the effective manager, firstly by reference to some of the **challenges** an individual manager has to face, in terms of the manager's dilemmas. We then discuss the type of **personal characteristics** a manager might have. Management involves dealing with **people**, but with the ability to concentrate on a **task**. We then expand into a broader discussion of **personality**.

1.3 In Section 3 we take the concept further. The effective manager has to have a number of **personal skills** and must act to ensure that these remain relevant to future developments. It is the combination of the manger's personality, knowledge and skills, and their deployment in the organisation that enable a manger to be effective. We ask you to **examine your own level of skills.** This forms the foundation of a personal development plan. One important trend of recent years has been managers taking increased responsibility for their own career development.

1.4 The **mix of skills** in the **management team** is also important. We also discuss in Section 3 how to review the mix of skills of the management team and to identify any skills gaps.

1.5 In Section 4 we cover various aspects of management training and development. People have different needs and learn in different ways, hence the discussion of learning styles, and can learn through formal training or experience. Many firms see management development as a benefit to the organisation.

Links with other papers

The effectiveness of 'good management' in motivating people is crucial for customer-facing activities, but it is a wider issue than merely being the boss. Good management sets the tone for the corporate culture, thereby supporting service quality at the marketing / customer interface.

2 WHAT ARE THE CHARACTERISTICS OF AN EFFECTIVE MANAGER?

2.1 *Charles Handy* identifies three aspects of being a manager.

- The manager as a **general practitioner**
- The managerial **dilemmas**
- The manager as a **person**

The manager as a general practitioner

2.2 The manager is the first recipient of an organisation's problems and has a number of tasks in dealing with them.

- **Identifying the symptoms** in the situation (eg low productivity, high labour turnover)
- **Diagnosing the cause** of the trouble
- Deciding how it might be dealt with
- **Prescribing a treatment** and monitor progress
- **Developing strategies** to prevent further problems

3: What makes a good manager ?

Action Programme 1

What characteristics would be needed by a person to undertake effectively the general practitioner roles described by Handy? Take ten minutes and jot your thoughts down on a sheet of paper. This can be the basis for your developing characteristics profile.

The managerial dilemmas

2.3 Managers face some constant dilemmas which they must resolve.

(a) **The dilemma of the cultures**. It is management's task to decide which culture of organisation and management is required for any particular task. Managers must be prepared to show flexibility and good judgement in their choice of organisation culture.

(b) **The dilemma of time horizons**. This is the problem of responsibility for both the present and the future at the same time.

(c) **The trust-control dilemma**. This is the problem of balance between management's wish to control the work for which they are responsible, and the necessity to delegate work to subordinates, thereby trusting them to do the work properly. The greater trust a manager places in subordinates, the less control he retains himself.

(d) **The commando leader's dilemma**. In many organisations, junior managers show a strong preference for working in project groups (or 'commando groups') with a clear task or objective outside the normal bureaucratic structure. Unfortunately, there can be too many project groups for the good of the organisation, and the management dilemma is to decide how much bureaucratic structure should be retained for the benefit of the total organisation despite the wishes of the subordinates.

Action Programme 2

Take a further ten minutes to consider the implied characteristics needed by a person to come to terms with these dilemmas. Add these to your list.

The manager as a person

2.4 Management is developing into a 'semi-profession' and managers expect to be rewarded for their professional skills. The implications for individual managers are that 'increasingly it will come to be seen as the individual's responsibility to maintain, alter or boost his/her skills, to find the right market for those skills and to sell them to the appropriate buyer'. In other words, **managers must continue to develop their own professional skills and sell them to the highest bidder.**

2.5 This view has implications that we touched on when considering the future role of the manager. Organisations are likely to select managers to meet specific needs. They will be less likely to take in young recruits, in order to create clones within the management team. As a result **new teams will be constantly evolving**. Managers will be valued increasingly for their wide range of experiences and the external view which they bring with them.

Part B: Personal effectiveness

Action Programme 3

Spend a final ten minutes completing your characteristics profile in light of this final issue identified by Handy.

2.6 Compare your list with ours. You may have included things we left out, or be able to add some of our suggestions to your list. If you are working with others you could now brainstorm the characteristics you would look for in an effective manager and produce an extended list.

Describing the manager

Decisive	Analytical
Leadership	Interested
Vision	Alert, Aware
Trusting	Trusted
Pro-active	Knowledgeable
Flexible	Sensitive
Agile thinker	Good judgement
Self-starter	Persuasive
Improver	Enthusiast
Communicator	A liker of people

2.7 A tall order? Well yes, but not all managers need to be excellent in all these respects. A more junior manager will need less vision than a director; and a financial manager may need to be less of a persuader than marketing colleagues.

2.8 An understanding and appreciation of the characteristics of an effective manager has some additional uses.

- It helps in the training and development of your own team's management potential.
- It helps in the process of selecting new managers.
- It provides benchmarks against which management's performance can be appraised and assessed.

Marketing at Work

Allied Domecq recognised that flatter organisation structures can leave middle managers in particular feeling demoralised as their peers have left the company, and there are limited opportunities for development.

Allied Domecq therefore introduced a development workshop which allowed managers to take stock of their own achievements, identify why they had achieved what they had achieved, and understand how their skills matched against the requirements of the business. This led to statements of career aspirations with development plans designed to gain the skills necessary to achieve their ambitions.

Personality

2.9 What kind of people display these desirable characteristics? Is it possible or useful to identify a personality type that might be particularly suited to the management function?

Action Programme 4

Think about managers you know. Do they share similar personalities or even similar characteristic strengths?

> **Key concept**
>
> **Personality** has been defined as: 'the total pattern of characteristic ways of thinking, feeling and behaving that constitute the individual's distinctive method of relating to the environment.'

2.10 The context in which individual and social behaviours develop is, for very many individuals, a work organisation. In such an organisation, individuals will be confronted by rules, norms, and expectations that others have of them; they will interact with other individuals; they will perform tasks and make decisions in ways that are consistent with the character traits they possess; they will suffer frustration or stress, or will be motivated and satisfied at work.

2.11 Organisations will make certain generalised assumptions about the personalities of the individuals they employ, about the type of individuals they would **wish** to employ and to whom they would wish to allocate tasks and responsibilities.

2.12 In organisations, particularly large organisations, it is however often **essential to concentrate on the characteristics which most individuals have in common**, because large organisations must develop rules, procedures and standards with which employees in general must conform. A casual and informal approach may not be suited to a highly bureaucratic and formal organisation. Carelessness may not be right for a task where attention to detail is critical.

> **Key Concept**
>
> The psychologist *Ernest Becker* argued that people are driven by an essential '**dualism**'.
> - The need to be part of something, a conforming member of a winning team (security instinct)
> - The need to stick out as an individual, to 'shine' in some way (self-expression instinct)

2.13 The implication of dualism for work behaviour affects the way in which individuals can be motivated and managed. As *Peters and Waterman* argue in *In Search of Excellence*, a strong 'central faith', which binds the organisation together as a whole, should be combined with a strong emphasis on individual self-expression, contribution and success: individuals should be given at least the 'illusion of control' over their destinies, while still being given a sense of belonging and a secure meaningful framework in which to act.

Action Programme 5

Do you think an assessment of personality should form part of an organisation's recruitment process? Does your answer apply equally whatever the job in question may be? How can an organisation assess a candidate's personality in any case?

Part B: Personal effectiveness

> **Action Programme 6**
>
> What would you classify as the most suitable personality traits for the following roles?
>
> - A market research officer
> - A key account manager for a creative agency
> - A creative director within the agency
> - A marketing director
> - A sales manager
>
> What criteria are you using to make your decisions? Knowledge and consideration of the role and tasks which they involve, or experience of people in similar jobs?

2.14 Whilst the danger of being too prescriptive in the desired characteristics or personality traits for a role should be avoided, it makes sense to use our knowledge and experience to ensure that the right people are selected for the right job. Round pegs in square holes are seldom effective.

2.15 Remember also to consider the implications of the culture of the organisation or sector. The personality of a salesperson working for a Funeral Home would perhaps need to be different from the salesperson in a travel agency!

> **Action Programme 7**
>
> In this and other Advanced Certificate and Diploma examinations, the examiners will be looking for evidence that you have the basic skills and characteristics associated with an effective marketing manager. You will need to ensure that you demonstrate them. For example you need to communicate clearly, and make decisions supported by and justified by your analysis. Therefore, before moving on, take time to do a strengths and weaknesses analysis of your own management traits and characteristics. Produce a list in three columns - the strengths, weaknesses which **could** be improved, and weaknesses which **must** be improved. Be honest, and ask a friend or colleague to review your analysis. Take time to do this thoroughly and identify priority development areas.
>
> This will be the foundation of your personal development programme which you will be producing later in this chapter.

3 ASSESSING MANAGEMENT SKILLS 6/00, 6/01

The individual personal skills audit

3.1 Knowing the skills needed to undertake a particular management role, or the management function in general, is only half of the picture. Before improvements in the effectiveness of the management function can occur, it is also necessary to establish the **current skills level and management performance**. This is not as easy as it may seem. Management is very much an art (though based on scientific frameworks) and assessing its 'quality' can be as difficult as evaluating the quality of a painting. You made a start by undertaking a personal strengths and weaknesses analysis at the end of the last section (Action Programme 7). How do you assess yourself? Three methods are outlined by *Pedler, Burgoyne and Boydell* (in *A Manager's Guide to Self Development*).

- Simple introspection. Consider yourself in the light of the management qualities outlined in paragraph 2.6.
- Conversation with a partner
- Filling in a specially designed questionnaire

3.2 Appraisal and self-evaluation are at the heart of skills audits for the individual. This is **not a matter simply for the organisation**, but, as Handy identified, **individual managers must also take responsibility for their own personal development**.

3.3 Although we brainstormed a list of the qualities of the manager as a person it might help to quote a list in which the manager's skills are put in the context of the work environment. After all, being a manager is about more than having a particular personality: it is about **exercising distinct skills**. Pedler, Burgoyne and Boydell indicate the following qualities influencing a manager's personal effectiveness.

(a) **Basic knowledge and information**

- **Command of basic facts** such as the organisation's plans
- **Relevant professional understanding**

(b) **Skills and attributes**

(i) **Continuing sensitivity to events**. This implies personal perceptiveness, and understanding of hidden agendas.

(ii) **Analytical, problem-solving and decision/judgement-making skills.** These are necessary for planning and decision-making; the manager needs to cope with uncertainty and ambiguity, and should be able to think and reason logically from the facts of the situation. Intuitiveness is as useful as rationality.

(iii) **Social skills and abilities** including communication, delegation and negotiation

(c) **Personal qualities**

(i) **Emotional resilience.** Managers have to exercise leadership and take sometimes unpleasant decisions affecting other people. Interpersonal conflict is often inevitable. This creates tensions, but the manager should not be destroyed by them.

(ii) **Proactivity - responding purposefully to events**. Successful managers do not merely react; instead they shape situations, and their responses always have some longer-term end in view.

(iii) **Creativity** is defined as 'the ability to come up with unique new responses to situations, and to have the breadth of insight to recognise and take up useful new approaches' even when presented from elsewhere.

(iv) **Mental agility**. Mental agility is the ability to sum up a problem, to react quickly, communicate fluently and deal with different problems in quick succession.

(v) **Balanced learning habits and skills**. We deal with the importance of learning later on in this section. Successful managers 'think and learn for themselves'. They relate abstract ideas (like 'the marketing concept') to concrete ones like what the customer wants from the product.

(vi) **Self knowledge**

3.4 There are a number of dimensions to this analysis for individuals.

(i) Do they have the skills necessary to do the job **today**? If they do not, training is essential.

(ii) Do they have the skills to do the job **tomorrow**? Circumstances may change and may be necessary to ensure the manager is prepared.

(iii) Do they have the skill to do **tomorrow's job**? They be promoted and new skills and knowledge will be needed. This is **management development** and would be a pro-active approach to succession planning, or a personal strategy to increase the chances of promotion.

(iv) Do they have the skills for a **different job** tomorrow? This is personal career development planning and investment and many managers are today taking responsibility for it.

Action Programme 8

You have already undertaken a personal strengths and weaknesses analysis of your current management and marketing competencies. You can add to that an **opportunities and threats** assessment which will encourage you to think about career prospects and future opportunities. This external analysis of your own personal job market should help you to extend and prioritise the areas of skill development you want to focus on.

Personal development plan

You are already undertaking your CIM Advanced Certificate so you are clearly committed to personal development. Your study time can have considerable added value if you use it to develop additional and specific management skills.

Select four skill areas you want to work on, or which your boss suggests might be beneficial.

(a) These may be areas of weakness like time management or presentation skills;
(b) or areas of strength like analysis and problem solving which you want to develop further.

Using the grid below identify each area, set a **quantified** objective for the next 6 months and give some thought to how to achieve this improvement (your strategy). The next section of this chapter has ideas on training and development which may stimulate some thoughts on strategy.

Here is our example. Note that the 'Area' can be anything which concerns you and it might include both the technical and managerial aspects of your work.

3: What makes a good manager?

Area	Objectives	Strategy
Time management	• To hit at least 90% of deadlines set over the last 6 months • To find at least 6 hours per week for CIM studies	• To spend time every morning planning my time • Agreeing a study plan and sticking to it • Taking measures to reduce timewasting

	Area	Objectives	Strategy
1			
2			
3			
4			
5			
6			
7			

Review Dates 1 ....
2 ....
3 ....

3.5 Planning is of no value unless it is followed up; review and feedback are essential so progress can be monitored and resources re-allocated and objectives and strategy modified as circumstances changed. It is important that the control element of every plan becomes routine. In the case of personal development, the role may change, new priorities emerge, the skill be acquired more quickly than forecast and so on.

Personal development plans

> **Key Concept**
> **Personal development plans (PDPs)** are essentially action plans for people's career development. It is the individuals responsibility to seek and organise training.

3.6 'Organisations no longer feel they can take prime responsibility for the future careers and development of their employees, and the PDP approach clearly places the development ball in the employee's court'. (*People Management*)

3.7 The most popular PDP schemes take account of people's wider needs and aspirations, rather than focusing simply on skills required to do their current job better. Such schemes are undoubtedly popular because of the changes in the employment market. Most people believe they need to obtain skills and experiences which will be of benefit should they move jobs. **As a result people are better able than companies to assess their training requirements**. They will choose courses, where the form and content assist their personal development, and will avoid courses which are of no value to their personal development.

3.8 This trend is also reflected in employee development programmes (EDPs), company-run schemes which offer employees a wide range of development opportunities, not necessarily related to the job. The effect of such schemes is to develop a culture in which learning and adaptability are valued as well as to enhance employee satisfaction and morale. Expense has hitherto confined EDPs to large companies such as Ford, Unipart and Rover.

The importance of personal development plans

3.9 Managers have to take responsibility for their own learning. Personal development needs to be considered and managed by the individual, working, where possible, in partnership with the employer.

- The habit of setting personal development targets should be a long-term commitment for the successful manager.
- In the examination you will be able to draw upon your experience of setting personal goals and the problems of achieving them.
- As a manager, you are likely to be faced with helping others with their personal development. Your personal experience of the process will be of some help then.
- The plans can be part of a **learning contract**, whereby targets are agreed with the employer, and their attainment is monitored.

Learning contracts

Key Concept
A **learning contract** is an agreement between the person undergoing the training or education or experience and the provider or the sponsor of the training, education or experience.

3.10 The learning contract will normally detail three things.
- The type of **learning process** involved
- The expected **achievement** (in terms of the increase in skills)
- The **timescale** required

The learning contract is a way for the individual to get a commitment out of the firm, by creating a moral obligation.

The organisation

Management team

3.11 How would you assess the quality of an organisation's management team? Answering this question is difficult, but perhaps the most important measure is the **outputs** they deliver.

- Do they achieve the organisation's objectives?

- Do they do so with the resources available?
- Have they in the process added value to the organisation in terms of image, training, new resources?
- Have they achieved the above without compromising the long-term future?

3.12 As an analogy, you might judge a football team by how many matches it has won. Does it matter if the football they play is 'safe', but unexciting and uninspiring? Perhaps it does, because in that case the needs of some of its stakeholders, the fans, would be unsatisfied. Managers need to recognise that **achieving objectives may not be enough, as the way they are achieved can also be important to the success of the organisation.**

3.13 People in an organisation are a valuable and critical resource. This is especially true of the management team since the responsibility for vision, culture, motivation and delivery are vested in them. Positive steps to identify current skill levels and action to develop areas of weakness must be taken. One way of completing a **skills audit** of the management team is to undertake a series of individual analyses. This will help if it is followed up by development actions to improve individuals' identified weaknesses.

3.14 However, assessing the **strengths of the team** on the basis of the strengths of the **individual members** in isolation has to be questioned.

- Does a collection of **expert managers** make the best team?
- Do **individual** improvements strengthen the team?

Consider the chart below. Half a dozen key management skills have been identified and a management team assessed individually against these and given a score from 1 to 10 (1=low) indicating their relative strength in that area. When aggregated we have a picture of the team's collective strengths in that area. With six managers in the team the maximum total score for each area is 60 (six people multiplied by the maximum score of 10).

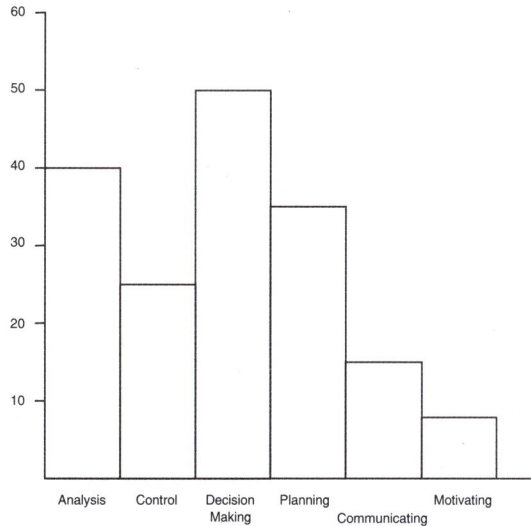

Individual development plans were undertaken during the year and collectively the team had improved its performance, **but** the critical areas of weakness are still clearly apparent.

Part B: Personal effectiveness

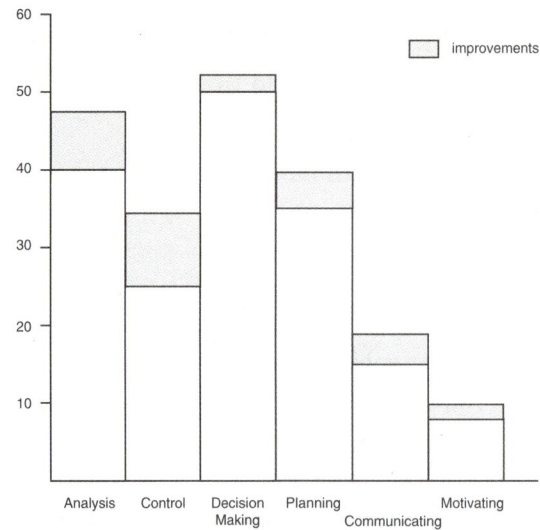

3.15 Looking at the management resource as a whole enables new and different insights into any skills gap. A better alternative in the situation above may be to strengthen the team by introducing a new member particularly skilled in motivation and communication who could take over responsibility for internal marketing of the plans. The other option would be to target the particularly weak areas as critical for development and introduce specific training and development for the **whole team**.

Action Programme 9

If you are working with a group of students, or have a team at work, devise a system for undertaking a skills audit and make recommendations for development to improve the team performance.

3.16 In practice, are teams likely to be so unbalanced? Sadly, the answer is 'quite probably'. A team of marketing managers may contain creative problem solvers and strong communicators, but weak analysts and controllers. A team of financial managers may show a mirror image of these traits. It is also possible for a team to select individuals who will 'fit in'. Taken to extremes, this can mean a whole group of people who have similar personality traits, strengths and weaknesses. Managers of all teams, including the senior management team, need to **monitor not only the skills of individuals but the combined skills of the team.** Identifying and filling gaps at all levels to help enhance the performance of the management function.

Organisational learning

3.17 A **learning organisation** is an organisation 'skilled at creating, acquiring and transferring knowledge, and at modifying its behaviour to reflect new knowledge and insights'. In other words, knowledge and expertise are not things to be jealously guarded. Instead it has to be shared to ensure the organisation can be continuously innovative.

3.18 *Peter Senge* (in *The Fifth Discipline - The Art and Practice of the Learning Organisation*) argues that to create a learning organisation, individuals and groups should be encouraged to learn five disciplines.

(a) **Systems thinking**. This is the ability to see particular problems as part of a wider whole, and to devise appropriate solutions to them.

(b) **Personal learning and growth**. Individuals should be encouraged to acquire skills and knowledge.

(c) **Challenging mental models**. Mental models are deeply ingrained assumptions and habits of thought. Organisations can use a number of group techniques to make these models explicit, and to challenge them.

(d) There must be a shared vision, but not one that is so strong as to discourage organisational learning. It should not filter knowledge.

(e) **Team learning**. Some tasks can only be done in groups. Teams, however, must be trained to learn, as there are factors in group dynamics which impede learning.

3.19 Organisational learning is about **group** communication and responsiveness. It also challenges some assumptions about creativity, such as that it resides only in the **individual**.

3.20 Finally, we need to note here two types of learning.

- Learning actual knowledge
- Learning **how to learn**, in other words how to acquire new knowledge

> **Exam Tip**
>
> The June 2001 exam also covered this area, but you had to focus your Personal Improvement Plan on three areas: report writing, handling customer problems and time management. You might therefore be given a **specific** area to improve. (Note that personal skills audit is not the same thing as appraisal!)
>
> The June 2000 exam also included a question on self development, including personal skills audit and an action plan for developing management skills.

4 TECHNIQUES FOR DEVELOPING MANAGEMENT SKILLS

4.1 Management development is the process of improving the effectiveness of an individual manager by developing the skills necessary achieve the organisation goals. Experience in the job will lead to some development, but the process is called **management development** when it is undertaken consciously.

> **Action Programme 10**
>
> Identify someone in your experience whom you would call a 'good manager'. How much of what made him or her a good manager would you put down to personality ('the way he/she is') and how much of it could have been developed through training, education and experience?

4.2 Management development is an aspect of the strategic progress of the organisation and should have a high priority. **A rational approach would compare the organisation's expectations with the manager's capabilities and make up any shortfall by training.** When a manager is fully competent consideration may be given to his or her capacity for promotion and further training provided in preparation for any possible move. The whole process is intimately linked to routine appraisal. Although we have been discussing the development of managers, staff appraisal is important for all grades of employees, and it is a topic we will be considering in more detail later in this Study Text.

Part B: Personal effectiveness

> REQUIRED LEVEL
> OF COMPETENCE
>
> *minus*
>
> PRESENT LEVEL
> OF COMPETENCE
>
> *equals*
>
> TRAINING NEED

4.3 Some options for developing management skills are indicated below. The selected methods should reflect three things.

- The individual's preferred **learning style**
- The level and type of skill development needed
- The needs of the organisation - in terms of budget, time and level of competence

Individual learning styles

> **Key Concept**
> It is believed that the way in which people learn best will differ according to the type of person they are: in other words, there are **learning styles** which suit different individuals.

4.4 *Honey and Mumford* have drawn up a popular classification of four **learning styles**.

(a) **Theorist**. This person seeks to understand underlying concepts before applying them in practice, and to take an intellectual, 'hands-off' approach based on logical argument. Such a person has distinct preferences about training.

- It should be programmed and structured
- It should allow time for analysis
- It should be provided by teachers who share his preference for concepts and analysis

Theorists find learning difficult if they have a teacher with a different style (particularly an **activist** style), material which skims over basic principles, a programme which is hurried and unstructured, or which encourages them to learn 'hands-on' by trial and error **before** they have studied the theory.

(b) **Reflector**. People who like to observe phenomena, think about them and then choose how to act are called reflectors. Such people need to work at their own pace and would find learning difficult if forced into a hurried programme, or required to attempt tasks before having a chance to observe and think about them first. Reflectors are able to produce carefully thought-out conclusions after research and reflection but tend to be fairly slow, non-participative (unless to ask questions) and cautious.

(c) **Activist**. These are people who like to deal with practical, active problems and who do not have much patience with theory. They require training based on hands-on experience. Activists are excited by participation, experimentation and pressure, such as making presentations and attempting new projects. Although they are flexible and optimistic, they may rush at things without due preparation, take risks and then get bored.

(d) **Pragmatist.** These people only like to study if they can see its direct link to practical problems - they are not interested in theory for its own sake. They are particularly good at learning new techniques in on-the-job training which they see as useful improvements. Their aim is to implement action plans and/or do the task better. Such a person is business-like and realistic, but may discard as being impractical good ideas which only require some development. They may even regard training, other than direct task-oriented training, as a waste of time.

The implications for management are that people react to problem situations in different ways and that, in particular, training methods should where possible be tailored to the preferred style of trainees.

Action Programme 11

John, Paula, Ringo and Georgette are learning French, as part of their firm's initiative to develop staff in a European market.

(a) John reckons that since he does not actually speak to clients, the whole scheme is a waste of time. He claims to be too busy to attend classes.

(b) Paula loves the classes, because they simulate real conversational situations. The trainees have to use whatever vocabulary they have to get their meaning across, guided and corrected by the tutor: Paula doesn't like learning grammatical rules - she's happy to pick up the phrases to fit the situations.

(c) Ringo doesn't mind the teaching method, either. He doesn't say anything for the first few minutes, though, just picks up what he can, gets it straight (allowing Paula to make the mistakes) and then comes out with a fluent response.

(d) Georgette is lost. She feels frustrated because, although she has learned the phrase for a given situation she is not sure it will apply in **other** contexts. She takes home a book of grammar at night, to bone up on the general principles and rules.

Who represents which learning style? What style has the course been designed for?

The learning cycle

4.5 Another useful model is the **experiential learning cycle** devised by *David Kolb*. Kolb suggested that classroom-type learning is 'a special activity cut off from the real world and unrelated to one's life': a teacher or trainer directs the learning process on behalf of a passive learner. Experiential learning, however, involves doing, and puts the learner in an active problem-solving role which encourages the learner to formulate and commit himself to his own learning objectives.

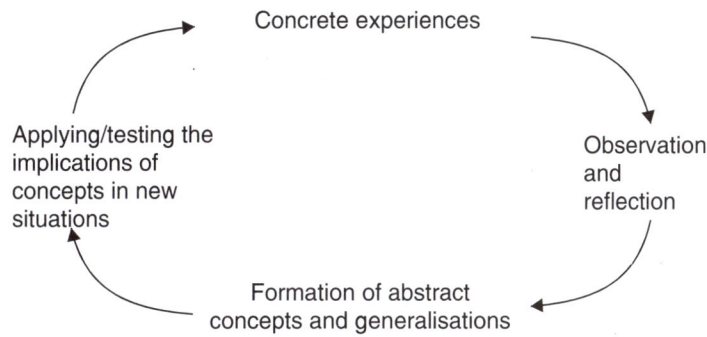

Say an employee interviews a customer for the first time (concrete experience). He observes his performance and the dynamics of the situation (observation) and afterwards, having failed to convince the customer to buy his product, he analyses what he did right and wrong (reflection). He comes to the conclusion that he had failed to listen to what the customer really wanted and feared, underneath her general reluctance: he realises that the key to communication is listening (abstraction/generalisation). In his next interview he applies his strategy to the new set of circumstances (application/testing). This provides him with a new experience with which to start the cycle over again.

Act

Analyse actions

Understand principles

Apply principles

This is the model for many of the modern approaches to training, and particularly management development, which recommend experiential learning - 'learning by doing', or self-learning. In effect, it involves elements of **all** the learning styles identified by Honey and Mumford.

4.6 How each individual learns best can be assessed by tests and procedures that may be available through the human resources or personnel department. Individual managers should be aware of their own preferred learning styles when planning personal development and the learning styles of others when recommending training opportunities or playing the part of the trainer.

4.7 **Training should take account of the current level of skill and tackle the training need.** Sending an already competent salesperson on a basic negotiation skills course is likely to be demotivating and unlikely to generate any positive outcomes. This makes life harder for the manager who must recognise that, though all his or her staff members need to achieve the same level of competence in a particular skill, each will need a different development plan.

4.8 The needs of the organisation should also be taken into account. If time is at a premium, an intensive course can be suggested (eg a language course, timed to take place before attending an overseas exhibition, from a specialist provider such as *Linguarama*). However, where budgets are tight, options like local college evening classes may be a preferred route.

4.9 *Constable and McCormick* formulated a useful distinction between management education, training and development.

(a) '**Education** is that process which results in formal qualifications up to and including post-graduate degrees.'

(b) **Training** is 'the formal learning activities which may not lead to qualifications, and which may be received at any time in a working career'; for example, a course in manpower forecasting or counselling skills;

(c) '**Development** is broader again: job experience and learning from other managers, particularly one's immediate superior, are integral parts of the development process.'

4.10 It is important to realise that 'education and training' **no longer implies bookwork, academic and theory-based studies.** *W A G Braddick (Management for Bankers)* suggests the kind of shift in focus that has occurred in management development methods in recent years. (The notes are ours.)

3: What makes a good manager?

From		To	Notes
Principles	→	Specifics	(Every organisation is unique)
Precepts	→	Analysis/diagnosis	(Address the issues)
Theory-based	→	Action-centred	(Understand it - but do it)
Academic	→	Real time problems	(Tackle 'live' problems)
Functional focus	→	Issue and problem focus	(Deal with 'whole' activities)
Excellent individual	→	Team members and leaders	(Develop people - together)
Patient	→	Agent	(Learn actively, take control)
One-off	→	Continuous	(Keep learning)

4.11 Thus management education and training now tends to focus on the real needs of specific organisations, and to be grounded in practical skills. In-house programmes and on-the-job techniques have flourished, as have techniques of off-the-job learning which simulate real issues and problems such as case study, role play, desk-top exercises and leadership exercises.

Approaches to training

4.12 Once the training needs, preferred learning styles and organisational constraints have been identified, the training options must be evaluated. There are a number of approaches.

- Formal learning methods include internal or external residential courses, day courses or lectures, distance learning, programmed learning and computer-aided learning.

- Less formal methods include on-the-job training, coaching and job-rotation.

- There is also the possibility of secondments to other departments and even other types of organisation.

Formal learning

4.13 Whether residential or short courses, internal courses are devised to meet the specific needs of the organisation and are not open to non-company staff. Whilst very good at meeting company needs, they are not so flexible at meeting different learning needs or styles of individuals.

- Internal programmes are a useful forum for meeting colleagues and can be used for presenting corporate strategy, and as a focus for team building and motivation.

- However they also tend to be inward-looking, particularly if staff have grievances or rivalries which end up dominating discussions. The more senior the managers, the less it is likely that such internal courses will provide the best opportunity for development.

4.14 Try the following exercise dealing with external courses.

Action Programme 12

What are the advantages and disadvantages of an external formal course for management development?

On-the-job training (OJT)

4.15 OJT has been the preferred method of training for decades in the UK. Managers learn by progressing from supervisory levels, through middle management and eventually to senior positions. They learn by mistakes and from other older and more experienced managers. Despite its informality, OJT must be carefully planned if it is to be worth while.

Part B: Personal effectiveness

Step 1. **Establish learning targets**. The areas to be learnt should be **identified, and specific, realistic goals** (eg completion dates, performance standards) stated by agreement with the trainee.

Step 2. **Plan a systematic learning and development programme**. This will ensure regular progress, appropriate stages for consolidation and practice.

Step 3. **Identify opportunities for broadening the trainee's knowledge and experience** (eg by involvement in new projects, placement on inter-departmental committees, suggesting new contacts, or simply extending the job, adding more tasks, greater responsibility etc).

Step 4. **Take into account the strengths and limitations of the trainee** in learning, and take advantage of learning opportunities that suit the trainee's ability, preferred style and goals.

Step 5. **Exchange feedback**. The supervisor will want to know how the trainee sees his or her progress and future. He or she will also need performance information in order to monitor the trainee's progress, adjust the learning programme if necessary, identify further needs which may emerge and plan future development for the trainee.

4.16 **Different methods of on the job training**.

Method	Detail
Coaching	The trainee is put under the guidance of an experienced employee who **shows the trainee how to do the job.** The length of the coaching period will depend on the complexity of the job and the previous experience of the trainee.
Mentoring	A senior staff member provides advice and support. Mentors can pass on practical skills and tips derived from their experience. They should be selected with care and trained appropriately. The mentor's workload should allow time for the mentoring, and regular discussions should take place to review progress.
Job rotation	The trainee is given several jobs in succession, to gain experience of a wide range of activities.
Temporary promotion	An individual is promoted into his/her superior's position whilst the superior is absent. This gives the individual a chance to experience the demands of a more senior position.
'Assistant to' positions	A junior manager with good potential may be appointed as assistant to the managing director or another executive director. In this way, the individual gains experience of how the organisation is managed at the top.
Committees	Trainees might be included in the membership of committees, in order to gain an understanding of inter-departmental relationships.
Project teams	A person's management skills and experience may be tested and enhanced by membership or leadership of a project team delegated to carry out a particular task. The trainee is responsible for a defined set of results, and management skills, such as planning and leadership, can be exercised on a project.
Internal secondment	Experience can be given by giving someone a few month's experience in a different department or different office.

4.17 OJT is very common, especially when the work involved is not complex. Unfortunately, this type of training will be unsuccessful if the assignments do not have a specific purpose from

3: What makes a good manager?

which the trainee can learn and gain experience; or the organisation is intolerant of any mistakes which the trainee makes. Mistakes are an inevitable part of on-the-job learning.

External experience

4.18 Practical experience can be gained outside the organisation, eg by secondment to other organisations (intermediaries or not-for-profit organisations). This can broaden the horizons and experiences of a young manager.

4.19 If you do not have the support of an organisation look around for opportunities to develop your skills externally. Look for charities and local clubs who would be glad of help in fund raising or marketing to attract new members.

Action Programme 13

Go back to the personal development grid which you completed earlier in this unit. What new ideas do you have for finding ways of achieving your objectives? Talk to personnel to identify appropriate short courses you could attend. Identify colleagues in the company who may be able to offer advice and support.

Exam Tip

The compulsory case study included a question on training and development in June 2000. The question was worth 17 marks and required the production of a training and development plan. It was necessary for the plan to tackle the clearly defined problems given in the scenario. The examiner commented that this question was the most poorly answered in part A. Better answers established how different methods of training could be used to meet different needs.

The message is this: make your answer as relevant as possible to the question.

Part B: Personal effectiveness

Chapter Roundup

- In order to perform the variety of roles expected of the manager he or she needs to have certain characteristics. The manager has to cope effectively with the three dimensions which Charles Handy identified as typical of the management job.

  The manager as a general practitioner (safeguarding the health of the organisation)
  Coping with the dilemmas of management
  Continually striving to develop personal management skills.

- You need an appreciation of the wide range of characteristics and skills needed by the successful manager both as a focus for your own personal development and to provide a basis for selecting and developing others.

- Whilst training and development can help develop skills, people have personalities and traits which tend to make them more suited to certain roles than others. Liking people is an important management trait. An understanding of personality and character traits can be helpful in the selection process.

- The skills of management, both as individuals and as a team, are a critical resource on which the success of the organisation depends. An audit or understanding of the current level of these skills is essential if any future improvements are to be made.

- The skills of individuals should not be the only aspect considered. The team as a whole is also important and needs careful analysis as to how its members work together.

- Many firms regard personal development as the responsibility of the employee. The process of undertaking a personal development plan during the six months of this course will provide you with invaluable experience for the examination and future rearrangement activities. A learning contract is an agreement between the firm and the employee.

- Once current skill levels are known, the gap between them and the levels needed by the organisation can be identified and filled with planned training and development.

- At its best, training needs to take into the needs and preferences of both individual and the organisation. There are a range of options and the strengths and weaknesses of each need assessing in each circumstance.

Quick Quiz

1. According to Handy, what are three aspects of the manager's position? (see para 2.1)
2. What are the management dilemmas identified by Handy? (2.3)
3. Identify a list of characteristics you might look for in a marketing manager. (2.6, 3.3)
4. What is 'personality'? (2.10 Key concept)
5. What are the implications of the dual need to conform and to be exceptional? (2.13)
6. What are personal development plans? (3.6 Key concept)
7. How would you evaluate the quality of the management within an organisation? (3.11)
8. Why might a business team's members share the same weaknesses? (3.16)
9. What is a learning organisation? (3.17)
10. How would you determine training needs? (4.2)
11. What factors should be considered before developing a specific training programme for an individual? (4.3)
12. What is mentoring? (4.16)
13. How would you advise a colleague not currently employed at a management level to develop some management experience? (4.18, 4.19)

3: What makes a good manager ?

Action Programme Review

5   There is room for you to have your own opinions on this topic. In practice, of course, job advertisements frequently do specify that they are looking for an 'outgoing personality', 'the ability to work in teams', 'a sense of humour' and so on. Sometimes, especially if certain skills are in short supply, the organisation has to accommodate the personality of the person who is otherwise best qualified for the job. Where social interaction is incidental to, rather than an actual part of, the job in question, a variety of different personalities might fit the bill equally well. Techniques for assessing personality include interviews, personality tests, psychometric tests, role-playing and even graphology (handwriting analysis).

We will be considering these later as part of the recruitment and selection criteria.

11 John is a pragmatist: Paula an activist; Ringo a reflector; Georgette a theorist. The course seems tailored for activists: reflectors would **cope**, but might not contribute enough to keep the classes going.

12

Advantages	*Disadvantages*
The level and style of course can be selected to meet individuals' preferences.	The focus of the course may not be an exact match for what the company needs.
An external view may introduce new ideas and approaches.	The different approaches may not be easily adopted in-house.
The opportunity to meet others and identify potential team members worth poaching!	Comparison of 'job benefits' with other course participants may cause discontent.
Because of the choice of course, there is more flexibility in timing.	There is no opportunity for achieving secondary objectives like team building etc.
Does not require several staff to be away at one time.	Staff can still be identified and called out to handle work problems.
Can make the manager feel valued and special and be a motivating experience.	Team members may not feel it is appropriate to be open and honest about their organisation and its problems.
Some added credibility (even certification) on an external programme.	
Staff not likely to be disturbed. Time to really concentrate on areas of development.	

Now try illustrative question 3 at the end of the Study Text

4 Time Management

Chapter Topic List	Syllabus reference
1 Setting the scene	
2 The importance of time management	2.3
3 Developing prioritisation skills	2.3, 3.1
4 Delegation	2.3
5 Other people's time management problems	2.3, 3.1
6 Managing projects and plans over time	2.3
7 Problem solving and decision making	2.3

Learning Outcome

- Students will be able to explain the theory underpinning effective management of self, other people, resources and client relationships.

Key Concepts Introduced

- Time management
- Prioritisation
- Delegation

1 SETTING THE SCENE

1.1 In the last chapter we asked the question: what makes a good manager? We listed a number of different management attributes. However, a manager should be able to deploy his or her skills effectively in order to satisfy the objectives of the organisation.

1.2 You have often heard the phrase: 'time is money'. This is pertinent to time management. Your time is a resource which the organisation is paying for, and you owe it to yourself and your employer to 'spend' it efficiently. In Section 2 we explore this point and then briefly introduce the skills you will need to manage how you spend your time. First of all you will need to log how you actually spend time at present, only then can you take steps to improve it.

1.3 In Section 3 we discuss **prioritisation**. Some things are more worthy of your time than others, in terms of their urgency and importance. Spending your time doing trivial tasks is a waste of time, so you have to learn how to rank all the demands made of you.

1.4 Of course the easiest way to get a task off your desk is to get someone else to do it for you; **delegation** is the subject of Section 4. Not only does this help you, but it provides one of the team members reporting to you with more interesting work. Delegation needs to be planned.

1.5 At times you may have to manage or co-ordinate other people's time management problems, the subject of Section 5, where we explore a case study. A common occurrence is having to deal with someone who has recently been promoted, but who has not developed the time management or delegation skills necessary for his or her new role.

1.6 In Section 6 we discuss the problems of managing projects and develop an approach to project scheduling.

2 THE IMPORTANCE OF TIME MANAGEMENT

2.1 **The scarcest resource any of us has is time**. No amount of investment can add more hours to the day or weeks to the year. All we can do is take steps to make more effective use of the time which is available to us. Planning how we spend our time is as normal to us as planning how we will spend our income, and you should already have considerable experience of both.

2.2 From the organisation's point of view, people's time is not only a scarce resource, but a very valuable one.

Action Programme 1

Have you ever worked out how much you cost your organisation by the hour? Deduct public holidays, sick days and days spent on training to calculate the number of working days per annum. Then add together the direct and indirect costs of your employment: remember the car, pension and office space (eg rental per square metre) before doing the calculation.

2.3 **To be worth his or her pay, every employee needs to add more value than he or she costs per hour.** If you do the same exercise for the whole team, you can see how expensive the time of your section actually is, and why keeping colleagues waiting to start a meeting or training course is more serious than just a breach of manners. It is important, therefore, that managers work as efficiently as possible.

Part B: Personal effectiveness

2.4 **Job management** means that the manager knows what the job is, as well as being able to do it in the most efficient way. The manager will then not waste time wondering what to do next, doing tasks that will not to achieve objectives, or doing tasks that might better be done by someone else. The manager ought to be thoroughly knowledgeable about the policies, systems and procedures of the organisation, and about the structure of authority and responsibility as well as about his/her own area of authority or expertise. This includes knowing where (or to whom) to go for information or assistance.

2.5 **Delegation** will be an important element in job management. Effective delegation will involve training subordinates to do their job properly and making it very clear what is expected of them. The manager must also give feedback on how well the job has been done.

2.6 The organisation must make sure that managers do not have unnecessary demands made on their time by work inappropriately referred upwards by subordinates, or downwards by senior managers. Training should be given at all levels on when to delegate and when to refer for a decision.

2.7 **Communication** skills can be used to speed up conversations, interviews and meetings. They can be used to say 'no', tactfully, when unhelpful interruptions present themselves. Learning to read faster, write more concise reports and sort out essential from non-essential information will also help efficient management of time. We will be considering improving communication skills in some depth in a later chapter.

Key Concept
Time management is the process of allocating time to tasks in the most effective manner

2.8 **Time management tasks**

   (a) **Identifying objectives** and the key tasks which are most relevant to achieving them - sorting out what the supervisor **must** do, from what he **could** do, and from what he would **like** to do. *Urgent* is not always the same as *important*. (See paragraph 3.4.)

   (b) **Prioritising and scheduling**: assessing key tasks for relative importance, amount of time required. Routine non-essential tasks should be delegated - or done away with if possible. Routine key tasks should be organised as standard procedures and systems. Non-routine key tasks will have to be carefully scheduled as they arise, according to their urgency and importance; an up-to-date diary with a **carry forward system** to follow-up action will be helpful.

   (c) **Planning and control**: Schedules should be regularly checked for disruption by the unexpected: priorities will indicate which areas may have to be set aside for more urgent items. Information and control systems in the organisation should be utilised so that problems can be anticipated, and sudden decisions can be made on the basis of readily available information.

2.9 In *Perfect Time Management*, Ted Johns notes some key assumptions behind the management of time. Do you agree with them?

   - Time **can** be managed.
   - Tasks can be **squeezed**, making time available for other tasks.
   - Your effectiveness depends on the extent to which you are **seen** to be effective, not whether you are actually effective.

4: Time management

- The secret is to **work smarter, not harder.**

2.10 Before moving on take some time to consider how effectively you manage your own time.

> **Action Programme 2**
> 1. Do you often miss deadlines for projects or activities you are responsible for at work?
> 2. Are you often late for meetings or appointments?
> 3. Do you have to work late regularly to get everything done?
> 4. Do you feel you are constantly trying to beat the clock?
> 5. Are you too busy to find time to plan?
> 6. Are you too busy to go on a time management course?
> 7. Do you seem to have more work to do than others?
> 8. Have you got a good balance between time spent on work, with family, on yourself?

Day ....

Time	Activities	Value (1-10)		Could someone else have done it? Yes ✓ No ✗	Interruptions as a % of time
		To me	To others		
8.00 - 8.15					
8.15 - 8.30					
8.30 - 8.45					
8.45 - 9.00					
etc					

2.11 You cannot make more effective use of your time until you know how you currently spend your time. Draw up a diary page with the headings shown above and divide your day into 15 minute blocks as shown. Complete this record for every day of the week or month that you intend to do this time management exercise. Add it to your diary at work and take time to fill it in at frequent intervals. Do not rely on your memory at the end of the day! Keep a note not only of **how** you spent your time, but also on how effectively you think it was spent. If it was a meeting how valuable was it to you? (or to others?). How much is your work interrupted, by whom and why? Try and establish a true picture of where your time is actually going.

2.12 Once you have completed a few days' diary sheets you will be able to analyse how efficiently and effectively you spend your time. Produce a breakdown of the way you spend your day or working day.

(a) What proportion of your time is spent:

- in meetings?
- on the phone?
- travelling?
- waiting?
- with customers?
- with subordinates?
- with superiors?
- with colleagues?
- socialising at work?
- doing routine administration?

(b) What is the typical breakdown of your time between:

Part B: Personal effectiveness

- work?
- home?
- yourself/social?

(c) What proportion of your time was spent in ways which:

- were important to you?
- were important to others?
- could have been delegated to others?

2.13 Once you have completed this audit of your own time you will be able to do four things.

- Help others undertake a similar analysis
- Identify activities which should be reviewed as they are of little value to you or others
- Identify activities which can be delegated to others
- Identify areas where time is not being used effectively and could be better organised

Improving time management 12/99, 6/00

2.14 **Plan each day**. A task list of things to be done each day will be a start, but a simple task list gives no idea of the priority of each task. The daily list should include the most important tasks you currently have as well as urgent but less important tasks. The effectiveness of the list will also be enhanced if you write down how long you think each task should take. You should review the list at the end of the day, partly to see what tasks should be transferred to the following day's list, but also to assess whether and why you completed less than you anticipated and spent less time on the important tasks.

2.15 **Produce a longer-term plan**. This can highlight the important tasks so that sufficient time is spent on them on a daily basis. A longer-term plan can also help you cope with more complicated jobs, by breaking them down into a number of stages. In addition long-term planning helps you anticipate busy periods so that you can ensure that backlogs of routine work are cleared during quieter times.

2.16 Assess the **opportunity costs**. If you use an hour in one way, you lose the ability to use it in another. The opportunity cost of using your time in a particular fashion is the benefit that would have been gained if you had used it in a different way. For example, travelling by car may be more convenient than travelling by train, but you may be able to work on the train.

2.17 Are you using travelling time effectively in other areas? Do you use the journey to and from work to read your CIM course materials, or plan your day? If you travel by car, use a tape to make a recording of key notes, revision materials and review this whilst driving.

2.18 Use the **ACIB method of in-tray management**. When a piece of paper comes into your in-tray, you should take **one** of the following approaches.

Act on the item **immediately**.

Co-opt someone else to act on it, ie delegate.

Input a time to your diary, when you will deal with it.

Bin it; if you're sure it is worthless.

A fifth way is not to receive the mail at all! You may be able to use your secretary to deal with certain routine correspondence. You should also be alert for any journals,

magazines etc from which you derive no value, and remove yourself from the distribution lists.

2.19 The **half open door**. Although having an open door is a common policy, **do not be available to all comers at all times**. There are several ways of preventing interruptions.

(a) Be **unavailable**. Use call-diverting facilities on your telephone (and/or ask your secretary, if you have one). Alternatively you can try working somewhere other than your usual desk or office.

(b) Set '**surgery hours**' during which your door is open to visitors.

(c) Determine which **people are 'urgent' or 'important'**. Your immediate boss might be asked to wait, whereas the Chief Executive must be attended to immediately.

(d) Arrange **regular meetings with people you have to deal with frequently** (immediate boss, subordinates). These meetings can be used to deal with routine business and also all but the most important problems.

(e) **Stay in control of meetings**, by asking people to come back later or saying that you can spare them X minutes (and no longer).

(f) **Do not allow people to by-pass the hierarchy**. Most people should deal with your staff first of all.

2.20 **Stay in control of the telephone**. The telephone can be a major barrier to good time management, by being a source of constant interruption and a means of communication which, through poor technique, is used inefficiently. The following are good ways of improving telephone time management.

(a) **Only take calls during certain times** and divert calls to your secretary during the rest of the day. Alternatively use your secretary as a screen so that only important calls are put through to you immediately.

(b) **Group calls** so that you make a number of calls together.

(c) If someone is unavailable when you call, say that you'll **ring back at a specified time**, rather than allowing the person to ring you back at an inconvenient time for you.

(d) You should **know what you aim to achieve by each telephone call**, also what information you will need to have handy and how long the call will take. We discuss good telephone techniques further in Chapter 5.

2.21 **Make appointments with yourself.** If you need to spend time alone, making plans, reviewing progress - or indeed making sure that you get personal time at work or at home for rest and relaxation - it is a good idea to treat this as if it were a meeting. Make a time for it in your diary, and stick to it: take it seriously, and do not let other activities encroach on it.

2.22 **Work to schedules and checklists**. Here is what you should do.

- Don't rely on memory for appointments, events and duties.

- Try to work on **one thing at a time**, and to **finish each task** you start.

- **Don't put off** large, difficult or unpleasant tasks simply because they are large, difficult or unpleasant. Today's routines will be tomorrow's emergencies, and today's emergencies will **still** be tomorrow's emergencies.

Part B: Personal effectiveness

- **Learn to anticipate** and allow for work coming up; recognise and set reasonable deadlines.

2.23 **Organise work in batches**, with relevant files to hand, machines switched on etc to save time spent in turning from one job to another.

2.24 Maintain a list of small jobs which can be completed whilst waiting for a meeting or telephone call.

2.25 **Take advantage of work patterns.** Self-discipline is aided by developing regular hours or days for certain tasks, like dealing with correspondence first thing or filing at the end of the day. If you are able to plan your own schedules, you might also take into account your personal patterns of energy, concentration and alertness. Large or complex tasks might be undertaken in the mornings before you get tired, or perhaps late at night with fewer distractions, while Friday afternoon is not usually a good time to start a demanding task in the office.

2.26 **Follow up tasks and see them through**. Uncompleted work, necessary future action, expected results or feedback should be scheduled for the appropriate time. Checklists are also useful for making sure an operation is completed, marking the stage reached in case it has to be handed over to someone else or temporarily laid aside.

2.27 In the examination you are likely to be faced with problems involving helping others with their time management. The list of ideas above may be useful examples, or suggestions for such questions, but add more of your own.

Action Programme 3

Ask around the office for people's favourite time management ideas. Make a list of them and circulate them. It is a good way of getting people to think about and value their time.

2.28 Time management is important because time equals cost, but also a failure to manage time can cause an immense amount of **stress. Working twelve hours a day to get the job done is not necessarily the sign of a keen and effective worker,** and instead might suggest someone who is failing to organise and plan. High levels of stress will result in poor health, worsening performance and even less effective time management. For example, assume that the office has been hectic and for two weeks you have been too busy to keep up with the routine filing. By week three you are spending an hour a day looking for papers which have not yet been filed, so making the time it takes to complete anything even longer.

2.29 Managers have a responsibility for their own health, that of their subordinates and colleagues. Failure to manage time is both a cause and symptom of stress.

2.30 Time management is becoming even more critical to today's managers, because flattening of the corporate hierarchy and delayering of management structures means that there are fewer of them with more responsibilities.

3 DEVELOPING PRIORITISATION SKILLS

3.1 Did you find when you completed your audit of your week (paragraph 2.12) that you were spending a lot your time on relatively unimportant tasks, and having to rush through the

4: Time management

important issues? Many managers find they only get around to the important things after everyone else has gone home.

3.2 Each of us has to identify a system for prioritising our work and this involves planning. If you treat work in a reactive and ad hoc way, then you will respond to tasks as they land on your desk with no consideration of their importance. Effective managers take the time to review what has to be done and consider each activity in terms of its importance, priority and urgency, as well as the potential for delegation.

> **Key Concept**
> **Prioritisation** involves identifying **key results** (objectives which *must* be achieved if the section is to fulfil its aims) and **key tasks** (those things that *must* be done on time and to the required standard if the key results are to be achieved).

3.3 A job will be **important** compared to other tasks, if it satisfies at least one of three conditions.

- It adds value to the organisation's mission.
- It comes from a source deserving high priority, such as a customer or senior manager.
- The potential consequences of failure are long-term, difficult to reverse, far reaching and costly.

3.4 One of the problems managers have in allocating their time, comes from determining what tasks are **important** as defined above and distinguishing these from **urgent** tasks, which may have a deadline but less importance.

- Tasks both urgent and important should be dealt with now, and given a fair amount of time.
- Tasks **not** urgent but still important will become urgent as the deadline looms closer. Some of these tasks can be delegated.
- Tasks urgent but not important should be delegated, or designed out of your job. The task might be urgent to someone else, but not to you.
- Tasks neither urgent nor important should be delegated or binned.

3.5 EXAMPLE

The telephone can be a particular problem. Its ringing is urgent! Few of us can ignore it, yet the reason for the interruption may be much less **important** than the project you were working on.

3.6 Use your own personal scale to grade the **importance** of activities for example:

    1 - 3   Unimportant
    3 - 6   Moderately important
    6 - 10 Very important

You will be surprised to find that **many 'urgent' things are actually relatively unimportant**.

3.7 As a manager, few of your requests should be urgent. You need to **plan your work so others have advance warning of your needs and can plan theirs**. Never ask for things urgently if

Part B: Personal effectiveness

they are not needed urgently, and take care to **find out what other important activities are being disrupted**.

3.8 Once your work has been allocated into importance categories, you can consider if any can be delegated and what you are left with. Take care to do some important, fairly important and routine tasks everyday. Remember what happens if the routine filing never gets completed!

3.9 A basic allocation might look like this:

> 3 hours on important tasks
> 2 hours on fairly important tasks
> 1 hour routine
> 2 hours contingency and dealing with urgent/unexpected issues
> ___
> 8 hours

4 DELEGATION

4.1 **Delegation** has already been mentioned on a number of occasions in this chapter and it is a key skill which managers must master if they are to be successful.

> **Key Concept**
> **Delegation** is the process whereby a supervisor gives someone else the authority to make decisions within a given sphere.

4.2 It is the way in which responsibility for decision-making is shared in the organisation. Although this is usually a line management activity it can also happen between colleagues, often through the medium of a meeting where activities are allocated to individuals who take responsibility for them.

4.3 It is generally recognised that in any large complex organisation, **managers must delegate some authority** for the following reasons.

(a) There are **physical and mental limitations** to the workload of any individual or group in authority.

(b) **Routine or less important decisions can be passed to subordinates**, freeing the superior to concentrate on the more important aspects of the work.

(c) The increasing size and complexity of organisations calls for **specialisation**, both managerial and technical.

(d) Employees in today's organisations have **high expectations with regard to job satisfaction**, including discretion and participation in decision making. Job enrichment is being seen as an important ingredient in encouraging development and motivation. This may become increasingly important as the opportunities for promotion within flatter management structures diminish.

(e) The managerial succession plan depends on junior managers gaining **some experience of management processes**.

(f) From the customer service viewpoint, subordinates may be better able to take certain decisions as they are closer to the problem.

4: Time management

> **Action Programme 4**
>
> What do you think are the problems associated with delegation which make managers reluctant to delegate?

4.4 **Effective delegation consists of four stages**

Step 1. *Select the appropriate person.* The subordinate should be allocated sufficient resources and authority to carry out the tasks at the expected level of performance.

Step 2. *Brief the subordinate.*

(i) *Appropriate instruction should be given*, and the expected performance levels should be clearly specified. These should be realistic, specific and measurable.

(ii) *The scope of the delegated authority must be specific.*

- A sales person may have the authority to negotiate up to 10% discount.
- A retail manager be able to offer a refund of up to £500 on goods.
- A research officer may have the authority to purchase secondary data up to a budget total of £10,000.

It is important to check that the subordinate understands what is expected and this should be confirmed by questioning him or her.

Step 3. *Support the subordinate.* The basic principle is to stay within the original parameters of control and responsibility levels. If problems have arisen, the subordinate should be encouraged to find ways to put matters right. Similarly, the manager should be available for support but should encourage the subordinate to find answers rather than giving the answer straightaway. This will encourage the subordinate to analyse the situation and come up with possible remedies.

Step 4. *Debrief at the end of the task.* The debriefing should cover performance and any problems that arose, including how the subordinate coped with them. The manager needs to consider whether the original briefing was adequate. The manager should also consider the implications of the delegation for the subordinate's long-term development, and whether the subordinate can be encouraged to develop further in particular areas.

4.5 The following organisational considerations will help overcome the reluctance to delegate.

(a) Provide a system of **selecting subordinates who will be capable of handling delegated authority** in a responsible way. If subordinates are of the right quality, superiors will be prepared to trust them.

(b) Have a system of **open communications, in which the superior and subordinates freely interchange ideas and information**. Subordinates who are given all the information needed to the job will make better-informed decisions. Similarly, superiors who know what is going on will have greater confidence. However, communication must not be used by superiors as a means of reclaiming authority.

(c) Ensure that a **system of control information** is established. Superiors are reluctant to delegate authority because they retain absolute responsibility for the performance of their subordinates. If an efficient feedback system is in operation, responsibility and

Part B: Personal effectiveness

accountability will be **monitored** at all levels of the management hierarchy, and the dangers of relinquishing authority to subordinates are significantly lessened.

(d) **Reward effective delegation by superiors** and the efficient assumption of authority by subordinates.

When to delegate

4.6 A supervisor or manager should be coached, if necessary, about the particular instances in which delegation should or should not be considered. The following issues would need to be considered.

(a) Whether the manager requires the **acceptance of the decision** by subordinates - for morale, good relationships or ease of implementation of the decision. If acceptance is the primary need and the decision itself is largely routine, for example in the case of canteen arrangements or office decor, delegation should be undertaken.

(b) Whether the **quality of the decision is most important, and acceptance less so**. Many financial decisions may be of this type, and should be retained by the superior, who alone may be capable of making them. If acceptance and quality are equally important, eg for changes in work methods or the introduction of new technology, **consultation may be advisable.**

(c) Whether the **expertise or experience of subordinates** is relevant or necessary to the task, or will enhance the quality of the decision. If an individual is required to perform a task which is not within his/her own specialised knowledge, it should be delegated to the appropriate person. The office manager may delegate repair and maintenance of machinery to an operations supervisor or the marketing director a research brief to the research manager etc.

(d) Whether, being as objective as possible, the manager feels he/she can trust in the **competence and reliability of subordinates**. The superior is accountable for his/her own area of authority, and should not delegate if **genuinely** there is a lack of confidence in the team (in which case there are other problems to solve).

(e) Whether the task or decision requires **tact and confidentiality**, or, on the other hand, maximum exposure and assimilation by employees. Disciplinary action, for example, should not be delegated, whereas tasks involving new procedures to which employees will have to get accustomed may be delegated as soon as possible.

(f) The supervisor's own personality and leadership style, and the culture of the organisation with regard to delegation and consultation, will also influence the decision.

Groups and decision making

4.7 **Group decision making** can be useful.

(a) Pooling skills, information and ideas from different functions, specialisms and levels in the organisation could increase the quality of the decision. Groups have been shown to produce better evaluated decisions than individuals working separately.

(b) Participation in the decision-making process makes the decision **acceptable to the group** either because it represents a compromise or consensus of all their views, or because the group has simply been consulted and given a sense of influencing the decision.

4.8 With **critical decisions,** where quality is the prime objective, it may be more helpful for a manager to involve work groups in areas such as problem definition and formulation of alternative solutions to take advantage of collective skills and experience and the creativity of group idea-generation. The decision might be best left to the manager responsible. Acceptance might have been enhanced by the consultative process.

4.9 The same criteria apply as deciding whether to delegate.

- Do you need employee acceptance?
- Do you have the power to do **without** employee acceptance?
- Do you trust employees' judgement and ability to reach consensus?
- Do you need employee input, or is the solution clear-cut?
- Do you need a fast decision or a well sold decision?

4.10 **Risks in group decision making**

- Shared responsibility can be **blurred responsibility**, and groups tend to make **riskier** decisions than individuals.

- The desire for consensus in a group can make it **ignore dissent** and any information that contradicts its pet theory.

- Groups may have their **own agenda** and make decisions to further their own objectives rather than the organisation's.

- Group decisions **take longer to reach** (although they are easier to implement later) especially if there is conflict and disagreement in the group. This is not regarded as a drawback by the Japanese, however. Argument leading to eventual consensus is common managerial practice in Japanese business.

Action Programme 5

What group(s) are you in at work that would have the authority to make or contribute to decisions (for example, quality circle, project group, committee or brainstorming session)? How much authority is the group actually given? Does it generate ideas, provide information, offer advice and criticism, make formal recommendations and/or make binding decisions?

Do you think it would be (a) useful and (b) practicable to consult and seek consensus for more decisions than are currently shared? If so, why - and if not, why not?

4.11 When considering delegation the manager must at all times remember that **responsibility cannot be delegated** or passed on to a subordinate. A manager may delegate **authority** to a subordinate but remains **responsible to his own boss** for seeing that the work gets done.

4.12 There should be a careful balance between delegated authority and responsibility in the organisation.

(a) A manager who is not held accountable for any area of authority is free to exercise it in a capricious way.   = risky.

(b) A manager who is held accountable for aspects of performance, but has not been given authority to control them, is in an impossible position. Sufficient authority must be given to enable individuals to do what is expected of them.

Part B: Personal effectiveness

5 OTHER PEOPLE'S TIME MANAGEMENT PROBLEMS

5.1 The **manager** has the added responsibility for the use of the scarce time resource of those working within his/her authority. Managing the time of others starts with ensuring that they all understand the importance of time management and have the skills necessary to enable them to manage their own time.

5.2 **It will be the job of those in authority to divide duties and allocate them to available staff**: departmental managers should have an overall understanding of the nature and volume of work to be accomplished, and the resources at their command.

5.3 **Planning is essential** in this division of labour, because although there are some obvious allocations, such as specialist tasks to specialists like computer programmers and market researchers, others may be more complicated.

(a) **Functions like filing and copying are not always centralised**, and do not always have the attention of a dedicated employee: who will do the work, and will it interfere with their other duties?

(b) **Peak periods in some tasks may necessitate re-distribution of staff** to cope with the work load. There should be flexibility in who does, and is able to do, various non-specialist tasks.

(c) **Status and staff attitudes must be considered**. A hierarchical organisation structure with job grades and different levels of authority and seniority can work towards efficiency, providing close control and motivation, but it can also cause planning problems. Flexibility in reassigning people from one job to another or varying the work they do may be hampered by an employee's perception of status. Planning must take into account experience and seniority, but it must also recognise that junior employees may desire challenges and greater responsibility.

(d) Individual abilities and temperaments differ, and **work should be allocated to the best person for the job**. Planning should allow for flexibility in the event of an employee proving unfit for a task, or more able than their present tasks indicate.

(e) **Efforts will be co-ordinated so that all those involved in a process work together as a team**. If the team is large, sub-groups may be formed for closer supervision and sense of unity. Work-sharing will also be more flexible for a unit with common skills and experience.

We will be considering team building and improving team performance in later chapters.

5.4 Timetabling and division of labour are only an aspect of efficiency. For either of these to be effective, a clear idea will be needed of three things.

- What tasks are to be performed *also*
- What resources they will require
- How the resources can be allocated to the tasks most efficiently

This will require further planning. Work procedures might be set out formally in a procedures manual. Alternatively, they might need to be planned by a manager (for the team) or by the individual worker.

5.5 A useful aid for any sequence of activities (routine and non-routine) is a checklist. It could be an action sheet with a list of activities, and spaces for start and completion. This shows immediately how far the process involved has gone, how far it still has to go, and whether anything has been missed out.

5.6 A **checklist** may be even simpler than this, namely a list of items or activities which can be checked off as they are completed.

5.7 EXAMPLE CASE STUDY

One of your customer services supervisors is consistently in trouble because his section always seems to be in a state of confusion. Work appears to be allocated on a haphazard basis; some people are overloaded, others have little to do. He does not produce information when required and he appears to be consistently harassed and preoccupied in trying to solve the latest crisis.

What steps can be taken to help him?

5.8 SOLUTION

The problem concerns a supervisor's failure to **plan** adequately, **control** the activities of his staff, **set targets** and **achieve results**. Possible reasons for this situation are the following.

(a) The supervisor has received little or no training in how to plan and control.

(b) The organisation has not adequately communicated its objectives to its employees. As a result, the supervisor does not know what is required of him and where the activities of his department fit into the overall corporate plan.

(c) The department may be short-staffed or the subordinates unable to do anything more than routine tasks.

(d) The supervisor may not be suited to leadership.

5.9 You should obtain relevant **details**.

(a) The supervisor's background, appraisals and training history

(b) Details of the activities of the department (such as what information it is required to produce and when and the importance of its output relative to other departments)

(c) The level and calibre of staff under the supervisor's control

5.10 The supervisor should be given a **counselling interview** and be asked to give his views of why his department is under-performing. He may point out that it is understaffed (so deadlines cannot be met) or that some staff cannot be entrusted with difficult work (so that capable staff have to be overloaded). It may even be the case that he receives little or no guidance or encouragement from his superiors so that he ends up 'firefighting'.

5.11 Depending on the reasons identified for the failure of the department, the following remedies could be suggested.

(a) The supervisor could be trained in the importance of planning and control and the management techniques available such as time management methods.

(b) More and better staff could be allocated to the department.

(c) Departmental duties might be revised and re-allocated so that the work becomes more manageable.

(d) Greater involvement should be requested from senior management, particularly in explaining the role of the department within the overall plan and being available to give advice and encouragement.

(e) The supervisor may need to be transferred to a less demanding job.

5.12 If the principal reason for the supervisor's under-performance is inability to plan and control, a **management by objectives** approach might be considered. The supervisor will be informed of corporate and departmental objectives, and key personal result areas. The supervisor will then be invited to co-operate in setting personal performance targets: achieving these should ensure that departmental goals are also achieved. In addition, the system for evaluating the supervisor's performance will be closely linked to the targets set. This should encourage the supervisor to plan the activities of the department efficiently and control them effectively, since this will help achieve the personal standards set.

Conclusion

5.13 Problems or failures may be an indication of other problems like time management. The customer service manager fails to plan because of firefighting to meet the day-to-day urgent demands on his department. Training is probably required.

Exam Tip

The June 2000 exam included a question on improving team effectiveness. While time management formed an important part of the answer, the appropriate techniques had to be selected carefully, so as to address the very specific problems in the setting. The question also required application of project management and delegation concepts. This is a typical approach. You **must** answer the question with relevant proposals. A 'theory dump' (as the examiner puts it) **will not do**.

5.14 Managers must keep alert for signs that their teams, or individuals within their teams, are not managing their time effectively. Here are some typical symptoms.

- Change in work patterns, with individuals working longer hours
- Increase in deadlines missed
- Late arrival at meetings
- Rushed work leading to poorer quality and more errors
- Lost papers, routine tasks not completed
- Working in isolation avoiding the rest of the group

5.15 Having worked through the time management review for yourself you will be better able to work with these staff to help them identify the cause and resolve their time management problems.

6 MANAGING PROJECTS AND PLANS OVER TIME

6.1 We have already begun to consider the importance of planning and scheduling projects when reviewing the time management of the team. Marketing is essentially a co-ordinating role and the management of a project from product launch to printing a new brochure is central to the marketer's role.

6.2 A **project** is 'an undertaking that has a beginning and an end and is carried out to meet established goals within cost, schedule and quality objectives'.

- It has specific **start and end** points
- It has a **well-defined objective**
- It is **self-contained** or a **one-off**
- It often **cuts across functional boundaries**

- It usually contains **cost and time schedules** for the duration of the project and **performance specifications** for the end result

6.3 Projects have their own special management problems.

(a) Projects require teamwork, but team members may belong to different business functions, with different specialist expertise, important at different times.

(b) The client/beneficiary of the project often sees no results until the project is completed.

(c) Some projects might cause conflict, for example new roads such as the Newbury bypass. The marketing manager might have to deal with different interest groups.

(d) It is hard to estimate the duration and cost of projects which involve new technology, or which are implemented in uncertain environmental conditions.

(e) Incomplete or changing specifications can make it impossible to adhere to the project's time and cost budget, and can damage the project's effectiveness.

6.4 **Objectives of project management**

- Quality (fitness for use) of the end result
- Keeping to budget
- Adhering to the agreed timescale

The project life cycle

6.5 A project has a life cycle (as it has a beginning and an end).

(a) **Conceiving and defining the project**. The project may be suggested in response to a problem. This must be explored and understood before a solution can be suggested.

- The project definition will be specified
- The overall project objective will state what the project should achieve
- Success criteria are determined
- Both the client and the supplier must have an agreed understanding as to what is required

(b) **Planning the project**. The aim is to ensure that the project's objectives in terms of quality, cost and time are achieved.

- Objectives for time, cost and performance must be specified
- The project must be broken down into manageable units
- The necessary resources must be estimated
- Usage of resources must be scheduled

These will be incorporated in a **project plan**. Detailed planning techniques are covered shortly.

(c) **Implementation and control**. A project manager or co-ordinator will often initiate and direct the work. The project manager should monitor performance against deadlines by inspections and progress reviews and take corrective action when necessary.

(d) **Completion and evaluation (post-audit)**. After the project is completed, two questions can be asked.

- Does the end result satisfy the project objective?
- Was the project itself well managed?

Analysis and estimation

6.6 In the **project planning** stage, one of the first tasks is to break the project down into parts. For example, the task of cooking a meal can be broken down into subtasks such as chopping onions, grinding spices, boiling water. This should be carried on until activities cannot be meaningfully broken down any further.

6.7 **Work breakdown structure** helps identify the sequence of tasks and the resources needed for the project. This is an important input to the estimation process. Cost estimation is often difficult. The project manager has to rely on individuals' assessments of the time it will take them to complete a task, and such estimates are unreliable.

6.8 Work breakdown structure has been applied to **new product development** where different teams work on different aspects of the same product simultaneously. However, coordination is needed to ensure that the output of each team is compatible. For example a number of **design teams** may work on different areas of a product under development, in order to speed up the process.

Scheduling techniques

6.9 The activities described in the work breakdown structure need to be performed in proper sequence. However some sequences can be carried out in parallel, and a number of tools are available to coordinate this.

Gantt charts

6.10 A **Gantt chart** illustrates the activities that are to be performed in a project and the time scale over which they must be performed. From these, **float times** can be identified, when there is a certain amount of leeway between the end of one activity and the start of another (eg if this subsequent activity depends on the completion of a number of earlier activities).

6.11 In 1993, the Diploma Analysis and Decision examination featured an airport seeking to open a third terminal. The following gives a view of how the timetables can be presented visually, indicating activities over time. In practice, Gantt charts may be much more detailed, depending on the project.

Terminal project progress and PR activities

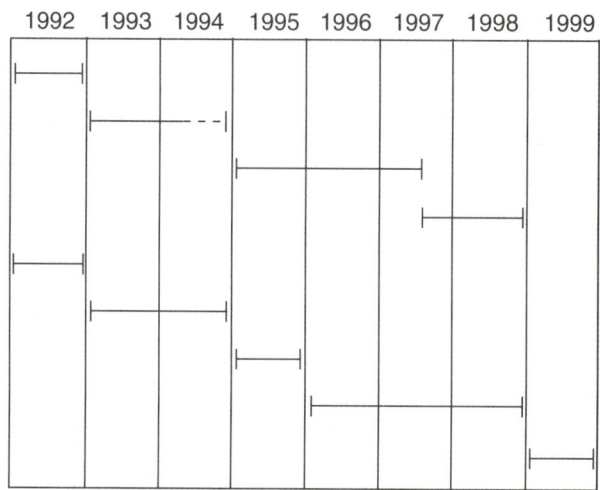

4: Time management

6.12 A plan for a project with an indicative budget is shown below. The plan deals with a firm's management of ecological and environmental issues.

Environmental policy

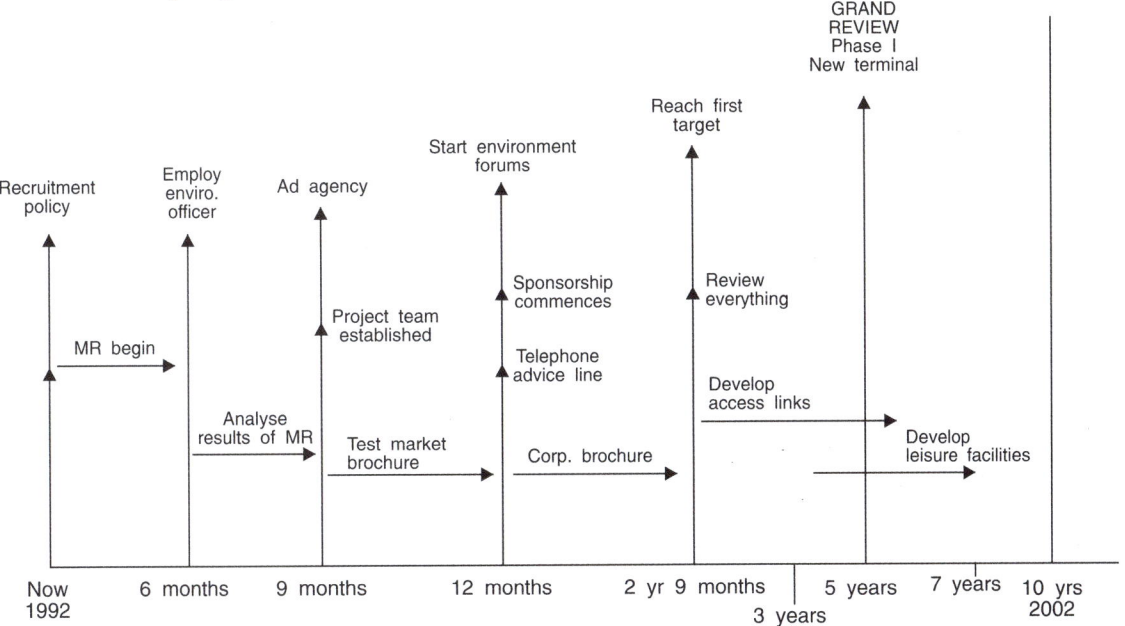

Budget for environmental policy

	£'000
Market research	60
Recruitment	50
Data analysis	15
Agency/campaign	400
Telephone service	20
Sponsorship	15
Joint ventures	-
Access/rail links	2,000
'Phased recycling'	1,000
Community forums	20
Total	3,580

6.13 It is almost certainly the case that you will need to allow for **contingencies**.

Critical path analysis (CPA)

6.14 Where the sequence of activities is complicated and where one task depends on another, in a chain, critical path analysis can be used. This is a term for project planning techniques which aim to map the activities in a particular project, the time they take, and the relationship between them. You are unlikely to use this in practice but you may come across it or need to refer to it in the exam.

6.15 CPA describes the **sequence** of activities, and how long they are going to take. These diagrams are drawn left to right.

(a) **Events** are represented by numbered circles. **Activities** are lettered and take place between **events**.

(b) The **critical path** is represented by drawing a thicker line along the most time consuming route through the network. It is the **minimum** amount of time that the project will take with normal resources.

Part B: Personal effectiveness

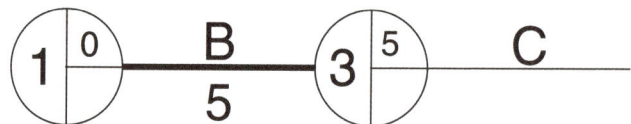

This means that the earliest possible completion time for B and start date for C is at the end of day 5.

6.16 An example of a network diagram is as follows. The critical path is AEG. These activities have to be completed in sequence.

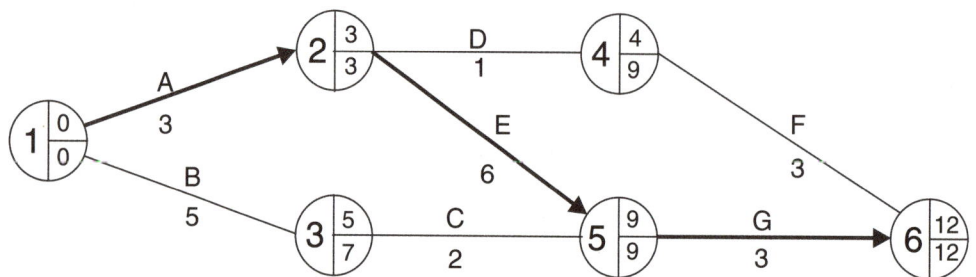

Activities B, D, C and F have **float**. They may be delayed without delaying the overall project.

6.17 **Advantages of this approach**:

- It identifies the shortest possible time for a project
- It identifies which activities can be scheduled simultaneously
- It may be possible to adjust the allocation of resources, by identifying activities that can be speeded up

7 PROBLEM SOLVING AND DECISION MAKING

7.1 A great deal of management time is spent dealing with problems and deciding what to do. It is possible to waste a great deal of time on these activities. The first stage in dealing with any problem is to decide whether any action at all is required. With limited management effort available, it is important that it is deployed where it **adds most value**. Very few organisations run in a perfect fashion but they do exist and compete and succeed. It may well be that some problems are not worth solving.

7.2 Even when it is clear that action must be taken, not all managers adopt a rational approach, and many seem constitutionally incapable of making decisions. There is no doubt that there is room for hunch and inspiration in business, just as it sometimes happens that a cautious and logical approach leads to an inadequate solution. However, the use of a disciplined technique can save time and produce acceptable solutions and all managers should know how to deploy such a technique.

7.3 The rational approach to decision making can be illustrated by a simple diagram.

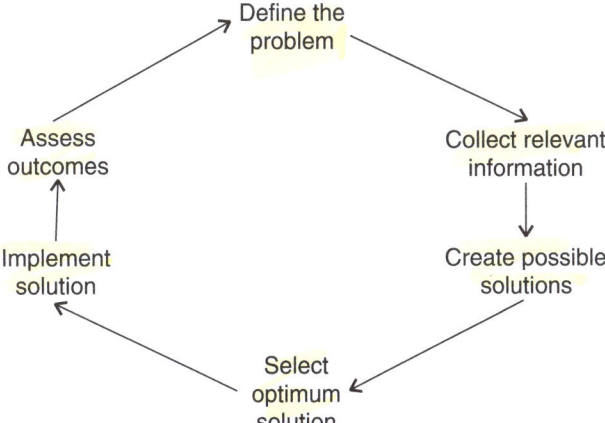

The decision process is **iterative**, that is, it allows for incremental improvements, each based on the outcome of its predecessor.

7.4 The process may be thought of as commencing at the top of the diagram. We become aware that there is a problem and we must do something about it. This may be the result of routine **monitoring of performance** or there may be a sudden shock such as a the successful launch of a revolutionary product by a rival. At this stage it is vital to **define the problem** very clearly, so that effort is focussed properly. For instance, in the case of the rival's product launch, is our problem the fact that we do not have a **similar product**, is it our general lack of **product development ability** or is it a failure of **market research** which should have indicated to us that such a product was needed?

7.5 The data collection phase may vary considerably in duration. Economic and scientific information is easily available but in huge quantities; the relevant information about a personnel problem may be quite limited but very difficult to obtain if it is obscured by people's attitudes and beliefs.

7.6 The next phase is the one which many of us miss out in our daily lives. We may be very rational about defining our problem and collecting information, but we then frequently leap to a conclusion. This intuitive process has its place and should not be totally discounted. Many solutions do become obvious at this stage. However, we should always be aware that there may be **more than one possible strategy**, especially in business where plans may be complex and open to adjustment.

7.7 Selection of the optimum solution is a second crucial stage, requiring the same care as problem definition. Experience will help, but the establishment of **decision criteria** will almost certainly be essential. In business decision making, for instance, the chosen solution must satisfy three criteria.

- It must be **suitable,** that is it must fit into the enterprise's current strategic and commercial stance
- It must be **feasible** in terms of the available resources
- It must be **acceptable** to those affected by it

7.8 The process of **implementation** requires its own skills of planning and management. Project management skills may be relevant here, or it may be possible to delegate this phase to a lower level.

7.9 We are now returning to the start point of the cycle. Assessment of outcomes is a continuing part of management control. Such feedback may reveal that we have not succeeded in totally solving our problem, or another aspect, previously obscured, may come to light. We must maintain our vigilance, since new problems are bound to arise.

Chapter Roundup

- Managers are responsible for managing their own time and the time of others, to ensure that projects are implemented effectively over time, the team's activities are co-ordinated and deadlines met.
- Time management cannot be improved until the current use of time is analysed. Keeping a 'time diary' is the first step in helping to improve time management problems.
- Careful analysis of how you spend your own time currently enables you to set benchmark time allocations to individual tasks and to measure improvements against them.
- There are a number of practical tips which can help the individual manage his/her time better. These need to be recognised and practised so that they become habitual.
- Failure to manage time effectively can cause considerable stress and lead to poor health.
- The ability **to prioritise** is fundamental to time management. Distinguishing between important and urgent is a big step on the way in ensuring effective use of time.
- Even routine tasks have to be completed. They may be **delegated** to others, but failure to do them will cause problems later.
- Delegation is needed to spread work throughout the organisation, to develop management skills in younger managers, and to create interest in the jobs for other staff.
- For effective delegation to take place, staff must be willing, have the resources and authority to do the task, and be clear on how their performance will be evaluated.
- Managers have to recognise that they can delegate authority, but responsibility is essentially theirs.
- Managers must watch out for poor time management in their subordinates.
- For projects, where time is of the essence, analysis of the project task and breaking it down into activities for scheduling can help planning.

4: Time management

Quick Quiz

1. Why is time management important? (see paras 2.1-2.2)
2. What must you do before you improve your time management? (2.11)
3. List five practical ways by which an individual might improve time management. (2.14 – 2.26)
4. What are the characteristics of an important or high priority job? (3.3)
5. How would you distinguish between important and urgent tasks? (3.4)
6. How would you define delegation? (4.2)(Key concept)
7. Why is delegation necessary? (4.3)
8. What are the stages of effective delegation? (4.4)
9. What problems might exist in allocating tasks to people? (5.3)
10. What are the problem-solving stages which will help you to tackle case studies and exam scenarios? (5.13) (Exam Tip)
11. What are the indicators which could signal that a member of your team is having problems with time management? (5.14)
12. What are the objectives of project management? (6.4)
13. List the stages of the project life cycle. (6.5)

Action Programme Review

1. An executive on £50,000 pa basic pay costs say £75,000 with all the extra costs of car, pension NI, PHI and bonus.

   She/he works 40 hours per week for 45 weeks of the year.

   $$\frac{£75,000}{45 \times 40} = \frac{£75,000}{1,800} = \text{approximately £41 per hour.}$$

2. If you answered yes to any of 1-7, and no to question 8, then you need to improve your time management. If you answered more than five of them this way then time management must be a priority, particularly whilst you are also trying to find time to take your CIM examinations.

4. (a) Low confidence and trust in the abilities of the subordinates, ie the suspicion that 'if you want it done well, you have to do it yourself'.

   (b) The burden of responsibility and accountability for the mistakes of subordinates, aggravated by (a) above.

   (c) A desire to stay in touch with the workload and staff. This may be particularly acute for the newly promoted supervisor, who does not feel at home in a management role, and misses aspects of the subordinate job.

   (d) An unwillingness to admit that subordinates could perform some of the superior's duties.

   (e) Poor control and communication systems in the organisation, so that the superior feels the need to do everything personally, in order to retain real control and responsibility, and know what is going on.

   (f) An organisational culture that has failed to reward or recognise effective delegation by superiors, so that they may not realise that delegation is positively regarded.

   (g) Lack of understanding that delegation does not involve giving subordinates total control and making the superior redundant.

Now try illustrative question 4 at the end of the Study Text

5 The Manager as a Communicator

Chapter Topic List	Syllabus reference
1 Setting the scene	
2 Identifying the role of communication in management	2.4
3 Communication processes and media	2.4
4 Oral and face-to-face communication: individuals	2.4
5 Oral and face-to-face communication: groups	2.4
6 Documentary and electronic communications	2.4
7 Improving communications	2.4, 3.8
8 Knowledge management	2.4
9 Effective management of meetings	2.4
10 Negotiation	2.4

Learning Outcomes

- Students will be able to determine communications problems typically faced by managers and describe strategies for improving and solving these problems.
- Students will be able to explain the principles and techniques of successful negotiation with internal colleagues and external customers, suppliers, distributors etc with a view to mutually successful outcomes.

Key Concepts Introduced

- Communication
- Negotiation

Example of Marketing at Work

- BA's staff communications initiative
- How to influence people

1 SETTING THE SCENE

1.1 For the marketing manager in particular, the ability to communicate well is a key component of his or her effectiveness, both within the company and with customers. We discuss this in Section 2.

1.2 In Section 3 we outline a **model of the communication process** and what can go wrong. Communication can be impeded by distraction in the environment (noise) or the inherent difficulties people have in getting on with each other. Money spent on expensive new methods of communication may be money wasted if staff are unwilling or unable to use them.

1.3 A way of minimising the barriers to communication is in the right use of **media,** and these form the subject of Sections 4 to 6. Sometimes, to ensure a message is understood, two communication media are used, for example a phone call and a letter to confirm what was said. Any manager must be skilled in oral communication, in interviewing situations for example, but needs to use written methods too.

1.4 Communication can be improved by attending to the way by which messages are sent, discussed in Section 7. This is an organisational issue, but managers need to improve their **individual skills in presentations, report writing and telephone manner**. Listening skills and the ability to interpret body language can be very valuable. You must also be able to present reports clearly - a vital skill for real-life of course, as well as this exam. In Section 8 we discuss the important topic of knowledge management. In Section 9 we discuss how to lighten a major burden on your time: meetings and in Section 10 we explain negotiation.

1.5 These skills apply in many different contexts. **Interviewing** skills are needed for recruitment (Chapter 7) and appraisal (Chapter 8), for example. Meeting skills are often needed for effective client relations (Chapter 10). Effective communication is vital for **change management** and **internal marketing.**

Links with other papers

1.6 Communication is fundamental to marketing and this chapter can be relevant to other papers, too.

- Marketing Operations: communication skills are essential in dealing with suppliers and in implementing the marketing plan.
- Marketing/Customer Interface: communication is essential in customer-facing service environments. Communication is also integral to the 'culture' of an organisation.

Exam Tip
Communication is relevant throughout and can feature in any question. The mini-case in December 2000 asked for a comprehensive audit of current internal communication activities including 'written, management style, interpersonal skills': underpinning this, perhaps, is the idea of culture.

Similarly, an exam question will require you to use one of a variety of formats.

2 IDENTIFYING THE ROLE OF COMMUNICATION IN MANAGEMENT 12/00

2.1 Communication is the lifeblood of the organisation. Without the free flow of communication the business cannot survive.

Key concept
The most basic definition of **communication** is the transmission or exchange of information.

Part B: Personal effectiveness

2.2 Communication is a universal human activity and has a number of **purposes**.

- Initiating action (eg by request, instruction or persuasion)
- Making known needs and requirements
- Exchanging information, ideas, attitudes and beliefs
- Establishing understanding, and perhaps also exerting influence or persuasion
- Establishing and maintaining relations.

Action Programme 1

Think about your organisation or one you know well. What are the reasons for communication within it? (Ignore for the moment external communications with customers and intermediaries.)

2.3 All this communication activity is focused on carrying information to and from managers who are central to the communication process and activity.

2.4 In any organisation, the communication of information is necessary for **planning, co-ordination** and **control**.

(a) Managers should be aware of what their departments are achieving, what they are not achieving and what they **should** be achieving.

(b) Communication between departments is needed so that interdependent systems **co-operate** in accomplishing the organisation's aims.

(c) Communication between individuals is needed. Employees should know what is expected of them and must liaise with management and fellow workers.

2.5 Managers must also communicate **decisions** to those affected by or involved with them, motivate people to implement plans and report on progress.

2.6 **Managers are at the hub of a communications system**. They are the place where information is exchanged. You might recall Mintzberg's discussion of managerial roles in Chapter 2. Many of these roles related to information.

Direction of communication

2.7 **Communication directions**

(a) **Vertical** communication may be **downwards** (from superior to subordinate) or **upwards** (from subordinate to superior).

(b) **Horizontal or lateral** communication takes place between people of the same rank, in the same section or department, or in different sections or departments.

Action Programme 2

What about the marketing manager as a communicator? What is the added dimension we should consider?

2.8 Formal vertical communication is an important part of the communication system. Formal mechanisms for meetings of employee representatives and management are useful, but tend to be applied in a limited number of situations such as negotiation and grievance. The organisation needs a system which offers a channel for employee complaints, comments and

suggestions from lower levels as to how work practices, systems or technology might be improved or problems solved. This may be achieved in several ways.

- Regular meetings with employee representatives
- Team meetings and brainstorming sessions to find solutions to problems or to discuss work issues
- Quality circles to discuss quality-related issues
- Suggestion schemes, perhaps with incentives for positive contributions
- Open door. A manager might be always available, or establish 'surgery' hours when employees are welcome to bring problems, suggestions or feedback.

> **Action Programme 3**
>
> What opportunities are there for you to put your ideas, opinions and suggestions to your boss, or for your team to communicate with you?
>
> (a) If there are team meetings, how do these differ from **team briefings** (where purely downwards information and instructions are given)?
>
> (b) If there is a suggestion scheme, does it work? If not, why not?
>
> (c) Do you think your in-house newspaper/journal (if any) gives you more than 'the official line'? Are there opportunities for you to contribute? Do you do so? If not, why not?
>
> (d) Can you talk informally to your boss? Do you? Do you listen to your own subordinates?
>
> Draw up a brief proposal, either for you to implement with your team or as a recommendation to your boss. Make sure that you include at least three practical suggestions for improving communication upwards from subordinates.

2.9 **Horizontal** communication occurs between people at the same hierarchical level in the organisation. It is necessary to co-ordinate the work of several people, and perhaps several departments, who have to co-operate to carry out a certain operation. Specialist departments which serve the organisation in general, such as personnel or information systems, have no clear line of authority linking them to managers in other departments who need their involvement. A sales supervisor, for example, may require the services of the personnel manager in a disciplinary procedure. Particular effort, goodwill and tact will be required in such situations.

Informal communications

2.10 Managers have a role play not only in formal communication but also in informal communication. The **formal** system of communication in an organisation is always supplemented by an **informal** one: talks in the canteen, at the pub, on the way home, on the telephone and so on.

2.11 The danger with informal communication is that it might be malicious, full of inaccurate rumour or wild speculation. This type of gossip in the organisation can be unsettling, and make colleagues mistrust one another. However managers need to be tuned in to it so that they can take action if needed. This is because the formal system may not carry certain types of valuable information, such as information about internal politics.

2.12 Formal communication systems do, however, need the support of a good informal system, which might be encouraged by in the following ways.

Part B: Personal effectiveness

(a) Setting up official communications to feed information into the informal system, such as **house journals or briefings** (though these will have to earn the attention and trust of employees).

(b) Encouraging and offering opportunities for **networking**. A network is a collection of people, usually with a shared interest, who tend to keep in touch to exchange informal information. Ordinary social exchanges should not be stifled at work.

2.13 The **grapevine** or bush telegraph is one aspect of informal communication. The grapevine works very fast and is selective: information is not divulged randomly but in a network of interested parties. The problem with the grapevine is that it tends to communicate rumour and gossip, which become further distorted in the retelling. Much of this inaccurate information will be negative in its effect, although the satisfaction involved in participating in the system may actually have a positive effect on morale.

2.14 Perhaps surprisingly, **the grapevine is only active when the formal communication network is also active**: the grapevine does not fill a gap created by an ineffective formal communication system, but co-exists with it.

2.15 Since the grapevine exists, and cannot be got rid of, management should learn both to accept it and to harness it towards achieving the objectives of the organisation. It is important for managers themselves to 'hook into' the grapevine, to be aware of what is going on - and what their subordinates think is going on.

Action Programme 4

Draw up an informal communication chart to reflect the communication networks in your organisation. The people with the most extensive and accurate information are often gatekeepers like security, portering and receptionist staff who may in formal organisational terms be at low levels in the hierarchy.

2.16 Marketing managers will be judged by the quality of their communication skills and so these are a high priority for improvement and development.

Internal marketing

2.17 The phrase **internal marketing** has been used in a variety of ways. Put most simply, it means applying the marketing concept to the organisation's internal affairs. There are then various applications for this idea.

(a) **Employees** in all departments and at all levels can be encouraged to focus their attention on how their work contributes to satisfying the external customer.

(b) Departments not dealing directly with the external customer can adopt the **internal customer concept**. This requires them to reappraise their objectives and performance in the light of the needs and expectations of the other parts of the organisation.

(c) This concept has been adopted in the system of **Total Quality Management** as a means of promoting consistently improved standards.

(d) Communication of management's plans and priorities can be seen as a marketing task where the work force is the target market. Marketing management may be required to produce an **internal marketing plan** for this purpose. This is a popular approach to **the management of change**, which is dealt with in Chapter 9.

2.18 Internal marketing in the sense of a form of communication may be very informal and hardly worthy of the title, but if a more structured approach is taken, the basic principles of the marketing mix should be applied.

Marketing at Work

From almost nowhere, internal communications has emerged as one of the few marketing disciplines that is experiencing growth, and one where that growth is expected to continue.

Everyone is talking about internal communications. The realisation that brand messages need to be consistent – in that messages on the shop floor need to be the same as £10m TV ad campaigns – has prompted senior management to spend more money communicating brands internally.

But there is still more talk than action, according to research conducted by brand consultants Dragon.

In its report 'One Company', Dragon says British businesses admit they could save millions of pounds a year 'by improving internal communications, doing away with old-fashioned rivalry within companies and encouraging people to work closer together.'

Despite this, only 19 per cent of those managers interviewed believe they have been successful in creating this 'one company' culture.

The report says: 'It is clear that most companies recognise that the bottom line benefits of generating a one company culture are there to be won ... but while companies are certainly talking the language of integration and involvement, and beginning to make the right moves, most would acknowledge there is some way to go to break down longstanding internal barriers.'

There are many reasons why there is still a gap between ideals and reality in this business: the short-termism of industry and the traditional boundaries between management and staff are only two.

According to Dragon's report, a lot of people are getting it wrong. It says: 'Companies need to increase activity in communicating common goals and reporting on the progress they achieve. Simply publishing a mission statement is not enough to create involvement ... Although 90 per cent of companies publish their mission and values, less than half report on performance to the whole workforce.'

The problem, according to Banner McBride chief executive Mike Pounsford, is that internal communications is not yet seen as a business issue.

'It's a "nice to have" not a "need to have",' he says.

But Pounsford points to those organisations which he believes that embraced internal communications where it has worked. 'For the past ten years, Tesco has been focused on internal branding. In the early Nineties, Tesco senior management took a conscious decision that if they didn't invest in the way people delivered the product they were wasting their time.

'Asda is the same. Archie Norman talks about his staff being brand ambassadors. The problem is a lot of chief executives don't put this issue high on the agenda.'

Jo-Anne Flack, Marketing Week, 10 August 2000

3 COMMUNICATION PROCESSES AND MEDIA

3.1 If you have studied for your Certificate examinations you will have completed the subject *Business Communication*, in which case treat this section as an opportunity to review the communication process. If, however, you are not yet familiar with the basic model and barriers to communication, take more time in working through this section.

The communication process

3.2 **Effective communication is a two-way process, perhaps best expressed as a cycle**. Messages are sent by the communicator and received by the other party, who sends back some form of confirmation that the message has been received and understood. This is enormously complicated in face-to-face communication: you may send a letter and receive

an acknowledgement back, which would correspond to a single cycle of communication, but face-to-face, the interplay of spoken and body language is much more complex.

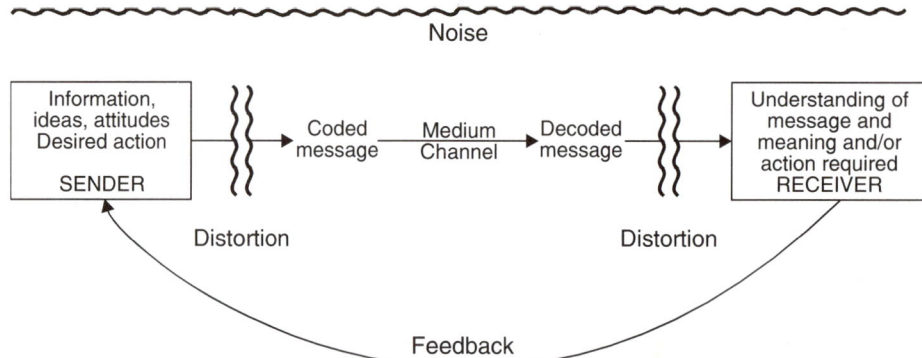

(a) **Coding of a message.** The code or language of a message may be verbal (spoken or written) or it may be non-verbal, in pictures, diagrams, numbers or body language.

(b) **Medium for the message.** There are a number of channels for communication, such as a conversation, a letter, a notice board or via computer. The choice of medium used in communication depends on a number of factors such as urgency, permanency, complexity, sensitivity and cost.

(c) **Feedback.** It is of vital importance that the sender of a message gets feedback on the receiver's reaction. This is partly to test the receiver's understanding of it and partly to gauge the receiver's reaction.

(d) **Distortion** leads to the loss of the meaning of a message in handling, that is at the coding and decoding stages. Usually the problem is one of language and the medium used; most of us have found, for instance, that it is far easier to get the wrong end of the stick in a telephone call than from a face to face conversation, since non-verbal language is missing.

(e) **Noise** includes distractions and interference in the environment in which communication is taking place. It may be physical noise (passing traffic), technical noise (a bad telephone line), social noise (differences in the personalities of the parties) or psychological noise (anger, frustration, tiredness). In multinational, or global corporations, it might be caused by differences in culture.

3.3 As illustrated in the above diagram, it is **feedback** that makes communication a two-way process rather than a series of send-receive events. Feedback is a vital and often neglected aspect of the process, which indicates to the sender whether or not his message has been successfully received, understood and interpreted. Failure to seek or offer feedback, or ignoring feedback offered, is one of the major problems in communication.

3.4 The management of interpersonal relations, inside and outside the organisation, depends on effective communication, and on correct understanding and interpretation. It is easy to misinterpret not only the surface meaning of words and numbers (eg for a customer who is not familiar with the terminology used in a technical brochure) but also the underlying meaning: tone of voice, metaphorical language or sarcasm could give quite the wrong impression; which defeats the purpose of communication.

3.5 Feedback can alert the sender if this is happening. It is now usual to talk in terms of two kinds of feedback, **positive** and **negative**. (Note that these terms are not being used in their strict *engineering* sense here.)

5: The manager as a communicator

Positive	Negative
Action being taken as requested	No action or wrong action being taken
A letter/note/memo confirming receipt of message and replying in an appropriate way	No written response where expected or request for more information, clarification or repetition
Accurate reading-back of message	Failure to read back message correctly
Smile, nod, murmur of agreement and so on	Silence, blank look, sound or gesture of protest or perplexity

3.6 Feedback allows you to monitor the effectiveness of your communication activity and if necessary modify or repeat the message, try a new channel or delivery method.

Reviewing the effectiveness of communications

3.7 The ultimate test of the effectiveness of internal communications, of whatever nature and however delivered, is that those who need information for whatever purpose receive it in a comprehensible form, in the right format, on time and in a state where it can be acted upon.

3.8 Analysing the effectiveness of internal communications is a difficult task; people may not know there are bad communications if messages do not get through at all.

3.9 A review of the current state of communications within an organisation would start off with a **position audit**.

(a) What media of **formal communication** are currently employed? Many managers, especially senior managers, prefer to use oral or informal methods of communication. Media of communication are subject to noise, which can inhibit messages from getting across.

(b) How do people at all levels in the organisation view communications? For example, a typical comment from a disgruntled worker might be: 'They never tell us anything'. This can relate to the overall direction of the company, or even operational instructions.

(c) Do managers consider they get enough information for planning, decision making and control? Or do they think they are critically dependent on people below them, who shape the information that they see fit?

(d) Have there been any instances where the organisation has suffered through an obvious failure of communication (eg two divisions within a decentralised firm might compete for the same business)?

(e) Are there problems in co-ordinating the work of different departments?

(f) Does information get to its destination quickly?

3.10 Once this exercise has been carried out, the it is appropriate to consider the overall communications needs of the organisation. Do people **need** information which they do **not** receive? Are existing communications needlessly complex? Do the managers have any communications objectives, to act as a benchmark to which the existing systems of communications can be compared?

3.11 Once the communication/information needs have been identified, current practice can be measured against it. If deficient, it can be improved. Team briefings, for example, may have been introduced in order to explain senior management policy to the workforce; a subsequent complaint may be that information flows only downwards.

Part B: Personal effectiveness

Barriers to communication

3.12 Barriers to communication are anything that prevents effective communication occurring. Barriers can be related to the perceptions of senders or receivers.

   (a) **Distortion or omission** of information by the sender

   (b) **Misunderstanding** due to lack of clarity or technical jargon

   (c) **Non-verbal signs (gesture, posture, facial expression) contradicting the verbal message**, so that its meaning is in doubt

   (d) **Overload**, that is, being given too much information to digest in the time available

   (e) Differences in social, racial or educational background, compounded by age and personality differences, creating barriers to understanding and co-operation

   (f) People hearing only what they want to hear in a message

3.13 There may also be particular **perception** difficulties in a work situation.

   (a) A general tendency to distrust a message in its retelling from one person to another

   (b) A subordinate mistrusting a superior and looking for hidden meanings in a message

   (c) The relative status in the hierarchy of the sender and receiver of information. A senior manager's words are listened to more closely and a colleague's perhaps discounted.

   (d) People or departments having different priorities or perspectives so that one person places more or less emphasis on a situation than another

   (e) Information which has no immediate use tending to be forgotten

   (f) Conflict in the organisation. Where there is conflict between individuals or departments, communications will be withdrawn and information withheld.

3.14 **The barriers to good communication arising from differences in social, racial or educational backgrounds, compounded by age differences and personality differences, can be particularly severe** and managers must be alert to them.

3.15 **Differences in background** can have a number of results.

   (a) Failure to understand the other's point of view and sense of values and priorities

   (b) Failure to listen to the information the other person is giving. The information is judged according to the person who gives it.

   (c) A tendency to give ready-formulated opinions instead of factual information which will enable recipients to formulate their own opinions

   (d) Lack of shared 'vocabulary', whether linguistic or symbolic, which might lead to lack of understanding of the message

3.16 Personal conflict or antagonisms will cause further communication problems.

   (a) Emotions (anger, fear, frustration) will creep into communications and further hinder the transmission of clear information.

   (b) Recipients of information will tend to hear what they want to hear in any message; to ignore anything they do not want to accept in a message; and blame it on the other person if problems arise later on.

> **Action Programme 5**
>
> | | Communication stage | Possible Problem |
> |---|---|---|
> | 1 | Sender | Poor perception of effect. Negative image projected |
> | 2 | The message | Inappropriate. Perceived irrelevant |
> | 3 | Encoding | Technical or vague language used |
> | 4 | The receiver | The wrong person gets the message |
> | 5 | Decoding | Tone of the message is misinterpreted |
> | 6 | Channel | The channel was expensive or didn't reach the intended audience |
> | 7 | Feedback | No monitoring of response |
>
> How might these problems be overcome?

Communication media available

3.17 **Face-to-face communication**

- Formal meetings
- Interviews
- Informal contact
- The grapevine

3.18 **Oral communication**

- The telephone
- Public address systems
- Video conferencing systems

3.19 **Written communication**

- Letters: external mail system
- Memoranda: internal mail system
- Reports
- Forms
- Notice boards
- House journals, bulletins, newsletters
- Organisation manual

3.20 **Visual communication**

- Charts
- Films and slides
- Video and videoconferencing

3.21 **Electronic communications**

- Email, the Internet
- Voicemail
- Electronic data interchange (EDI) between computers (see paragraph 6.15)

3.22 We discuss these types of communication in the rest of this chapter.

Part B: Personal effectiveness

Marketing at Work

An example of the role of communications in managing a business is provided by British Airways.

After privatisation, BA cut its staff by almost 20,000 to 35,000 although since then staff levels have increased to 53,000 as airline traffic has expanded.

BA attaches great importance to internal corporate communications, as it wishes to make staff feel involved.

(a) At a series of business seminars, costing £750,000, senior board members made detailed presentations to 4,500 junior and senior mangers, and, as importantly, invited - and received - feedback and criticism. BA's senior managers 'say they benefit enormously from hearing how staff feel that BA can continue to improve its performance'.

(b) BA is investing possibly £2m pa 'in an experimental news video service ... to bring together on a daily basis thousands of staff dispersed around the world at BA's 10 locations'. Staff 'will be able to plug in at our centres to find out what BA is doing, and they will be able to ask questions as well. If we had a serious industrial relations problem at Terminal One, we would not be afraid to interview one of our managers, and we would not interfere editorially unless libel was a problem. But the staff however far away would feel instantly involved.'

Communication of the role of marketing

3.23 Communication about marketing's role can be an important part of the communication process. Other departments may not understand the variety of tasks the marketing department undertakes, and hence fail to appreciate how marketing can help them. The marketing department can communicate with other departments in various ways.

(a) Other departments can be encouraged to make suggestions and give feedback.

(b) Members of the marketing team can enhance their understanding by contact with the user departments. An example of this is a newly privatised water authority, which had staff working with plumbers and sewer repair teams. This sort of shadowing can also work in the other direction.

(c) Individual members of the marketing department can be made responsible for contacts with particular operational departments or senior staff.

(d) A network of marketing contacts within operational departments can be developed. Marketing can keep in touch with these contacts on a regular basis and invite them for seminars or training in marketing techniques. The idea will be to build up links from whom informed comment and criticism can be obtained, and who will act as champions of the marketing department.

(e) Other means of increasing marketing visibility include a newsletter, highlighting the variety of activities undertaken by the marketing department.

4 ORAL AND FACE-TO-FACE COMMUNICATION: INDIVIDUALS

4.1 **Face-to-face communication** is useful for:

- Generating new ideas
- On the spot feedback, constructive criticism and exchange of views
- Encouraging co-operation and sensitivity to personal factors
- Spreading information quickly through a group of people

4.2 However, discussions can be non- or counter-productive.

- The terms of reference (defining the purpose and power of the meeting) must be clear
- The people attending must be skilled and willing communicators
- There must be sufficient guidance and leadership to control proceedings

Interpersonal skills

4.3 **Interpersonal skills** are needed in order to understand and manage roles, relationships, attitudes and perceptions. They enable us to communicate effectively and to achieve our aims when dealing with other people.

4.4 **Interpersonal skills**

- The ability to interpret **body language** and to use it to reinforce messages
- The ability to **listen attentively and actively**
- The ability to put others at their ease, to persuade and to smooth over difficult situations
- The ability to **identify when false or dishonest arguments** are being used, and to construct logical ones
- The ability to recognise how much information, and of what kind, another person will **need and be able to take in**
- The ability to **use communication media effectively**: to speak well, write legibly, use appropriate vocabulary and use visual aids where required
- The ability to **sum up** or conclude an argument clearly and persuasively
- The ability to communicate and show enthusiasm, ie **leadership** or inspiration

4.5 The above list is by no means exhaustive.

4.6 Here are some more important things to consider in interpersonal relations.

Factor	Comment
Goal	What does the other person want from the process? What do you want from the process? What will both parties need and be trying to do to achieve their aims? Can both parties emerge satisfied?
Perceptions	What, if any, are likely to be the factors causing distortion of the way both parties see the issues and each other? (Attitudes, personal feelings, expectations?)
Roles	What roles are the parties playing? (Superior/subordinate, customer/server, complainer/soother?) What expectations does this create of the way they will behave?
Resistances	What may the other person be afraid of? What may he or she be trying to protect? (His or her ego/self-image, attitudes?) Sensitivity will be needed in this area.
Attitudes	What sources of difference, conflict or lack of understanding might there be, arising from attitudes and other factors which shape them (sex, race, specialism, hierarchy)?
Relationships	What are the relative positions of the parties and the nature of the relationship between them? (Superior/subordinate? Formal/ informal? Work/non-work?) What style is appropriate to it?
Environment	What factors in the immediate and situational environment might affect the issues and the people? (eg competitive environment customer care; pressures of disciplinary situation nervousness; physical surroundings formality/ informality)

Marketing at Work

How to influence people

More and more of us rely on people over whom we have no authority in order to achieve results at work. They may be our opposite number in another function, a management colleague, a technical specialist or a more senior manager. Without their backing for our ideas or their willingness to reconsider a hasty decision, our effectiveness in the job can be compromised. That is why influencing skills – the ability to gain commitment from others – are increasingly important.

Organisations exist in a state of dynamic tension. We are all working under so much pressure that one person's good idea is often another's extra workload; one person's long-term investment is another's short-term cost. The trick is to remember that not everyone shares the same logic.

We need to help others use their own logic to persuade themselves. Instead of piling on the facts to support out logic, we need to cause them to think. And the simplest way of doing this is to ask them questions set within a four-stage framework known as the 'persuasive funnel'.

1 Probe and listen

It can take a great deal of self-discipline to listen to another person when you are keen to talk. But if you do listen, you will increase the likelihood that they will then listen to you – and that you will be able to make your proposal in terms that they might find attractive.

2 Summarise

It is not enough to understand; you have to prove that you do. So summarise. As you summarise, you can emphasise the points that you are about to make.

3 Refer to

When the other person is happy with your summary, you can refer to something that supports your proposal, such as a point that has already been agreed, one of their priorities or another aspect of company policy.

4 Suggest

Lastly, you can suggest (don't insist) on a solution that flows naturally from the points made at the previous stage. Suggesting, rather than insisting, along with the quantity of listening that you have been doing, improves the chances of the other person's agreement.

Rapport-breakers – seven behaviours to avoid

- **Talking more than listening.** People would rather be listened to than talked at. We become defensive when someone is trying hard to influence us. Probe, listen and try hard to influence us. Probe, listen and try hard to understand them. Eventually they will tell you what you need to say to influence them.

- **Formal-speak.** In ordinary conversations, people don't use terminology such as 'in the fullness of time', 'has not been forthcoming' and 'it has been brought to my attention that'. Ineffective influencers feel that such phrases boost their case. They don't use the terminology that you would employ in everyday conversations.

- **Parental language.** Adults talking to children often use autocratic words such as 'can't', 'must', 'should' and 'ought'. Delivered to an adult, these irritate and increase resistance.

- **Using 'irritators'.** Phrases such as 'with respect', 'I hear what you say', 'let's be realistic' and 'I'm being perfectly reasonable' all convey the opposite message loud and clear to the other person. These terms are all influencing no nos.

- **Doing their thinking for them.** 'What you don't seem to realise is...', 'what you clearly haven't taken account of is...' and similar phrases suggest that you are telepathically gifted. They sound insulting and have no persuasive potential. Most people react to them negatively.

- **Arguing.** Disagreeing with someone produces 60 per cent chance that they will disagree back. It's better to probe and understand their point of view.

- **Being dogmatic.** The harder you push people, the harder they resist.

Terry Gillen, *People Management*, 5 April 2001

Interviewing

4.7 You know, from your own experience, what an interview is, but if you had to define it, you might call it a **planned interaction** at work, characterised by **objectives**. It is conducted in order to achieve a specific **purpose** for at least one of the parties involved, such as information gathering, problem solving or behaviour change.

4.8 An interview must be **planned** if it is to be effective. An agenda can be drawn up on the basis of objectives, and should be structured with an introductory phase, main body and concluding phase. Knowing what the opening will be (to start the interview off fluently), and knowing what you want from the close (to achieve objectives) are as important as drafting questions and topics for the main part of the interview.

4.9 An interview is an **interaction, not a monologue**.

(a) During an investigation, the interviewer must ask questions that elicit useful answers and listen to them.

(b) Interviews usually involve interaction between people **in their roles** as, for instance, representative and customer, superior and subordinate. In addition, there is a role difference between interviewer and interviewee: the interviewer should take control of proceedings.

(c) The degree of **formality** in the interview will depend on the circumstances and personalities involved, but the interaction of roles implies some formality in the work context. The fine line between formality and tension will need to be managed.

4.10 **Five basic stages to the interview process**.

- Preparation
- Opening
- Conducting
- Closing
- Follow-up

Preparation

4.11 First of all, **the objectives of the interview must be determined.** The interviewer should also be aware of any unstated objectives the interviewee may be bringing as a hidden agenda: scoring points off a supervisor, perhaps. The basic framework of the interview can then be planned, with ideas for any points that must be made or information that must be obtained or given; there should be enough flexibility, however, so that the interviewer can listen and respond to the interviewee's input and questions where relevant. It is particularly important to anticipate how the interviewee will react at the start of the interview and at key stages during it, and how the interviewer's approach may have to be modified as a result.

4.12 There may be some **preparation** to do for the content of the interview: information to be gathered on the interviewee or the topic under discussion. For a customer interview, for example, you will need to know what services the customer uses and requires, and you will need to know about the company's products and services. Interviews for appraisal, grievance and discipline require considerable prior information and thought if they are to be handled constructively.

4.13 **Physical preparations** include obtaining suitable time and accommodation for the interview, usually somewhere private and free from distraction. The setting can be

Opening

4.14 **The purpose of the interview should be clearly laid out** as a preliminary to engaging in any discussion.

(a) The tone and atmosphere of the interview will also be established by the first impressions the parties have of each other, and the interviewer's opening remarks. The interviewer should clarify the purpose of the interview. It is usually desirable to put the interviewee at ease, but the interviewer's strategy may be to maintain or even increase the tension, perhaps to test a candidate under pressure, to underline the seriousness of a disciplinary interview, or to assert control in other situations.

(b) In less extreme conditions, even the desk alone can distance the interviewer from the interviewee. If this is felt to be undesirable, for example in a customer interview, the physical setting may be changed or the interviewer may take particular care to set a positive, supportive and welcoming tone in opening the interview.

Conducting the interview

4.15 Ask the right questions. Listen to the answers.

4.16 Questions should be paced and put carefully. The interviewer should not try to confuse the interviewee; nor should he allow the interviewee to digress or gloss over important points. The interviewer must retain control over the information-gathering process.

4.17 **Open questions** should be used, so that interviewees have to put together their own responses in complete sentences. This is a lot more revealing than using **closed questions** which invite 'yes' or 'no' answers. **Closed questions** have several disadvantages.

(a) They elicit answers only to the question asked: there may be other questions and issues that have been anticipated but will emerge if the interviewee is given the chance to speak.

(b) They do not allow interviewees to express their personalities so that interaction can take place on a deeper level.

(c) They make it easier for interviewees to conceal things ('you never asked me....')

(d) They make the interviewer work very hard.

4.18 The interviewer should not ask leading questions, giving the interviewee ideas about how to respond: the response may be adjusted to please or impress. Leading questions include: 'Don't you agree that...?' and 'Surely...?'.

4.19 The interviewer must listen to and evaluate the responses, to distinguish between what the interviewee wants to say; is trying not to say; is saying but doesn't mean, or is lying about; and is having difficulty saying. It is also necessary to distinguish between what the interviewer needs and does not need to know.

4.20 Interviewers must also be **self aware**. They must recognise when they are being told what they **wish to hear** and ensure that their own attitudes do not colour their perception of what interviewees say.

4.21 **Non-verbal signals or body language** should also be taken as relevant feedback. The **interviewer should look for signs of stress** (nervous movements, pallor), dishonesty (failure to meet the eye), irritation (frown, tapping foot), positive response (smile, nod, leaning forward) and so on. The interviewer can also **use** non-verbal signs to create a desired impression (smart appearance, smile, firm handshake) and to provide feedback (raised eyebrow, encouraging nod).

Closing the interview

4.22 A **summary of proceedings or findings** is usually a good way of confirming information, signalling the extent to which objectives have been achieved, and 'winding down' the interview towards closure. If a decision is required, it should be given: but only if the interviewee has the authority and has acquired the information to do so. The general 'position' of the parties should be clarified, especially if a compromise or agreement has been reached, or if one or both parties is not yet satisfied. Further action required should be agreed or communicated to the interviewee. A courteous closure (handshake, goodbye) should end the proceedings.

Follow-up

4.23 Once the interviewee has left, the interviewer should complete a permanent record of the interview and initiate any actions agreed at or required by the interview.

> **Action Programme 6**
>
> List the types or purposes of interview a supervisor in your branch might have to conduct. What are the role/relationship problems special to each type?
>
> Are there procedures laid down for these interviews: a checklist, perhaps, or guidance notes? Are supervisors trained in interview technique?
>
> Think of an interview you have recently had - either as interviewer or as interviewee. How could the interview have been made more effective?

Telephone

4.24 **The telephone is the most common method of oral communication** between individuals in remote locations, or even within an organisation's premises. It provides all the interactive and feedback advantages of face-to-face communication except body language, while saving travel time. It is, however, **more impersonal than an interview** for the discussion of sensitive personal matters, and it **does not provide the concreteness of written media**. The latter disadvantage can be remedied by written confirmation of a telephone call. Developments like **teleconferencing** and **video-conferencing** are increasingly featuring in communication options.

5 ORAL AND FACE-TO-FACE COMMUNICATION: GROUPS

Meetings

5.1 Formal meetings, such as the Board meeting of a company are governed by rules about a variety of matters. Many people regard such rules and conventions as a hindrance to free and effective communication. However a well-organised, focussed and well-led meeting can be extremely effective. We discuss how you can ensure that you are effective in meetings later in this chapter.

Committees

5.2 Within an organisation, committees can consist entirely of executives or may be an instrument for joint consultation between employers and employees.

5.3 **Purposes of committees**

   (a) **Creating new ideas**. Group creativity may be achieved by a brainstorming committee or think tank (see below).

   (b) They can be an excellent means of **communication**. For example, they can be used to exchange ideas before a decision is taken or to inform managers about policies, plans, actual results and so on.

   (c) They are democratic, because they allow for greater **participation** in the decision-making process.

   (d) **Combining abilities**. Committees enable the differing skills of its various members to be brought together to deal with a problem. In theory, the quality of committee decisions should be of a high standard.

   (e) **Co-ordination**. Committees should enable the maximum co-ordination of all parties involved in a decision to be achieved, for example in co-ordinating the budgets of each department and compiling a master budget.

   (f) **Representation**. Committees enable all relevant interests to be involved in the decision-making process and they bring together the specialised knowledge of working people into a working combination.

Drawbacks of committees

5.4 **Disadvantages of committees**

   (a) They are **apt to be too large for constructive action**, since the time taken by a committee to resolve a problem tends to be in direct proportion to its size.

   (b) Committees are **time-consuming and expensive**. In addition to the cost of highly paid executives' time, secretarial costs will be incurred.

   (c) **Delays may occur if matters of a routine nature are entrusted to committees**; committees must not be given responsibilities which they would carry out inefficiently.

   (d) **Operations may be jeopardised by the frequent attendance of executives at meetings**, and by distracting them from their real duties.

   (e) **Incorrect or ineffective decisions** may be made, if members are unfamiliar with the issues. Occasionally, there may be a **total failure to reach any decision at all**.

   (f) Certain members may be **apathetic**, owing to pressure of work or lack of interest, resulting in superficial action.

   (g) The fact that there is no individual responsibility for decisions might invite **compromise** instead of clear-cut decisions. Moreover, members may avoid responsibility for poor results arising from decisions taken in committee. Weak management can hide behind committee decisions.

   (h) Committees lack **conscience**.

   (i) **Proceedings may be dominated by outspoken or aggressive members**.

5: The manager as a communicator

5.5 **Misuses of committees**

(a) **To replace managers**. A committee cannot do all the tasks of management (eg leadership) and therefore cannot replace managers entirely.

(b) **To carry out research work**. A committee may be used to create new ideas, but work on those ideas cannot be done effectively by a committee itself.

(c) To make **unimportant** decisions. This would be expensive and time-consuming.

(d) **To discuss decisions beyond the authority of its participants**. This might occur, for example, when an international committee of government ministers is created, but ministers send deputies in their place to meetings, without giving the deputy sufficient authority to enable the committee to make important decisions.

5.6 **Using committees successfully**

(a) Well-defined areas of authority, timescales of operations and purpose should be specified in writing.

(b) The chairman should have the qualities of leadership to co-ordinate and motivate the other committee members.

(c) The committee should not be so large as to be unmanageable.

(d) The members of the committee should have the necessary skills and experience to do the committee's work; where the committee is expected to liaise with functional departments, the members must also have sufficient status and influence with those departments.

(e) Minutes of the meetings should be taken and circulated, with any action points arising out of the meetings notified to the members responsible for doing the work.

(f) Above all, an efficient committee must provide benefits that justify its cost.

(g) Finally, if at all possible, the committee should be allowed plenty of time to reach decisions, enabling members to form sub-groups.

Brainstorming

5.7 **Brainstorming** sessions aim to produce ideas to solve a particular problem. Ideas are produced but **not** evaluated at these meetings, so that originality is not stifled by fear of criticism. Brainstorming sessions rely on the ability of members to feed off each other's ideas. They have been used in many organisations and might typically occur, for example, in advertising agencies to produce ideas for a forthcoming campaign.

Team briefings

5.8 Team briefings are a form of face-to-face communication mechanism which is designed to increase the commitment and understanding of the workforce.

5.9 A team briefing is given by a team leader, who should have been thoroughly trained and briefed, or, occasionally, a more senior member of management. Its purpose is to communicate and explain management decisions and policies. There should be between four and eighteen people in the team. The briefing, which should take place at regular intervals, should last about half an hour.

5.10 A survey by the Manchester School of Management found that most workers welcomed such schemes, although acknowledging that they did not really affect their commitment to

the organisation. They also said there was no change in their understanding of management decisions. Moreover, a majority said that team briefings failed to indicate a more open management style.

5.11 A probable reason for failure is lack of senior management commitment to the discussion of matters of real importance.

6 DOCUMENTARY AND ELECTRONIC COMMUNICATIONS

Letters

6.1 **The letter** is widely used for **external communication** and provides a **record and confirmation** of the matters discussed. Various facilities are provided by the Post Office for the delivery of letters, with special arrangements for guaranteed, insured or urgent deliveries in the UK or internationally. Couriers may also be used for urgent or important letters and documents. A letter may be used **internally** in certain situations where a **confidential written record is necessary** or personal handling required, for instance to announce redundancy or record disciplinary action. **Faxes** are faster and increasingly used in business to confirm oral discussions.

Memoranda

6.2 **The memorandum** is the equivalent of the letter in internal communication; it is versatile and concrete.

Reports

6.3 Formal reports allow a number of people to review complex facts and arguments on which they have to make a decision.

6.4 The written report does not allow for effective discussion or immediate feedback, as does a meeting, and can be a time-consuming and expensive document to produce. However, as a medium for putting across a body of ideas to a group of people, it has advantages.

   (a) Recipients can study the material in their own time, rather than arranging to be present at one place and time.

   (b) No time is wasted on irrelevancies and the formulation of arguments, as may occur in meetings.

   (c) The report can be presented objectively; emotional reactions or conflicts may be avoided.

Forms

6.5 Routine information flow is largely achieved through the use of forms. A well-designed form can be filled quickly with relevant information. They are simple to file, and information is quickly retrieved and confirmed. Staff do not usually have to exercise discretion in the selection and use of this medium: a form either is, or is not, available to meet a particular need.

Notice board

6.6 **Noticeboards** allow the organisation to present a variety of information to a large number of people. Items may have a limited time span of relevance but will at least be available for verification and recollection for a while. However they can easily become untidy or irrelevant or be sabotaged by graffiti. Also, they are wholly dependent on the intended recipient's curiosity or desire to receive information.

House journal

6.7 Larger companies frequently run an internal magazine or newspaper to communicate with employees. The journal usually avoids being controversial. It may not deal with sensitive issues such as industrial relations or pollution of the environment, and may stop short of criticising policy, management and products; it is, after all, designed to improve rather than threaten communication and morale, and it may be seen by outsiders (especially customers) who might get an unfavourable impression of the organisation. Journals are sometimes regarded by the workforce as predictable, uninteresting and not to be taken seriously: on the other hand, they can provide a legitimate means of expression and a **sense of corporate identity**.

Organisation manual

6.8 An organisation (or office) manual is useful for drawing together and keeping up to date information and procedures. Typically it will cover the topics below.

- The structure of the organisation, perhaps giving an organisation chart
- The organisation's products, services and customers
- Rules, regulations and procedures
- Standards and procedures for health and safety
- Procedures for grievance, discipline, salary review and so on

6.9 **Manuals and handbooks must be regularly updated and reissued**, which can be expensive and time-consuming: a loose-leaf format permitting additions and amendments is a common solution, though the circulation of loose amendment sheets (which may or may not get inserted) may not prove efficient.

6.10 Organisation manuals are useful in stable organisations. Businesses that are constantly evolving in response to changing conditions will find them less useful.

Electronic communications

6.11 The introduction of personal computer networks facilitates new sorts of communication, of which **email** is the most prevalent and particularly useful in organisations which are widely dispersed over several sites in one or more countries.

6.12 A 1997 *Financial Times* survey highlighted possible drawbacks with using email. In some companies it was used because it avoided the need for face-to-face contact. In other cases the volume of email was excessive. emails were being sent for trivial reasons, eg to find the owner of a pen left by the coffee machine.

6.13 Another drawback with using email is the **potential for legal problems.** During 1997 Norwich Union was forced to pay damages to a rival health insurer, Western Provident Association, because Norwich Union's staff had circulated untrue email messages about

Part B: Personal effectiveness

Western's financial stability. Asda were also successfully sued by a disgruntled customer because untrue rumours that the customer was guilty of fraud had been circulated via the company's email system.

6.14 Other companies have faced problems through employees ordering pornographic material or drugs through email. In America there have been successful prosecutions for sexual and racial harassment via email.

6.15 These legal problems emphasise the need for internal guidance on how email should be used. If email is used to communicate with other customers or suppliers, it should be treated in the same way as other business correspondence, including obtaining appropriate authorisation. The guidance should prohibit defamatory or other abusive messages. Above all employees should be made aware that communication by email is permanent and not transitory in nature.

6.16 **Electronic data interchange** (EDI) is a form of direct communication between computers and may be used between organisations. For instance, production scheduling software may send orders directly to a supplier's stock handling computer via a telephone link.

> **Action Programme 7**
>
> How good is your organisation at internal communication? Review any internal communication examples you have. During the next week, do a communications audit on messages received (and sent) by your department.
>
> (a) How are they encoded? What image is the department or sender creating?
>
> (b) How are internal telephone calls handled?
>
> (c) Do meetings exemplify good communication practice from start to finish, or are they a waste of time?
>
> (d) Is there a consistent style or image created by communications sent?
>
> Produce a checklist of five things you could do to improve the effectiveness of your internal communication. Consider discussing this with others,

7 IMPROVING COMMUNICATIONS

7.1 The most appropriate method of internal communication in any given circumstances will depend on a variety of considerations.

  (a) The **time necessary to prepare and transmit the message,** considering its urgency. A phone call, for example, is quicker than a letter: a memo is quicker than a full-scale report.

  (b) The **complexity of the message:** A written message, for example, allows the use of diagrams, but if some things needs to be explained and questions answered on the spot, a discussion may be preferred.

  (c) The **distance the message is required to travel** and in what condition it must arrive.

  (d) **The need for a written record,** eg for confirmation of transactions.

  (e) **The need for interaction**. It is often preferable to meet customers, for example, in order to discuss complex problems or attempt to sell the benefits of a service.

(f) The **need for confidentiality** or, conversely, the dissemination of information widely and quickly. A notice board is obviously different in application from a private interview or confidential letter.

(g) **The need for tact, personal involvement, or impersonality**. The effect of a letter and a face-to-face discussion in announcing redundancies, for example, will be quite different.

(h) **Cost,** considered in relation to all the above, for the best possible result at the least possible expense.

Action Programme 8

Having completed the general audit of department communication try a more focused people watching exercise.

Make a note to pay careful attention to communication in the office.

(a) Note the amount of verbal communication (face to face or by telephone) going on. What kinds of noise are interfering with it?

(b) Note the methods of communication you use in a day. How do you decide whether to see someone, use the phone, write, use post or fax, leave a note or send a confidential memo? Do others have a different approach?

(c) **Watch** people talking to each other. What facial expressions, gestures and postures do they adopt? Would they want to use the same kind of body language with a customer, or a superior, as they would with a colleague?

Action Programme 9

What communication pattern is dominant in your organisation?

What alternatives could you suggest and how would you justify it in terms of its implications for the team members and the organisation?

7.2 We considered earlier many of the actual barriers to communication and possible strategies for overcoming them. It will be apparent to you from this that communication problems fall into three broad categories.

- There may be a **bad formal communication system**
- There may be **misunderstanding** about the actual **content** of a message
- There may be **interpersonal difficulties** causing a break-down even though the formal communications of the organisation may be adequate under normal circumstances

7.3 **Bad organisation** must be improved. The aim should be to set up more or better communication links in all directions. Standing instructions should be recorded in easily accessible manuals which are kept fully up-to-date; management decisions should be sent in writing to all people affected by them.

7.4 To improve upward communication, regular staff meetings or formal consultation with staff associations or trade union representatives should be held. For the same reason, there should be formal appraisal interviews between a manager and his subordinates, to discuss

Part B: Personal effectiveness

job performance, career prospects, how they feel about their work, and how it could be improved. The **informal** organisation should supplement these measures.

7.5 Communication between superiors and subordinates will be improved when trust exists. Exactly how this is achieved will depend on the management style and the attitudes and personality of the individuals involved, and other factors. Some people have advocated '**management by walking around**' and informality in superior/subordinate relationships as a means of establishing closer links.

Information overload?

> 'The manager has a specific tool: information. He does not "handle" people; he motivates, guides, organises people to do their own work. His tool - his only tool - to do all this is the spoken or written word or the language of numbers. No matter whether the manager's job is banking, engineering, accounting or selling, his effectiveness depends on his ability to listen and to read, on his ability to speak and to write. He needs skill in getting his thinking across to other people as well as skill in finding out what other people are after'.
> *Peter Drucker*

7.6 Just as you would not want to have to read a whole encyclopaedia to find out one fact, so good information should be **no more** as well as **no less** than strictly necessary to fulfil its purpose. **Management by exception** is the term used for a system whereby managers are not overloaded with routine information. Only deviations from routine are reported to them, and they only get involved in matters which are new or outside the responsibilities which they have delegated to subordinates. The system for processing and storage of data should be designed for the amount of information handled. It is difficult for manual systems to cope with very large volumes of information, but computer systems can handle more, more quickly.

7.7 Since information should have a purpose, there ought to be a clear idea of **who needs it**. The information-users must be identifiable. Others are not targeted, to avoid them becoming the victims of information overload.

Action Programme 10

What do you think should characterise good information?

7.8 Time spent planning and developing useful information systems will reduce communication problems. There are a number of aspects.

- Identifying what decisions managers must make
- Identifying what information is needed to make them and when
- Identifying how managers will measure the effectiveness of their actions
- Developing systems which will generate this information in a timely and useable format

Action Programme 11

What monitoring do **you** perform? Where do you find your information, and to whom do you pass it on? Are you supported by an effective information system?

Do you regard monitoring external information (keeping up to date with competitors' actions, changing customer needs etc) as part of your **job?** Does your boss?

Despite the best efforts, communication problems are bound to occur. What can the manager do about them?

Action Programme 12

Take a few minutes to consider the following scenarios. For each, consider:

- what has gone wrong?
- what action would you take?
- what could have been done (if anything) to prevent the problem?

(a) A memo has been sent to all field sales staff indicating that there is excess production capacity forecast during July - September. As a result, a special volume discount has been authorised and a sales incentive to reflect this has been developed.

Informally it is being rumoured by competitors and suppliers that the company is 'price cutting' because it is in financial difficulties. This is not the case. Sales are always down in the summer quarter: the new volume discount scheme is in fact a new marketing plan to change this seasonality.

(b) There are rumours in the company that a new appraisal scheme being introduced is the first stage in a large redundancy programme. Several key staff are therefore actively looking for new positions.

7.9 Managers need to be ready to tackle any communication problems as soon as they are identified. The following checklist should help you.

Step 1. Identify the cause (not just the symptoms) of the problem.
Step 2. Identify options for dealing with the problem and preventing it from reoccurring.
Step 3. Select the approach and implement your plan.
Step 4. Monitor its effectiveness.

Improving communication skills

7.10 In the rest of this section we examine some ways in which communications can be made more effective.

Listening

7.11 Listening in the communications model is about decoding and receiving information. Effective listening has three consequences.

- It encourages the sender to listen effectively in return to what you have to say
- It reduces the effect of noise
- It helps resolve problems by encouraging understanding from someone else's viewpoint

Part B: Personal effectiveness

7.12 **Advice for good listening**

(a) **Be prepared to listen.** Put yourself in the right frame of mind and be prepared to grasp the main concepts.

(b) **Be interested.** Make an effort to analyse the message for its relevance.

(c) **Keep an open mind.** Your own beliefs and prejudices can get in the way of what the other person is actually saying.

(d) **Keep an ear open for the main ideas.** An awareness of how people generally structure their speech can help the process of understanding. Be able to distinguish between the thrust of the argument and the supporting evidence.

(e) **Listen critically.** This means trying to assess what the person is saying by identifying any **assumptions, omissions and biases**.

(f) **Avoid distraction.** People have a natural attention curve, high at the beginning and end of an oral message, but sloping off in the middle.

(g) **Take notes,** although note taking can be distracting.

Presentations

7.13 Make a particular effort to develop **presentation skills**. A lack of confidence through inexperience makes nerves worse for many. Use opportunities to make presentations and speak in public. Be prepared. Produce a plan for your presentations.

Planning a presentation

7.14 **Purpose**. A presentation should have clear and specific objectives. If the presentation is instructional, the objective should be in terms of a precise statement of behaviour required of a trainee by the end of training (eg, the trainee will be able to answer customer queries using the computerised sales system). Here are some possible purposes.

(a) **Technical information** or **briefing**, for example informing management of research findings, or new legislative provisions affecting operations

(b) **Instruction:** telling others how to perform a task, or use new equipment

(c) **Persuasion:** getting the audience to think as you do on the matters you are presenting **and** to respond in the way you wish them to (eg to buy your product, accept your proposal or share your positive attitude)

7.15 You must consider a number of aspects of **content**.

(a) The main **objective** of the presentation
(b) The **main ideas** of the presentation
(c) **Supporting facts,** examples and illustrations
(d) What the audience will understand
(e) What the audience will be interested in or motivated by
(f) **How much time to spend on each part** of the presentation, and its overall length

7.16 There are many ways in which content can be used to **clarify the message**.

(a) **Logical links** between one topic or statement and the next

(b) **A framework for the whole argument,** giving the audience an overview and then filling in the detail

5: The manager as a communicator

(c) **Anecdotes** inviting the audience to relate an idea to a real-life situation

(d) **Explanation**, showing how or why something has happened or is so, to help the audience understand the principles behind your point

(e) **Definition**, explaining the precise meaning of terms that may not be shared or understood by the audience

(f) **The use of facts, quotations or statistics**

7.17 **Visual aids**

(a) **Slides** are usually still photographs, but may include text and diagrams, projected on to a screen or other surface. They allow the use of photography, including colour, which can be very powerful in creating a mood or impression. They give good definition of detail and a larger picture. The swiftness with which one image follows another is particularly suited to messages of contrast or comparison: two products, say, or before and after scenarios.

(b) **Film and video** allow powerful, realistic and pre-designed images to be projected onto a screen or TV monitor. Moving images are particularly good at holding the audience's attention.

(c) An **overhead projector** can display pre-prepared transparencies or may be used like a blackboard with blank transparent rolls.

(d) Whatever aids you use, ensure that are **appropriate to your message**, in content and style or mood. Only use them if they support the purpose of your presentation.

(e) Ensure that all equipment and materials are available and working and that you operate them efficiently and confidently.

(f) Ensure that aids do not become distractions.

7.18 **Introduction.** Establish your credibility and gain the audience's interest early, when their concentration is at its peak. Give the audience an overview of your presentation, to guide them through it.

- Make an initial impact to focus the audience's attention and establish your credibility.
- Give them a taste of the subject to arouse their interest, and focus their thoughts.
- Prepare the audience for the content and structure of your presentation.
- State the objectives of your presentation.

7.19 **Conclusion.** People tend to rally their concentration when they realise the end of a talk is approaching.

- Draw together the points you have made.
- Reinforce the audience's recall of the content of your talk, and the response they are expected to make as a result.

Exam note

7.20 You can expect examination questions to be expressed in terms of preparing for a presentation. An outline for a presentation appears below.

7.21 In your daily work, take time to produce professional visual aids to support presentations. Learn about the equipment you can use from overhead projectors and flipcharts to 35mm

Part B: Personal effectiveness

slides, video and computer aided presentation facilities. See if you can go on an internal training course. This will help you develop your own style whilst emphasising fundamental points about good presentation.

7.22 Encourage others in your team to gain experience. Ask individuals to make mini presentations within team meetings, and undertake some communications techniques training within the same context. Get the team to brainstorm a list of the team's communication strengths and weaknesses and draw up an action plan to improve on these.

Title
Equipment and aids
Aims
Opening
Introduction - Aims - Approach

Main body	
Key points	Aids
Close	
Revisit Aim	
Summarise	
Action/outcomes	
Questions?	

Written communication

7.23 Review samples of your own and your team's written communication. Check memos, letters and reports for style, tone and image. Produce a strengths and weaknesses analysis to help you identify areas for improvement.

Action Programme 13

Review all the correspondence received from a supplier or contact. How could it be improved? What image does it create? Is there a clear house style?

Now repeat the exercise by collecting examples of all the paperwork a client would typically receive - from invoices and delivery notes, to sales brochures, newsletter and promotional merchandising. How can these be improved?

Report writing

7.24 **The basics of report writing**

- Plan ahead
- Analyse the material in total

- Classify it into logical groups
- Put these groups into a logical order such as of time, of importance, of familiarity, of cause and effect

7.25 There are three main considerations when writing a report

- Planning the report
- Formatting the report
- Report style

Planning the report

7.26 Without planning the information will not be put together and communicated effectively. Ask yourself these questions.

- Who is the user?
- What type of report will be most useful?
- What exactly does the user need to know, and for what purpose?
- How much information is required, how quickly and under what cost constraints?
- Do judgements and recommendations need to be given, or just information?

7.27 You will then be able to establish the basic aspects of the report.

(a) The objective of the report - providing the required information in the necessary way

(b) The reasoning required in the report, particularly if the report is to contain analysis of facts. Any assumptions should be stated

(c) The sources of information used

(d) The type of conclusion required, usually a summary or a recommendation

(e) The structure of the report, including headings, subheadings and appendices

Formatting formal and informal reports

7.28 When a formal request is made by a superior for a report to be prepared, the format and style of the report should be formal as well, using impersonal constructions and avoiding emotive or colloquial expressions.

7.29 An informal request for information will result in an informal report, in which the structure is less rigid, and the style slightly more personal.

Report style

7.30 **Objectivity and balance**

Subjective value-judgements and emotions should be kept out of the content and style as far as possible: bias, if recognised, can undermine the credibility of the report and its recommendations.

(a) Emotional or otherwise loaded words should be avoided.

(b) In more formal reports, **impersonal constructions** should be used.

It became clear that ...
Investigation revealed that ...

(c) Colloquialisms and abbreviated forms should be avoided in formal written English. 'I've', 'don't' for example, should be replaced by 'I have' and 'do not'.

7.31 **Ease of understanding**

(a) Avoid technical language and complex sentence structures for non-technical users.

(b) Organise the material logically, especially if it leads up to a conclusion or recommendation.

(c) Relevant themes should be signalled by appropriate headings or highlighted for easy scanning.

(d) The layout of the report should display data clearly and attractively. Figures and diagrams should be used with discretion, and it might be helpful to highlight key figures which appear within large tables of numbers. Large volumes of supporting date may be relegated to an annex.

Exam note

7.32 You are often asked by examiners to write a report. A sample format is offered on the following page. This should cover all eventualities. You should tailor it to the requirements of the question.

Telephone communication

7.33 The telephone is of central importance to all business people, but those in sales and marketing are likely to be using the phone to communicate with customers as well as colleagues. Proper use of the telephone starts before you make the call.

(a) **Know why** you are making the call and result you are aiming at.

(b) **Know to whom** you should be talking.

(c) **Know what** you want to say, and the order and manner in which you want to say it. A checklist of points will be an invaluable reminder.

(d) Make sure you will not be interrupted once you have dialled.

7.34 Once through to your target, remember that the cost of the call rises with the time you are spending on it. Make it as satisfying as possible, in as brief a time as possible, consistent with courtesy.

Step 1. Identify your organisation, name and function.

Step 2. State the purpose of the call.

Step 3. Greet the other person by name if at all possible.

Step 4. Prepare the ground by briefly explaining the **context** and **purpose** of your call.

Step 5. Remember that the other person cannot see you to. You will have to speak clearly and use your **tone of voice** to convey friendliness, enthusiasm or firmness.

Step 6. Pace your message so that the other person can refer to files or take notes.

Step 7. Check your own notes as you speak, and make fresh ones of any information you receive.

Step 8. You may easily be misheard or misinterpreted over the telephone line, so you will have to seek constant feedback. If you are not receiving any signals, ask for some ('Have you got that?', 'Can you read that back?', 'Am I going too fast for you?', 'OK?')

Step 9. Close the call effectively. Emphasise any action you require, and ask the other person to read back or otherwise confirm that he has understood the gist of your message and your further expectations (if any). Thank him politely for his time, concern or help: you may need his co-operation in the future.

FORMAT FOR A REPORT

To: [Name(s)/position(s) of recipient(s)]
From: [Sender - but NEVER use your own name in an exam]
Date:
Subject: [Effectively this will be the title of your report, such as **Communication Media in A Ltd**]

Contents: [Here you outline the structure of the report. This is optional, but looks nice. It should help you plan, but if pressed for time, leave until the end. If the worst comes to the worst, leave out. Here is an example.]

1. Terms of reference and work undertaken
2. Executive summary
3. Findings
4. Operational issues
5. Management issues
6. Conclusion and recommendations

Annex: Supporting Data

1 **Terms of reference and work undertaken**

1.1 [Here is laid out the scope and purpose of the report: what is to be investigated, what information is required, whether recommendations should be made. In the exam, the Terms of Reference may be given in the question - so don't waste time repeating it - leave this to the end]

1.2 [You might also describe the work you did, how you collected the data, documents consulted, visits made and so on. This gives some indication of the scope of your work, for example, whether it was a detailed investigation or a only cursory glance. This information might go in a separate section of a report. In an exam only include it if it is specifically asked by the question. All the information has been given in the case study.]

2 **Executive summary** [Many reports have a brief description of their key points at the top. Leave this until last, though if you are running out of time in an exam an executive summary indicates to the examiner that you have considered the key issues even if you have not been able to explore them.]

3 **Findings**

3.1 [The remaining sections in the report will depend on the question. If we had followed the table of contents, this section would have been Section 3]

3.2 [You might like to use numbered paragraphs like this, with sub-paragraphs organised like the BPP Study Text. But avoid too many **sub**-paragraphs]

3.3 [The content in this and the following sections should be complete but concise and clearly structured in chronological order, order of importance or any other logical relationship.]

4 [**More findings**]

5 [**More findings**]

6 **Conclusion and recommendations**

6.1 [This section allows for a summary of the main findings and their implications. However, you may not have time for a summary in the exam, but you should at least try to indicate their implications.]

6.2 [If you are required to make recommendations, and not all questions will ask for these, they could come here, referenced, if necessary, to the findings of the earlier section. The recommendations will allow the recipient to make a decision if necessary.]

7.35 If you anticipate receiving calls, keep your message pad, pen and appointments diary handy, together with a list of internal extensions, in case you have to transfer a call.

> **Action Programme 14**
> (a) Call your competitors to see how your query is handled.
> (b) Call your own company. How long do you wait? How friendly and helpful are the staff?
> (c) How could your telephone skills be improved?

Non-verbal communication: body language

7.36 The hidden messages in face-to-face communication can be a common cause for communication breakdown, as they cause decoding problems. Observe others, in meetings, presentations, interviews or just talking in the bar. Notice the signs of boredom or disagreement, support and interest. Picking up these signals will help you improve your own communication skills.

7.37 Whilst watching others, also become more aware of yourself. Be aware of the signals you are sending and transmit only those you intend to.

7.38 Non-verbal communication can be controlled and used for several purposes.

   (a) It can **provide appropriate feedback** to the sender of a message (a yawn, applause, clenched fists, fidgeting)

   (b) It can **create a desired impression** (smart dress, a smile, punctuality, a firm handshake)

   (c) It can **establish a desired atmosphere** or conditions (a friendly smile, informal dress, attentive posture, a respectful distance)

   (d) It can **reinforce spoken messages** with appropriate indications of how interest and feelings are engaged (an emphatic gesture, sparkling eyes, a disapproving frown)

7.39 If we can learn to **recognise** non-verbal messages, our ability to listen is improved.

   (a) When we are speaking, non-verbal **feedback** helps us to modify our message.

   (b) We may recognise people's **real feelings** when their words are constrained by formal courtesies (an excited look, a nervous tic, close affectionate proximity).

   (c) We can **recognise existing or potential personal problems** (the angry silence, the indifferent shrug, absenteeism or lateness at work, refusal to look someone in the eye).

7.40 **Non-verbal cues**

   - Facial expression
   - Gesture
   - Posture and orientation
   - Proximity and contact
   - Movement and stillness
   - Silence and sounds
   - Appearance and grooming
   - Response to norms and expectations

> **Exam Tip**
>
> Non verbal communication has not been specifically examined since the old syllabus. It is, however, a subject that can be used to add value to your answers to almost any question involving face to face communication. It will be particularly relevant when you are asked to prepare a presentation, since you could include a note about your own non-verbal cues and the audience's non-verbal responses.

8 KNOWLEDGE MANAGEMENT

8.1 Knowledge management is a relatively new concept in business theory. It is connected with the theory of the **learning organisation** and founded on the idea that knowledge is a major source of competitive advantage in business. The aim of knowledge management is to exploit existing knowledge and to create new knowledge so that it may be exploited in turn. This is not easy. All organisations possess a great deal of data, but it tends to be unorganised and inaccessible. It is often locked up inside the memories of people who do not realise the value of what they know. Even when it is recorded in some way it may be difficult and time consuming to get at, as is the case with most paper archives.

8.2 Studies have indicated that 20 to 30 percent of company resources are wasted because organisations are not aware of what knowledge they already possess. *Lew Platt*, Chief executive of *Hewlett Packard*, has articulated this, saying 'If only HP knew what HP knows, we would be three times as profitable'.

Data, information and knowledge

8.3 There is an important conceptual hierarchy underpinning knowledge management. This distinguishes between **data, information** and **knowledge.** The distinctions are not clear-cut and, to some extent, are differences of degree rather than kind. An understanding of the terms is best approached by considering the relationships between them.

8.4 We start with **data.** Data typically consists of individual facts, but in a business context may include more complex items such as opinions, reactions and beliefs. It is important to realise that a quantity of data, no matter how large, does not constitute **information.**

8.5 **Information** is data that is **organised** in some useful way. For instance, an individual credit sale will produce a single invoice identifying the goods, the price, the customer, the date of the sale and so on. These things are data: their usefulness does not extend beyond the purpose of the invoice, which is to collect the sum due. Even if we possess a copy of every invoice raised during a financial year, we still only have data. However, if we **process** that data we start to create information. For instance, a simple combination of analysis and arithmetic enables us to state total sales for the year, to break that down into sales for each product and to each customer, to identify major customers and so on. These are pieces of information: they are useful for the **management** of the business, rather than just inputs into its administrative systems.

8.6 Nevertheless, we still have not really produced any **knowledge.** Information may be said to consist of the **relationships between** items of data, as when we combine turnover with customer details to discover which accounts are currently important and which are not. We need to go beyond this in order to create knowledge.

8.7 The conceptual difference between data and information is fairly easy to grasp: it lies chiefly in the **processes** that produce the one from the other. The difference between

information and knowledge is more complex and varies from setting to setting. This is not surprising, since knowledge itself is more complex than the information it derives from.

8.8 A good starting point for understanding the difference is an appreciation of the importance of pattern: **knowledge tends to originate in the discovery of trends or patterns in information**. To return to our invoicing example, suppose we found that certain combinations of goods purchased were typical of certain customers. We could then build up some interesting customer profiles that would enhance our market segmentation and this in turn might influence our overall strategy, since we could identify likely prospects for cross-selling effort.

8.9 Another important aspect of the differences between data, information and knowledge is the relevance of **context**. Our sales invoice is meaningless outside its context; if you, as a marketing person, found an invoice in the office corridor, it would be little more than waste paper to you, though no doubt, the accounts people would like it back. However, if you found a list of customers in order of annual turnover, that would be rather more interesting from a marketing point of view. The information is **useful outside of its original context** of the accounts office.

8.10 This idea also applies to the difference between information and knowledge. If you were a visitor to a company and found a copy of the turnover listing, it would really only be useful to you if you were trying to sell the same sort of thing to the same customers. Its value outside its context would be small. However, if you found a marketing report that suggested, based on evidence, that customers were becoming more interested in quality and less interested in price, that would be applicable to a wide range of businesses, and possibly of strategic importance.

8.11 Here is a table that summarises the progression from data to knowledge.

	Data	**Information**	**Knowledge**
Nature	Facts	Relationships between processed facts	Patterns discerned in information
Importance of context	Total	Some	Context independent
Importance to business	Mundane	Probably useful for management	May be strategically useful

8.12 There is one final important point to note here and that is that the **progression** from data to knowledge is not the same in all circumstances. The scale is moveable and depends on the general complexity of the setting. Something may be **information** within its own context. Something similar may be **knowledge** in a different context. The difference will often be associated with the scale of operations. Take the example of a customer going into insolvent liquidation with £200,000 outstanding on its account. For a small supplier with an annual turnover of, say, £10 million, a bad debt of this size would be of strategic importance and might constitute a threat to its continued existence. Advance notice of the possibility would be valuable **knowledge**. However, for a company operating on a global scale, the bad debt write-off would be annoying but still only one item in a list of bad debts – **data**, in other words.

5: The manager as a communicator

Knowledge management systems

8.13 Recognition of the value of knowledge and understanding of the need to organise data and make it accessible have provoked the development of sophisticated IT systems.

8.14 **Office automation systems** are IT applications that improve productivity in an office. These include word processing and voice messaging systems.

8.15 **Groupware**, such as **Lotus Notes** provides functions for collaborative work groups. In a sales context, for instance, it would provide a facility for recording and retrieving all the information relevant to individual customers, including notes of visits, notes of telephone calls and basic data like address, credit terms and contact name. These items could be updated by anyone who had contact with a customer and would then be available to all sales people.

8.16 Groupware also provides such facilities as messaging, appointment scheduling, to-do lists, and jotters.

8.17 An **intranet** is an internal network used to share information using Internet technology and protocols. The **firewall** surrounding an intranet fends off unauthorised access from outside the organisation. Each employee has a browser, used to access a server computer that holds corporate information on a wide variety of topics, and in some cases also offers access to the Internet. Applications include company newspapers, induction material, procedure and policy manuals and internal databases.

(a) Savings accrue from the elimination of storage, printing and distribution of documents that can be made available to employees on-line.

(b) Documents on-line are often more widely used than those that are kept filed away, especially if the document is bulky (eg manuals) and needs to be searched. This means that there are improvements in productivity and efficiency.

(c) It is much easier to update information in electronic form.

8.18 An **expert system** is a computer program that captures **human expertise** in a limited domain of knowledge. Such software uses a knowledge base that consists of facts, concepts and the relationships between them and uses pattern-matching techniques to solve problems. For example, many financial institutions now use expert systems to process straightforward loan applications. The user enters certain key facts into the system such as the loan applicant's name and most recent addresses, their income and monthly outgoings, and details of other loans. The system will then:

(a) Check the facts given against its database to see whether the applicant has a good previous credit record.

(b) Perform calculations to see whether the applicant can afford to repay the loan.

(c) Make a judgement as to what extent the loan applicant fits the lender's profile of a good risk (based on the lender's previous experience).

A decision is then suggested, based on the results of this processing.

8.19 Other applications of expert systems include medical and legal advice; diagnosis of equipment breakdowns; and surveillance, for example of the number of customers entering a supermarket in order to decide when more checkouts need to be opened. Expert systems are not suited to high-level, unstructured problems as these require information from a wide range of sources rather than simply deciding between a few known alternatives.

8.20 IT systems can be used to store vast amounts of data in accessible form. A **data warehouse** receives data from operational systems, such as a sales order processing system, and stores it in its most fundamental form, without any summarisation of transactions. Analytical and query software is provided so that reports can be produced at any level of summarisation and incorporating any comparisons or relationships desired.

8.21 The value of data warehouse is enhanced when **datamining** software is used. True datamining software **discovers previously unknown relationships** and provides insights that cannot be obtained through ordinary summary reports. These hidden patterns and relationships constitute **knowledge**, as defined above, and can be used to guide decision making and to predict future behaviour. Datamining is thus a contribution to organisational learning.

8.22 The American retailer *Wal-Mart* discovered an unexpected relationship between the sale of nappies and beer! Wal-Mart found that both tended to sell at the same time, just after working hours, and concluded that men with small children stopped off to buy nappies on their way home, and bought beer at the same time. Logically, therefore, if the two items were put in the same shopping aisle, sales of both should increase. Wal-Mart tried this and it worked.

8.23 Here is an amended version of our earlier table. This one includes the relevant IT systems.

	Data	Information	Knowledge
Nature	Facts	Relationships between processed facts	Patterns discerned in information
Importance of context	Total	Some	Context independent
Importance to business	Mundane	Probably useful for management	May be strategically useful
Relevant IT systems	Office automation Data warehouse	Groupware Expert systems Report writing software Intranet	Datamining Intranet Expert systems

8.24 We will conclude this section with an example of the modern approach to knowledge management. You will notice that the IT system eventually developed looks like something half way between groupware and a database. However, the strategic impact of the system and its ability to create new corporate knowledge mean that it is properly described as a knowledge management system.

8.25 Notice also that the knowledge originates with people who are fairly low down in the hierarchy and who would not normally be described as knowledge workers. This illustrates the very important principle that valuable knowledge can be found at all levels and is not the prerogative of an elite.

Marketing at Work

Servicing Xerox copiers

Our story begins with researchers working on artificial intelligence who wanted to see if they could replace the paper documentation that Xerox technicians used on the road with an expert system.

The team found that it was indeed possible to build software that could do just that. But when they showed their first efforts to technicians, the response was underwhelming.

What kept technicians from finding fixes was not that the documentation was paper-based but that it didn't address all the potential problems. And not all problems were predictable. Machines in certain regions could react to extreme temperatures in different ways. A can of Mountain Dew overturned in one part of a machine could wreak havoc in another seemingly unconnected part. Technicians could handle these mishaps quickly only if they had seen them before or if another technician had run into a similar problem and shared the results.

Once the conversations with technicians revealed this gap in information sharing, the researchers realised that AI was the wrong approach. What Xerox needed instead was knowledge management. It wasn't a smart computer program that was going to fix these things, it was sharing the best ways to make these repairs.

When the researchers realised they needed to look at the way technicians work, they spent time in the field, following the technicians from call to call. What they observed proved invaluable – knowledge sharing was already unofficially ingrained in the organisation. Most striking was not how technicians solved common problems, but what they did when they came up against a tricky, intermittent one. Often they called one another on radios provided by the company. And in informal gatherings they shared vexing problems and their fixes.

Meanwhile, another researcher was busy comparing the way French and U.S. technicians worked. He discovered that, while French technicians appeared to work from immaculate, uniform documentation put out by headquarters, their real solutions also came from a second set of documentation – notes they carried with them detailing what they'd learned. It was from that database that researchers started building the first laptop-based knowledge-sharing system.

The researchers took the first iteration to France and began a series of exhaustive sessions with the French experts in the Xerox headquarters outside Paris. In those sessions, something magical happened: The system took on the shape of the people working on it, evolving with each suggestion from the actual users.

But the worldwide customer service group didn't take the project seriously. Nobody believed that the knowledge of the technicians was really valuable. So, working stealthily, outside the realm of worldwide management, the research team gave laptops and the fledging program to 40 technician and matched them with a control group of technicians who relied solely on their own knowledge when fixing machines. After two months, the group with the laptops had 10 percent lower costs and 10 percent lower service time than those without – and the control group was jealous of those with the system.

By 1998, the system was officially deployed in the United States and began to make its way around the globe. Today it has more than 15,000 user tips, with more being added every day. The hope is that by 2002 it will be distributed worldwide to the company's 25,000 technicians. And already success stories abound. One technician in Montreal authored a tip about a 50-cent fuse-holder replacement that caused a chronic problem with a high-speed colour copier. A Brazilian technician had the same problem, and his customer wanted the $40,000 machine replaced. When he found the tip from Montreal, he fixed the machine in minutes. Current estimates have the system saving Xerox at least $7 million in time and replacement costs. It's tales like those that make senior management happy.

Adapted from Meg Mitchell, www.darwinmag.com February 2001.

9 EFFECTIVE MANAGEMENT OF MEETINGS 6/01

9.1 In the chapter on time management we identified the value of an hour of a manager's time. The effectiveness of every hour the individual spends in a meeting has to be considered in terms of opportunity cost. What are the benefits derived from the meeting against the costs of being there?

9.2 A problem with committee meetings is that they can so easily grow. Meetings seem to have an inbuilt dynamic which spurs their expansion.

Part B: Personal effectiveness

- Meetings grow in duration
- Meetings grow in terms of the number of participants
- Meetings multiply, with sub-meetings and eventually meetings to plan meetings

9.3 When you consider the real cost of a meeting lasting three hours involving of half a dozen senior managers, you can see how expensive meetings are. The question which has to be asked is: do you get value for money? Are the effort and scarce resources devoted to a meeting generating real added value for the business?

Action Programme 15

Try and calculate the amount of time which you, or your manager spent in meetings during the last month. Calculate as a percentage of salary what this costs the organisation.

9.4 Once you have analysed how much time is spent in meetings you can begin to analyse whether there are opportunities to make your meeting time more effective. Use the following checklist to help.

1. What is the purpose of the meeting? Is it important that I attend?
2. Can someone else attend in my place?
3. Are the right people involved?
   - (i) Those who will need to make decisions or take actions must be included.
   - (ii) Those whose involvement is more indirect can perhaps be excluded and briefed later.
4. Is the meeting arranged at a location which minimises the collective travelling time and at a time which minimises disruption to the rest of the working day?
5. Is the meeting well planned, with important papers etc circulated in advance? (see the next section).
6. How important is the outcome of the meeting to you and how will it be followed up?

Action Programme 16

Identify an opportunity to sit and observe a meeting - preferably not of a team you work closely with. If this is not possible at work, sit in on a social committee meeting at your sports club or a more formal public meeting like a meeting of the Planning Committee at the Local Council.

- How well is this organised?
- How efficiently does it progress through its business?
- Does everyone attending get to make a contribution?
- Who manages the meeting? Do they do it well?
- What roles do the various participants adopt?

A note about team roles

9.5 In an effective meeting the team members will take on different roles. This is essential if the outcome of the meeting is to be productive and valuable.

9.6 *Belbin*, in a study of business-game teams in 1981, discovered that a differentiation of influence among team members (agreement that some members were more influential than others) resulted in higher morale and better performance. Belbin's picture of the most effective character-mix in a group involves eight necessary roles which should ideally be balanced and evenly spread in the group.

(a) The **co-ordinator (or chairman)** presides and co-ordinates. This person is balanced, disciplined, and good at working through others.

(b) The **shaper** is highly strung, dominant, extrovert, passionate about the task itself, and a spur to action.

(c) The **plant** is introverted, but intellectually dominant and imaginative. This person is a source of ideas.

(d) The **monitor-evaluator** is analytically rather than creatively intelligent and so dissects ideas and spots flaws. This person is possibly aloof and tactless, but is necessary.

(e) The **resource-investigator** is popular, sociable, extrovert, relaxed. He or she is a source of new contacts but is not an originator.

(f) The **implementer (or company worker)** is a practical organiser, turning ideas into tasks, scheduling and planning. This person is trustworthy and efficient but not excited (or exciting, often), and is not a leader, but an administrator.

(g) The **team worker** is most concerned with team maintenance: supportive, understanding, diplomatic, popular but uncompetitive and noticed only when absent.

(h) The **finisher** chivvies the team to meet deadlines and attend to details.

Note that more than one role may be played by each person at a meeting. Also, Belbin subsequently added a further role: the **specialist** who is brought into the team when required.

Action Programme 17

Over the next month make a note of the sort of roles you play in meetings and group situations. Are any of the roles absent from the group? Did this make the task harder than necessary in hindsight?

If there is the opportunity, perhaps in syndicate work at college, make a conscious effort to take on a different role.

Stages in running effective meetings

9.7 If you think about the people hours spent in meetings as a valuable and scarce resource, the need to plan meetings effectively becomes apparent.

Decide if the meeting is necessary

9.8 If the meeting will purely be a forum for disseminating information, a memo may be a more efficient means of communication.

Plan the meeting

9.9 Decide on the objectives of the meeting. Unclear objectives will lead to irrelevancies being discussed.

9.10 It is also necessary to decide who should attend the meeting. Only those people with a genuine need to be at a meeting should be invited.

9.11 When involving a number of people, particularly when they do not work at the same location, co-ordinating diaries to establish a convenient time can be an extremely challenging operation. Remember to allow plenty of time - this increases the chance of people being free. If one or two people are unable to attend, ask if they can send deputies.

Part B: Personal effectiveness

9.12 A **formal notification** of the meeting with either an **agenda** or a request for any further items for the agenda should be supplied. It is worth reminding people about a meeting a few days beforehand, if the meeting was arranged a long time in advance.

9.13 Paperwork sent out before the meeting should include the agenda, location maps if it is being held away from the normal place of work and any relevant background papers.

Drafting the agenda

9.14 A detailed agenda can contribute heavily to the success of a meeting. It gives attendees time to prepare themselves properly.

(a) The agenda should be in a **logical order**.

(b) The agenda should give details about the **purpose of each item.**

(c) The agenda should show the **start and finish times** of the meeting, and also roughly how much time will be allocated to each item.

(d) **Any other business** should be used (if at all) for minor matters. Anything significant should be on the main agenda.

Conduct of the meeting

9.15 The conduct of the meeting will depend on the degree of formality - but normally you would expect someone (not necessarily the manager) to take the chair. This person has a number of responsibilities.

- All items on the agenda should be thoroughly considered
- Future action should be agreed and minuted
- Everyone should have an opportunity to contribute to the discussion and decision making
- Time must not be wasted by sidetracking or leaving the agenda
- Everyone must understands agreed action
- Future meetings should be arranged as necessary

9.16 **Poor chairing can have several adverse consequences**. It can mean that too much time is spent on unimportant matters and not enough on significant matters. It can also mean that the meeting is hijacked by a few participants, whilst others do not have the chance to contribute properly.

9.17 **The choice of chair may be influenced by the objective of the meeting**. If the objective of the meeting is primarily to inform, it is likely that the person in the chair will take the lead in informing and explaining. On the other hand, if the purpose of the meeting is primarily to discuss matters, there is much to be said for giving the chair to someone other than the person who is likely to contribute most to the discussion. The problem with giving the chair to the most talkative person is that the meeting can become little more than a monologue. A more reticent chair may well be better able to see whether everyone is contributing fully and obtaining maximum benefit from the meeting; this type of chair may also be better able to sum up the discussion and indicate what has been achieved.

Minutes

9.18 After the meeting the person responsible for taking minutes needs to check with the chair that minutes and action points are a fair reflection of events. Action points should specify the action to be taken, by whom the action should be taken, and by when. There should be follow up and progress check on those with responsibilities before the next meeting.

More effective meetings

9.19 As we indicated earlier, meetings can represent a significant investment and it is important to get good value out of them. There are a number of actions which can be taken to help improve the effectiveness of meeting time. Here is a checklist.

> **Meeting effectiveness checklist**
> 1 Ensure all those involved are trained in meeting skills.
> 2 Encourage teams to analyse the effectiveness of their own meetings and to establish targets for improvement.
> 3 Establish a culture that takes meetings seriously.
>   - People should arrive at meetings on time and be thoroughly prepared.
>   - Paperwork and follow up points should be completed quickly and thoroughly.
> 4 Encourage short/sharp meetings with clear indications of time to be spent on each agenda item.
> 5 Set targets for the maximum time per month for meetings:
>   (a) encourage managers and teams to review to see if meetings are necessary or the best method of communication
>   (b) encourage managers to delegate attendance at meetings to others.

> **Exam Tip**
>
> The June 2001 exam included a question on the use of meetings for a new product launch. You were asked to suggest how meetings might be made more productive and creative.
>
> You must be very careful about questions of this kind: they look like invitations to write down all you know on a given topic. This approach will **never** produce a satisfactory answer. You must **always** apply theory to the setting of the question.
>
> In this case, for instance, a new product launch will have its own peculiar problems, such as the need to get everybody to contribute creatively without descending into chaos.

10 NEGOTIATION 12/99, 6/00

10.1 Negotiation is an important skill at all levels of management. At board level there may be pay negotiations with trade unions; at lower levels, working practices and organisational changes may have to be discussed. It is also common for managers to enter into negotiation with each other on operational matters, especially when a department's work impinges on that of another. The Marketing Manager is particularly likely to be involved in this type of negotiation, since the marketing orientation should reach into all parts of the organisation.

Part B: Personal effectiveness

> **Key concept**
> A **negotiation** is a conference between parties who have different views on how an issue should be resolved. Both parties accept that agreement between them is necessary.

10.2 It is important to differentiate negotiation from **consultation**. **Negotiation** implies that both parties have **power** over the issue and must reach **agreement**. In consultation, there is no over-riding requirement for agreement and one of the parties will have final discretion over the solution. Managers should avoid giving the impression that they are negotiating (in this strict sense) when they do not need to. However, the use of the word 'negotiation' can be a useful ploy to defuse conflict when all that the manager intends is to provide an opportunity for letting off steam.

10.3 Negotiation is only one way of dealing with conflict and other approaches are used.

(a) **Smoothing** is to use 'honeyed words in exhortation or discussion where the emphasis is on the value of teamwork' (*Torrington and Hall: Personnel Management*). This technique assumes that disagreement is superficial and there is common ground at a fundamental level.

(b) To **compromise** is to split the difference without much in the way of discussion. The drawback of this approach is that both sides are dissatisfied.

(c) **Avoidance** is a popular strategy in autocratic organisations. No opportunity is given for opposing views to be heard on any topic. The potential for conflict is ignored and hence its expression is stifled. The danger is that it will eventually break out in an overwhelming form. However, many businesses are run like this.

(d) **Suppression** of conflict is rather different. Expressions of dissent occur but they are attacked and stamped out.

10.4 The need for negotiation may be **enshrined in procedure**, as with most wage negotiations, or it may become apparent from **circumstances**. In the latter case, it is important to **recognise what is happening**, in order to avoid losing the initiative.

10.5 The parties to a negotiation will each aim to reach agreement on terms which are as close as possible to their **starting** positions. Some form of compromise is almost inevitable. An important aspect of negotiation is that the parties reach agreement feeling that their needs have been respected, even if they have not achieved everything they wished for. It may be wise, therefore, for the stronger party to be generous.

10.6 **Conventions of negotiation**. Negotiation has its conventions; they are valuable because they help the parties to reach a conclusion.

(a) Both parties actually wish to reach a settlement and accept that some compromise may be necessary.

(b) Civilised behaviour is desirable, but hard words and loss of temper are sometimes used as tactics to emphasise determination. Outbursts should not be allowed to undermine commitment to the process.

(c) Some discussion may take place off the record.

(d) Firm offers and concessions should not be withdrawn.

(e) A final agreement should be implemented without amendment or further manoeuvring.

Preparing for negotiation

10.7 When negotiations are to be conducted in a more or less formal manner, appropriate arrangements should be made, as for any other meeting. These should include the establishment of an agenda, which may itself be the subject of negotiation, and provision of a suitable meeting room.

10.8 **Opening positions.** If the parties are realistic, they will have established in their own minds not only their **ideal** outcomes, but also a **minimum acceptable** outcome. This is actually quite difficult to do and requires careful thought. If the acceptable outcomes overlap, it should be relatively easy to reach a **mutually acceptable** result. If they do not, the task becomes much harder. It is clearly very useful for a negotiator to have a good idea of what the other side's minimum position really is, and, equally, to conceal his or her own.

10.9 **Negotiating teams.** In more formal negotiations, there may be more than one negotiator from each side. It is important that the members of a team understand their roles. There should be a single **principal advocate** who controls the team's work. A free for all does not enhance the likelihood of progress. Other members of the negotiating team may attend to provide specialist advice or simply to observe. Careful attention to the opposing team's **reactions** can be very rewarding.

Conducting the negotiation

10.10 **Opening.** The opening position should be stated clearly and realistically. The opposing position should be challenged on its merits; it is important to leave the opponent with room for manoeuvre. It is desirable to say as little as possible at this stage and to concentrate on assessing the other side's strengths and weaknesses. A bargaining phase may then ensue.

10.11 **Bargaining.** The bargaining phase is a process of argument and persuasion. There are some important tactics.

(a) Do not allow elements of the dispute to be settled **piecemeal**. This limits room for subsequent manoeuvre.

(b) Any concession should be **matched** by a concession from the other side.

(c) To avoid one-sided concessions, make proposals which are conditional on the other side moving too: 'If you do this I will agree to that'.

10.12 **Closing.** Closing a negotiation is similar to closing a sale; it means attempting to bring the process to a conclusion. There are several techniques.

(a) Offer to trade a concession for an agreement to settle.

(b) When there is a single outstanding issue, offer to split the difference.

(c) Offer a choice between two courses of action.

(d) Summarise the arguments, emphasise the concessions that have been made and state a final position. However, a bluff runs the risk of being called.

Part B: Personal effectiveness

Successful negotiation

10.13 *John Hunt* lists some characteristics of successful negotiators in his book *Managing People at Work*.

(a) They avoid direct confrontation

(b) They consider a wide range of options

(c) They hold back counter proposals rather than responding immediately

(d) They use emollient verbal techniques: 'would it be helpful if we...'

(e) They summarise on behalf of all involved

(f) They advance single arguments insistently and avoid long winded, multiple reason arguments

10.14 Negotiation skills are difficult to learn other than from experience. Role plays and simulations can help, but the best way is to attend live negotiations as a junior member of a team.

Exam Tip
Negotiations are internal and external. In June 2000, a question put you in the position of trying to appease 'management' and the 'team'.

5: The manager as a communicator

Chapter Roundup

- Communication is a central business activity, without which the organisation cannot function. It is essentially a two-way process involving the sending and receiving of information.
- Managers are at the heart of this process. Marketing managers are also directly responsible for organisation/customer communication, and so have a critical responsibility for communication.
- Managers need to use both formal and informal communication channels and need to become expert in their knowledge of the various communication options open to them.
- Listening skills are as important as sending skills. Organisations and managers can establish systems of feedback, suggestion schemes etc to help them listen.
- Interviews, meetings, committees and presentations all involve the manager in face-to-face communication. Here an understanding of both verbal and non-verbal communications will be useful.
- Planning the structure of interviews is necessary, and conducting them requires a number of personal and interpersonal skills. Managers need to consider their own interview performance and take steps to improve on this dimension of their work.
- Written communications are also important - not least for your exam.
- Information **overload** can be as big a problem as inadequate communication. Communication should be carefully thought through to ensure it is targeted at the right person, and offering information in the right format.
- **Everyone** in the organisation, no matter how skilled, should be constantly reviewing his or her communication skills and identifying opportunities for improvement. Self-analysis, and development and support groups within teams or colleges can help with this.
- The amount of time managers spend in meetings is considerable. To be effective meetings must be taken seriously, well planned and controlled.
- Knowledge management exploits existing knowledge and creates new knowledge.

	Data	Information	Knowledge
Nature	Facts	Relationships between processed facts	Patterns discerned in information
Importance of context	Total	Some	Context independent
Importance to business	Mundane	Probably useful for management	May be strategically useful
Relevant IT systems	Office automation	Groupware	Datamining
	Data warehouse	Expert systems	Intranet
		Report writing software	Expert systems
		Intranet	

- Negotiation is an important skill for all managers. Do not confuse it with consultation.
- When negotiating, establish in your own mind what is your minimum acceptable position.
- The negotiating process uses different techniques in the opening, bargaining and closing phases.
- Successful negotiators avoid confrontation but maintain their position firmly. They are flexible and take their time to respond to proposals.

Part B: Personal effectiveness

Quick Quiz

1. How would you define communication and what are its purposes? (see para 2.2 (Key concept), 2.4)
2. List different types of upwards and downwards communication. (2.8)
3. Is it true that the 'grapevine' only works when formal communication breaks down? (2.14)
4. What is the role of feedback in the communication process? (3.3) Identify three positive and three negative items of feedback you may receive as a communicator. (3.5)
5. List as many barriers to communication as you can. (3.12 - 3.16)
6. Why are interpersonal skills important to the manager? (4.3) List some interpersonal skills. (4.4)
7. What are the five stages of the interview process? (4.10)
8. What should the manager do after the end of an interview? (4.23)
9. For what purposes may committees be used? (5.3)
10. What is the function of reports? (6.3)
11. What criteria would you use to help you select the most appropriate method for internal communication? (7.1)
12. According to Peter Drucker, what is the manager's main tool? (7.6)
13. Produce a framework for the delivery of a presentation (7.22)
14. Outline a report format. (7.32)
15. What is non-verbal communication and why is it relevant to the manager? (7.36 - 7.40)
16. What is the distinction between data and information? (8.5)
17. What is datamining? (8.21)
18. What goes wrong with meetings if they are not controlled? (9.2)
19. What factors should you consider when asked to attend a meeting? (9.4)
20. What actions can you take to encourage people to make a more effective use of meeting time? (9.19)
21. What are the conventions of negotiation? (10.6)
22. What are the three stages a negotiation goes through? (10.10 – 10.12)

Action Programme Review

1. Types of communication in the organisation:
    - Giving instructions
    - Giving or receiving information
    - Exchanging ideas
    - Announcing plans or strategies
    - Comparing actual results against a plan
    - Laying down rules or procedures
    - Job descriptions, organisation charts or manuals (communication about the structure of the organisation and individual roles)
    - Providing feedback or data

2. The marketing and sales managers not only have to cope with managing internal communication flows, but are also the communication exchange between the organisation and its customers or stakeholders.

    Marketing managers **have** to be excellent communicators, not only in their role as managers, but also because of their central responsibility for external communication.

5: The manager as a communicator

3   As an integral part of quality initiatives, and as a mechanism for involving and interesting staff in the activities of the organisation, suggestion schemes can be used. When taken seriously organisations:

   (a)   set targets for suggestions per employee per annum
   (b)   take **all** suggestions seriously and respond to them or acknowledge them promptly
   (c)   offer incentive and bonus schemes to reward those whose ideas are implemented
   (d)   value and respect the contributions of all, no matter what role or position they hold.

5   The individual problems are easily diagnosed. However, improving matters will be more difficult. There may be a place for **training** in communications techniques. Also, managers at all levels should both take great care with their own communication practices and encourage their subordinates to do the same.

6 | Interview type | Problems |
    |---|---|
    | Routine, work-related | Finding time, interruptions |
    | Discipline |) See Chapter 8 |
    | Grievance |) |
    | Appraisal | Is it a box ticking exercise? Or is it constructive? |
    | Internal vacancy/promotion | Will anything new come out of the interview? |
    | Exit | Interviewee may be hostile or boat-happy |

7   Easy ways to better communication

   (a)   When speaking, in meeting or on the telephone, think first. Decide what you want to say, say it then shut up.

   (b)   Whether speaking or writing don't use two words where one will do. Words are precious. Ration them.

   (c)   When running a meeting, make sure everyone is heard but don't allow blather. Some people think that if they say the same thing over and over again they will convince everyone else of their case.

   (d)   When you have written or typed something, **read it through** Have you said what you meant to say? Have you made any errors of grammar, spelling or punctuation? Is it clear? In particular, are there any ambiguities or other opportunities for misinterpretation?

   (e)   When you have had a conversation on an important topic, especially if a decision was made, make a note of it. You could even send a memo or e-mail summarising it. This is particularly important when talking to superiors who tend to be vague.

10 Information is data processed to having meaning and purpose.

   - It should be **relevant** for its purpose
   - It should be **complete** for its purpose
   - It should be **sufficiently accurate** for its purpose
   - It should be **clear** to the user
   - The user should have **confidence** in it
   - It should be **communicated to a person who needs it** to do his job
   - There should not be more than the user can take in
   - It should be **timely**
   - It should be communicated by an **appropriate channel**
   - It should be provided at a **cost less than the value** of its benefits

12 (a)
   - What has gone wrong? The message has not been decoded in a way which was intended? The perception is of trouble - possibly the views of the sales team who are communicating their worries to customers.

   - What action would you take? A sales briefing to put the whole picture and present the strategy to the sales team. Some attempt to generate positive PR through press releases about new products etc might help to quell the external rumours. If serious then a briefing for key account customers and suppliers could also be considered.

   - What could have been done? A briefing to start with would perhaps have prevented the problem. The sales team may have had some useful ideas for tackling the seasonal variations!

(b)
- What has gone wrong? A lack of consultation has left staff feeling worried and apprehensive about the proposed appraisal system. The benefits have not been communicated to them - they fear a hidden agenda.
- What action would you take? Immediate consultation and discussion with staff using both formal and informal channels will clarify matters. A postponement of the implementation of formal appraisals may help to allay suspicions. Briefings about future plans, particularly if they involve expansion, will help.
- What could have been done? The issue of appraisals could have been treated more sensitively. Staff could have been more directly involved, and possibly informal appraisals and training implemented, before a formal system was introduced.

Now try illustrative questions 5 to 7 at the end of the Study Text

Part C
Managing people

6 Managing the Team

Chapter Topic List	Syllabus reference
1 Setting the scene	
2 Teams and groups: dynamics and needs	3.2
3 Forming teams	3.2
4 Effective and ineffective teams	3.2
5 The manager's role within the team	2.1, 3.2

Learning outcome

- Students will be able to explain concepts of building and managing effective teams and the role of leadership.

Key Concepts Introduced

- Group dynamics
- Leadership style
- Theory X and Theory Y

Examples of Marketing at Work

- The innovation squad
- Nationwide Building Society
- The Hawthorne Studies

1 SETTING THE SCENE

1.1 In Chapter 5, we finished off with a section about meetings, and we described the variety of roles that people play in meetings, according to Belbin's classification: somebody co-ordinates, somebody has ideas, and so on.

1.2 In many respects, this is characteristic not only of meetings as such, but of working in a team in general. Especially where tasks are complex, a range of different skills is needed, and people have to work **together.**

1.3 In this chapter, we discuss some of the issues in managing a team. In Section 2 we discuss teams and groups in general, why they are needed, what they do, some examples in a marketing context, and some key management issues.

1.4 In Section 3, we discuss the problems of forming new teams, and the type of developmental stages a team goes through before it can get down to work. Team formation in difficult or unusual circumstances has been stressed as important for this paper. In Section 4, we offer some rules of thumb for you to assess whether a team is effective or not, with the proviso that a team which is too cohesive can be blind to new or different ideas - group think.

1.5 In Section 5 we focus on your role, as a possible team leader. Teams often need some sort of direction, but the approach to leadership you adopt (leadership style) can vary, depending on the task and the followers.

1.6 In this chapter we offer some detailed examples for you to try out your diagnostic skills.

1.7 In Chapter 7, we discuss the procedures for recruiting and introducing new individuals to the organisation or team; in Chapter 8 we discuss how the performance of individual team members can be improved.

2 TEAMS AND GROUPS: DYNAMICS AND NEEDS

2.1 In *Understanding Organisations,* *Handy* defines a group as '**any collection of people who perceive themselves to be a group**'. The point of this definition is the distinction it implies between a random collection of individuals and a group of individuals who share a **common sense of identity and belonging.**

> **Key Concept**
> **Group dynamics** is the name given to the system of relationships and behaviour which exists in any group of people. Membership of a group tends to modify or develop personal characteristics to the extent that the group appears to have a personality of its own.

2.2 A group has certain attributes that a random crowd does not possess.

- **The members have a sense of identity**: there are acknowledged boundaries to the group which define it.

- **Members are loyal to the group**, and conform to the norms of behaviour and attitude that bind the group together.

- **Purpose and leadership**. Most groups have a **purpose or set of objectives** and will, spontaneously or formally, choose individuals or sub-groups to lead them towards those goals.

Why people form groups

2.3 People are drawn together into groups for many reasons.

- The **need to belong and to make a contribution** that will be noticed and appreciated
- **Familiarity**: a shared office or canteen
- **Common** rank, specialisms, objectives and interests
- The attractiveness of a particular **group activity** (for example joining a club)
- **Power** greater than the individuals alone could muster (for example a trade union)

Formal and informal groups in organisations

2.4 Some groupings will be part of the **formal organisation**: for example, specialists may be in a committee investigating a particular problem; a department split into small work teams to facilitate supervision. Other groups are **informal**.

(a) **Formal groups** will have a formal structure; they will be consciously organised for a function allotted to them by the organisation, and for which they are held responsible - they are task oriented, and become **teams**. Leaders may be chosen within the group, but are typically given authority by the organisation. Permanent formal groups include work sections and management teams such as the board of directors. **Temporary** formal groups include ad hoc committees and project teams.

(b) **Informal groups** will invariably be present in any organisation. Informal groups include workplace cliques and networks who socialise outside work. They have a constantly fluctuating membership and structure, and leaders usually emerge because of their personal qualities. The purposes of informal groups are usually related to group and individual member satisfaction, rather than to a task.

The functions of groups

2.5 From the organisation's standpoint groups and teams have several purposes.

- Performing tasks which require the collective skills of more than one person
- Testing and ratifying decisions made outside the group
- Consulting or negotiating, especially to resolve disputes within the organisation
- Creating ideas
- Collecting and transmitting information and ideas
- Co-ordinating the work of different individuals or other groups
- Motivating individuals to devote more energy and effort into achieving the organisation's goals

2.6 There may be no strict division between these different functions. They will inevitably overlap in practice. A group will be most effective if its members are not attempting to cope with different functions simultaneously.

2.7 From the individual's standpoint, groups also perform some important functions.

- They satisfy social needs for friendship and belonging.
- They help individuals in developing images of themselves.

Part C: Managing people

- They enable individuals to help each other on matters which are not necessarily connected with the organisation's purpose, for example, people at work may organise a baby-sitting circle.

- They enable individuals to share the burdens of any responsibility they may have.

Examples of groups

2.8 **Examples of groups** or teams in marketing:

(a) **Quality circles** discussing and improving quality of service

(b) **Project groups**
- A **new product development team**
- A **key account team** responsible for all aspects of a marketing for a key client or customer segment
- A **specialist marketing function team** responsible for research or the creative dimensions of marketing

(c) **Brainstorming groups,** brought together to generate new ideas and suggestions, for problem-solving or planning

(d) **Training or study groups**

Action Programme 1

What (a) formal and (b) informal groups are you involved with? What are their functions? Why can these functions be performed better by a group than by an individual?

Pick a group of which you are a member. How do you define who is 'in' the group and who isn't? Does the leader of the group make a positive effort to keep the group close-knit and to make it **feel** like a team? Would you say your department or section was a team?

Do you personally **like** working in a group, or do you prefer to be and function better alone? Do you think you could succeed by being either a team player or a loner? Or does your work and the marketing culture require you to be both, at appropriate times?

Issues in managing groups

2.9 John Adair's work on leadership identified **three** overlapping sets of **needs** which need to be satisfied when teams are managed, and the **roles the team leader needs to play** to satisfy these needs.

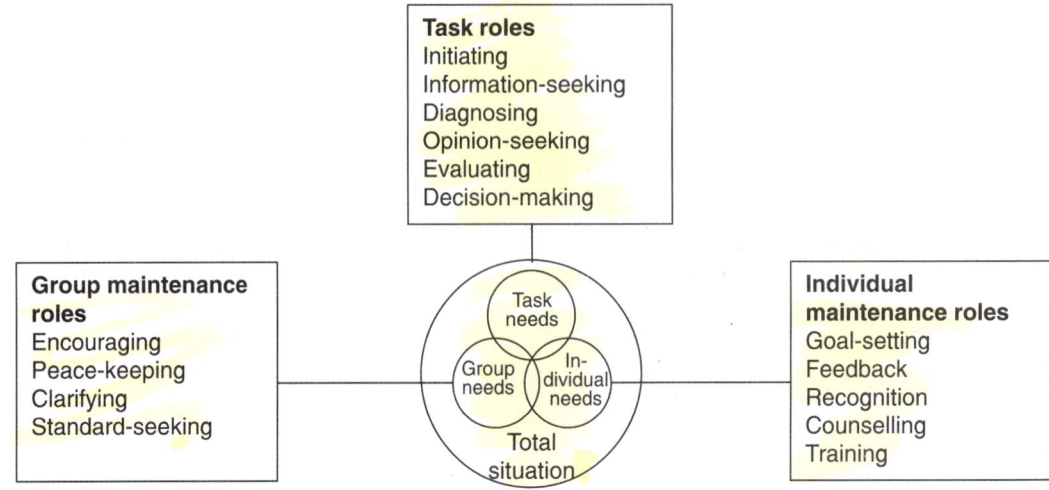

6: Managing the team

2.10 For effective performance all three sets of needs must be identified and satisfied. Without an overlap of these three circles, the group will be unsuccessful.

2.11 The total situation dictates the relative priority that must be given to each of the three sets of needs. Effective leadership involves identifying and acting on those priorities to create a balance between the needs. Meeting the various needs implies specific management roles.

2.12 Around this framework, Adair developed a scheme of leadership training based on precept and practice in each of **eight leadership activities** as applied to task, team and individual.

- Defining the task
- Planning
- Briefing
- Controlling
- Evaluating
- Motivating
- Organising
- Setting an example

2.13 Adair argued that the common perception of leadership as 'decision-making' was inadequate to describe the range of action required by the complex situations in which managers find themselves. This model is therefore more practical. It clearly identifies the responsibilities of the manager or leader in ensuring that the required task is achieved, but also that team and individual needs are satisfied as part of the process.

New trends

2.14 Teams and groups will become increasingly popular in a marketing context, and will replace the type of hierarchical organisation structure we discussed in Chapter 1. *Freeling* suggests that teams from a number of business functions will carry out most marketing functions.

- '**Integrators** are responsible for serving each distinct consumer, channel or product.' They will co-ordinate the organisation's resources for the customer's benefit. They will lead teams with a variety of skills.

- '**Specialists** will create competitive advantage by helping the company build world class skills in the two or three most important areas of marketing.' A team might contain a pricing specialist and a specialist in database marketing, for instance.

    'The teams will be organised around key **cross functional** business processes like building **brand unity** and ensuring superior **customer service**.'

A problem is the need to adjust people's behaviour. The 'integrators' are co-ordinators, not bosses: they rely on the **specialist** expertise of the people in the team.

Exam Tip

A question in the December 2000 exam asked about improving teams from a customer perspective. In answering a question like this, use a mental checklist and ask yourself what the implications of such a project are in terms of the main theoretical topics you have studied. You will have a clearer idea of what they when you have worked through the rest of this book, but in general terms we might divide them into ideas about the **individual**, the **team**, the **organisation** the **manager**, and **the customer**.

Part C: Managing people

3 FORMING TEAMS 12/99

3.1 Simply bringing a group of individuals together does not make a team. A team implies some synergy. Its output collectively would be greater than the sum of the outputs of individuals working in isolation.

3.2 But what constitutes a team? The eleven players on the football field may seem to be a team, but their manager is seldom a player and there are dozens of others supporting their activities behind the scenes.

3.3 If you are faced with starting a team from scratch, you can begin by identifying what the task is and what skills and characteristics are needed to achieve it. Then group members can be identified from within or outside the organisation.

3.4 In the supposedly flatter more matrix structured organisation of today the formation of teams for relatively short periods is becoming more common. These may be **project teams** which bring together individuals from different disciplines, backgrounds and even different companies. In these situations the manager has two key roles.

- Selecting the right mix of individuals
- Actively working to turn individuals into effective teams in as short a time as possible

3.5 Imagine for a moment you are free to choose individuals to make up a new business team: perhaps a creative marketing team. Who would you choose? All the best known experts in their fields? Common sense would suggest that a team of the best must generate the best results.

3.6 In practice, however, this is not always the case. A team drawn from a combination of stars and workhorses is more likely to be effective. The individual needs of stars can sometimes take precedence over the needs of group or task.

3.7 Once you have a group of individuals selected (or inherited) as your basis, you now have the task of turning them into a team.

Marketing at Work

Nicky Wnek in described the 'innovation squad' in *Marketing Business*

'**Mr Blue Skies** is the broad thinker who keeps the long-term vision but needs to be kept-in-touch with reality. His colleague, **Mr Margin** gets margins up and thus delivers the all-important profit. However, he cannot see that innovation relies on intangibles such as faith and judgement.

Ms Misery takes her name from her tendency to focus on the negative. But innovation needs her rigorous approach.

Ms Me-Too could bring about a first-to-market situation by keeping a valuable eye on the competition - for instance an innovation abroad. Every innovation needs someone to champion the cause but **Mr Hobby-Horse** can be in danger of backing the wrong horse. **Mr Cavalier** is the classic self-confident entrepreneur with high energy levels and a healthy disregard for the established way of doing things; he genuinely cares about a result and is faster at effecting change.

Ms Brands is the player who contributes the strong understanding of the consumer, but unfortunately not everyone shares her passion for her particular brand. **Mr Out-of-Depth** is unlikely to have that big idea, but he is keen, hard-working and sufficiently junior to do the essential donkey work.'

Team development

3.8 Groups are not static. They mature and develop. Four stages in this group development were identified by *Tuckman*.

- Forming
- Storming
- Norming
- Performing

Forming

3.9 During the first stage **the group is just coming together.** Each individual wishes to impress his or her personality on the group, while its purpose, composition, and organisation are being established. The individuals will be trying to find out about each other and about the aims and norms of the team. Objectives may be unclear and a leader may not have emerged.

3.10 This **settling down** period is essential; the group will not be used to being autonomous, and will probably not be efficient at planning its activities. It may resort to complex bureaucratic procedures to ensure that what it is doing does not get its members into trouble.

Storming

3.11 The second stage frequently involves more or less **open conflict** between group members. There may be changes agreed in the original objectives, procedures and norms established for the group. If the team is developing successfully this may be a fruitful phase as more realistic targets are set and trust between the group members increases.

Norming

3.12 The third stage is a period of **settling down**. There will be agreements about work sharing, individual requirements and expectations of output. The enthusiasm and brainstorming of the second stage may be less apparent, but norms and **procedures may evolve** which enable methodical working to be introduced and maintained.

Performing

3.13 In the fourth stage the group sets to work to **execute its task.** Difficulties of growth and development no longer hinder the group's objectives.

3.14 This is theoretical analysis and it would be misleading to suggest that these four stages always follow in a clearly defined progression, or that the development of a group must be a slow and complicated process. Where the task to be performed is urgent, or where team members are highly motivated, the fourth stage will be reached very quickly while the earlier stages will be hard to distinguish.

Marketing at Work

It may be possible to apply Tuckman's ideas to the **management of work groups**.

The Nationwide Building Society has introduced self-managed teams into its administrative centre. The progress of the change can be described in Tuckman's terms. The project also illustrates how *management input* can contribute to the process.

Part C: Managing people

At the **forming** stage, management provided extra training in team building, conflict management and job-specific skills. Leaders were appointed, but in coaching rather than directive roles. The need to learn new skills produced a temporary dip in performance.

The **storming** stage started at the same time, with some leaders fearing a loss of control and some team members objecting to what they saw as more work for the same rewards.

Norming was an important part of the project and crucial to the management's intentions. One management input was the publication of a series of **performance measures** for each team. A **sense of ownership and responsibility** caused the teams to work to improve their results. For instance, peer pressure led to a 75% reduction in sickness absence. Similarly, a low-achieving group took advice from other groups and made a significant improvement in its performance. Consistent comment from team members during annual appraisals indicates that they are now committed to the new norms.

The **performing** stage has now been reached. Productivity is up by 50% and the centre's staff are now at the top of the organisation's annual staff survey in terms of job satisfaction.

Exam Tip

There was a question in the December 1999 exam that asked about team building in an organisation culture focussed on individuals. The examiner complained wearily about answers that consisted of little more than a Tuckman theory dump. This is a very important point. Theory is very important but you must **apply** it to the setting given in the question. In this particular question there was an emphasis on the use of temporary teams to respond to changing customer requirements.

Action Programme 2

What norms and customs are there in the group you are part of or familiar with? What do you have to do to become part of its culture? Is there a non-conformist in the group - someone who doesn't fit in: how is that person treated?

Creating an effective team

3.15 The criteria of group effectiveness are:

   (a) fulfilment of task and organisation goals
   (b) satisfaction of group members

3.16 A useful way of looking at the problem of how a supervisor or manager can create an effective team is to take a **contingency approach**. Handy suggested that group effectiveness (**outcomes**) depends on the **givens** and **intervening factors** in the diagram below.

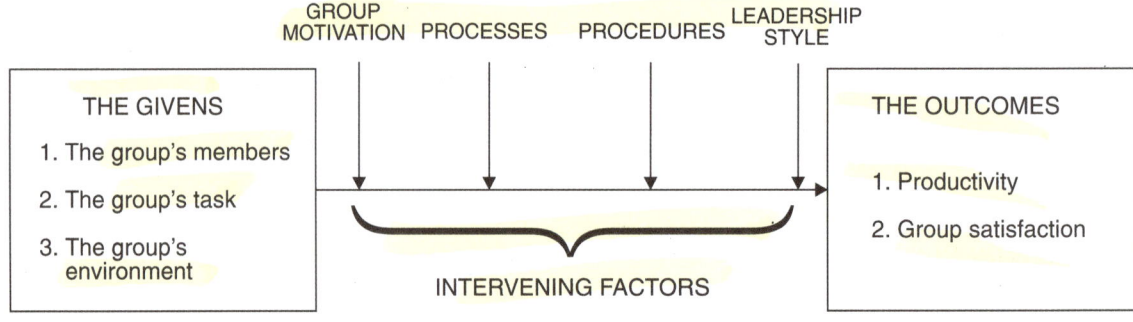

6: Managing the team

The givens

3.17 The personalities of the members of the team, and their personal goals, will help to determine the group's personality and goals. Individuals are likely to be influenced more strongly by a small group than by a large group in which they may be unable to participate effectively in team decisions.

3.18 The nature of the task must have some bearing on how a group should be managed.

- If a job must be done urgently, it is often necessary to dictate how things should be done, rather than to encourage a participatory style of working.

- Jobs that are routine, unimportant and undemanding will be insufficient to motivate either individuals or the group as a whole.

3.19 The group's environment relates to the physical surroundings at work and to inter-group relations. An open-plan office, in which the members of the group are closely situated, is conducive to group cohesion. A group's attitudes will also be affected by its relationship with other groups, which may be friendly, neutral or hostile. Where groups are in competition with other groups, they become more closely knit among themselves, are better motivated and more task-focused. Teams playing games show this kind of motivation.

Intervening factors

3.20 Of the intervening factors, we will be discussing motivation in more detail later and we will go on to talk about leadership and leadership style in the following section. With regard to processes and procedures, groups are much the same as individuals: research indicates that a team which tackles its work systematically will be more effective than one which muddles through. Note that it is the intervening factors that a manager is likely to be able to manipulate.

The outcomes

3.21 Ideally, the group and its work will be managed so that efforts towards high productivity will also lead to the satisfaction of personal and group needs such as job satisfaction, respect and cohesion. A **participative style of management** (see below) may contribute to this. However, as in the Bank Wiring observation room discussed below, individuals and the groups may have goals which prevent high output.

Marketing at Work

Elton Mayo's work sheds light on the importance of groups within an organisation. The '*Hawthorne Studies*' were conducted at the Hawthorne plant of the Western Electric Company.

(a) **Stage one**. The company investigated the effects of lighting on production. To management's surprise, **output increased whatever they did with the lighting** - even when the experimental group was subjected to very poor lighting conditions. Mayo was called in to identify the 'mystery' factor at work.

(b) **Stage two**. The **Relay Assembly Test Room**. Six women were separated from the others in a different room, where they were observed under changing working conditions. In most cases, the women were consulted in advance about the changes. Productivity rose - whatever the changes, good or bad! Mayo concluded that this was what was later called '**the Hawthorne effect**': **the response of the women appeared to be affected by their sense of being a group singled out for attention.**

(c) **Stage three**. Stage two had suggested that employee attitudes and values were important. The company set up an interview programme designed to survey attitudes towards supervision, jobs and working conditions. The major conclusion was that relationships with people at work were important to employees.

Part C: Managing people

(d) **Stage four**. The **Bank Wiring Observation Room**. Fourteen men were put in an observation room to work under more or less normal conditions. **The group was seen to set its own rules, attitudes and standards of output**. Its behaviour became oriented towards its own interests in a way that seemed beyond the supervisor's control. In other words, the group had developed into a powerful, self-protecting informal organisation.

The conclusions of the studies were that individual members must be seen as part of a group, and that **informal groups exercise a powerful influence in the workplace:** supervisors and managers need to take account of **social needs** if they wish to secure commitment to organisational goals.

4 EFFECTIVE AND INEFFECTIVE TEAMS 12/00

4.1 Characteristics of an ideal team

(a) Each individual gets the **support of the team and a sense of identity and belonging** which encourages loyalty and hard work on the group's behalf.

(b) **Skills, information and ideas are shared**, so that the team's capabilities are greater than those of the individuals.

(c) New ideas can be tested, reactions taken into account and persuasive skills brought into play in **group discussion for decision making and problem solving.**

(d) Each individual is encouraged to participate and contribute and thus becomes personally **involved in and committed to the team's activities.**

(e) Goodwill, trust and respect can be built up between individuals, so that **communication is encouraged** and potential problems more easily overcome.

4.2 Unfortunately, team working is rarely such an undiluted success.

(a) Awareness of **group norms** and the desire to be acceptable to the group may **restrict individual personality** and flair.

(b) **Too much discord.** Conflicting **roles and relationships** can cause difficulties in communicating effectively.

(c) **Personality problems** will harm performance if one member dislikes or distrusts another; is too dominant or so timid that the value of his ideas is lost; or is so negative that constructive communication is rendered impossible.

(d) **Rigid leadership** and procedures may **strangle initiative and creativity** in individuals.

(e) **Differences of opinion** and political conflicts of interest are always likely.

(f) **Too much harmony.** Teams work best when there is room for disagreement. The cosy consensus of the group may prevent consideration of alternatives, constructive criticism or conflict. *I L Janis* called this **group think**. Similarly, efforts to paper over differences lead to bland recommendations.

(g) **Corporate culture and reward systems.** Teams may fail if the company promotes and rewards the individual at the expense of the group.

(h) **Too many meetings.** Teams should not try to do everything together. Not only does this waste time in meetings, but team members are exposed to less diversity of thought.

(i) **Powerlessness.** People will not bother to work in a team or on a task force if its recommendations are ignored.

6: Managing the team

Appraising group effectiveness

4.3 Supervisors who wish to improve the effectiveness of their work groups must be able to identify the different characteristics of an effective and an ineffective group. No one factor on its own will be significant, but taken collectively the factors may indicate how well or badly the group is doing.

> **Action Programme 3**
>
> How would you determine whether a team was effective or ineffective? Think about both quantitative and qualitative factors which may characterise the two extremes. Remember that individual attitudes will affect many things, as well as the dynamics of the group.

> **Action Programme 4**
>
> Consider your group at work. How effective is it in terms of (a) doing what the organisation wants it to do in the way of tasks and (b) offering satisfaction to its members?
>
> What can you (or your manager) do to improve the effectiveness of the group? Think about your contribution, if you are a member, and your ability to adjust the 'intervening factors' in the group situation, if you are its leader. What is there in the group membership, the task and the environment (ie the 'givens') that hold the group back from being as effective as it might be?

4.4 EXAMPLE CASE STUDY

You have recently been appointed to manage a group of 10 people and you have found evidence that all is not well. The output of the section is not high. Although overtime is regularly worked, there are substantial backlogs and targets are missed. Absenteeism is high with the same people absent regularly. They produce poor excuses or none at all. People fall out over trivial issues and the lack of co-operation impairs efficiency. You feel a general air of lethargy, if not hostility. What do you propose to do about it? How will you know when you are succeeding?

4.5 SOLUTION

There are various possible causes of this serious situation. The failure to achieve targets might be due to inadequate planning, failure of the manager to tell individuals what their targets are, and lack of a feedback and control system to ensure that action is taken when needed. Some individual group members might be unsuited to their jobs and this might help to explain poor efficiency. Inadequate working conditions and poor organisation of the group's work routines might also be at fault. The workload of the group might be excessive so that group members no longer try to achieve targets. However, an improvement in efficiency would increase output and the group is clearly not performing well enough.

4.6 The problem of absenteeism might be caused by low morale, but the absence of disciplinary action against persistent offenders can only create a sense of unfairness amongst the others. This could help to explain the hostility and conflicts over trivial matters between group members.

Part C: Managing people

4.7 The lack of co-operation might be caused by poor planning and supervision, or by poor motivation of staff and inter-personal dislikes. Staff have clearly been reluctant to refer matters to their manager, since conflicts have arisen over trivial matters. Good supervision should prevent minor disagreements from escalating into conflict in the first place.

What should be done?

4.8 The effectiveness of the group should be assessed initially in terms of the group itself, the group's task and the group's working environment.

(a) The **personalities, characteristics, skills and experience** of each individual group member should be assessed. Inter-personal hostility between particular individuals should be identified. Habitual absentees should be identified.

(b) The **tasks** of the group should be assessed. Are the tasks of the group too difficult for the group members? Is the workload too heavy for a group of ten?

(c) The **environment** of the group should be examined. Do the individuals who have to co-operate closely with each other actually sit close together? Is the equipment used by the group adequate for their job?

4.9 After an initial assessment of these matters, you should call a group meeting. At the meeting, you should express disquiet at the state of affairs, and explain why. The group members should be encouraged to state their own views, after which you should state your intention to do something about the problem. An outline of the proposed steps should be given.

(a) The group as a whole must know what its **planning targets** are, and each individual member of the group should be given standards or targets to work towards.

(b) If there is a need for **overtime**, the quantity of overtime that ought to be required should be built into the plan. You should ask individuals whether they are unable or unwilling to work these amounts of overtime. If there is a need for more staff, you could pursue the matter through your superior, and let the staff know what is happening about it.

(c) There should be regular **feedback** to individual group members on their performance, against target. If performance is below standard, you should discuss what control action or remedies might be necessary.

(d) **Persistent absenteeism** must be **stopped**. It should be made clear to all group members that disciplinary measures will be taken against offenders. You should than apply discipline consistently and keep to your word.

(e) The need for **co-operation** between group members should be made clear and can be improved by good planning. You should set a timescale for improvements and use regular group meetings to review progress, identify problems and work out difficulties.

(f) You should give **time and attention to individual members** of the group. **Training needs** should be identified, and group members given appropriate training where required. You should get to know each individual, identifying their needs and interests, and trying to encourage them. If some individuals continue to show personal animosity, or to perform badly, you should express concern, and indicate that their next formal appraisal will not be favourable.

(g) The **techniques and equipment** used by the group should be improved where necessary (and if resources are available). You should make whatever alterations to the office layout and environment seem beneficial and practicable.

6: Managing the team

How to gauge success

4.10 Two things should happen when matters are improving.

- The **productivity of the group should improve** and targets will be achieved.
- There should be an apparent improvement in the **attitudes** of group members.

4.11 More specific improvements will occur. Several of these can be quantified and monitored.

- **Absenteeism** should be much lower.
- There should be **higher output**.
- Individual targets as well as group targets should be achieved.
- Individuals should display a **greater commitment** to their work and the achievement of targets.
- **Communication** between group members should be more free and open.
- **Conflicts** over minor matters should no longer occur.
- Group members should show signs of trying to help each other by offering **constructive suggestions and ideas**.
- Group members will show signs of wanting to develop their abilities further.

4.12 It is the manager's responsibility to monitor the effectiveness of the group and be constantly seeking ways of improving it. The manager should bring in new ideas and people and set new challenges and targets Although there is a tendency not to change a winning team, **even a successful group can become complacent and stale**.

Action Programme 5

Draft a short report to the manager of a team you are involved with. In it you should make three specific recommendations for improving team performance and the ways in which you suggest the effect of these changes is monitored.

The dangers of group think

4.13 *Handy* notes that 'ultra-cohesive groups can be dangerous because in the organisational context the group must serve the organisation, not itself'. If a group is completely absorbed with its own maintenance, members and priorities, it can become dangerously blinkered to what is going on around it, and may confidently forge ahead in a completely wrong direction.

4.14 The cosy consensus of the group may prevent consideration of alternatives, constructive criticism or conflicts. There are several symptoms of **group think**.

- A sense of invulnerability and blindness to the risk involved in pet strategies
- Rationalisation of inconsistent facts
- Moral blindness and a feeling that might is right
- A tendency to stereotype outsiders and enemies
- Strong group pressure to quell dissent
- Self-censorship by members
- Mutual support and solidarity to guard decisions

4.15 Group think is rife at the top and centre of organisations. Victims take great risks in their decisions, fail to recognise failure, and are highly resistant to unpalatable information. Such

groups must actively encourage **self-criticism**; welcome **outside ideas** and evaluation; and respond positively to **conflicting evidence**.

5 THE MANAGER'S ROLE WITHIN THE TEAM   12/99, 12/00

As a leader

5.1 **Leadership** is the process of influencing others to work **willingly** towards a goal, and to the best of their capabilities. 'The essence of leadership is **followership**. In other words it is the willingness of people to follow that makes a person a leader' (*Koontz, O'Donnell, Weihrich*).

5.2 Leadership comes about in a number of different ways.

- A manager is **appointed** to a position of authority within the organisation. Leadership of subordinates is a function of the position.
- Some leaders are **elected**.
- Other leaders **emerge** by popular choice or through their personal drive.

5.3 The personal, physical or expert power of leaders is more important than position power alone. Within teams and groups of equal colleagues leadership can and does change.

5.4 If a manager has indifferent or poor leadership qualities then the team would still do the job, but not efficiently. A good leader can ensure more than simply a compliance with orders. **Leadership and management are different. Managing** is concerned with logic, structure, analysis and control. If done well, it produces predictable results on time. **Leadership** requires a different mind set and the leader has different tasks.

- **Creating a sense of direction**
- **Communicating the vision**
- **Energising, inspiring and motivating**

All of these activities involve dealing with people rather than things. A manager needs leadership skills to be effective.

Leadership traits

5.5 Early writers believed that leadership was an inherent characteristic: you either had it, or you didn't: leaders were born, not made. Studies on leadership concentrated on the personal traits of existing and past leadership figures.

5.6 It is now felt that leadership appropriate to a given work situation can be learned.

Action Programme 6

Think about your own supervisor or manager. Would you consider him or her a leader? Are you a leader to your subordinates (if you are in an appropriate position)? Why, or why not?

Identify someone who you would consider a real leader. What qualities can you identify in that person that makes them a leader in your eyes? Could those qualities be taught somehow?

Does your organisation create or encourage leaders? What training courses offered by your employer are aimed at developing leadership qualities and skills?

6: Managing the team

> **Key concept**
> Managerial style was briefly discussed in Chapter 2. **Leadership style** is a similar, though wider ranging concept, concerning the basic assumptions managers make when dealing with their subordinates.

Leadership styles

5.7 Four different types or styles of leadership were identified by *Huneryager and Heckman*.

  (a) **Dictatorial**. The manager **forces** subordinates to work by threatening punishment and penalties.

  (b) **Autocratic**. Decision making is centralised in the hands of the leader, who does not encourage participation by subordinates; indeed, subordinates' ideas might be actively discouraged and obedience to orders would be expected from them.

  (c) **Democratic**. Decision-making is decentralised, and shared by subordinates in **participative group action**. To be truly democratic, the subordinate must be willing to participate.

  (d) **Laissez-faire**. Subordinates are given **little or no direction at all**, and are allowed to establish their own objectives and make all their own decisions.

5.8 A similar spectrum from autocratic to democratic, but without the extremes at either end, was suggested by the research unit at Ashridge Management College (**the Ashridge studies**).

  (a) The **autocratic or *tells* style**. This is characterised by one-way communication between the manager and the subordinate, with the manager telling the subordinate what to do. The leader makes all the decisions and issues instructions, expecting them to be obeyed without question.

  (b) The **persuasive or *sells* style**. Managers make all the decisions, but believe that subordinates need to be **motivated** to do what is required.

  (c) The **consultative style**. This involves discussion between the manager and the subordinates involved in carrying out a decision, but the manager retains the right to make the decision.

  (d) The **democratic or *joins* style**. The leader joins the group of subordinates to make a decision on the basis of consensus. It is the most democratic style of leadership. The joins style is most effective where all subordinates have equal knowledge and can therefore contribute in equal measure to decisions.

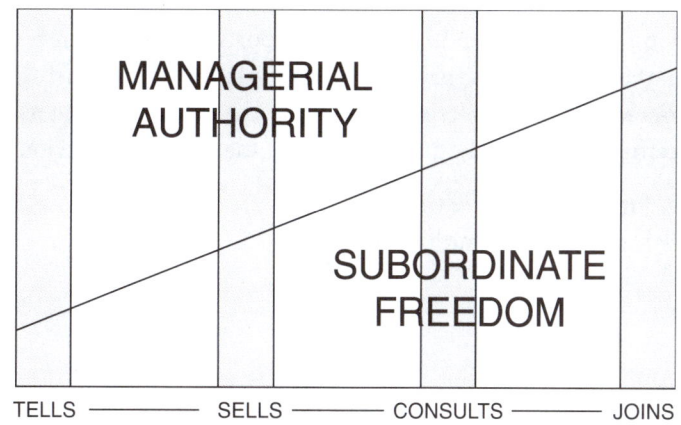

5.9 These four divisions of management style are really a simplification of a continuum or range of styles, from the most dictatorial to the most laissez-faire.

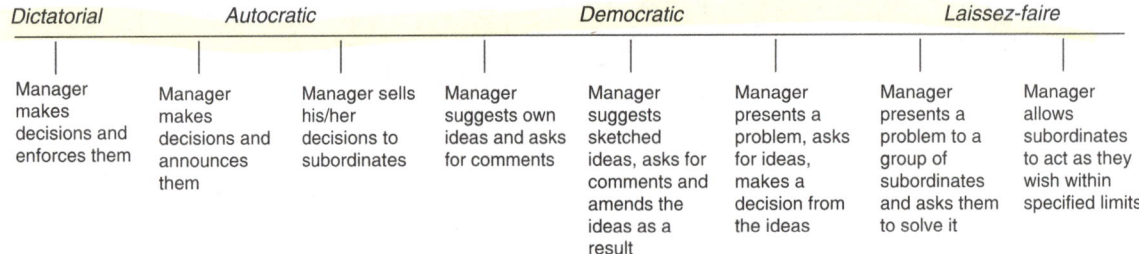

Dictatorial	Autocratic		Democratic				Laissez-faire
Manager makes decisions and enforces them	Manager makes decisions and announces them	Manager sells his/her decisions to subordinates	Manager suggests own ideas and asks for comments	Manager suggests sketched ideas, asks for comments and amends the ideas as a result	Manager presents a problem, asks for ideas, makes a decision from the ideas	Manager presents a problem to a group of subordinates and asks them to solve it	Manager allows subordinates to act as they wish within specified limits

This **continuum of leadership styles** was first suggested by *Tannenbaum and Schmidt*.

5.10 There are differing views as to which of these leadership styles is most effective. The probable truth is that the degree of effectiveness of a particular leadership style will depend on the work environment, and the character of the leader and subordinates.

5.11 The Ashridge studies made the following findings with regard to leadership style and employee motivation.

(a) Subordinates preferred the **consults** style of leadership, but mainly thought their managers exercised the **tells** or **sells** style.

(b) The attitude of subordinates towards their work was most favourable amongst those who thought that their boss exercised the 'consults' style.

(c) The least favourable attitudes were found amongst subordinates who were unable to perceive a consistent style of leadership in their boss. In other words, subordinates are unsettled by a boss who chops and changes between autocracy, persuasion, consultation and democracy.

Action Programme 7

Take some time to consider these four styles and produce a list of the strengths and weaknesses of the following leadership styles.

Tells
Sells
Consults
Joins

Blake and Mouton

5.12 By emphasising style of leadership and the importance of human relations, it is all too easy to forget that a **manager is primarily responsible for ensuring that tasks are done** efficiently. *Blake and Mouton* tried to address the balance of management thinking, with their **management grid** based on two aspects of managerial behaviour.

- Concern for production, ie the **task**
- Concern for people and human relations

6: Managing the team

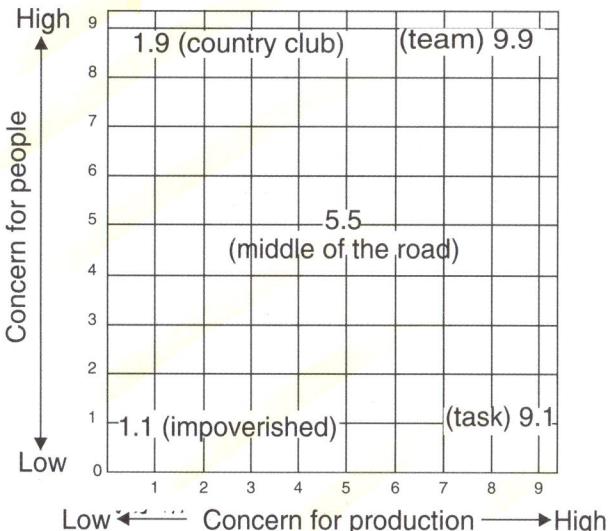

5.13 The extreme cases shown on the grid are:

(a) 1.1 **impoverished**: manager is lazy, showing little effort or concern for staff or work targets.

(b) 1.9 **country club**: manager is attentive to staff needs and has developed satisfying relationships. However, little attention is paid to achieving results.

(c) 9.1 **task management**: almost total concentration on achieving results. **People's needs are virtually ignored** and conditions of work are so arranged that people cannot interfere to any significant extent.

(d) 5.5 **middle of the road or the dampened pendulum**: adequate performance through balancing the necessity to get out work while maintaining morale of people at a satisfactory level.

(e) 9.9 **team**: high performance manager who achieves high work accomplishment through leading committed people who identify with the organisational aims.

Action Programme 8

Think about yourself and other managers you know. Where would you place them on the grid?

Exam Tip

A December 1999 question asked about management style in a context of organisational change. The examiner commented on the relevance of the setting to current real world developments.

You should try to keep abreast of what is happening in the world of management by reading the business pages of a good newspaper. You will then be able to give relevant examples in your ansers. You will also find that the questions themselves seem less threatening, because they are often based on contemporary developments.

A December 2000 question asked about the role of the leader in improving team performance. So the issue of task-centred and people-centred leadership is relevant here. You could also have brought in appraisal.

Part C: Managing people

> **Key concept**
>
> **Theory X and Theory Y**
>
> McGregor discussed the way in which managers handle people according to the **assumptions** they have about them, and about what kind of management style will obtain their efforts. He identified **two extreme sets of assumptions (Theory X and Theory Y)** and explored how management style differs according to which set of assumptions is adopted.

5.14 **Theory X** is the theory that the average human being has an **inherent dislike of work** and will avoid it if possible. Human beings **prefer to be directed**, wishing to avoid responsibility. They have relatively little ambition and want security above all. They are self-centred, with little interest in the organisation's needs. They are **resistant to change**, gullible and easily led. They **must be coerced, controlled, directed, offered reward or threatened with punishment to get them to put forth adequate effort** towards the achievement of the organisation's objectives.

5.15 According to **Theory Y**, however, the expenditure of physical and mental effort in **work is as natural as play or rest**. The ordinary person does **not** inherently dislike work: according to the conditions it may be a source of satisfaction or punishment. Extensive control is not the only means of obtaining effort. **People exercise self-direction** and self-control in the service of **objectives to which they are committed**: they are not naturally passive, or resistant, to organisational objectives, **but have been made so by experience**.

5.16 The most significant reward that can be offered is the satisfaction of the individual's need for personal growth and development. The average human being can learn not only to accept but also to seek responsibility. Managements should create conditions and methods that will enable individuals to integrate their own and the organisation's goals, by personal development.

5.17 McGregor intentionally polarised his theories, and recognised that managers' assumptions may be somewhere along the line between the two extremes. He also recognised that the **assumptions were self-perpetuating**. If people are treated as though they are Theory X people, because of management assumptions, Theory X behaviour will in fact be induced - thus confirming management in its beliefs and practices.

> **Action Programme 9**
>
> What is the most common leadership style used in your office? What is it about the culture and work of the firm, or the personalities involved, that make this the most-used style?
>
> What style would you like your boss to adopt? What drawbacks, if any, can you see in that style from the leader's point of view?

5.18 **EXAMPLE CASE STUDY**

Derek is a young retail manager who, after completing his Advanced Certificate examinations recently, was transferred to a small old-established company outlet.

At his first progress review with his superior, he was very confident and enthusiastic about numerous initiatives which he had already taken or was about to take. Derek expressed disappointment that his staff were so reactionary and unco-operative.

Enquiries by Derek's superior among the staff uncovered general dissatisfaction about Derek's leadership. The younger ones are frightened of him, and feel he has no interest in

them. They say he is always in a hurry, and they have no idea of whether their work is up to his requirements or not.

The older ones, who have worked in the company for years, are very worried about his apparently arbitrary and risky decisions. Others are resentful and frustrated that Derek never bothers to listen to their ideas. Derek has been informed of these comments.

Recommend the behaviour which Derek should adopt to improve the situation.

5.19 SOLUTION

Derek's problem is one of leadership style.

5.20 We are told that Derek is very confident and takes many initiatives, but does not understand why others resist his decisions. He appears to take decisions without consulting his subordinates and then tells them what his decision is. Having taken decisions, he appears to leave his staff to get on and shows no obvious interest in what they are doing. This is a self-contradictory combination of the **autocratic** and **laissez-faire** styles.

5.21 The problems with his leadership style are evident in the dissatisfaction of the subordinates.

(a) The younger ones want to do their job well but get no personal interest or attention from Derek. They do not know whether they are doing well or badly nor by what standards they may be judged.

(b) Some people are frustrated because they are not allowed to participate in the decision-making process. Their opinions are not asked for, and their ideas are ignored.

(c) The older ones are upset by Derek's radical approach to the decisions he takes. Derek is failing to explain his reasons and persuade the older ones of the need for change.

Advice to Derek

5.22 The advice to Derek should be to urge him to **recognise his supervisory responsibilities**.

(a) He seems unaware of the problems his leadership style is causing. His performance will be judged on the achievements of his store **as a whole**, not just on his own personal efforts. If his subordinates are performing badly, he will be held responsible.

(b) His attitude to his staff should change. In general terms, a more participative style of leadership is needed.

(c) Derek should give each of his staff individual attention, counselling and encouragement. He must find time to devote to this task, and he must not be too busy with other work to bother about his subordinates.

(d) In addition to giving subordinates individual attention, he should also try to encourage a group identity and cohesiveness. Regular meetings in a group with his subordinates should be recommended to him.

Derek should tackle each of the specific worries of his staff.

5.23 The younger ones require **closer supervision**, and Derek should spend more time with them. He should set clear standards for their work and, at regular appraisal sessions, let them know whether they are meeting these standards.

5.24 In the case of those who are **resentful** that Derek never listens to their ideas, Derek should be much more prepared to **listen**. Their ideas might not always be good ones, but a task of

supervision is to develop staff. This can be done by encouraging ideas and initiatives, discussing them, and then explaining why they might or might not be good ones. A more consultative or participative style of leadership will almost certainly reduce their frustrations, and also help to develop his own skills and experience.

5.25 The older staff have a lot of experience in the department and Derek should try to see the benefit of making use of that. Derek should explain his reasons for changes. Knowing why change is needed helps to reduce resistance to it. He should also explain how the staff will be affected personally by any changes, and how they can adapt to them. Their specific responsibilities and targets as a result of any change should be spelled out clearly, and Derek should try to convince them that they are capable of carrying out new tasks well. Their experience should be used constructively, whereas currently it is being expressed negatively in frustration and resistance to change.

5.26 It is not easy for a manager to change his leadership style overnight, and Derek should seek advice as to how to introduce the necessary changes. Regular staff meetings would be one suggestion.

5.27 Derek should be counselled regularly by his boss as he tries to change. A formal review of his success in changing his style, and the effects of his new approach on the branch's performance and attitudes, should be made after some months.

The manager as a team member?

5.28 Besides taking the role as leader the manager may also be a team member. The marketing director may lead the marketing team, but be a member of the senior management team. Recognising which 'hat' you are wearing is important in these situations. There is only room for one leader at a time and it is important not to usurp the authority of the established leader. A team player should support by playing a full part, contributing to discussions but not overriding the leader's approach.

6: Managing the team

Chapter Roundup

- A group is 'any collection of people who perceive themselves to be a group'. An 'effective' group is one which achieves its allotted task **and** satisfies its members. Teams are becoming more important as a means of organising work.

- Groups function through interaction between individual members and the blend of their skills and abilities.

- Collections of individuals develop into groups. A common pattern to this process has been identified by Tuckman.

    Forming (ie getting together, to know each other);
    Storming (conflict and creativity);
    Norming (the 'settling down' stage);
    Performing (becoming effective and 'getting on with it').

- Groups prize loyalty, which usually expresses itself in conformity to **norms of behaviour** which bind the group together. Groups are capable of exerting considerable social pressure on individuals to conform.

- Belbin developed a model of the eight **roles** required - evenly spread - in an effective team.

- The management problem is how to create an efficient work group.

- If managers can motivate groups (and individuals) to work well, the sense of pride in their own competence might create **job satisfaction** through belonging to the group and performing its tasks; it will also mean fulfilment of those tasks and hence the organisation's goals.

- Handy takes a **contingency approach** to the problem of group effectiveness which is constructed out of the **givens**, and **intervening factors** which generate **outcomes**. Management can operate on both 'givens' and intervening factors' to affect the 'outcomes'.

- **Leadership is** the process of influencing others to work willingly towards the achievement of organisational goals. Theories of leadership have taken several different approaches.

    Traits (common characteristics of leaders, which are innate)
    Styles which can be adopted, lying on one of several continuum
    Dictatorial to autocratic to democratic to laissez-faire
    Tells to sells to consults to joins
    Wholly task centred to wholly human relations centred
    Theory X and **Theory Y** assumptions
    Functions, in the context of task, group and individual needs.

- Leadership is fundamental to the effective working of a group and **skills of leadership can be learnt and improved**.

Part C: Managing people

Quick Quiz

1. What attributes distinguish a group or team from a random collection of individuals? (see para 2.2)
2. What are the functions of groups from the point of view of the organisation? (2.5)
3. What are the main issues to be taken into account when managing a group? (2.9)
4. What stages does a team go through as it matures? (3.8)
5. What happens during the norming stage? (3.12)
6. What does Handy mean by the term 'outcomes' in his contingency approach? (3.21)
7. List four of the characteristics you would expect in an ideally functioning group. (4.1)
8. How will you know when your measures to improve the performance of a team are being successful? (4.11)
9. What is meant by the term *group think* and why is it a problem? (4.14 - 4.15)
10. How does leadership come about? (5.2)
11. Are all managers leaders? (5.4)
12. What were the four leadership styles identified by Huneryager and Heckman? (5.7)
13. What leadership style, if any, do employees prefer? (5.11)
14. What are the axes of the management grid? (5.12)
15. What is Theory X? (5.14)

Action Programme Review

3

Effective teams	Ineffective teams
Quantifiable factors	
Low rate of labour turnover	High rate of labour turnover
Low absenteeism	High absenteeism
High output and productivity	Low output and productivity
Good quality of output	Poor quality of output
There are few stoppages and interruptions to work	Much time is wasted owing to disruption of work flow
Qualitative factors	
There is a high commitment to the achievement of targets and organisational goals	There is a low commitment to targets
There is a clear understanding of the group's work	There is no understanding of organisational goals or the role of the group (or there are no clear organisational goals)
There is a clear understanding of the role of each person within the group	There is confusion about the role of each person and uncertainty
There is free and open communication between members of the group and trust between members	There is mistrust between group members and suspicion of group's leader
There is idea sharing	There is little idea sharing
The group is good at generating new ideas	The group does not generate any good new ideas
Group members try to help each other out	Group members make negative and hostile criticisms about each other's work
There is group problem solving which gets to the root causes of the work problem	Work problems are dealt with superficially, with attention paid to the symptoms but not the cause.
Group members seek a united consensus of opinion	Group members hold strongly opposed views
The group is sufficiently motivated to be able to carry on working in the absence of its leader	The group needs its leader there to get work done

Style	Characteristics	Strengths	Weaknesses
Tells (autocratic)	The manager makes all the decisions, and issues instructions which must be obeyed without question.	(1) Quick decisions can be made when speed is required. (2) It is the most efficient type of leadership for highly-programmed routine work.	(1) It does not encourage the sub-ordinates to give their opinions when these might be useful. (2) Communications between the manager and subordinate will be one-way and the manager will not know until afterwards whether the orders have been properly understood. (3) It does not encourage initiative and commitment from subordinates.
Sells (persuasive)	The manager still makes all the decisions, but believes that subordinates have to be motivated to accept them in order to carry them out properly.	(1) Employees are made aware of the reasons for decisions. (2) Selling decisions to staff might make them more committed. (3) Staff will have a better idea of what to do when unforeseen events arise in their work because the manager will have explained his intentions.	(1) Communications are still largely one-way. Sub-ordinates might not accept the decisions. (2) It does not encourage initiative and commitment from subordinates.
Consults	The manager confers with subordinates and takes their views into account, but has the final say.	(1) Employees are involved in decisions before they are made. This encourages motivation through greater interest and involvement. (2) An agreed consensus of opinion can be reached and for some decisions consensus can be an advantage rather than a weak compromise. (3) Employees can contribute their knowledge and experience to help in solving more complex problems.	(1) It might take much longer to reach decisions. (2) Subordinates might be too inexperienced to formulate mature opinions and give practical advice. (3) Consultation can too easily turn into a façade concealing, basically, a sells style.
Joins (democratic)	Leader and followers make the decision on the basis of consensus.	(1) It can provide high motivation and commitment from employees. (2) It shares the other advantages of the consultative style (especially where subordinates have expert power).	(1) The authority of the manager might be undermined. (2) Decision-making might become a very long process, and clear decisions might be difficult to reach. (3) Subordinates might lack enough experience.

Now try illustrative questions 8 and 9 at the end of the Study Text

7 Recruitment and Selection

Chapter Topic List	Syllabus reference
1 Setting the scene	
2 Expanding the team: the importance of search and selection	2.5
3 Planning and managing the search process	2.5
4 Recruitment interviews and selection	2.5
5 Integrating new members into the team	2.5

Learning Outcome

- Students will be able to describe the role of HRM planning and its contribution to ensuring effective levels of marketing staffing and skills.

Examples of Marketing at Work

- Management style at Texas Instruments
- Proctor and Gamble
- Internal recruitment at Logica

1 SETTING THE SCENE

1.1 Chapter 6 discussed how teams might be formed and managed, but often the membership of a team or department changes. As people leave, or the department grows, new people are needed.

1.2 In Section 2, we start with the circumstances in which the need for new recruits is identified, and we show how the overall human resources needs of a firm can be broken down into the need for individuals to fill specific jobs.

1.3 In Section 3, we discuss the labour market in which the firm is perhaps a seller. The firm needs to identify the people it is advertising to, draw up an appropriate job description, and develop the right job advertisements in the right media: after all, the firm is 'selling' the job to a potential 'customer', the successful recruit.

1.4 We then discuss in Section 4 what happens to those applicants who apply, and here we show the use of application forms, selection interviews and testing. Finally, in Section 5 we describe the recruit's first few days in the office.

1.5 In Chapter 8, we go on to see how employees' performance can be appraised and improved. New recruits - and existing workers - need training and appraisal.

Links with other papers

1.6 Recruitment and human resources underpin the effectiveness of *Marketing Operations* and you may find your knowledge useful in the context of the **Marketing/Customer Interface**. The availability or lack of availability of resources can be a key component of the marketing plan.

2 EXPANDING THE TEAM: THE IMPORTANCE OF SEARCH AND SELECTION   12/99, 12/00

Human resource planning

2.1 Human resource planning concerns the acquisition, utilisation, improvement and return of an enterprise's human resources. Human resource planning deals with:

- Recruitment
- Retention (company loyalty, to retain skills and reduce staff turnover)
- Downsizing (reducing staff numbers)
- Training and retraining to enhance the skills base

Part C: Managing people

2.2 The process of human resources planning

```
1. STRATEGIC ANALYSIS
  • of the environment
  • of the organisation's manpower strengths    [SWOT]
    and weaknesses, opportunities and threats
  • of the organisation's use of manpower
  • of the organisation's objectives
          ↓
2. FORECASTING
  • of internal demand and supply
  • of external supply
          ↓
3. JOB ANALYSIS
  • investigating the tasks performed in each job
  • identifying the skills required
          ↓
4. IMPLEMENTATION
  • training and developing existing staff
  • recruiting required staff
```

2.3 It will often be necessary to bring new people into the team.

- To fill an identified skills gap
- To replace staff who have been promoted or who have left
- Because the work of the team has expanded

The process of recruitment is very important. Getting the wrong person can cause problems within the existing group, and the person will require either extensive training and development, or will require replacing, with all the attendant disruption this involves.

2.4 The overall aim of the recruitment and selection process is to obtain the employees required by the human resource plan, with maximum efficiency. This process can be broken down into three main stages:

(a) **Definition of requirements**, including the preparation of job descriptions and specifications.

(b) **Recruitment.** The identification and attraction of potential applicants, inside and outside the organisation.

(c) **Selection.** Selection is the part of the employee resourcing process which involves choosing between applicants for jobs: it is largely a 'negative' process, eliminating unsuitable applicants.

2.5 A marketing manager may have the help and support of **human resources (HR) specialists** during the process but in smaller organisations, he or she will be responsible for all aspects of the search and selection process. Many firms outsource the early stages of the process to consultants or agencies.

An approach to recruitment and selection

2.6 If not approached systematically, the process of recruitment and selection can become costly and time-consuming. A methodical approach will probably involve the following stages:

(a) Detailed **human resource planning,** defining what resources the organisation needs to meet its objectives. At marketing team level, this activity would require an analysis of the future marketing skills needed. This requirement will flow from the overall marketing plan which, in turn, is one of the outputs from the wider **corporate planning** process. The recruitment of an individual member of marketing staff is thus set in the context of the overall strategic control of the organisation.

(b) **Job analysis,** so that for any given job there are two things.

- **A job description** describing the nature and responsibilities of the job
- **A person specification** describing the ideal candidate for the job

(c) An identification of **vacancies,** from the requirements of the human resources plan or by a **job requisition** from the section needing a new post holder.

(d) Evaluation of the **sources of labour,** which should be in the HR plan. Internal and external sources, and media for reaching both, will be considered.

(e) **Advertising** has three functions.

- To attract the attention and interest of potentially suitable candidates
- To give a favourable (but accurate) impression of the job and the organisation
- To tell candidates how to apply

(f) **Processing applications** and assessing candidates

(g) **Notifying applicants** of the results of the selection process

Action Programme 1

Find out what the recruitment and selection procedures are in your organisation and who is responsible for each stage. A procedures manual might set this out, or you may need to ask someone - perhaps in the Personnel or Human Resources department. In your own experience, what part does the manager play in these procedures? Get hold of some of the documentation your company uses. We show specimens in this chapter, but practice and terminology varies, so your own 'house style' will be invaluable. Try to find three things.

- The job description for your job
- The personnel specification (if any) for your job
- If your firm is currently recruiting, a full set of the paperwork including the job ad

2.7 None of the stages in the recruitment process can be ignored or taken lightly if the best candidate for the post is to be found. Practical advice for running an interview is included in section 4 of this chapter.

2.8 Before the search process can begin managers have a great deal to do. When the need for a new member of the team is recognised, a careful review should be undertaken to ensure that an extra full time post is justified by the contribution the person is expected to make. Particular care is needed when the vacancy is due to a team member leaving. Simple replacement is not always appropriate. During the job holder's time in the job, the task itself may have changed, or the individual may have shaped the role differently from how it was advertised originally.

Part C: Managing people

Recent trends

2.9 Recent trends towards flexibility and multi-skilling have encouraged an approach which is oriented towards fitting the job to the person rather than fitting the person to the job.

(a) In a highly innovative market or technological environment rigid job descriptions would not be suitable. In order to 'thrive on chaos' (*Peters*), organisations should look at the skills and attributes of the people they employ, and gifted outsiders, and ask: 'What needs doing that this person would do best?'

(b) In a relatively informal environment, where all-round knowledge, skills and experience are highly valued and suitable external labour resources scarce, for example in management consultancy, this approach would give much-needed flexibility. The organisation would try to recruit, flexible, motivated and multi-skilled people without reference to any specific job description.

However, the **selection** approach is still the most common, and is suitable for most organisations with fairly well defined goals and structures.

Job analysis

2.10 **Job analysis** is 'the determination of the essential characteristics of a job' (British Standards Institute) - that is, the process of examining a job to identify its component parts and the circumstances in which it is performed.

2.11 Information elicited from a job analysis includes both **task-orientated** and **worker-orientated** details.

(a) **Initial requirements** of the employee include aptitudes, qualifications, experience and training required.

(b) **Duties and responsibilities** include physical aspects, mental effort, routine or requiring initiative, difficult or disagreeable features, consequences of failure, responsibilities for staff, materials, equipment or cash and so on.

(c) **Environment and conditions** include physical surroundings, with particular features (eg temperature, noise, hazards), remuneration, other conditions such as hours, shifts, travel, benefits, holidays, career prospects, provision of employee services (eg canteens, protective clothing).

(d) **Social factors** include size of the department, teamwork or isolation. The sort of people dealt with (eg senior management, the public), the amount of supervision and job status.

2.12 A job analysis may cause some concern among employees from fear of standards being raised, rates cut or redundancy imposed. The job analyst will need to gain confidence; this can be done in a variety of ways.

- Communicating (explaining the process, methods and purpose of the analysis)
- Being thorough and competent in carrying out the analysis
- Respecting the work flow of the department, which should not be disrupted
- Giving feedback on the results of the appraisal, and the achievement of its objectives

7: Recruitment and selection

Recruitment process

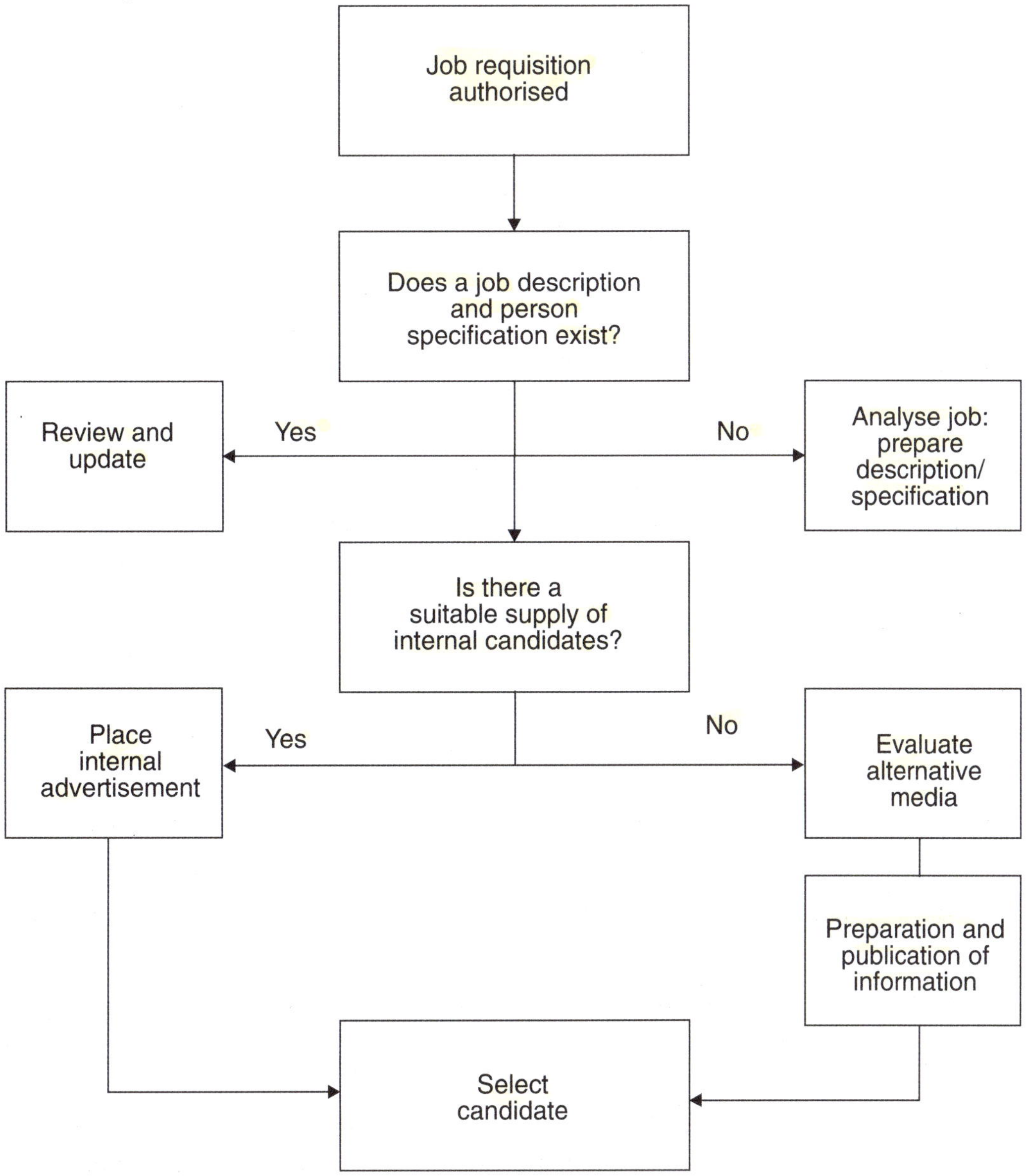

```
                    ┌─────────────────────┐
                    │   Job requisition   │
                    │     authorised      │
                    └──────────┬──────────┘
                               ▼
                    ┌─────────────────────┐
                    │ Does a job description │
                    │   and person         │
                    │ specification exist? │
                    └──────────────────────┘
     ┌──────────────┐  Yes          No  ┌──────────────┐
     │  Review and  │◄─────────  ──────►│ Analyse job: │
     │    update    │                   │   prepare    │
     │              │                   │ description/ │
     │              │                   │specification │
     └──────┬───────┘                   └──────┬───────┘
            │                                  │
            └──────────────┬───────────────────┘
                           ▼
                ┌─────────────────────┐
                │     Is there a      │
                │ suitable supply of  │
                │ internal candidates?│
                └─────────────────────┘
   ┌──────────┐  Yes                No  ┌──────────────┐
   │  Place   │◄────────     ──────────►│  Evaluate    │
   │ internal │                         │ alternative  │
   │advertis. │                         │    media     │
   └────┬─────┘                         └──────┬───────┘
        │                                      ▼
        │                          ┌──────────────────┐
        │                          │ Preparation and  │
        │                          │  publication of  │
        │                          │   information    │
        │                          └──────┬───────────┘
        │          ┌──────────────┐       │
        └─────────►│    Select    │◄──────┘
                   │  candidate   │
                   └──────────────┘
```

2.13 The product of the job analysis is usually a **job specification**. This is defined by *Bennett* (*Dictionary of Personnel and Human Resource Management*) as 'a detailed statement of the physical and mental activities involved in a job and (where appropriate) a description of the environment in which work is undertaken. Job specifications are usually expressed in terms of **what the worker has to do and the knowledge and judgements required** for successful completion of duties.'

Marketing at Work

Some companies tie some of their human resource requirements to the **product life cycle.** Armstrong states that 'Texas Instruments believes that it is necessary to match management style to product life cycle. As a product moves through different phases of its life cycle, different levels of management skills become dominant. It could be disastrous, for instance, to put risk taking entrepreneurs in charge of mature cash flow businesses'.

Part C: Managing people

Job description

2.14 A **job description** is prepared from the job analysis. It is a broad statement of the purpose, scope, duties and responsibilities of a job. It describes the content of a job; and its relative importance in comparison with other jobs.

2.15 The job description states the principal details of the job.

- Job title
- Location of the job (department, place)
- The relationship of the job to other positions such as who the job holder is responsible to and who are the job-holder's subordinates
- The main duties and responsibilities of the job
- The limits to the job holder's authority
- Any equipment for which the job holder is responsible

2.16 In many organisations, there is no proper job analysis, job specification or person specification for a given post, but a broad job description does exist. Such a job description can then be used for a number of purposes.

(a) To decide what skills (technical, human, conceptual, design etc) and qualifications are required of the job holder. When interviewing an applicant for the job, the interviewer can use the job description to match the candidate against the job

(b) To ensure that the job provides a sufficient challenge to the job holder. Job content is a factor in the motivation of individuals

(c) To determine a rate of pay which is fair for the job, if this has not already been decided by some other means, eg a separate job evaluation exercise

(d) To provide information from which particular job vacancies can be advertised

Person specification

2.17 Once the job has been clearly defined, the organisation can decide what kind of person is needed to fill it effectively. A **person specification** identifies the **type of person** the organisation should be trying to recruit - his or her character, aptitudes, qualifications, career aspirations, special abilities and experience.

2.18 A person specification is often used as an **all-purpose selection assessment plan** for recruiting younger people in fairly large numbers into a fairly junior grade. Research has been carried out into what a person specification ought to assess. Two designs of specification are **Rodger's Seven Point Plan** and J Munro Fraser's **Five Point Pattern of Personality**.

The Seven Point Plan

2.19 This person specification highlights seven points about the candidate.

- **Background circumstances**
- **Attainments** such as educational qualifications
- **Disposition** or manner
- **Physical attributes** such as neat appearance, ability to speak clearly, health
- **Interests** (practical, social, intellectual and physical)

7: Recruitment and selection

- **General intelligence**
- **Special aptitudes** such as speed and accuracy, numeracy, written communication skills

The mnemonic for this is BAD PIGS.

Five Point Pattern of Personality

2.20 This draws the selector's attention to five important aspects of the candidate's personality.

- Impact on others
- Acquired knowledge or qualifications
- Innate ability
- Motivation
- Adjustment and emotional balance

> **Action Programme 2**
>
> Do you have a job description? (If you don't, draw one up.) Determine a person specification for the job. How far do you match the ideal requirements of your job?

2.21 **EXAMPLE**

	ABC Business Machines Ltd: Job description for sales office manager	
1	Job title	Sales Office Manager
2	Branch	Head Office
3	Job summary	To provide effective office support for field sales and an efficient re-ordering system for customers.
4	Job content	Typical duties will include: (a) Ensuring staffing as needed of sales office (b) Providing telesales training to new staff (c) Dealing with customer complaints.
5	Reporting to:	Sales Director
6	Responsible for:	4 Telesales staff 1 General assistant
7	Experience/Education	At least 4 years telesales. Some supervisory experience.
8	Training to be provided	Initial on-the-job training.
9	Hours	38 hours per week
10	Personal characteristics required	Organised, friendly, manner and enthusiastic.
11	Objectives and appraisal	Ensure smooth operation of telesales.
12	Salary	£15-18K According to experience.
	Job Description prepared by: Sales Director 4/98	

Part C: Managing people

3 PLANNING AND MANAGING THE SEARCH PROCESS

3.1 The objective at this stage of the process is to identify candidates who are likely to be most suited to the vacancy. It is an exercise in segmentation and promotional targeting which marketers are well trained to manage. A strategic approach is needed.

3.2 *Connock* identifies two important demographic variables.

(a) **Long-term demographic trends.** These include the fall in the number of young people and the increase in overall labour force size because of increased female participation.

(b) **Education trends.** The proportion of school leavers going into higher education is expected to increase, but with **fewer school leavers in total**.

3.3 **Equal opportunities.** Any organisation that employs more than a few people should have a clear equal opportunities policy. This should promote equal opportunities in recruitment and career progression. There are three reasons for this.

(a) It is ethically desirable.

(b) Anti-discrimination legislation in most advanced countries will impose significant sanctions on organisations that do not comply.

(c) It is to the organisation's benefit to recruit using objective criteria of suitability. This widens the pool of potential recruits at all levels of ability.

Marketing at Work

Proctor and Gamble

P&G, maker of everything from Pampers nappies to Old Spice deodorant to Pringles crisps, has a huge variety of customers and wants its workforce to reflect that.

'Our success depends entirely on our ability to understand these diverse consumers' needs,' Alan Lafley, the CEO told his company last year. A diverse organisation will out-think, out-innovate and out-perform a homogenous organisation every single time. I am putting particular importance on increasing the representation of women and minorities in leadership positions at all levels.'

P&G UK has a fairly good record already. Ethnic minority employees make up 6 per cent of P&Gs UK workforce, compared with 5.4 per cent of the British population. 'But that is not a reason to be happy with ourselves. We primarily recruit graduates and 17 per cent of the students in this country are from ethnic minorities,' says Neil Harvey-Smith, UK Diversity Manager.

Why is PG not recruiting more of those students? 'It's not the case that people applying aren't getting in. It's that they're not applying.' Why not? 'It's probably fair to say that people perceive that we are a white company or an American company.'

Provided it fits in with their jobs, P&G staff of either sex can share jobs and change their hours. New parents can take up to a year's unpaid leave beyond their statutory maternity or paternity leave entitlements. The result is that the number of women appointed director or associate director in P&G Europe rose to eight last year from its previous rate of one or two a year.

Mr Harvey-Smith says the UK organisation has also made progress in attracting disabled recruits. It designed a computer programme that could read out the questions on a problem-solving test so that a blind applicant could complete it. The technology is now being used by P&G in the US.

Financial Times

Tapping unused labour resources — eg B&Q

3.4 **Older workers** are a possible labour market. This was a feature of the mid 1980s, when some companies in the retail sector targeted older workers (over-40s and over-45s). They bring important qualities.

- Skills and experience
- High regard for customer service
- Stabilising influence on younger staff
- Contribution to better staff retention rates

3.5 **Women returners.** There are a number of factors determining a woman's return to work.

(a) **Child care facilities.** If these are easily obtainable, a mother is likely to use them. Employers can provide them. Private child care is expensive. Some organisations, which do not wish to provide child care facilities themselves, might offer **child care vouchers**.

(b) **Career break schemes** have been introduced in particular in the financial services sector. Women are allowed to take time off for a few years to have children and return to the same job. Some organisations require a 'satisfactory performance record'. Other factors affecting retention include equal opportunity training schemes and assertiveness courses.

3.6 It is useful to remember throughout this process that **the objective is not to fill the post at any cost**. The wrong appointment will always be a more costly mistake than leaving the post unfilled. But likewise the **ideal** candidate will be hard to find. The reality often means accepting a good candidate and developing his or her skills in areas of identified weakness.

Internal recruitment

> **Action Programme 3**
>
> What would be the benefits of attracting an internal candidate? What would be the possible problems?

3.7 **Internal candidates** can be considered before advertising outside or they can be included in the process as candidates. It is worth remembering, though, that an internal candidate who fails to be offered a post requires much more sensitive handling, as there will be a strong sense of rejection and this can sour an otherwise happy team. The individual may resent the successful candidate and be unco-operative. In the worst case you might even lose what is otherwise a key member of the team, thereby creating a new search and selection problem.

Marketing at Work

Personnel Management reported an innovative approach to **internal recruitment** at computer company Logica. As part of a more flexible and international approach (including performance-related pay, appraisal and training), Logica is implementing a global 'resource management system' in which a central database of employees' skills and experiences is being established. 'As well as holding employees' CVs, this will be the first medium to advertise vacancies on a global basis within the company.'

Job advertisements

3.8 Despite these options, in the end many posts will be advertised. The advertisement is, in a way, already part of the selection process, because it will be placed where suitable people are likely to see it, and will be worded in a way that further weeds out people who would not be suitable for the job (or for whom the job would not be suitable). Obviously, for marketing posts, the advertisement is the recruit's first sight of the firm's marketing communications.

Part C: Managing people

3.9 In order for this pre-selection to be effective, the advertisement will have to contain details of the organisation and the job.

- Employer's **location** and **business**
- **Rewards**: the salary or wage benefits, training
- **The job**: title, main duties and responsibility, special factors
- **Career prospects**
- **Qualifications and experience required**/preferred, other aptitudes
- **How to apply**

It will have to present an attractive image, but also an honest one, so as not to disillusion successful applicants.

3.10 Preparation of the job information requires skill and attention in order to fulfil its objectives of attraction and preselection. It should meet a number of criteria.

(a) It should be **concise**, but comprehensive enough to be an accurate description of the job, its rewards and requirements.

(b) It should be **targeted** to attract the attention of the maximum number of the right sort of people.

(c) It should be **attractive**, conveying a favourable impression of the organisation, but not falsely so.

(d) It should be **relevant** and appropriate to the job and the applicant. Skills, qualifications and special aptitudes required should be prominently set out, along with special features of the job that might attract or deter applicants, such as shiftwork or extensive travel.

3.11 The way in which a job is advertised will depend on the type of organisation and the type of job. A factory is likely to advertise a vacancy for an unskilled worker in a different way from a company advertising vacancies for clerical staff. Managerial jobs may merit national advertisements, whereas semi- or unskilled jobs may only warrant local coverage, depending on the supply of suitable candidates in the local area. Specific skills may be most appropriately reached through trade, technical or professional journals, like *Marketing Week*.

3.12 The **choice of advertising medium** will depend upon three considerations.

(a) The **cost** of advertising. It is more expensive to advertise in a national newspaper than on local radio, and more expensive to advertise on local radio than in a local newspaper.

(b) The **type and number of readers** of the medium, and its suitability for the number and type of people the organisation wants to reach.

(c) The **frequency** with which the organisation wants to advertise the job vacancy. A monthly magazine or weekly newspaper are probably only useful for advertising a vacancy once. This is probably sufficient for a specialist or professional, or for a senior management position, since those who are interested will be on the look-out for vacancies advertised in certain magazines or newspapers.

3.13 **Methods and media for advertising jobs**.

(a) **In-house magazines and notice-boards**

(b) **Professional and specialist newspapers or magazines**, such as *Personnel Management*, *Marketing* or *Computing*

(c) **National newspapers**, especially for senior management jobs or vacancies for skilled workers, where potential applicants will not necessarily be found through local advertising. **Local newspapers** would be suitable for jobs where applicants are sought from the local area

(d) **Local radio, television and cinema**. These are becoming increasingly popular, especially for **large-scale campaigns, for large numbers of vacancies**

(e) **Job centres**. On the whole, vacancies for unskilled work (rather than skilled work or management jobs) are advertised through local job centres, although in theory any type of job can be advertised here

(f) **School and university careers offices**

(g) The **Internet**, especially for IT professionals and to attract candidates internationally

(h) **Employment agencies and recruitment consultants** for unusual or specialist posts

Other methods of reaching the labour market

3.14 Various **agencies** exist, through whom the employer can reach the public.

(a) **Institutional agencies** exist to help their own members to find employment: for example, the career services of educational institutions such as schools and colleges, and the employment services of professional institutions and trade unions.

(b) **Private employment agencies** have proliferated in recent years. There is a wide range of agencies specialising in different grades of staff and areas of skill. Private agencies generally offer an immediate pool of labour already on their books, and many also undertake initial screening of potential applicants, so that the recruitment officer sees only the most suitable.

3.15 There are also more **informal recruitment methods,** not directly involving advertising.

(a) **Unsolicited applications** are now frequently made to organisations, especially where there are few advertised vacancies. Some applicants may have heard about impending vacancies through the grapevine.

(b) Some vacancies may be filled through **informal contacts** and on the **recommendation** of established workers.

(c) **Head hunting** has become increasingly popular. Informal approaches are made to successful executives currently employed elsewhere.

3.16 The role of the **recruitment consultant** is to perform the staffing function on behalf of the client organisation. This involves a number of activities.

- Analysing the organisation's requirements
- Helping to draw up job descriptions and person specifications
- Designing job advertisements
- Screening applications and short-listing for interview
- Advising on the constitution and procedures of the interview

3.17 The decision whether or not to use consultants will depend on a number of factors.

(a) **Cost** will be an important consideration when recruiting for lower grades, since an expert recruitment decision will not be so crucial, and the fees may not therefore be cost effective.

(b) **The level of expertise and specialist techniques or knowledge which the consultant can bring to the process**. Consultants may be expert in using interview techniques,

Part C: Managing people

analysis of personnel specifications and so on. In-house staff, on the other hand, have experience of the particular field and of the culture of the organisation into which the recruits must fit.

(c) **The level of expertise, and specialist knowledge, available within the organisation**. The cost of training in-house personnel in the necessary interview and assessment techniques may be prohibitive.

(d) Whether there is a **need for impartiality** which can only be filled by an outsider trained in objective assessment. If fresh blood is desired in the organisation, it may be a mistake to have staff selecting clones of the common organisational type.

(e) **Supply of labour**. If there is a large and reasonably accessible pool of labour from which to fill a post, consultants will be less valuable. If the vacancy is a standard one, and there are ready channels for reaching labour (such as professional journals), the use of specialists may not be cost effective.

3.18 Managing the search process can be summarised in the following steps.

> 1 Confirming the profile of the ideal candidate
> 2 Identifying possible sources of such candidates
> 3 Reviewing possible internal sources and external options
> 4 Developing an attractive but realistic advertisement
> 5 Determining the appropriate media
> 6 Placing the advertisement
> 7 Handling the applications.

Action Programme 4

Select any two job advertisements from a notice board, magazine, journal or newspaper. Note three things.

- The elements of information given
- The tone and style of the advertisement
- The visual presentation, and the impression it makes on you

Decide what sort of person each advertisement is trying to attract. How (if at all) are the advertisers going about attracting that sort of person and discouraging applications from others?

4 RECRUITMENT INTERVIEWS AND SELECTION

Application forms

4.1 Applicants who reply to job advertisements are usually asked to fill in a job application form, or to send a letter giving details about themselves and their previous job experience and explaining why they think they are qualified to do the job. An application form should elicit sufficient information to screen candidates into two groups.

- Those obviously unsuitable for the job
- Those who might be of the right calibre, and worth inviting to an interview

4.2 **Application forms have two important aspects.**

(a) An open-ended element, which will enable a candidate to give information about his or her abilities and achievements, including academic qualifications, work experience, activities and interests, career expectations and why the candidate thinks he or she is suitable.

7: Recruitment and selection

(b) The closed element is much more structured. In this case the candidate is required to answer detailed questions (eg basic biographical information) which are posed in a restricted format (eg tick boxes). This element of an application form enables easier comparison between candidates.

4.3 A skeleton application form which you can adapt and expand to meet the needs of a specific post is given below. Candidates should be asked to sign, and date their applications as they will become part of the details of the contract of employment, if appointed, and dishonesty will be grounds for dismissal.

4.4 An alternative approach is simply to request applicants to send CVs. This will usually contain all the information needed for shortlisting and in itself is a good indication of a candidate's written communication skills.

APPLICATION FORM

Post applied for: _____ Date:

Surname: Mr/Mrs/Miss/Ms   First names:
Address:

Post Code: Telephone:

Age: Date of birth: / /
Nationality

EDUCATION AND TRAINING

Place of education (including schools/professional body after 11 years)	Dates	Examinations passed/qualifications

EXPERIENCE

Name of employer and main business	Position held	Main duties	Reason for leaving	From	To

OTHER INFORMATION
Please note your hobbies and interests, and any other information you would like to give about yourself or your experience.

May we contact any of your previous employers?   Yes ☐   No ☐

If yes, please give the names of any managers to whom we may speak.

If you are offered the post, when would you be able to start? / / .

Signature: Date:

Part C: Managing people

The selection interview

4.5 The selection interview is the next stage of the selection process. Interviewing is a crucial part of the selection process.

- It gives the organisation a chance to assess applicants directly
- It gives applicants a chance to learn more about the organisation, and to decide whether or not they are still interested

4.6 The interview has a three-fold purpose.

(a) To find the best person for the job.

(b) To ensure that applicants understand what the job is and what the career prospects are. They must be allowed a fair opportunity to decide whether or not they want the job.

(c) To make applicants feel that they have been given fair treatment in the interview, whether they get the job or not. Current applicants may still be future employees or customers.

4.7 **The interview must be prepared carefully**, to make sure that the right questions are asked, and relevant information obtained to give the interviewers what they need to make their selection.

(a) The **job description should be studied** to review the major demands of the job.

(b) The **person specification should be studied and questions should be planned** which might help the interviewer make relevant assessments of the applicant's character and qualifications. The interview may concentrate on the following aspects:

 (i) Confirming and expanding factual knowledge about the candidate. This means, for example, asking about the major problems the candidate faced in previous jobs

 (ii) Gauging the candidate's level of knowledge

 (iii) Judging how quick the candidate is to respond to questions

 (iv) Finding out likes and dislikes

 (v) Establishing a trend in his or her thinking

(c) Each application form should be carefully studied, in order to decide on questions or question areas for the individual applicant.

4.8 The interview should be conducted in such a way that the information required is successfully obtained during the interview.

(a) The **layout of the room** and the **number of interviewers** should be planned carefully. Most interviewers wish to put candidates at their ease, and so it would be inadvisable to put the candidate in a 'hot seat' across a table from a large number of hostile-looking interviewers. However, some interviewers might want to observe the candidate's reaction under severe pressure, and deliberately make the layout of the room uncomfortable and off-putting.

(b) The **manner of the interviewers**, the tone of their voice, and the way their early questions are phrased can all be significant in establishing the tone of the interview.

(c) **Questions should be put carefully.** The interviewers should not be trying to confuse the candidate, but should be trying to obtain the information that they need.

7: Recruitment and selection

(d) It is necessary to ask relevant questions, but the time of **the interview should be taken up mostly with the candidate talking,** and not with the interviewers asking questions. The more a candidate talks, the easier it should be to assess their suitability for the job. As a rule of thumb, the candidate should be talking for 70% of the time.

(e) **The candidate should be given the opportunity to ask questions.** Indeed well-prepared candidates should go into an interview knowing what questions they may want to ask. The choice of questions might well have some influence on how the interviewers finally assess them.

(f) Similarly the interviewer should be aware of the questions candidates are likely to ask. Candidates may well try to probe behind the statements made about the business, by asking for example why the interviewer chose or has remained with the organisation. Some candidate questioning may be a sign that the interviewer has failed to impart key information - for example the candidate's likely role within the organisation or the opportunities for advancement.

4.9 After each interview has been completed, notes should be made and, if more than one interviewer was present, impressions compared. Each candidate should be evaluated against the criteria for appointment. There are then three possible outcomes for each candidate.

(a) A job offer, possibly subject to conditions.

- Taking up references
- Obtaining evidence of educational and professional qualifications
- Medical examination

(b) An invitation to a **second interview**. Some organisations have a two-stage interview process, whereby first stage interview candidates are reduced to a short-list for a second stage interview. The second stage of the interview might well be based on a group selection method (see below). In many instances, the recruitment consultant might carry out the first stage interview.

(c) Rejection.

4.10 The diagram at the end of this section outlines the stages of the selection process.

The limitations of selection interviews

4.11 Interviews have often been criticised because they **fail to select suitable people** for job vacancies.

(a) **Assessment may be unclear.** The opinion of one interviewer may differ from the opinion of another. They cannot both be right, but because of their different opinions, a suitable candidate might be rejected or an unsuitable candidate offered a job.

(b) **Interviews fail to provide accurate predictions** of how a person will perform in the job.

(c) **The interviewers are likely to make errors of judgement** even when they agree about a candidate. There are several reasons for this.

(i) A **halo effect**. This is a tendency for interviewers to make a general judgement about a person based on one single attribute, which will colour the interviewers' opinions and make them mark the person up or down on every other factor in their assessment.

(ii) **Stereotyping** candidates on the basis of insufficient evidence, for example on the basis of dress, hair style or accent of voice.

(iii) **Contagious bias**. This is a process whereby an interviewer changes the behaviour of the applicant by suggestion. The applicant might be led by the wording of questions or non-verbal cues from the interviewer and change what he is doing or saying in response to the signals being received.

(iv) **Incorrect assessment of qualitative factors** such as motivation, honesty or integrity. Abstract qualities are very difficult to assess in an interview.

(v) **Logical error**. An interviewer might draw conclusions about a candidate from what is being said or done when there is no logical justification for those conclusions. For example, an interviewer might decide that a person who talks a lot in a confident voice must be intelligent, when this is not the case.

(vi) **Incorrectly used rating scales**. For example, if interviewers are required to rate a candidate on a scale of 1-5 for a number of different attributes, there might be a tendency to mark candidates in the middle range for safety or consistently above or below average for every attribute, because of **halo effect**.

(vii) **Misleading environment.** The interview can be a tense occasion for both parties, and as a result become very formal with interviewer and applicant on their best behaviour.

(d) The candidate may be adept at being interviewed. Many will have received training, including video debriefs, in presenting themselves.

Action Programme 5

What assumptions might an interviewer make about **you**, based on things like these:

(a) Accent
(b) School
(c) Clothes and hair-style
(d) Stated hobbies and interests
(e) Taste in books and TV programmes

To what extent would any of these assumptions be fair?

For objectivity, you might like to conduct this exercise in class. What assumptions do you make about the person sitting next to you?

4.12 It might be apparent from the list of limitations above that a major problem with interviews is the **skill and experience of the interviewers themselves**. Any interviewer is prone to bias, but a person can learn to reduce this problem through training and experience. Inexperienced interviewers have other problems as well.

- **Inability to evaluate** properly information about a candidate

- **Inability to compare** a candidate against the requirements for a job or a personnel specification

- Bad interview planning

- A **tendency to talk too much** in interviews, and to ask questions which call for a short answer

- A tendency to act as an inquisitor and make candidates feel uneasy.

To some extent the problems can be overcome with training.

> **Action Programme 6**
>
> Some careers officers give tuition in interview techniques to people looking for jobs. What do you think this says about interviewing, as opposed to testing, as a means of selection?

Selection testing

4.13 Interviews are often supplemented by some form of **selection test**. The interviewers must be certain that the results of such tests are reliable, and that a candidate who scores well in a test will be more likely to succeed in the job. The test will have no value unless there is a direct relationship between ability in the test and ability in the job. The test should be designed to be discriminating (ie to bring out the differences in subjects), standardised (so that it measures the same thing in different people, providing a consistent basis for comparison) and relevant to its purpose.

4.14 There are **four** types of test commonly used in practice.

(a) **Intelligence tests** aim to measure the applicant's general intellectual ability.

(b) **Aptitude tests** are designed to predict an individual's potential for performing a job or learning new skills.

(c) **Proficiency tests** are perhaps the most closely related to an assessor's objectives, because they measure ability to do the work involved. An applicant for an audio typist's job, for example, might be given a dictation tape and asked to type it.

(d) **Psychological tests** may measure a variety of characteristics, such as an applicant's skill in dealing with other people, ambition and motivation or emotional stability. To a trained psychologist, such questionnaires may give clues about the dominant qualities or characteristics of the individuals tested, but wide experience is needed to make good use of the results.

Sometimes applicants are required to attempt several tests (a **test battery**) aimed at giving a more rounded picture than would be available from a single test.

4.15 **This kind of testing must be used with care** as it suffers from several limitations.

(a) It was mentioned above **that there must be a direct relationship between ability in the test and ability in the job**. One way of assessing a test is to try it on existing employees whose capabilities are already known. It is very unlikely that tests alone will be sufficient to assess an applicant's suitability. They should be supplemented by other information, such as that derived from interview.

(b) **The interpretation of test results is a skilled task**, for which training and experience is essential. It is not something a marketing manager would undertake.

(c) Particular difficulties are experienced with particular kinds of test. For example, an aptitude test measuring arithmetical ability would need to be constantly revised; otherwise, its content might become known to later applicants. Personality tests can often give misleading results because applicants seem able to guess which answers will be looked at most favourably.

(d) It is difficult to exclude **bias against racial and ethnic minorities** from these tests.

Part C: Managing people

Personality testing

4.16 Personality tests attempt to detect the main characteristics of a candidate's personality. Despite the statistical method, however, **there is a certain amount of human subjectivity involved in the wording of questions and the interpretation of results**.

4.17 There are **other limitations** to the use of personality tests based on fitting subjects into pre-conceived trait moulds.

   (a) The **hypothetical yes/no question** used in most personality tests may be **irrelevant** to an individual's experience, and **inaccurate** as a reflection of complex thought processes.

   (b) The data is not in any case designed for predicting individual behaviour (such as might be most useful to a manager) but for comparison.

   (c) The **conditions of being tested may falsify the response**. Most subjects of such tests are willing and interested enough to try to be honest, but may be hostile to unqualified 'yes or no' questions, with no room for self-expression or middle ground. They may also be inclined to give what they think is the normal response (particularly in view of the value judgements commonly attached to character analysis).

   (d) **It is easy to cheat or falsify the data deliberately**. Even the lie scale questions, designed to test the respondent's general honesty in answering, are easy to spot and answer 'correctly'.

Group selection methods

4.18 **Group selection methods** might be used by an organisation as the **final stage of a selection process for management jobs**, particularly since most managers are required to manage and operate in a team. They consist of a series of tests, interviews and group situations involving a small number of candidates for a job. Typically, six or eight candidates will be invited to an assessment centre for two days. After an introductory chat to make the candidates feel at home, they will be given one or two tests, one or two individual interviews, and several group situations in which the candidates are invited to discuss problems together and arrive at solutions as a management team.

4.19 These group sessions might be thought useful for a number of reasons.

   (a) They give the organisation's selectors a longer opportunity to study the candidates.

   (b) They reveal more than application forms, interviews and tests alone about the ability of candidates to persuade others, negotiate with others, and explain ideas to others and also to investigate problems efficiently. These are typically management skills.

   (c) They reveal more about the candidates' personalities - stamina, interests, social interaction with others (ability to co-operate and compete) intelligence, energy and self confidence.

4.20 Since they are most suitable for selection of **potential managers** who have little or no previous experience of group selection, these methods are most commonly used for selecting university graduates for management trainee jobs.

4.21 Drawbacks of **group selection methods**

   - Time and cost
   - The need to provide training for the assessors

- The rather unreal nature of the group situations in which candidates are expected to participate may lead them to behave in a contrived way.

4.22 Once the selection process is complete those involved need to compare their views and decide which candidate should be offered the post. Even though this may be at the end of a long day this process should not be rushed. If the interviewers have used an interview form to record their observations and impressions they will have a standard format to use in the following discussions.

4.23 It is better not to rush the decision if there is a considerable debate and to avoid the danger of selecting the most middle of the road candidate simply because they are 'uncontroversial'.

4.24 **Selection methods reviewed**

In 1994 Smith and Abrahamsen described a scale that predicts how well a candidate will perform at work if offered that job. This is known as a predictive validity scale. The scale ranges from 1 (meaning a method that is right every time) to 0 (meaning a method that is no better than chance). On this basis, they produced the following results.

Method	% use	Predictive validity
Interviews	92	0.17
References	74	0.13
Work sampling	18	0.57
Assessment centres	14	0.40
Personality tests	13	0.40
Cognitive tests	11	0.54
Biodata	4	0.40
Graphology	3	0.00

The results are most revealing as they show a pattern of employers relying most heavily on the least valid selection methods for their recruitment purposes. Interviews, in particular (and for the reasons given earlier) seem not much better than tossing a coin.

References

4.25 References provide further confidential information about the prospective employee. This may be of varying value, **as the reliability of all but the most factual information must be in question.** A reference should contain two types of data.

(a) Straightforward **factual information** confirming the nature of the applicant's previous job(s), period of employment, pay, and circumstances of leaving

(b) **Opinions** about the applicant's personality and other attributes, which should obviously be treated with some caution.

The offer

4.26 Once a selection is made the candidate should be approached with a formal offer. It is best not to notify a suitable second choice until the candidate has accepted. Unsuccessful candidates should be notified as quickly as possible.

Part C: Managing people

4.27 **The organisation should be prepared for its offer to be rejected at this stage.** Applicants may have received and accepted other offers. They may not have been attracted by their first-hand view of the organisation, and may have changed their mind about applying; they may only have been testing the water in applying in the first place, gauging the market for their skills and experience for future reference, or seeking a position of strength from which to bargain with their present employers. **A small number of eligible applicants should therefore be kept in reserve.**

> ### Action Programme 7
>
> Some companies have run into trouble from disgruntled employees because the companies have given them poor references. Certain companies have therefore tried to deal with this situation by giving references along the following lines: 'You will be lucky to have this person working for you.'
>
> What are the potential problems with that reference?

7: Recruitment and selection

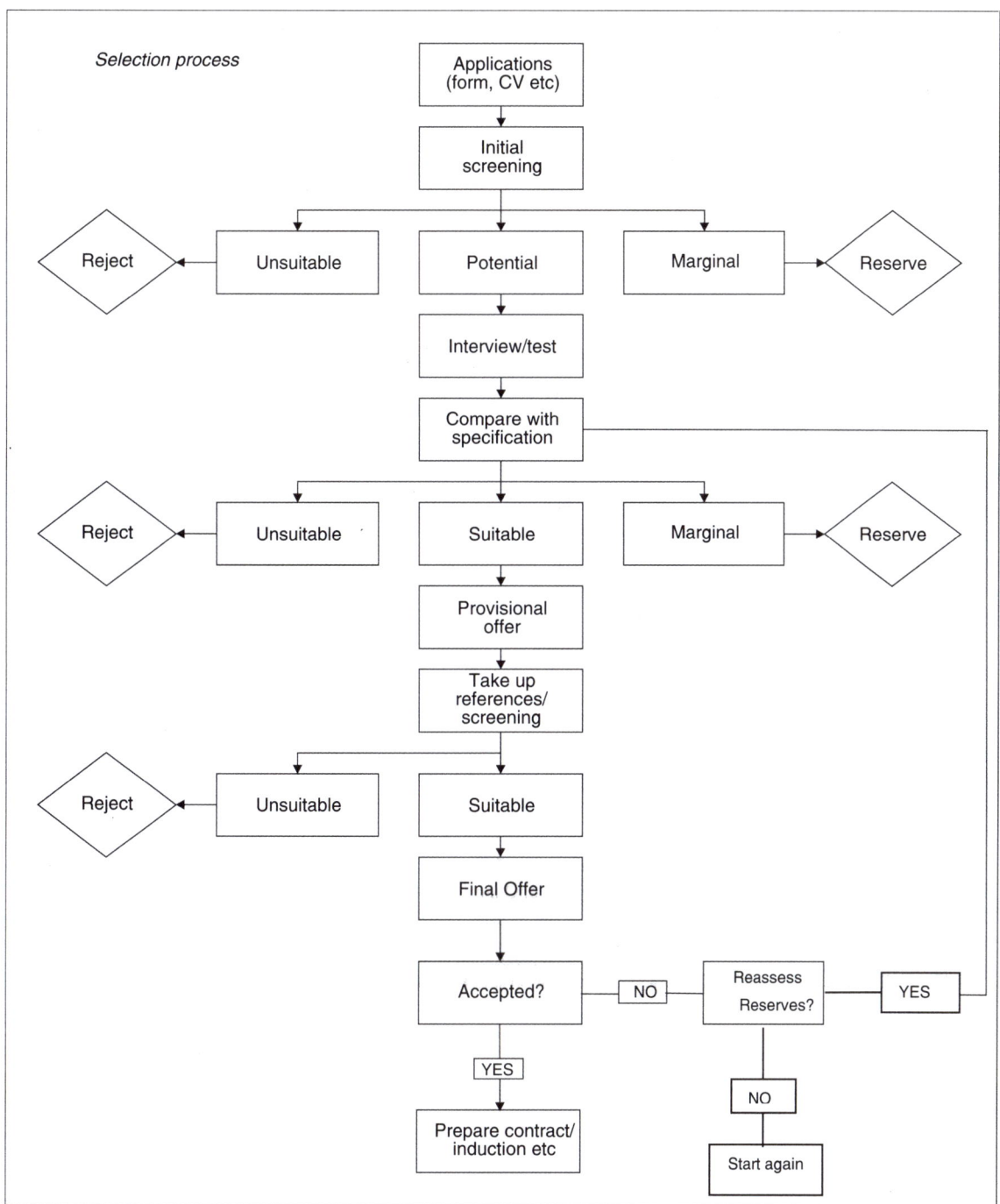

5 INTEGRATING NEW MEMBERS INTO THE TEAM   6/00, 12/00

5.1 Selection is only a beginning. Candidates have to be helped through the transition to a new job so that they become productive and integrated team members. Any change to the team can upset its dynamics, potentially pushing it back from **performing** to **storming**.

5.2 Giving someone the job does not magically convert that person from an acceptable or good fit for the post to an ideal one. Action to fill the gaps with training or even to modify the job is needed.

5.3 The manager should be sensitive to potential problems and take action to help new team members settle in quickly and make a positive contribution. They might need new skills or knowledge and experience for the job, or their existing skills might need developing.

Part C: Managing people

5.4 Once an applicant for a job is offered the job and accepts it, he or she has to be introduced to the job. This is **the process of induction.** If you are examined about the induction process, you should be able to draw on your own experience on first starting work.

5.5 Good induction should set out performance targets and encourage quality work. It should also maintain the motivation of starters and develop a commitment to the company.

5.6 Induction starts before the first day with **joining instructions**. These should tell the joiner where, when and to whom to report, and also the documentation they need to bring in with them.

5.7 On the first day, a senior person should welcome the new recruit. The seniority of this manager is likely to vary according to the size of the organisation, and the size of the section where the recruit will be working. In smaller organisations a recruit is more likely to see a manager in a more senior position than in larger organisations. The manager might discuss in broad terms what is required from people at work, working conditions, pay and benefits, training opportunities and career opportunities and should then introduce the new recruit to the person who will be the recruit's immediate manager.

5.8 The immediate line manager should then take over the **continuing process of induction and development.** This involves a number of tasks.

(a) **Pinpoint** the **areas** that the **new staff member will have to learn** about **in order to start** his or her job. Some things (such as detailed technical knowledge) may be identified as areas for later study or training. A list of learning priorities should be drawn up so that the recruit and the manager are clear about the rate and direction of progress required.

(b) Explain first of all the **nature of the job, and its goals, in the context of the department as a whole.** This will help the recruit to work to specific targets and to understand how his or her tasks relate to the organisation as a whole.

(c) Explain the **structure** of the department - and introduce those who will be working with or for the new team member. He or she should meet all the members of the immediate work team. One colleague may be assigned to a recruit as a **mentor** for the first few days, to keep an eye and show the ropes.

(d) Plan and implement an appropriate **training programme** for whatever technical or practical knowledge is required. The programme should have a **clear schedule and set of goals** so that the recruit has a sense of purpose, and so that the programme can be efficiently organised to fit in with the activities of the department. Training should cover general information about the business and also the specific skills that the employee will need to perform properly.

(e) **Coach and train** the recruit; check regularly on progress. **Feedback** information on how he or she is doing will be essential to the learning process, correcting any faults at an early stage and building the confidence of the recruit.

(f) **Integrate** the recruit into the **culture** of the organisation. Much of this may be done informally to reinforce commitment by rewarding evidence of loyalty, hard work and desired behaviour.

5.9 **Note that induction is a continuing process which might last for several months or even longer.**

(a) The manager must arrange for the recruit's training programme to start.

(b) The recruit will only gradually learn the job through continued on-the-job training.

(c) The person responsible for induction should keep checking up on the new recruit, to make sure that he or she is settling in well and is learning the ropes.

(d) The senior manager should check on the recruit from time to time (in particular, to find out how the training is progressing).

5.10 After an appropriate period, the performance of a new recruit should be formally appraised. The recruit should then be subject to the normal appraisal cycle and procedure.

Exam Tip

A question in the December 1999 paper asked about the role of human resources planning in meeting the need for marketing skills. The examiner's report pointed out that the question was not merely about recruitment and selection, but about the wider strategic purposes those activities serve.

Note that a simple statement of theory or technique will rarely produce a satisfactory answer in this exam. You must always address the wider setting of the question and **apply** your knowledge to the business situation.

A question in the December 2000 exam was very specifically about recruitment, asking what sort of people you would need for a specific role and how you would go about recruiting them. This was a very factual question, without too much room for manoeuvre or confusion. With a question, like this you must be able to deploy the relevant theory accurately, making sure that it is, in fact, relevant.

Induction was also covered in the December 2000 mini-case: an induction programme for new actors joining the Royal Shakespeare Company. So, add the performing arts to the type of businesses you might have to deal with in the exam.

Part C: Managing people

Chapter roundup

- All teams will need to recruit new members at some time and the marketing manager will be very involved in that process, possibly supported by Human Resource specialists.

- The process of search and selection needs to be thoroughly planned and professionally managed if the right candidate for the post is to be identified.

- The aim of recruitment and selection is to provide the quantity and quality of human resources needed to fulfil the organisation's objectives.

    Recruitment is concerned with finding applicants.
    Selection is concerned with choosing between applicants.

- The first critical stage is a **job analysis**, from which the **job specification** and/or **job description** and **person specification** can be generated. Care and attention here will ensure the manager knows the kind of person needed to suit the needs of both the task and the group.

- The process of search uses many marketing skills, to help segment the labour market and target the right sources of potential candidates.

- Internal applicants should be considered, but the relative advantages and disadvantages of making an internal or external appointment should be considered. It may be best to assess the internal candidate against external alternatives.

- The objective of the selection process is to find the most suitable candidate for the post. This is the best match between the job requirements and the individual's competences, approach and experience. A variety of techniques can be used to help in the selection process. Companies use a combination of them, particularly for more senior appointments.

- Whatever techniques are used, the process must be thought through, and managers must make the time to plan and undertake the selection of new staff. Mistakes can be **very** damaging to the team and to the output of the department.

- Once a candidate is selected, equal attention must be given to the process of **induction**. This ensures that new team members settle in quickly, and have the induction and training needed to make a productive contribution.

- References should be sought, although they must be used with care.

Quick Quiz

1. What is human resource planning? (see para 2.1)
2. Outline a methodical approach to recruitment and selection. (2.4)
3. What goes into a job description? (2.14)
4. What is a person specification? (2.17)
5. List the factors included in the Five Point Pattern of Personality. (2.20)
6. What long-term demographic trends must organisations consider? (3.2)
7. List four disadvantages of recruiting an internal candidate (Action Programme 3)
8. What details should be included in a job advertisement? (3.9)
9. What factors would you consider before selecting the advertising medium for a vacancy? (3.11)
10. What is the purpose of an application form? (4.1)
11. How should selection interviews be conducted? (4.8)
12. What are the limitations of selection interviews? (4.11)
13. List four types of selection test. (4.14)
14. What are the limitations of personality testing? (4.17)
15. Why is the induction process important? (5.1 - 5.3)

Action Programme Review

3.

For Internal	Against Internal
Knows the people, systems and the business	May have pre-conceived ideas and an established and unsuitable image/reputation from current post
Fits in with the culture: knows 'how we do things here'	No new ideas, creativity or challenge to the culture and systems
Motivating to the individual and others to have an internal promotion	A post will still need filling - this person's old post!
Quicker, cheaper and less risky than an outside appointment	This person may not be the best qualified or most able candidate
The induction period will be quicker.	

6. If interview techniques are taught, it might imply that, in the absence of any other selection criteria, your success at interview will have more to do with your ability to present yourself in an interview situation than you ability to do the job. On the other hand, an interview is a test of how well you perform under pressure, in an unfamiliar environment and with strangers. This might reflect some of the interpersonal skills required in a job.

7. The reference is deliberately ambiguous. The writer hopes that the subject will be satisfied with it while any potential employer is warned by it. The opposite might occur, possibly leading to protest from either party.

Now try illustrative question 10 at the end of the Study Text

8 Improving Team Performance

Chapter Topic List	Syllabus reference
1 Setting the scene	
2 Motivational theory and its value to the manager	3.3
3 Motivating teams and individuals	3.1, 3.2, 3.3
4 The role of appraisal	3.1, 3.4
5 Training and development for staff	3.5
6 Counselling and advice	3.1, 2.4
7 Discipline and grievance	3.1, 2.4
8 Managing peripheral workers	3.1

Learning Outcomes

- Students will be able to devise methods for motivating marketing staff to improve individual and team effectiveness.
- Students will be able to devise training and development plans for marketing personnel to improve individual and team effectiveness.

Key Concept Introduced

- Motivation

Examples of Marketing at Work

- Delegation and job enrichment
- Empowerment at Harvester Restaurants
- Motivation
- Measuring performance at British Airways and Burger King
- Service awards at Whitbread pubs
- Marketing training for operations departments
- BT's plans for teleworking

1 SETTING THE SCENE

1.1 Having recruited, trained and inducted a new team member, all described in Chapter 7, we have to ensure the new member's and the team's optimal performance. It is very easy to fall into simplistic, common sense attitudes of the Theory X/Y variety which we saw in Chapter 6 when wondering how to get employees to work well. The motivation theories described in this chapter will help you avoid falling into this trap.

1.2 In Section 2 we discuss **different approaches to motivation** and what factors encourage people to work hard and well, and how the manager can understand and use these factors: do people have needs which managers can satisfy? Do people weigh up the options?

1.3 In Section 3, we go on from identifying the needs which people have to how they can be satisfied, using pay, the job itself, participation and empowerment to enhance motivation. **People are often motivated by things other than money**, and in times when funds are scarce, attention to the non-financial aspects can help motivate a team.

1.4 Motivation has to be translated into performance: a person can be well motivated but incompetent. Consequently we have to review **the performance of the individual or team**, the subject of Section 4. Of course, as you will recall from Chapter 1, there are many aspects to a job. The purpose of **appraisal** is to develop a review of a person's performance, with a view to improving it. Sometimes this might be achieved by training, which we discuss in Section 5: you have already encountered some of the relevant issues in Chapter 3.

1.5 On occasions, performance may be such that people require **counselling or advice** outside of the normal appraisal system. In extreme cases, **disciplinary action** might be necessary. We discuss these aspects in Sections 6 and 7. You must appreciate the differences between appraisals, counselling and disciplinary interviews.

1.6 Information technology and the new flexible job market can affect the management of the team, so in Section 8 we highlight some of the issues relating to people who work from home and/or who are not part of the organisation's full-time, permanent workforce.

1.7 Special considerations apply to situations of change, which we discuss in Chapter 9.

2 MOTIVATIONAL THEORY AND ITS VALUE TO THE MANAGER

> **Key Concept**
> **Motivation** is simply reasons for behaviour. People at work display varying degrees of motivation to achieve the goals set by management. It is an important task of managers at all levels to enhance the individual's motivation to work effectively.

2.1 Managers can provide the team with the opportunity and resources to work, but without motivation, little effective work will result. Motivation is the magic ingredient or catalyst which the manager has to add to the work situation to generate results.

2.2 Earlier we considered the role and responsibilities of the leader. Responsibility for motivation is an integral part of that job. You must be aware of the theory and importance of motivation and be able to suggest solutions to motivational problems for the examiner.

2.3 Marketers may have a head start in this area of management, as they have studied motivation frequently in the context of understanding customer behaviour.

Part C: Managing people

Why is motivation important?

2.4 You may be wondering why motivation is important. It could be argued that a person is employed to do a job, and so will do that job and no question of motivation arises. A person who does not want to do the work can resign. The point at issue, however, is the **efficiency** with which the job is done. It is suggested that if individuals can be motivated, by one means or another, they will produce a **better quality of work**.

Motivators and motivation

2.5 In the most basic terms, an individual has **needs** which he or she wishes to satisfy. The means of satisfying the needs are **wants**. For example, an individual might feel the need for power, and to fulfil this need, might want money and a position of authority. Depending on the strength of these needs and wants, she/he may take action to achieve them. If successful in achieving them, she/he will be satisfied. This can be shown in a simple diagram.

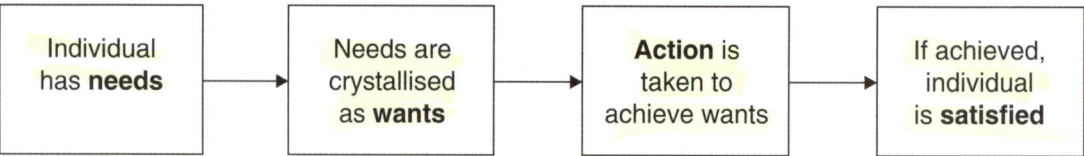

2.6 **Motivators** can be established which act as the wants of the individual. For example, the position of sales director might serve as a want to satisfy an individual's need for power, or access to the senior executive's dining room might serve as a want to satisfy a need for status. **Motivators may exist which are not directly controllable by management**; for example, an individual might want to be accepted by work mates, to satisfy a need for friendship and affiliation with others, and might therefore choose to conform to the norms and adopt the attitudes of the work group, which are not necessarily shared by the organisation as a whole.

2.7 Management has the problem of creating or manipulating motivators which will actually motivate employees to perform in a desired way.

> **Action Programme 1**
>
> Before you start reading about motivation theories, answer the following questions. What factors in yourself or in your organisation motivate you:
>
> - to turn up at work at all?
> - to do an average day's work?
> - to 'bust a gut' on a task or for a boss?
>
> Go on - be honest!
>
> Talk to friends and colleagues - find out what makes them tick.

Motivation theories

2.8 What we believe motivation is and what can be done with it will influence all our attitudes to individuals in organisations and to our management style.

(a) Some suggest that a **satisfied** worker will work **harder**, although there is little evidence to support the assumption. Satisfaction may reduce labour turnover and absenteeism, but will not necessarily increase individual productivity. Some hold that people work best within a compatible work group, or under a well-liked leader.

(b) There is a common assumption that individuals will work harder in order to obtain a desired reward. **Incentives** can work if certain conditions are satisfied.

- The individual perceives the increased reward to be worth the extra effort
- The performance can be measured and clearly attributed to that individual
- The individual wants that particular kind of reward
- The increased performance will not become the new minimum standard

2.9 One way of grouping the major theories of motivation is by making the following distinction.

(a) **Content theories,** which assume that human beings have a 'package' of needs which they pursue and try to define and explain them. *Maslow's* **need hierarchy** and *Herzberg's* **two-factor theory** are two of the most important approaches of this type.

(b) **Process theories,** which explore the process through which outcomes are pursued by individuals. This approach assumes that people are able to select goals and choose the paths towards them, by a conscious or unconscious process of calculation. *Vroom's* **expectancy theory** and *Handy's* **motivation calculus** are theories of this type.

> **Exam Tip**
> You will not be asked detailed questions on the theories of motivation in this examination but you will be required to understand the process and alternative approaches to motivation. It will be useful to have a feel for the ideas of the leading writers on motivation which you can call upon to illustrate your work.

Content theories

Maslow's hierarchy of needs

2.10 In his motivation theory, Maslow put forward certain propositions about the motivating power of people's **needs**.

(a) Every person's needs can be arranged in **a hierarchy of relative strength**.

(b) Each **level of need is dominant until satisfied;** only then does the next higher level of need become a motivating factor.

(c) A **need which has been satisfied no longer motivates** an individual's behaviour. The need for self-actualisation can never be satisfied.

Part C: Managing people

2.11 There is a certain intuitive appeal to Maslow's theory. After all, you are unlikely to be concerned with status or recognition while you are hungry or thirsty, primary survival needs will take precedence. Likewise, once your hunger is assuaged, the need for food is unlikely to be a motivating factor.

2.12 Maslow's theories may be of general interest, but they have no clear practical application.

(a) The same need may cause different behaviour in different individuals. One person might seek to satisfy his need for esteem by winning promotion whereas another individual might seek esteem by leading a challenge against authority.

(b) It is occasionally difficult to reconcile the willingness of individuals to forgo the immediate satisfaction of needs and to accept current suffering to fulfil a long-term goal (eg the long studentship of the medical or accounting professions), in terms of Maslow's hierarchy.

Herzberg's two-factor theory of job satisfaction

2.13 Herzberg contrasted the factors which cause job **dissatisfaction** and those which can cause job **satisfaction**. He called the former **hygiene** or **maintenance** factors, because they are essentially preventative. They prevent or minimise dissatisfaction **but do not give satisfaction,** in the same way that sanitation minimises some threats to health, but does not ensure good health.

Action Programme 2

What factors can you identify which cause dissatisfaction at work?

2.14 The important point is that **motivation** cannot be achieved by addressing the above-mentioned factors. All that will be attained is a neutral state in which there is neither motivation or dissatisfaction.

2.15 **Motivator factors** actively **create job satisfaction** and *are* effective in motivating an individual to superior performance and effort.

- Status (although this may be a hygiene factor as well as a motivator factor)
- Advancement
- Recognition
- Responsibility
- Challenging work
- Achievement
- Growth in the job

2.16 Herzberg saw two separate need systems in individuals.

(a) **A need to avoid unpleasantness.** This need is satisfied at work by **hygiene factors. Hygiene satisfactions** are short-lived; individuals come back for more as their expectations rise.

(b) **A need for personal growth.** This is satisfied by **motivator factors.**

2.17 Some individuals are not **mature** enough to want personal growth; these are '**hygiene seekers**' because they are only bothered about hygiene factors. A lack of motivators at work will encourage employees to concentrate on shortcomings in hygiene factors. These may be real or imagined. The result will be an endless series of demands relating to pay and conditions of work.

2.18 Herzberg suggested means by which motivator satisfactions could be supplied. Stemming from his fundamental division of motivator and hygiene factors, he encouraged managers to **study the job itself** (the type of work done, the nature of tasks, levels of responsibility) rather than **conditions of work**. Only this way will motivation improve. (Concentrating on hygiene factors will merely stave off job dissatisfaction.)

2.19 If there is sufficient challenge, scope and interest in the job, there will be a lasting increase in satisfaction and the employee will work well; productivity will be above 'normal' levels. The extent to which a job must be challenging or creative to a motivator seeker will, in relation to each individual, depend on his ability and his tolerance for delayed success.

2.20 Herzberg specified three typical means whereby work can be revised to improve motivation.

(a) **Job enrichment**: this is the main method of improving job satisfaction and can be defined as 'the planned process of up-grading the responsibility, challenge and content of the work'. Typically, this would involve increasing **delegation** to provide more interesting work and problem solving at lower levels within an organisation.

(b) **Job enlargement**: although often linked with job enrichment, it is a separate technique and is rather limited in its ability to improve staff motivation. Job enlargement is the process of increasing the number of operations in which a worker is engaged This is more limited in value, since a person who is required to complete several tedious tasks is unlikely to be much more highly motivated than a man performing one continuous tedious task.

(c) **Job rotation**: this is the planned operation of a system whereby staff members exchange positions with the intention of breaking monotony in the work and providing fresh job challenge.

These ideas are discussed in more detail in section 3.

McClelland's typology

2.21 *McClelland* identified three types of motivating needs.

(a) **The need for power**. People with a high need for power usually seek positions of leadership in order to influence and control.

(b) **The need for affiliation**. People who need a sense of belonging and membership of a social group tend to be concerned with maintaining good personal relationships.

(c) **The need for achievement**. People who need to achieve have a strong desire for success and a strong fear of failure. They might set themselves **low targets** in order to feel successful.

Process theories

Vroom's expectancy theory

2.22 *Victor Vroom* suggested that the strength of an individual's motivation to do something will depend on the extent to which he expects the results of his efforts to contribute towards his personal needs or goals, to reward him or to punish him. Put another way, expectancy theory states that people will effectively decide how much they are going to put into their work as a result of two considerations.

Part C: Managing people

(a) The **value** that they place on the expected outcome, whether the positive value of a reward, or the negative value of a punishment. Vroom called this '**valence**'.

(b) The strength of their **expectation** that behaving in a certain way will in fact bring out the desired outcome. Vroom called this **expectancy**.

> **E**xpectancy x **V**alence = **F**orce of motivation.

Handy's motivation calculus

2.23 Handy suggests that for any individual decision, there is a conscious or unconscious **motivation calculus** which is an assessment of three factors.

(a) The individual's needs

(b) The job performance expected from the individual

(c) 'E' factors. Handy suggests a set of words beginning with 'e', that describe what the individual puts into the job. As well as effort, there is energy, excitement in achieving desired results, enthusiasm, emotion, and expenditure of time and money.

2.24 The **motivation decision** (how strong the motivation to achieve the desired results will be) will depend on the individual person's judgement about three things

- The strength of his/her needs
- The expectancy that expending 'E' will lead to high performance
- How far the result will be instrumental in satisfying his/her needs

A person may have a high need for power. To the degree that he believes that a particular result, such as a completed task, will gain him promotion (expectancy) **and** that promotion will in fact satisfy his need for power (instrumentality) he will expend 'E' on the task.

2.25 In terms of organisation practice, Handy suggests that several factors are necessary for the individual to complete the calculus, and to be motivated.

(a) **Intended results should be made clear**, so that the individual can complete the calculation, and know what is expected, what will be rewarded and how much 'E' it will take.

(b) Without knowledge of **actual results**, there is no check that the 'E' expenditure was justified (and will be justified in future). **Feedback on performance**, good or bad, is essential, not only for performance but for confidence and prevention of hostility.

2.26 Handy's calculus helps to explain various phenomena of individual behaviour at work.

(a) Individuals are more committed to specific goals, particularly those which they have helped to set themselves.

(b) If individuals are **rewarded** according to performance tied to standards ('management by objectives'), however, they may well set **lower** standards: the likelihood of success and reward is greater if the standard is lower, so less expenditure of 'E' is indicated.

Models of man

2.27 *Schein* summarises the historical development of thinking about motivation by describing **three sets of assumptions about people**. These correspond to the scientific management,

human relations and Maslow/Herzberg schools of thought. Schein then describes his own model, which may be thought of as a **contingency approach**.

(a) **Rational-economic man is primarily motivated by economic incentives.** He is mainly passive and can (and must) be manipulated by the organisation into doing what it wants. In the context of an employing organisation, such a person would be influenced mainly by salary and fringe benefits. Fortunately, not all people are like this, and the self-motivated, self-controlling individuals must assume responsibility for those that are.

(b) **Social man looks for self-fulfilment in social relationships.** In the context of an employing organisation, this would imply that an individual's major motivation would be not so much the job itself as the opportunity to mix with other people. Considerable implications exist here for the development of home working (see Section 6).

(c) **Self-actualising man is influenced by a wider range of motivations.** Ultimately, the self-actualising man wishes to realise his own full personal potential. He is capable of maturity and autonomy and will (given the chance) voluntarily integrate his goals with the organisation.

(d) **Complex man represents Schein's own view of people.** According to his model, individuals are variable and driven by many different motives. The motives influencing a particular individual may change from time to time, and their relative importance may also vary, depending on the situation. The complex man will respond to no single managerial strategy, but will consider its appropriateness to circumstances and his own needs.

Psychological contracts

2.28 According to Schein a **psychological contract** exists between individuals in an organisation and the organisation itself. An individual belongs to many organisations, and he or she has a different psychological contract with each. A psychological contract might be thought of as a **set of expectations**.

(a) The individual expects to derive certain benefits from membership of the organisation and is prepared to expend a certain amount of effort in return.

(b) The organisation expects the individual to fulfil certain requirements and is prepared to offer certain rewards in return.

2.29 Three types of psychological contract can be identified.

(a) **Coercive contract.** The individual feels that he is being forced to contribute his efforts and energies involuntarily, and that the rewards he receives in return are inadequate compensation. For example, if an individual believes that he does not receive enough pay for the work he does, or if he is forcibly transferred to another job he does not like, there would be a coercive psychological contract between the individual and the organisation.

(b) **Calculative contract.** This is a contract, accepted voluntarily by the individual, in which he expects to do his job in exchange for a readily identifiable set of rewards (for example pay, promotion, job content, status, or simply having a job of work to keep him occupied). This form of contract is the most frequent in industrial and commercial organisations. With such psychological contracts, motivation can only be increased if the rewards to the individual are improved. If the organisation demands greater efforts without increasing the rewards, the psychological contract will revert to a coercive one, and **motivation may become negative**.

(c) **Co-operative contract**. This is a contract in which the individual **identifies himself with the organisation and its goals**, so that he actively seeks to contribute further to the achievement of those goals. **Motivation comes out of success at work, a sense of achievement, and self-fulfilment**. The individual will probably want to share in the planning and control decisions which affect his work, and co-operative contracts are therefore likely to occur where employees **participate in decision making**. Since these contracts are likely to result in high motivation and high achievement, the lesson for management would be that employee participation in decision making is the most desirable way to structure manager-subordinate relations at work, but **only if subordinates want participation**.

2.30 Motivation happens when the psychological contract, within which the individual's motivation calculus operates for new decisions, is viewed in the same way by the organisation and by the individual.

Action programme 3

In *Brits at Work*, John Mole (a former manager) describes various work environments which he explored in order to gain a worm's eye view of life in British companies. In this quotation he is talking to a manager about scientists and researchers.

'"...but once you've provided them with the money (ie resources to finish research projects) and support (laboratory assistants), what motivates them?" "They motivate themselves, don't they?" There were certainly no material incentives for working in medical research. After a degree and a doctorate...you might be taken on at the salary I used to pay my secretary!'

Why is the narrator slightly confused?

3 MOTIVATING TEAMS AND INDIVIDUALS

3.1 We have already talked about job satisfaction in connection with the work of Herzberg. He conducted a survey of employees in Pittsburgh and analysed their accounts of times when they 'felt good' about their jobs; this was taken to be a sign of **job satisfaction** (as opposed to **job dissatisfaction**, arising from events which made them 'feel bad' about their jobs).

3.2 *Drucker* suggested that motivation through employee satisfaction or morale is not a useful concept because it is such a wishy-washy idea. It has no particular meaning, and if it is to have meaning, it must be defined more constructively. His suggestion was that employee satisfaction comes about through encouraging employees to accept responsibility. There are four ingredients to this.

(a) **Careful placement of people in jobs**. The person selected should see the job as one which provides a challenge to their abilities. There will be no motivation for a university graduate in the job of shop assistant, whereas the same job can provide a worthwhile challenge to someone of lesser academic training and intelligence.

(b) **High standards of performance in the job**. Targets for achievement should be challenging. However, they should not be imposed in an authoritarian way by the employee's bosses. The employee should be encouraged to set high standards of performance.

(c) **Providing the worker with the information needed to control personal performance**. The employee should receive routine information about how well or badly they are doing without having to be told by the boss. Being told by a boss comes as a praise or reprimand, and the fear of reprimand will inhibit performance. Access to information as a routine matter overcomes this problem of inhibition.

(d) **Opportunities for participation in decisions that will give the employee managerial vision.** Participation means having some say and influence in the way the employee's work is organised and the targets for work are set.

Methods of improving motivation and job satisfaction

3.3 There are various ways in which managers can attempt to increase the motivation of their subordinates.

(a) Herzberg and others recommended better **job design**.

(b) Various writers have suggested that subordinates' **participation in decision making will improve** motivation through self-realisation and **empowerment**.

(c) **Pay and incentive schemes** are frequently regarded as powerful motivators.

We shall discuss each of these ways in turn.

Job design

3.4 Job design is the process of deciding three issues.

- The **content** of a job in terms of its duties and responsibilities
- The **methods** to be used in carrying out the job, in terms of techniques, system and procedures
- The **relationship** that should exist between the job holder and his/her superiors, colleagues and subordinates

> **Action Programme 4**
>
> Write out a job design for the work you do. Assess the design in terms of motivation.

3.5 The objectives of the job design process are to improve productivity, efficiency and quality and to satisfy the individual's needs for interest, challenge and accomplishment.

Job enrichment

3.6 **Job enrichment is planned, deliberate action to build greater responsibility, breadth and challenge of work into a job.** A job may be enriched in a variety of ways, such as allowing the employee in the job greater freedom to decide how the job should be done.

3.7 Job enrichment attempts to add further responsibilities to a job by giving the job holder decision-making opportunities of a higher order.

Part C: Managing people

Marketing at Work

At first, a **market researcher's** responsibilities for producing quarterly management reports ended at the stage of producing the figures. These duties were then extended so that she prepared the actual reports and submitted them, under her own name, to the senior management. This alteration in responsibilities not only enriched the job but also increased the work-load. This in turn led to delegation of certain responsibilities to clerks within the department. These duties were in themselves job enrichment to the clerks and so a cascading effect was obtained. This highlights one of the basic elements of job enrichment - that what is tedious, mundane detail at a high level can represent significant job interest and challenge at a lower level in the organisation where a person's experience and scope is much less.

3.8 Some experiments have been made whereby **work groups** were given collective job enrichment. *Child* gives the example in the UK of the Dutch company, *Phillips*. A work group responsible for manufacturing television sets carried out the entire assembly operation and also had authority to deal directly with purchasing, stores and quality control, without a supervisor acting as intermediary. The change in work organisation meant, however, that the **company had to incur additional costs in re-equipment and training**.

3.9 The opportunity for job enrichment may be constrained.

- Technology and working conditions may dictate how work must be done.
- Jobs utilising a low level of skill may be difficult to enrich.
- Job enrichment should be wanted by subordinates.

3.10 Job enrichment alone will not automatically make employees more productive. If jobs are enriched, employees will expect to be paid fairly for what they are doing. It might be more correct therefore to say that **job enrichment might improve productivity through greater motivation, but only if it is rewarded fairly**.

Action Programme 5

In what ways could your work or the work of your team be enriched?

Job enlargement

3.11 **Job enlargement** is frequently confused with job enrichment. **Job enlargement is the attempt to widen jobs by increasing the number of operations in which a job holder is involved.**

3.12 This has the effect of lengthening the cycle time of repeated operations; by reducing the number of repetitions of the same work, the dullness of the job should also be reduced. Job enlargement is therefore a horizontal extension of an individual's work, whereas job enrichment is a vertical extension. For most **knowledge workers**, like marketing staff, this may be less useful than job enrichment.

3.13 Job enlargement is the opposite of the **micro-division of labour** approach to the organisation of work, in which a job is divided up into the smallest number of sequential tasks possible. Each task is so simple and straightforward that it can be learned with very little training.

3.14 There are several arguments against the micro-division of labour:

8: Improving team performance

(a) The work is monotonous and makes employees bored and dissatisfied. The consequences will be high labour turnover, absenteeism and spoilage.

(b) People, unlike machines, work more efficiently when their work is varied.

(c) Excessive specialisation isolates the individual in his work and inhibits social contacts with work-mates.

3.15 **Aspects of well-designed jobs**

- Scope for the individual to set work standards and targets
- Individual control over the pace and methods of working
- Provision of variety by allowing for inter-locking tasks to be done by the same person
- Opportunity to comment about the design of the product, or job
- Feedback to the individual about performance

3.16 Arguably, **job enlargement is limited in its ability to improve motivation** since, as Herzberg points out, to ask a worker to complete three separate tedious, unchallenging tasks is unlikely to motivate him more than asking him to fulfil one single tedious, unchallenging task.

Job enrichment and job enlargement combined

3.17 Nevertheless, job enlargement might succeed in providing job enrichment as well, provided that the nature of the extra tasks to be done in the bigger job are possible and give the employee a greater challenge and incentive.

3.18 Enlarged jobs might also be regarded as high status jobs within the department, and as stepping stones towards promotion.

Job rotation

3.19 Job rotation may take two forms.

(a) An employee might be transferred to another job in order to give him or her a new interest and challenge, and to bring a fresh person to the job being vacated.

(b) Job rotation might be regarded as a form of training. Trainees might be expected to learn a bit about a number of different jobs, by spending six months or one year in each job before being moved on.

Job rotation is often practised unofficially among the members of small work groups.

3.20 No doubt you will have your own views about the value of job rotation as a method of training or career development. It is interesting to note *Drucker's* view: 'The whole idea of training jobs is contrary to all rules and experience. A person should never be given a job that is not a real job, that does not require performance from him'.

Participation in decision making and empowerment

Participation

3.21 Much research suggests that if a superior invites subordinates to participate in planning decisions which affect their work, if the subordinates voluntarily accept the invitation, and if results about actual performance are fed back regularly so that they can make their own control decisions, then the subordinates' **motivation will rise**.

Part C: Managing people

- Efficiency may rise
- They may become more conscious of the organisation's goals
- It may be possible to raise planning targets to reasonably challenging levels
- They may be ready to take appropriate control actions when necessary

3.22 It is obvious that participation will only be feasible if the superior is willing to apply it, and if it is acceptable within the culture of the organisation.

What does participation mean and why is it desirable?

3.23 Handy commented that: 'Participation is sometimes regarded as a form of job enlargement. At other times it is a way of gaining commitment by workers to some proposal on the grounds that if you have been involved in discussing it, you will be more interested in its success.

3.24 **Merits of participation schemes**

(a) **They bring into play the employees' own experiences to decide the best methods**. Someone who is actually doing the job may be able to see where improvements can be made, and where the impact of decisions will be.

(b) **Employees may actually set targets higher than managers expect.** In the Hawthorne experiment, a group who participated in decisions affecting them became much more productive.

(c) **If employees can control their performance, many supervisory jobs will be removed** making supervision more effective and helping in the **delayering of organisations**.

(d) **Improved quality of work may result where employees are interested**. A group that feels involved will perform better.

(e) **Unexpected events will not be so traumatic.** Employees will have learned to think for themselves and will be willing to take decisions. This may have the additional effect of greater job satisfaction and reduced labour turnover and absenteeism.

3.25 The advantages of participation should also be considered from the opposite end: what would be the disadvantages of not having participation? The answer to this is that employees would be told what to do, and would presumably comply with orders. However, their compliance would not be enthusiastic, and they would not be psychologically committed to their work.

3.26 Participation can involve employees and make them committed to their task, if the following conditions are met.

(a) **Participation should be genuine.** It is very easy for a manager to invite participation from his subordinates and then ignore their views. A culture change may be needed within management.

(b) The efforts to establish participation by employees should be pushed over a long period of time and with a lot of energy. However, 'if the issue or the task is trivial...and everyone realises it, participative methods will boomerang. Issues that do not affect the individuals concerned will not, on the whole, engage their interest'. (Handy).

(c) The **purpose** of the participation of employees in a decision is made quite **clear** from the outset. 'If employees are consulted to make a decision, their views should carry the decision. If, however, they are consulted for **advice**, their views need not necessarily be accepted.'

8: Improving team performance

   (d) The **individuals** must have the **abilities** and the **information** to join in decision making effectively.

   (e) The supervisor or manager **wishes** for participation from the subordinates, and does not suggest it merely because he/she thinks it is the done thing.

3.27 Worldwide social and educational trends show that **people's expectations** have risen above the basic requirement for money. The current demand is for more interesting work and for a say in decision making. These expectations are a basic part of the movement towards greater participation at work.

Empowerment

3.28 It might have been expected that the world economic recession of the 1980s and 1990s would divert management theorists' attention away from such issues.

3.29 However, competitive pressures have encouraged processes such as **delayering** (cutting out levels of (mainly middle) management) and **downsizing**, leading to **flatter hierarchies**, with more delegation and more decentralisation of authority. All this involves **shifting responsibility** to employees further down the management hierarchy, a process recently given the broad name of **empowerment.**

3.30 The argument is that by empowering workers the job will be done more effectively.

3.31 This thinking is very much in line with that of the neo-human relations theorists such as Maslow, Herzberg and McGregor, who believed that organisational effectiveness is determined by the extent to which people's higher psychological needs for growth, challenge, responsibility and self-fulfilment are met by the work that they do.

Marketing at Work

The validity of this view and its relevance to modern trends appears to be borne out by the approach to empowerment adopted by **Harvester Restaurants**, as described in *Personnel Management*. The management structure comprises a branch manager and a 'coach', while everyone else is a team member. Everyone within a team has one or more 'accountabilities' (these include recruitment, drawing up rotas, keeping track of sales targets and so on) which are shared out by the team members at their weekly team meetings. All the team members at different times act as 'co-ordinator' - the person responsible for taking the snap decisions that are frequently necessary in a busy restaurant. Apparently all of the staff involved agree that empowerment has made their jobs more interesting and has hugely increased their motivation and sense of involvement.

Pay and incentive schemes

Pay as a motivator

3.32 Employees need income to live. The size of that income will affect the standard of living, and although they would obviously like to earn more, they are probably more concerned about two other aspects of pay.

- That they should **earn enough**
- That pay should be **fair in comparison** with the pay of others

There is no doubt that pay does have some motivating effect, but it is fundamentally a **hygiene** factor.

Part C: Managing people

Incentive schemes

3.33 Pay as a motivator is commonly associated with **payment by results** or incentive schemes, where a worker's pay is dependent upon output. These are common in production settings but less appropriate for knowledge workers.

3.34 All such incentive schemes are based on the principle that people are willing to work harder to obtain more money. However, the work of *Mayo* has shown that there are several constraints which can nullify this basic principle.

(a) The average employee is not generally capable of influencing the timings and control systems used by management.

(b) Employees remain suspicious that if they achieved high levels of output and earnings then management would **alter the basis of the incentive rates** to reduce future earnings. As a result they **conform to a group output norm**. The need to have the approval of their fellow workers by conforming is more important than the money urge.

(c) **High taxation rates** would mean that workers do not believe that extra effort produces an adequate increase in pay.

3.35 A short-term incentive scheme involves a direct observable link between personal or team efforts and the reward gained. However a long-term scheme such as a profit sharing scheme, has a less personal relevance and a slower pay-back.

Common types of short-term incentive schemes

3.36 **Individual payment by results**, such as a sales bonus over and above a basic wage for achieving set standards of sales over a prescribed period. There is thus a direct link between performance and earnings for each individual so the motivating effect is strong. However, it has its disadvantages.

(a) The system is complex and expensive to administer.

(b) If **quantity** of sales is the relevant index, margins may suffer as sales staff negotiate lower prices to make sales.

(c) Employees may **manipulate** sales, because of fears that high sales will become a new norm, with a reduction in the pay incentive.

(d) **Employees outside the scheme may resent the wages levels of those inside**: pay differentials may be eroded. It has been known for top sales people to earn more than the Managing Director.

3.37 **Group payment by results** such as team bonus schemes mean that bonus pay for group performance is distributed equally among members. The cohesion of the team may then be built up in an effort to improve collective performance. This type of scheme works well where individual contributions are hard to isolate: the calculation is fairer. However, there are still disadvantages to schemes of this type.

(a) In addition to the disadvantages of the individual system, the **larger the group, the less direct the link** between individual effort and reward - so the motivating effect may be reduced.

(b) The system may be **unfair to harder-working individuals** within the group.

(c) Political conflicts and rivalries **between groups** may work to the detriment of the organisation as a whole.

3.38 It has become clear from the experiences of many companies that profit sharing schemes, incentive schemes (productivity bonuses) and joint consultation machinery do not in themselves improve productivity or ease the way for work to get done. Company-wide profit sharing schemes cannot be related directly to extra effort by individuals and are probably a hygiene factor rather than a motivator.

Non-financial incentives

3.39 Marketing managers may already have considerable experience at developing non financial incentives to influence sales teams and the purchase behaviour of customers. Competitions, gifts and prizes can all be utilised as the basis of specific motivation schemes. They create interest, add status for the winner and often have a higher **perceived value** than financial incentives do. Non financial incentives can be cheaper than their cash equivalent; for example, retail vouchers can be purchased at a discount on face value.

3.40 Such incentives must satisfy two conditions.

- They must give recipients a choice.
- They must be valued by recipients.

3.41 Offering extra time off or holiday are typically very acceptable and an early finish on a Friday is the sort of incentive which can often be organised fairly informally at team level.

Marketing at work

Motivation

UK organisations spent more than £900 million last year on non-cash incentives. At least a quarter of that sum was spent on trying to improve people's performance at work.

Understandably, it is the more off-the-wall ideas that attract attention. A computer company in Oxfordshire, for example, appointed an 'apology man', who was employed to say sorry to individuals on behalf of others for day-to-day misunderstandings. The directors claim this saves a lot of management time and makes for a happier and more productive workforce.

Business systems specialist SAS also achieved some notoriety recently when it gave up providing free jelly beans to all employees and switched to providing share options instead. Such examples can cause people to take employee incentives less seriously, but millions of pounds of investment cannot be wrong. There are sound principles behind the work of Freud and Jung, and the idea that most people's actions are driven by the pursuit of pleasure and the fear of pain.

Clark Hull was the first academic to establish that behaviour is rooted in the individual's inner drive, habits and the incentive to change. Within a business context, we all recognise that some people appear well motivated all the time, while others need to establish a behaviour pattern or habit before they begin to perform well. A third group of people perform at their best only when there is something in it for them.

But all individuals make choices based on maximising personal pleasure. We see this when organisations set incentive or behaviour targets. Employees are usually very canny at working out whether the effort to change is worth the reward. Several studies have shown that few individuals will change their behaviour for less than 10 per cent of their take-home benefits. I'm afraid that the idea of jelly beans all round simply doesn't cut it.

In 1938 personality theorist Henry Murray established 20 basic human needs that could be exploited in order to improve people's performance. They included the need to accomplish something difficult; to master, manipulate or organise objects, human beings or ideas; and to rival and surpass other people.

All of these needs feed straight into recognition systems and methods of devising challenging work that have their origins in the studies of Maslow, Herzberg and other job enrichment specialists.

> **Incentive strategy**
>
> To devise effective incentive programmes, employers need to:
>
> - take account of the corporate environment and trading background of the organisation
> - combine goals with emotions
> - keep organisational goals congruent with each other
> - use success stories to spur people on
> - provide adequate skills training
> - establish a gradual change process, rather than a sudden switch
> - respond to feedback from employees quickly and directly

John Fisher, People Management, 11 January 2001

4 THE ROLE OF APPRAISAL   12/99, 12/00

> **Exam Tip**
>
> Both questions set so far on appraisal required you to write a report in general terms about the benefits of an appraisal system and how you would implement one. Of course your answers have to be sensitive to the context when it is given in the question: in December 2000, a large travel agency.

4.1 Motivation is concerned with attempts to improve the performance of groups and individuals. We saw in the last section how important regular **feedback** was to the basic concepts of motivation. Appraisal is a systematic approach to providing that feedback and for putting praise and criticism in context. It also provides an assessment of current performance against which future improvements can be measured and **training needs** established.

4.2 The general purpose of any staff assessment system is to improve the efficiency of the organisation by ensuring that the individuals within it are performing to the best of their ability and developing their potential for improvement. Within this overall objective, staff assessments have several specific purposes.

- To review **performance**, to plan and follow up training and development programmes; and to set targets for future performance
- To review **potential**, as an aid to planning career development by predicting the level and type of work the individual will be capable of in the future
- To increase **motivation by providing feedback**
- To review **salaries**: measuring the extent to which an employee is deserving of a salary increase as compared with peers

4.3 **Features of a typical system**

- **Identification of criteria for assessment**, perhaps based on job analysis, performance standards and person specifications
- The preparation by the subordinate's manager of an **assessment report**
- An **appraisal interview**, for an exchange of views about the results of the assessment and targets for improvement
- **Review of the assessment by the assessor's own superior**, so that the appraisee does not feel subject to one person's prejudices. Formal appeals may be allowed, if necessary to establish the fairness of the procedure
- The preparation and implementation of **action plans** to achieve improvements and changes agreed
- **Follow-up**: monitoring the progress of the action plan

4.4 There may not need to be standard forms for appraisal (and elaborate form-filling procedures should be avoided) as long as managers understand the nature and extent of what is required, and are motivated to take it seriously. Most systems, however, provide for assessments to be recorded, and report forms of various lengths and complexity may be designed for standard use, A written record of some form is essential to prevent doubts and uncertainties at a later date.

The assessment report

4.5 The basis of assessment must first be determined. Assessments must be related to a **common standard**, in order for comparisons to be made between individuals, and of a particular individual's progress over time. They should also be related to meaningful performance criteria, which take account of the critical variables in each different job.

4.6 Various appraisal techniques may be used.

(a) **Overall assessment** is the simplest method, simply requiring the manager to write in narrative form judgements about the appraisee, possibly with a checklist of personality characteristics and performance targets to work from. There will be no guaranteed consistency of the criteria and areas of assessment, however, and managers may not be able to convey clear, effective judgements in writing.

(b) **Guided assessment** requires assessors to comment on a number of specified characteristics and performance elements, with guidelines as to how the terms (eg 'application', 'integrity', 'adaptability') are to be interpreted in the work context. This is a more precise, but still rather vague method.

(c) **Grading** adds a comparative frame of reference to the general guidelines, whereby managers are asked to select one of a number of levels or degrees to which the individual in question displays the given characteristic. These are also known as **rating scales**, and are much used in standard appraisal forms. Their effectiveness depends to a large extent on the **relevance** of the factors chosen for assessment and the definition of the agreed standards of assessment.

   (i) Numerical values may be added to ratings to give rating 'scores'. Alternatively a less precise **graphic scale** may be used to indicate general position on a plus/minus scale, for example:

   Factor: job knowledge

   High ———————————— Average ——✓———————— Low

   (ii) The principal drawback of such schemes is that the subordinate may not agree with the precise ratings given. This may lead to the subordinate questioning the judgement of the appraiser. The appraisal may degenerate into an argument about the appraiser's use of the grading system rather than what the assessment tells the subordinate about his or her performance.

(d) **Results-orientated schemes.** The above techniques will be concerned with results but are commonly based on behavioural appraisal. A wholly results-orientated approach, such as Management by Objectives, reviews performance against specific targets and standards of performance agreed in advance by manager and subordinate together. Such an approach has a number of advantages.

   (i) The subordinate is more involved in appraisal because success or progress is measured against specific, jointly agreed targets.

Part C: Managing people

(ii) The manager is relieved, to some extent, of the role of critic, and becomes a **counsellor**.

(iii) Learning and motivation theories suggest that clear and known targets are important in modifying and determining behaviour.

(e) **Self-appraisals**, where the individuals carry out their own self-evaluation, can be an alternative to management/subordinate appraisals. They have the advantage that the system is evidently aimed at the needs of the individual. Self-appraisal schemes can also be combined with training schemes where the individuals decide on the training they require.

4.7 The effectiveness of any scheme will depend on the realistic and clear statement of targets; and the commitment of both parties to make it work. The **measurement of success or failure is only part of the picture**: **reasons** for failure and opportunities arising from success must be evaluated.

4.8 Managers will need guidance, or perhaps training to help them make a relevant, objective and helpful report. Most large organisations with standard review forms also issue detailed guidance notes to aid assessors with the written and discussion elements.

Appraisal interview

4.9 The report may be shown to the appraisee and thus form a basis for discussion. Some organisations, however, do not show the report to the employee; this is likely to lead to resentment and anxiety about the correctness or otherwise of its contents.

4.10 **Approaches to appraisal interviews**

(a) The **tell and sell** method. The manager gives details of the assessment to the subordinate and then tries to **gain acceptance** of the evaluation and the improvement plan. This requires unusual human relations skills in order to convey constructive criticism in an acceptable manner, and to motivate appraisees to alter their behaviour.

(b) The **tell and listen** method. The manager gives the assessment and then **invites response**. The manager no longer dominates the interview, and there is greater opportunity for counselling. The employee is encouraged to participate in the assessment and the working out of improvement targets and methods. Managers using this method will need to have good listening skills.

(c) The **problem solving** approach. The manager abandons the role of critic altogether, and becomes a counsellor and helper. The discussion is centred not on the assessment, but on the employee's work problems. The employee is encouraged to think solutions through, and to commit to the recognised need for personal improvement.

4.11 Many organisations waste the opportunities for **upward communication** embedded in the appraisal process. In order to get a positive contribution from employees, the appraisal interviewer should ask positive and thought-provoking questions. Here are some examples.

- What parts of your job do you do best?

- Could any changes be made in your job which might result in improved performance?

- Have you any skills, knowledge, or aptitudes which could be made better use of in the organisation?

4.12 **Follow-up procedures**

- Having the report agreed and counter-signed by a more senior manager
- Informing appraisees of the final results of the appraisal, if this has been contentious in the review interview
- Carrying out agreed actions on training, promotions and so on
- Monitoring the appraisee's progress with agreed actions
- Taking necessary steps to help the appraisee for example by guidance, providing feedback or upgrading equipment

The effectiveness of appraisal

4.13 In practice, the system often goes wrong.

(a) There may be a divergence between the subordinate's and interviewer's perceived and actual needs. A subordinate may want praise but need constructive criticism. The interviewer may wish to concentrate on criticising, whereas the appraisal could be used to give feedback on management practice.

(b) Appraisal interviews are often **defensive on the part of the subordinate,** who believes that any criticism will bring sanctions. There may also be some mistrust of the validity of the scheme itself.

(c) Interviews are also often **defensive on the part of the superior**, who cannot reconcile the role of judge and critic with the constructive intent of the interview. As a result there may be many unresolved issues left at the end.

(d) The superior might show **conscious or unconscious bias** in the report. Systems without clearly defined standard criteria will be particularly prone to the subjectivity of the assessor's judgements.

(e) The general level of ratings may vary widely from manager to manager.

(f) Appraisals may deal with specific problems which should have been dealt with at the time they arose by counselling. Appraisals ought to concentrate on ongoing matters that are important to career development.

(g) Appraisals may be seen merely as a bureaucratic form-filling exercise or as no more than an annual formality.

Upward appraisal

4.14 A notable modern trend, adopted in the UK by companies such as *BP*, *British Airways*, *Central TV* and others, is upward appraisal, whereby **employees are not rated by their superiors but by their subordinates.** The followers appraise the leader. The advantages of this method were set out by Adrian Furnham in the *Financial Times* (March 1993).

(a) Subordinates tend to know their superiors better than superiors know their subordinates.

(b) An assessment based upon ratings given by several people is likely to be more accurate than a single opinion.

(c) Subordinates' ratings have more impact because it is more unusual to receive ratings from subordinates.

Part C: Managing people

4.15 Problems with the method include fear of reprisals, vindictiveness, and extra form processing. Some managers in strong positions might refuse to act, even if a consensus of staff suggested that they should change their ways.

Peer rating

4.16 An alternative approach to individual appraisal (which also removes the link between past performance and reward) is **peer rating** in which an individual is judged and counselled by workmates or colleagues. It has been argued that peer rating will be devoid of mistrust and fear of missing promotion and will therefore be more honest and constructive, thus aiding the individual to develop in his job. It may be a useful strategy amongst professionally qualified staff.

360-degree appraisal

4.17 A final variant on appraisal schemes is the 360 degree appraisal. In this case, effectiveness is appraised by all the people with whom the subject has dealings - superiors, subordinates, customers and suppliers, internal and external.

Marketing at Work

(a) At BA, managers will have measurable performance targets based on customers' perceptions of service: 'the manager of the cabin crew on an aircraft will be judged, for example, on how many customers think staff were warm and friendly.' The internal customer is not forgotten, either. 'In the case of departments that do not deal directly with passengers, such as engineering, those who use their services within the airline will be asked to evaluate them.'

(b) Burger King has an appraisal scheme for some of its regional managers - the outlets are asked to give feedback on individual managers' performance.

4.18 The aim is to get an all-round picture of a manager's effectiveness. A manager who achieves some objectives by alienating staff might be taking a short-term view; if this increases staff turnover in the long run. 360-degree appraisal identifies areas where a manager can do better, the manager's superior cannot always offer the wide perspective necessary.

4.19 **Advantages** of 360-degree feedback

- It **highlights every aspect** of the individual's performance, and allows comparison of the individual's self-assessment with the views of others.

- Feedback tends, overall, to be balanced, covering strengths in some areas with weaknesses in others, so it is less discouraging.

- The assessment is based on the normal work environment and circumstances. The feedback is thus felt to be fairer and more relevant, making it easier for employees to accept.

4.20 Potential **pitfalls** of 360-degree feedback

- **Negative emphasis.** Feedback on weaknesses should be balanced by positive feedback on strengths and potential, to encourage the employee to develop.

- '**Flavour of the month approach**'. The technique and its results are seen as interesting but no thought has been given to follow-up action.

- **Lack of confidentiality.** Respondents must be anonymous, or they may fear to tell the truth in an assessment.

- **Poor communication about the purpose of the exercise.** It can be daunting, and employees need to understand that it is not a political exercise, or a rod to beat anyone.
- **Lack of action and support.** The organisation must support the employee in the development suggested by the feedback.

> ### Action Programme 6
>
> Peter Ward gives an example of the kind of questionnaires that might be used as the instrument of 360-degree feedback.
>
> 'A skill area like "communicating", for example, might be defined as "the ability to express oneself clearly and to listen effectively to others". Typical comments would include "Presents ideas or information in a well-organised manner" (followed by rating scale); or: "Allows you to finish what you have to say".'
>
> Rate **yourself** on the two comments mentioned here, on a scale of 1-10. Get a group of friends, fellow-students, even a tutor or parent, to write down, **anonymously**, on a piece of paper **their** rating for you on the same two comments. Keep them in an envelope, unseen, until you have collected several.
>
> Compare them with your self-rating. If you dare...

5 TRAINING AND DEVELOPMENT FOR STAFF 6/00

5.1 Procuring the most appropriate human resources for the task and environment is an on-going process. It involves not only recruitment and selection, but the training and development of employees prior to employment, or at any time during their employment, in order to help them meet the requirements of their current, and potential future job.

5.2 **Purposes of selection and training**

- Fitting people to the requirements of the job
- Securing better occupational adjustment
- Defining performance criteria against which the success of the process can be monitored

5.3 Training may be defined as: 'the systematic development of the attitudes, knowledge and skill patterns required by an individual in order to perform adequately a given task or job'.

The contribution of training

5.4 Modern business is increasingly dynamic, with changes in technology, products, processes and control techniques. The need for planned growth combined with this dynamism mean that a working organisation's competitiveness depends increasingly on the continuous reassessment of training needs and the provision of planned training to meet those needs.

5.5 Training can contribute to success, but has its limitations.

(a) It must be the correct tool for the need: it cannot solve problems caused by faulty organisation, equipment or employee selection.

(b) Reasons for neglecting training must be overcome: these include cost, inconvenience, apathy and an unrealistic expectation of training in the past.

(c) Limitations imposed by intelligence, motivation and the psychological restrictions of the learning process must be understood.

5.6 Internal formal training courses are run by the organisation's training department. External training courses are available in many forms.

- **Day-release courses**
- **Evening classes**, which make demands on the individual's time outside work
- **Revision courses** for professional examinations
- **Block-release courses** which may involve some weeks at a college followed by a period back at work
- **Sandwich courses**, usually involving six months at college then six months at work, in rotation, for two or three years
- A sponsored **full-time course at a university or polytechnic** for one or two years

5.7 **Disadvantages of formal training**

(a) Individuals will not benefit from formal training unless they want to learn. The individual's superior may need to provide encouragement in this respect.

(b) If the subject matter of the training course does not relate to an individual's job, the learning will be quickly forgotten.

(c) Individuals may not be able to accept that what they learn on a course applies in the context of their own particular job. For example, managers may attend an internal course on management that suggests a participatory style of leadership, but may consider it irrelevant, because their subordinates are 'too young' or 'too inexperienced'.

On-the-job training (OJT)

5.8 OJT is very common, especially when the work involved is not complex. Trainee managers require more coaching, and may be given assignments or projects as part of a planned programme to develop their experience. Unfortunately, this type of training will be unsuccessful if the assignments do not have a specific purpose or the organisation is intolerant of any mistakes which the trainee makes.

Action Programme 7

What different methods of on-the-job training can you identify?

Coaching

5.9 **Coaching** is a common method of OJT; the trainee is put under the guidance of an experienced employee who demonstrates how to do the job and helps refine the trainee's technique.

5.10 All forms of training require the commitment of the organisation to the learning programme. It must believe in training and developing employees, and be prepared to devote both the money and the time. The manager will largely dictate the department's attitude to these things.

8: Improving team performance

A training programme

5.11 Training is often concerned with teaching a person how to do a particular job, or how to do it better. Many firms have structured training programmes.

5.12 A **systematic approach to training**

- **Identify areas** where training will be beneficial.
- **Establish learning targets**. The areas where learning is needed should be identified and specific, realistic goals stated, including standards of performance.
- Decide on the **training methods to be used**.
- **Plan a systematic learning and development programme**. This should allow for practice and consolidation.
- **Identify opportunities for broadening the trainee's knowledge and experience** such as involvement in new projects, extending the job or greater responsibility.
- **Take into account the strengths and limitations of the trainee**. A trainee from an academic background may learn best through research-based learning like fact-finding for a committee; whilst those who learn best by doing may profit from project work.
- **Implement** the scheme in full.
- **Exchange feedback**. The manager will want performance information in order to monitor the progress, adjust the learning programme, identify further needs and plan future development.
- **Validate the results** to check that the training works and benefits exceed costs.

Analysis of training needs

5.13 **Training needs** can be identified by considering the **gap** between **job requirements**, as determined by job analysis, job description and so on, and the **ability of the job holder**, as determined by testing or observation and appraisal.

5.14 The training department's management should make an initial investigation of the problem. Even if work is not done as well as it could be, training is not necessarily the right answer. We have seen that poor working standards might also be caused by other factors.

Marketing at Work

People Management reported that a number of Whitbread pubs had improved performance as a result of a change in the company's training scheme. Previously the company's training scheme had aimed to improve the service standards of individuals, and there were also discussions with staff on business developments. It was felt however that other companies in the same sector had overtaken Whitbread in these respects.

Whitbread therefore introduced an integrated approach to assessment of the performance of pubs. Assessment is by four criteria; training (a certain percentage of staff have to have achieved a training award), standards (suggested by working parties of staff), team meetings and customer satisfaction. Managers are trained in training skills and they in turn train staff, using a set of structured notes to ensure a consistent training process.

Pubs that fulfil all the criteria win a team hospitality award, consisting of a plaque, a visit from a senior executive, and a party or points for goods scheme. To retain the award and achieve further points, pubs have then to pass further assessments which take place every six months.

The scheme seemed to improve standards. Significantly staff turnover was down and a survey suggested morale had improved, with a greater sense of belonging particularly by part-time staff. A major cause of these improvements may well be the involvement of staff and management in the design process.

Part C: Managing people

Training objectives

5.15 If the training department concludes that the provision of training could improve work performance, it must **analyse the work in detail in** order to decide what the **requirements** of a training programme should be. In particular, there should be **a training objective or objectives.** These are tangible, observable targets which trainees should be capable of reaching at the end of the course.

5.16 The training objectives should be **clear, specific and measurable**, for example: 'at the end of a course a trainee must be able to describe ..., or identify ..., or list ..., or state ..., or distinguish x from y ...'. It is insufficient to state as an objective of a course 'to give trainees a grounding in ...' or 'to give trainees a better appreciation of ...'. These objectives are too woolly, and actual achievements cannot be measured against them.

Training methods

5.17 Having decided what must be learned and to what standard of achievement, the next stage is to decide what method of training should be used.

5.18 **Course training methods**

(a) **Lectures.** Lectures are suitable for large audiences and can be an efficient way of putting across information. However lack of participation may lead to lack of interest and/or failure to understand by most of the audience.

(b) **Discussions.** Discussions aim to impart information but allow much greater opportunities for audience participation. They are often suitable for groups up to 20 and can be a good means of maintaining interest.

(c) **Exercises.** An exercise involves a particular task being undertaken with pre-set results following guidance laid down. They are a very active form of learning and are a good means of checking whether trainees have assimilated information.

(d) **Role plays.** Trainees act out roles in a typical work situation. They are useful practice for face-to-face situations. However, they may embarrass some participants and may not be taken seriously.

(e) **Case studies.** Case studies identify causes and/or suggest solutions. They are a good means of exchanging ideas and thinking out solutions. However trainees may see the case study as divorced from their real work experience.

5.19 **Programmed learning** can be provided on a computer terminal, but it is still associated with printed booklets which provide information in easy-to-learn steps. The booklet asks simple questions which the trainee must answer. If they are answered correctly, the trainee is instructed to carry on with more learning. If the questions are answered wrongly, the booklet gives an alternative set of instructions to go back and learn again. Programmed learning has a number of advantages.

(a) Trainees can work through the course in simple stages and continually checks their progress. Misunderstandings are quickly put right.

(b) Trainees are kept actively involved in the learning process because they must keep answering questions put to them in the booklet.

(c) Giving correct answers immediately reinforces the learning process.

(d) Trainees can work at their own pace.

Cost/benefit analysis of training

5.20 The training course should only go ahead if the **likely benefits are expected to exceed the costs** of designing and then running the course. **Costs** include training materials, the salaries of the staff attending training courses, their travelling expenses, the salaries of training staff and training overheads. **Benefits** might be measured in a variety of ways.

- Quicker working and therefore reductions in overtime or staff numbers
- Greater accuracy of work
- More extensive skills
- Improved motivation

5.21 As you will appreciate, the **benefits are more easily stated in general terms than quantified in money terms.** Indeed, it is often difficult to measure benefits such as increased identification with business objectives and increased cohesion as a team, but these benefits may nevertheless be significant.

Implementation and evaluation of training

5.22 When the training course has been designed, **a pilot course may be run.** The purpose of the test would be to find out whether the training scheme appears to achieve what it has set out to do, or whether some revisions are necessary. After the pilot test, the scheme can be implemented in full.

5.23 Implementation of the training scheme is not the end of the story. The scheme should be **validated** and **evaluated**.

   (a) **Validation** means observing the results of the course, and measuring whether the training objective has been achieved.

   (b) **Evaluation** means comparing the actual costs of the scheme against the assessed benefits which are being obtained. If the costs exceed the benefits, the scheme will need to be re-designed or withdrawn.

5.24 **Validation methods**

   (a) **Asking the trainees** whether they thought the training programme was relevant to their work, and whether they found it useful. This is rather inexact and does not measure results for comparison against the training objective.

   (b) **Measuring what the trainees have learned** on the course, perhaps by means of a test at the end of the course.

   (c) Studying the **subsequent behaviour of the trainees** in their jobs to measure how the training scheme has altered the way they do their work. This is possible where the purpose of the course was to learn a particular skill.

   (d) Finding out whether the training has affected **the work or behaviour of other employees not on the course.** This form of monitoring would probably be reserved for senior managers in the training department.

   (e) Seeing whether training in general has contributed to the **overall objectives of the organisation.** This too is a form of monitoring reserved for senior managers and would perhaps be discussed at board level in the organisation.

Marketing at Work

An article in *Marketing Business* in March 1998 highlighted recent trends in marketing training, particularly its interaction with the rest of the organisation. This reflects a change in emphasis in the role of marketing in many companies, away from product management and towards anticipating and supplying customer needs.

Companies are supplying increased marketing training to operating departments in topics such as brand awareness and are giving marketing departments training which consists of two parts. The first part focuses on normal technicalities such as research and promotional techniques. The second gives marketers a wider perspective on the rest of the company, focusing on issues such as systems, distribution, customer service and financial management. Motivating operating departments to become more innovative and centred on the customer is seen as being very important.

Action Programme 8

Devise a training programme for a new recruit who will be doing a job similar to yours.

6 COUNSELLING AND ADVICE

6.1 To **advise** is to propose solutions to someone else's problems. To **counsel** is to assist someone through the process of finding his or her own solutions. The counselling approach involves a number of considerations.

- **Discerning the need** for counselling
- **Ensuring privacy and time**
- **Encouraging openness** and ensuring confidentiality
- **Using specific examples** to illustrate points discussed and avoiding abstract comments
- Emphasis on **constructive interaction** including personal rapport and trust
- Sensitivity to the subject's beliefs and values
- Guidance in **evolving the subject's own solutions** rather than giving advice
- **Avoiding arguments** but instead getting the subject to discuss reasons for disagreement
- **Supporting the solution** devised
- **Monitoring the progress of the solution**

6.2 You will note that **counselling** requires a systematic approach, with careful planning and a range of interpersonal skills being brought into play. Particularly important are listening skills. It requires the support of the organisation, to train counsellors, to back the solutions reached and to allow time for the counselling and monitoring period. Some organisations formalise this in a counselling programme, with qualified counsellors, while others prefer to support managers in particular counselling situations.

6.3 **Advising** is a much more common and on-going process. Because, unlike counselling, advising is not essentially a co-operative process, the **effectiveness of advice depends on the willingness of the recipient to accept suggestions**. It also depends on the **soundness of the advice itself**: unlike counselling, advising has very little beneficial effect **in itself**.

6.4 A counselling approach is now often applied to interviewing situations previously regarded as purely informative or judgmental, for example, disciplinary and grievance interviews, and appraisal interviews.

6.5 An open door management policy or supervisory style may encourage employees to come forward with a wide range of work and even personal problems which require counselling. Some organisations may have a welfare officer to provide counselling.

The role of counselling in organisations

6.6 Effective counselling is not merely a matter of pastoral care for individuals, but is very much in the organisation's interests.

- Appropriate use of counselling tools can **prevent underperformance, reduce labour turnover** and **absenteeism** and **increase commitment** from employees.

- Workplace counselling recognises that the **organisation** may be contributing to the employees' problems and therefore it provides an opportunity to **reassess organisational policy and practice.**

> **Action Programme 9**
>
> How do you react when people try to give you advice at work? Have you ever been counselled? If so, did you feel differently about that experience?
>
> Who (if anyone) is responsible for formal counselling in your company: a specialist or line manager? Is the availability of counselling clearly communicated to staff, and in a way that will encourage them to come forward? Do people go to informal counsellors among their colleagues instead: if so, to whom and why?

7 DISCIPLINE AND GRIEVANCE 6/00

Disciplinary principles

7.1 Maintaining discipline among employees is an integral part of leadership, and requires human relations and communication skills. Discipline is a condition of orderliness in which the members of the enterprise behave sensibly and conduct themselves according to the standards of acceptable behaviour as related to the goals of the organisation. Once employees know what is expected of them and feel that the rules are reasonable, **self-disciplined** behaviour becomes a part of group norms.

7.2 Self discipline must start at the top: the manager should comply with certain requirements, such as being on time, observing safety rules, no smoking and no drinking rules, and dressing and behaving in a manner expected of the position.

7.3 There are some employees in every organisation who will fail to observe the established rules and standards even after having been informed of them. These employees simply do not accept the responsibility of self discipline. Firm action is required to correct those situations which interfere with the accepted norms of responsible employee behaviour.

7.4 **Disciplinary action can lead to significant legal problems**. The employee may be dismissed or regard the disciplinary action as amounting to **substantive dismissal**. In either case, an **action for wrongful or unfair dismissal** may result. This can be very

Part C: Managing people

expensive for the employer. **Managers commencing any formal disciplinary procedure would be well advised to consult the HR department first**.

7.5 There are many types of disciplinary situations which require attention by the supervisor or manager.

- Excessive absenteeism
- Excessive lateness in arriving at work
- Poor attitudes which influence the work of others or harm the firm's image
- Improper personal appearance
- Breaking safety rules
- Open insubordination

7.6 In addition to these types of situations managers might be confronted with disciplinary problems stemming from employee behaviour **off the job** such as a drinking problem or involvement in some form of law breaking activity. In such circumstances, whenever an employee's off-the-job conduct has an impact upon the organisation the manager must be prepared to deal with such a problem within the scope of the disciplinary process.

7.7 **Managers must not ignore disciplinary problems**, however unpleasant they are for everyone. If a manager does not take firm and appropriate action, some other employees may be encouraged to break the rules because they think they can get away with it. It is also unfair to these members of staff who do observe the rules.

The manager-subordinate relationship in disciplinary situations

7.8 Any disciplinary action must be undertaken with sensitivity and sound judgement on the manager's part. Disciplinary action must have as its goal the improvement of the future behaviour of the employee and other members of the organisation.

7.9 Even if the manager uses sensitivity and judgement, imposing disciplinary action tends to generate resentment because it is an unpleasant experience.

7.10 Following the basic rules set out below will help the manager to reduce the resentment inherent in all disciplinary actions.

(a) **Immediacy** means that the manager takes disciplinary action as speedily as possible; the full circumstances may not be known or there may be doubt as to the penalty which should be imposed. The nature of the incident may make it advisable to have the offender leave the premises quickly, but the ACAS Code of Practice requires that **investigation** be made **before action is taken**. Consideration should be given to the employee's record and all pertinent details of the situation in preparation for the disciplinary interview.

(b) **Advance warning**. In order to have employees accept disciplinary action as fair, it is essential that they know in advance what is expected of them. Many companies find it useful to have a disciplinary section in an employee handbook, which every new employee receives. However, each new employee should also be informed orally about what is expected.

(c) **Consistency**. Consistency of discipline means that each time an infraction occurs appropriate disciplinary action is taken. Inconsistency lowers morale, diminishes respect and creates doubt.

8: Improving team performance

(d) **Impersonality**. It is only natural for an employee to feel some resentment towards a manager who has taken disciplinary action against him or her. The supervisor can reduce the amount of resentment by making disciplinary action as impersonal as possible. Penalties should be connected with the act and not based upon the personality involved. Once a disciplinary action has been taken, the manager should treat the employee in the same way as before the infraction.

(e) **Privacy**. As a general rule, unless the manager's authority is challenged directly and in public disciplinary action should be taken in private.

Action Programme 10

Outline a disciplinary incident in which you have been involved as the person imposing discipline - even if it is only an informal telling off you've given someone. What were the interpersonal difficulties involved: the attitudes and feelings that made the situation awkward? (If it wasn't awkward at all, stop and think: were you just insensitive to the other person's feeling at the time - or were there **real** reasons why the encounter was friendly and positive, in which case, what were they?)

The structure of a disciplinary interview

7.11 Preparation

(a) Gather the facts about the alleged infringement.

(b) Determine the organisation's position. How valuable is the employee, is there a past record and how far will the organisation go to help him/her improve?

(c) Determine the specific aims of the interview

- Punishment?
- Deterrence?
- Improvement?
- Establish future behaviour standards?

7.12 **Correct procedure must be followed**.
Informal oral warnings must precede formal sanctions. The employee must be given adequate notice of the interview and be informed of the charge and the right to be accompanied by a colleague or representative.

7.13 **Content of the interview**

(a) The manager will explain the purpose of the interview.

(b) The charges against the employee will be delivered, clearly, unambiguously and without personal emotion.

(c) The employee should be given the opportunity to comment, explain, justify or deny.

(d) The manager will explain the organisation's position with regard to the issues involved: disappointment, concern, need for improvement, impact on others.

(e) **The organisation's expectations should be made clear** with as positive an emphasis as possible on the employee's capacity and responsibility to improve.

- They should be specific and quantifiable, performance related and realistic.
- They should be related to a practical but reasonably short time period and so a date should be set to review progress.

- The manager may agree to measures to help the employee should that be necessary.

(f) The **manager** should explain the reasons behind any **penalties** imposed on the employee, including the entry in his/her personnel record of the formal warning. The manager should also explain how the warning can be **removed** from the record, and what standards must be achieved within a specified timescale. There should be a clear warning of the **consequences of failure** to meet improvement targets.

(g) The **manager** should explain the organisation's appeals procedure. There should be a right of appeal to a higher manager.

(h) Once it has been established that the employee understands all the above, the **manager** should summarise the proceedings briefly.

Records of the interview will be kept for the employee's personnel file, and for the formal follow-up review and any further action necessary.

Grievance interviews

7.14 The dynamics of a **grievance interview** are broadly similar to a disciplinary interview, except that it is the **subordinate** who primarily wants a positive result from it.

7.15 Prior to the interview, the manager should have some idea of the complaint and its possible source. The meeting itself can then proceed through a number of stages.

(a) **Exploration**. What is the problem: the background, the facts, the causes, manifest and hidden? At this stage, the manager should simply try to gather as much information as possible, without attempting to suggest solutions or interpretations.

(b) **Consideration**. The manager should do three things.

- Check the facts
- Analyse the causes - the problem about which the complaint has been made may be only a symptom
- Evaluate options for responding to the complaint, and the implication of any response made

It may be that information can be given to clear up a misunderstanding, or the employee will, having aired the matter, withdraw the complaint. However, the meeting may have to be **adjourned** while the manager gets extra information and considers extra options.

(c) **Reply**. The manager, having reached and reviewed conclusions, reconvenes the meeting to convey and if necessary justify a decision, and to hear counter-arguments and appeals. The outcome (agreed or disagreed) should be recorded in writing.

7.16 Grievance procedures should be seen as an employee's right. To this end, managers should be given formal training in the grievance procedures of their organisation, and the reasons for having them. Managers should be persuaded that the grievance procedures are beneficial for the organisation and are not a threat to themselves (since many grievances arise out of disputes between subordinates and managers).

Exit interviews

7.17 Employees may resign for any number of reasons, personal or occupational. Some or all of these reasons may well be a reflection on the structure, management style, culture or

personnel policies of the organisation itself. When an employee announces the intention to leave, verbally and/or by letter, it is important for the manager to find the real reasons why they are leaving, in an exit interview. This may lead to a review of existing policies on pay, training, promotion, the work environment, the quality and style of supervision and so on.

8 MANAGING PERIPHERAL WORKERS

8.1 You may have read about job insecurity and the decline of the permanent, full-time job. Whilst this development can be exaggerated, there are a **number of new ways in which people are employed and managed**. A firm might have a **core workforce** of permanent, full-time employees. This core might be supplemented by a **periphery** of people employed on a number of other bases, such as part-timers, people on short-term employment contracts which may or may not be renewed and freelances who are contracted to work when needed.

8.2 As a result of such arrangements, the organisation saves money and gains **flexibility**. However there might be concerns as to the **commitment** of the peripheral workforce. After all, if management can dispose of them at will, why should they be committed to the long-term future of the organisation? Such problems are truer for some organisations than others.

(a) Many part-timers welcome the opportunity to work part-time and the flexibility it provides.

(b) People on short-term contracts might hope that their performance will result in a full-time job eventually. Even if not, they might welcome the opportunity for personal learning and skill development.

(c) Freelances, will welcome the opportunity for more work - but they will also be hunting around elsewhere.

8.3 Another development is **telecommuting** or **teleworking,** which involves the use of IT to work at home but remain in close contact.

Marketing at Work

One in 100 of British Telecommunications' 100,000 UK employees could find their home transformed into their office in Britain's most ambitious experiment in teleworking.

The UK's largest telecoms operator is hoping to persuade at least 10,000 of its office staff to work from home, communicating with customers and managers by fax machine, telephone and the internet.

BT estimates it would save at least £134m a year in costs and an unquantifiable amount in terms of reduced stress, commuting delays and fuel. *Financial Times* (12 May 1999).

8.4 Working at home (**homeworking**) is not new in itself: there are many pieceworkers in the textile industry who do certain jobs at home, but it is relatively new to the management of the office.

8.5 **Advantages to the organisation of homeworking**

(a) **Cost savings on space.** Office rental costs and other charges can be very expensive. Firms can save money if they move some of their employees to homeworking.

(b) **A larger pool of labour.** The possibility of working at home might attract more applicants for clerical positions, especially from people who have other demands on their time.

(c) If the homeworkers are freelances, then the organisation need only pay them when they are actually working. However organisations should consider whether lack of benefits means that homeworkers are regarded as having second-class status.

(d) **Improved customer service** may result from a better match between available and required hours.

8.6 **Advantages to the individual of homeworking**

- **No time is wasted commuting to the office.**
- **The work can be organised flexibly** around the individual's domestic commitments.
- **Jobs which require concentration can sometimes be done better** at home without the disruption of the office.
- **It makes employment possible in remote areas.**

8.7 Managers who practise close supervision will perhaps feels a worrying **loss of control**. Managers who take the Theory X view of human nature might view homeworking as an opportunity for laziness and slack work.

8.8 However, these problems of control are partly illusory. There are **real problems for the organisation**.

(a) **Co-ordination** of the work of different homeworkers. The job design should ensure that homeworkers perform to the required standard. They should have the opportunity to ask for help, and supervisors should visit on a regular basis.

(b) **Briefing**. If a homeworker needs a lot of help on a task, this implies that the task has not been properly explained. So, briefing must be thorough.

(c) **Culture**. A homeworker is relatively isolated from the office and therefore, it might be assumed, from the firm. However, questions of **loyalty and commitment** do not apply for an organisation's sales force, whose members are rarely in the office. There should be regular meetings of homeworkers, and other regular contacts with the office.

(d) **Health and safety**. Health and safety regulations apply to homeworkers as well as office-based staff.

8.9 **Other management issues**

(a) When introducing homeworking for the first time, it is best done voluntarily. Homeworking is likely to be a change in conditions of employment.

(b) When recruiting, employers need to check that the home environment is suitable, and the candidates will be suited to working at home.

(c) The induction process for new employees is likely to have to be more extensive for homeworkers, since they cannot pick things up whilst being in the office.

(d) Homeworkers will have the same training and development needs as office-based workers, but may not be able to attend training courses. Distance learning packages can be used. Homeworkers should also have regular appraisals.

8.10 **Problems for homeworkers**

(a) **Isolation**. Work provides people with a social life, and many people might miss the sense of community if they are forced to work at home. Some firms get round this by having meetings where groups of homeworkers can get together.

(b) **Intrusions**. A homeworker is vulnerable, by definition, to interruptions especially from members of his or her family forgetting that the worker is **working** at home, in time that the employer is paying for.

(c) **Adequate space**. It is not always possible to obtain a quiet space at home in which to work.

(d) In practice many homeworkers, especially if they are freelances, have **fewer employment rights**. They are not entitled to sick pay or holiday pay. They have limited security, as the firm can dispense with their services at whim.

(e) **Technology.** Successful homeworking using IT requires systems that the homeworkers are able to use, and the availability of support in case there are technical problems with hardware or software.

8.11 The most important question that has to be decided is how homeworkers should be paid. Homeworkers should be rewarded equally for work of equal value, but the organisation has to decide how that work is to be measured. Using timesheets to determine hours worked may not be satisfactory since work patterns may be irregular. It may be better to pay for **output**, with average pay equivalent to an office wage. There can be some standardisation of pay so that minor output variations do not change wages.

8.12 Evidence suggests that work processes which are ideal for homeworking tend to be individually driven, require few instructions, need not be performed at set times and produce outputs that can be measured precisely.

Exam Tip

The 40 mark case study in the December 1998 exam was concerned with people management issues in a changing work environment. There were questions on communication, team building and customer service, all with an implied need to consider motivation.

Questions on improving the performance of individuals or teams are very common in this exam, and you must have the basics at your fingertips. These are **motivation, training, appraisal,** and **discipline**.

An important feature of this question was the management of **temporary staff.** There are several issues here, including training, experience, familiarity with products and methods and continuity, but generally, temporary staff may be treated in the same way as permanent staff.

Chapter roundup

- Motivation is an essential ingredient in ensuring that the individual and the team perform efficiently and effectively.
- Management writers have devoted considerable time to understanding motivation because it is believed improvements here can generate competitive advantage.
- There are basically two types of motivational theories

    Process theories - motivation describes how people make choices
    Content theories - motivation satisfies 'needs'
- Herzberg's work was important because it encourages managers to recognise the **hygiene factors**, which can cause dissatisfaction if they are absent, but are unlikely to generate positive motivation.
- Herzberg also highlighted the motivational opportunities from job enlargement, enrichment and rotation, all of which are quite commonly used for both motivation and for training and development.
- Drucker identified that motivation of individuals starts with putting the right people in the right jobs.
- A wide variety of options are available to motivate the individual and the team. The important thing is to develop motivational strategies which suit both the situation and the individual. Schemes should be simple to administer, easy to understand and perceived to be fair, and any incentives should be clear.
- **Participation** and **feedback** are key factors in motivating a team. **Appraisal** can help by providing a formal system of feedback which is also a useful benchmark for monitoring performance changes. Most appraisal systems require a manager to appraise a subordinate, but alternatives can be suggested.
- As with all interviews, an appraisal interview must be well planned and taken seriously. It should be part of an appraisal system or scheme which is seen to be of value to both appraiser and appraisee. It should encourage two-way communication.
- Appraisals can be damaging and de-motivating if not undertaken professionally. Managers involved must give them time, be well prepared and pay attention to the follow up.
- One of the common follow-up outcomes will relate to **training and development**, and identified training needs.
    - To tackle an identified weakness
    - To develop skills in anticipation of a change in the job, environment or technology
    - In preparation for promotion
- Training methods are many and varied. They must be selected with care to be best suited to the needs of the organisation in terms of cost, time, approach and the individual in terms of level, style, relevance and commitment needed.
- In addition to appraisal people often require help. Advice is often unrequested, although it might be to do with a specific problem. **Counselling** is a more formal, long-term process with a specific objective.
- **Disciplinary proceedings** are, sadly, sometimes necessary, for a variety of reasons relating to behaviour at work. People should know what is expected of them and discipline should be fair.
- Occasionally employees will have a **grievance**. In a grievance interview, the facts are checked and examined, and remedies are suggested.
- Many firms are experimenting with alternatives to full-time, office-based employment: a core workforce is surrounded by a periphery of temporary and/or part-time employees. Particular management problems relate to generating commitment.
- Technology enables many people to work from home. Supervisory problems include control.

8: Improving team performance

Quick Quiz

1. What is motivation and why is it important? (see para 2.4)
2. What are the levels in Maslow's hierarchy? (2.10)
3. What problems are associated with Maslow's theory? (2.12)
4. Briefly describe Herzberg's 'two-factor' theory. (2.13 - 2.16)
5. What is 'expectancy theory'? (2.22)
6. Identify and describe three types of psychological contract. (2.29)
7. Drucker suggested that, in order to persuade employees to accept responsibility, four ingredients are needed. What are they? (3.2)
8. What methods have been suggested for increasing motivation generally? (3.3)
9. Describe job enrichment, job enlargement and job rotation. (3.6 - 3.13 and 3.19)
10. What are the advantages of participation? (3.24)
11. Describe two types of short-term incentive scheme. (3.36 – 3.38)
12. What are the benefits of non-financial incentives? (3.39)
13. What is the purpose of appraisal? (4.2)
14. What general appraisal techniques could you use? (4.6)
15. Describe three types of approach to appraisal interviews. (4.10)
16. What would you expect to happen as part of the follow up to appraisal? (4.12)
17. What is upwards appraisal? (4.14 - 4.15)
18. What is 360 degrees appraisal? (4.17 - 4.20)
19. List the stages in developing a training programme. (5.12)
20. What is the difference between advice and counselling? (6.1)
21. What is the heart of discipline? (7.2)
22. What are the basic rules you can follow to help reduce the resentment involved in a disciplinary interview? (7.10)
23. What will be the structure of a disciplinary interview? (7.13)
24. List the stages of grievance interviews. (7.15)
25. What is the purpose of exit interviews? (7.17)
36. Distinguish between 'core' and 'peripheral' employees. (8.1)
27. What are the problems of teleworking? (8.8, 8.10)

Action Programme Review

2. Hygiene factors, which cause dissatisfaction at work

   - Company policy and administration
   - Salary
   - The quality of supervision
   - Interpersonal relations
   - Working conditions
   - Job security

3. Perhaps the narrator is contrasting economic man with self-actualising man. For some people the enjoyment of the job itself is satisfaction enough. People will accept less money to pursue an interest.

Part C: Managing people

5   Typical features of enrichment are challenge; a whole job rather than part of one; responsibility for results; trust in small matters such as access to stores and making small purchases; and the power to take decisions, even if only small ones.

7   (a) Coaching: the trainee is put under the guidance of an experienced employee who shows the trainee how to do the job. The length of the coaching period will depend on the complexity of the job and the previous experience of the trainee.

   (b) Job rotation: the trainee is given several jobs in succession, to gain experience of a wide range of activities. (Even experienced managers may rotate their jobs to gain wider experience; this philosophy of job education is commonly applied in the Civil Service, where an employee may expect to move on to another job after a few years.)

   (c) Temporary promotion: an individual is promoted into his/her superior's position whilst the superior is absent due to illness. This gives the individual a chance to experience the demands of a more senior position.

   (d) 'Assistant to' positions: a junior manager with good potential may be appointed as assistant to the managing director or another executive director. In this way, the individual gains experience of how the organisation is managed at the to'.

   (e) Committees: trainees might be included in the membership of committees, in order to obtain an understanding of inter-departmental relationships.

8   Don't forget administrative items like where the lavatories are, nor health and safety issues. Allow time for the recruit to ask questions and make some allowance for checking that the training has achieved its objectives. You did start with objectives, didn't you?

Now try illustrative questions 11 to 14 at the end of the Study Text

9: Managing Change

Chapter Topic List	Syllabus reference
1 Setting the scene	
2 The need for organisational change	3.7
3 Innovation, growth and decline	3.7
4 Changing organisation structure	3.7
5 The impact of change on individuals	3.7
6 The role of the manager in facilitating change	3.7
7 The internal marketing of plans and change	3.7, 2.4

Learning Outcome

- Students will be able to describe the principles of managing change that minimise resistance and maximise successful outcomes and the role of marketing in the management of change and achieving a marketing orientation.

Key Concepts Introduced

- Change management

Examples of Marketing at Work

- Shifting emphasis at Ericsson
- Overcoming resistance to change at Butlins

Part C: Managing people

1 SETTING THE SCENE

1.1 In Chapter 1, we touched on some of the new factors in the environment that managers have to cope with. They offer challenges to all managers, not just marketing managers, who might have to implement change.

1.2 In Section 2 we identify the **types of changes that might be necessary** and where change comes from - the environment, technology and so forth. Organisations therefore have to innovate to grow or even to survive (section 3). Organisations have to respond to these changes by changing themselves - a change in organisation structure, discussed in Section 4, is sometimes needed.

1.3 Change inevitably affects established ways of working which individuals have grown used to and feel comfortable with. The ease with which change is implemented in part depends on **how individuals respond to it**. Their possible reactions are discussed in Section 5.

1.4 As a manager, you may be responsible for making changes yourself, or implementing changes which your superiors have decided. The **broad outlines** of what a manager has to do, including a brief model of how to implement a change process, are discussed in Section 6. (Obviously, you may also need to apply some of the leadership skills we discussed in Chapter 6.)

1.5 Finally, as a marketer, you may find yourself involved in internal communications and **internal marketing**, and you can use sound marketing principles, as elaborated in Section 7, to communicate to the people affected by change. Sometimes the changes you have to market will affect the company's whole way of doing things, at other times it will be a change in a specific aspect of operations, maybe even the company's system of internal communications.

2 THE NEED FOR ORGANISATIONAL CHANGE

2.1 The business environment is constantly changing and businesses must respond if they are to survive and prosper. Environmental change thus drives internal change.

- **Changes in the market** include competitors' responses, changes in fashion and changes in promotional methods.
- **Technological change** can introduce new product possibilities and more efficient ways of working.
- **Social, legal and political developments** can extend or constrain the acceptability of products and business practices.

2.2 The organisation must respond by instituting its own **internal changes**. These can include:

- New or developed **products or services**
- Changed **working practices**
- Entry into **new markets** or withdrawal from old ones
- New **organisational structures and philosophies**

2.3 *Buckley and Perkins* (1984) made a distinction between **change**, which is gradual and small and **transformation**, which is change on a significant scale.

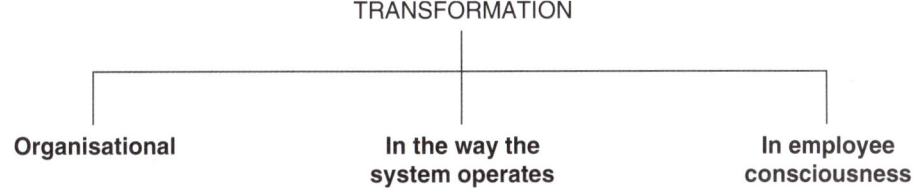

```
                          TRANSFORMATION
        ┌─────────────────────┼─────────────────────┐
   Organisational        In the way the         In employee
                         system operates        consciousness

   major changes in      major changes in       major changes in the
   job definitions,      communication patterns, way that things are viewed,
   reporting lines       working relationships   involving shifts in attitudes,
   (lines of authority)  and processes           beliefs and myths
   and so on
```

3 INNOVATION, GROWTH AND DECLINE

> **Key concept**
> **Change management** is the process of planning and implementing change within organisations.

Innovation

3.1 **Innovation** is a term that is often associated with change. Innovation is something completely new. Some changes might result in going back to something that was done before. Innovation creates change, but change isn't always innovative.

3.2 The rate of change might be fast or slow, depending on the organisation's circumstances, and the environment in which it operates. Organisations which operate in a rapidly changing environment need to be highly innovative and responsive to change if they are to survive and grow.

The value of innovation

3.3 The chief object of being innovative is to ensure that organisation's **survival** and **success** in a **changing world**. It may develop prompt and imaginative **solutions** to problems (through use of project teams), and generate greater **confidence** inside and outside the organisation in its ability to cope with change.

Encouraging innovation

3.4 To encourage innovation management should aim to create a more outward looking organisation which actively seeks new products, markets, processes and ways to improve productivity.

Marketing at work

Team creativity

What have we discovered about how to promote creativity and innovation in teams at work? Here are six tips.

1 **Recognise that creativity and innovation are not easy**

   Conflict is a common characteristic of innovation, observable principally in resistance to change.

   Innovation, by definition, represents a threat to the status quo. For a team to implement innovation successfully, its members must manage conflict, with the attendant emotional pain and difficulty. They must overcome resistance to change. They must persist in ensuring the successful implementation of

Part C: Managing people

their innovative proposal. And they must accept that, after all that, the innovation may turn out to have been a mistake.

2 **Pick creative people with wide experience and knowledge, put them in a supportive environment and challenge them**

Creativity requires individuals with creative characteristics who feel free from threat and pressure and who work in a supportive environment.

Learning and innovation will occur only when team members trust other members' intentions.

3 **Give the team members interesting jobs**

Jobs that stimulate individual innovation are likely to score highly on the following characteristics.

- **Skill variety**. The degree to which a job requires different activities in order for the work to be done, and the degree to which the full range of skills and talents of the person working in the role is used.

- **Task identity**. The extent to which a job is not a small part of a larger task.

- **Task significance**. The job's impact upon other people within the organisation or in the world at large.

- **Level of autonomy**. The amount of discretion vested in employees.

- **Task feedback**. People who receive feedback on their performance are more likely to become aware of the performance gaps. This also implies that they have clear job objectives.

4 **Emphasise team creativity, not only productivity, and make them stop work**

One of the implications of our findings is that organisations need to encourage teams by focusing on creativity and innovation as important performance outcomes, rather than only on productivity.

5 **Encourage constructive conflict and dissent and treasure team errors**

Dissent can stimulate team innovation when it occurs in a co-operative context. It allows individuals in small teams to change the views of the majority by being consistent and persistent.

Learning about the causes of errors as a team – and then devising innovations to prevent future errors – were possible only in those teams that discussed them.

6 **Does the organisation inspire the team?**

Organisations can create an ethos within which creativity is either nurtured and blooms into innovation or is starved of support.

Across the world, companies use a range of schemes to support team innovation. The US-based firm 3M, which produces Post-it Notes and adhesive tape, has 30,000 employees. Its technical staff are encouraged to spend 15 per cent of their time 'bootlegging' – working on pet projects that they hope will become new products for the company. They are given the time to pursue these ideas and, if necessary, they can apply for money to buy equipment or hire extra help.

For an idea to be taken further at 3M, it must win the backing of one member of the board. Once this occurs, an inter-disciplinary venture team of researchers, engineers, marketing people and accountants is set up to push the idea further. If a director is not willing to support the idea, it returns to the drawing board. But teams are not penalised for failure.

Michael West, People Management, 8 March 2001

Creativity

3.5 Creative ideas can come from anywhere and at any time and management should try to provide an organisation structure in which innovative ideas are encouraged.

(a) Creative ideas must then be rationally analysed to decide whether they provide a viable commercial proposition.

(b) A system of organisation must exist whereby a viable creative idea is converted into action. In marketing terms constructive new product development frameworks would need to be established.

9: Managing change

3.6 Management can also create conditions in which risk taking, creativity and enthusiasm for change is **impossible**. Below are the ideas of *Rosabeth Moss Kanter* on how to **stifle innovation**.

> 1 Regard any new idea from below with suspicion.
> 2 Insist that people who need your approval first go through several other levels of management.
> 3 Get departments/individuals to challenge each other's proposals.
> 4 Express criticism freely, withhold praise, instil job insecurity.
> 5 Treat identification of problems as signs of failure.
> 6 Control everything carefully. Count everything in sight - frequently.
> 7 Make decisions in secret, and spring them on people.
> 8 Do not hand out information to managers freely.
> 9 Get lower-level managers to implement your threatening decisions.
> 10 Above all, never forget that you, the higher-ups, already know everything important about the business.

Action Programme 1
Fishpaste Ltd is a business making adhesives. One of the employees, during the course of some research into adhesives, discovers a dryish glue that will not quite stick properly. It holds things in place, but two pieces of paper stuck together with this glue can be easily separated without damage to either. What do you do with the tub of glue and the employee?

Growth

3.7 An organisation will usually seek to grow by increasing its **range of products** and **markets**, its **sales turnover** and its **profits**. Companies might seek to grow **organically**, by developing their own internal resources, or else to grow by merger and acquisition. Many companies seek growth through a combination of the two strategies.

Innovation and growth

3.8 If a company operates in a market with a good prospect for growth, it can grow **organically** either by exploiting existing product-market opportunities or by diversifying. However, **because existing products have a finite life, a strategy of organic growth must include plans for new product development.**

Innovation and stability

3.9 **Stability calls for innovation too.** An organisation cannot rely on its existing products and markets for ever. An organisation which wants to maintain its sales and profits must also, therefore, develop new or improved products, or new markets, to replace the old ones in decline. Product development involves R&D costs and, often, heavy capital expenditure to set up a new product or new market opinion.

3.10 An innovation strategy should take a broad view of what sort of innovations should be sought. A product might be completely new, or just a different quality version of an existing product. A new product is not necessarily much different from existing products; rather, the essential characteristic is that it should be distinguishable from its predecessors **in the eyes of its customers**.

Part C: Managing people

3.11 The car industry provides a very good example of the different types of product innovation. Some years ago, the hatchback was a fairly major innovation. Modifications to existing models are made regularly, to keep consumers interested and wanting to buy.

Leaders and followers

3.12 Some firms **lead the way** with technological innovation, and actively seek new products for their markets. Other firms **react to what the leaders do**. Either approach can be a successful strategy for innovation, but later entry is a more successful approach than leadership, because the leader will make mistakes that the followers can learn from and avoid. Research shows that the eventual leaders in high-technology industries usually enter several years after the pioneers. The failure rate for pioneers is almost 50%.

New product strategies

3.13 Innovation can mean creating new markets as well as new products, creating extra demand from existing customers or creating new demand from new customers.

Motives for growth

3.14 *Starbuck* suggested various motives for organisational growth

(a) Organisations attempt to realise their ultimate **objective**. This may involve providing **a more complete service** to customers, perhaps by expanding geographically or by vertical integration.

(b) Executives might like the **challenge and adventure** of a new gamble. Boredom with the existing situation might prompt changes.

(c) The **status, power and job security** of individuals may be enhanced by growth.

(d) Executive **salaries** are likely to rise as a result of increasing **turnover** (rather than by increasing profits).

(e) Growth may lead to **profit maximisation**.

(f) Growth may lead to **economies of scale**.

(g) Large organisations tend to be more **stable** than small ones. The desire for stability may lead to growth.

The management of contraction

3.15 Change might involve a contraction of the organisation and its business, rather than growth. **Divestment** means getting rid of something. In strategic planning terms, it means selling off a part of a firm's operations, or pulling out of certain product market areas.

3.16 One reason for divestment is economic recession. A more common reason is to **rationalise** a business as a result of a strategic appraisal. A company might decide to concentrate on its **core businesses** and sell off fringe activities to **sell off subsidiaries** where performance is poor, or where growth prospects are not good.

3.17 **Advantages of divestment**

(a) By selling off parts of the business that are not performing as well as others, a firm can concentrate on areas of its business that provide better results.

(b) Selling off a subsidiary will bring in funds that can be invested in other projects. [opportunity cost of continuing with product/service against stopping/selling off & investing in alternative.]

3.18 If a firm goes into a product market area and finds that it has made a mistake or that, after some years of good returns, the market is declining, it makes good commercial sense to pull out. There is no point carrying on with an operation just through reluctance to let things go. However, divestments will probably mean significant redundancies among staff, which might meet strong resistance from employees and their trade unions.

> **Action Programme 2**
>
> In what way is your business changing? How is this change being managed?

4 CHANGING ORGANISATION STRUCTURE

4.1 Changes in what an organisation **does** could lead to a need for **restructuring**.

4.2 However, this is not the only reason why a new structure might be needed.

(a) **Changes in the environment** such as **greater competition** might create pressures for cost cutting, and hence **staff cuts**.

(b) **Diversification into new product market areas** demands better lateral and vertical integration as an organisation becomes more complex and differentiated. A possible role exists for **special co-ordinators**. Also there is the problem of when to switch from a **functional to a divisional organisation structure**.

(c) **Growth** of staff numbers creates problems of extended management hierarchies and poor communication.

(d) **New technology** can change the way things are done.

(e) **Changes in the capabilities of personnel employed** may lead to new approaches. There have been changes in education levels, the distribution of occupational skills and employee attitudes to work. The growth of knowledge-based work has accelerated.

4.3 Initially, there is [*may be*] a problem of identifying the need to reorganise. The need for restructuring might become apparent when the existing organisation shows signs of weakness and strain, for example through management overload, insufficient innovation or weakening control.

4.4 Restructuring is not always necessary every time changes take place in an organisation's circumstances. When a problem arises out of an organisational deficiency, managers have to analyse and diagnose the fault. They might ask a number of questions.

[handwritten: Too much restructuring in NHS + Education → confusion + focus away from what should be the core focus.]

- What is the extent of the problem?

- What is the source of the problem? It is relatively easy to spot personal problems, if a manager is not doing the job properly, or if there are personal rivalries and conflicts, but it is not so easy to diagnose faults in organisational structure.

- Is the problem temporary or permanent or recurrent?

- At what level in the management hierarchy and organisation structure is the problem located?

> **Exam Tip**
>
> A sideways approach to this topic was taken in June 2001 when you were asked about the differences in employee relations and expectations in the context of two companies engaging in strategic alliance.

Part C: Managing people

The stages in an organisation development programme

4.5 Basic stages of an organisation development programme

(a) Management must first become aware of deficiencies and faults in its method of operations and lay down in broad terms what is to be done. A **change agent** or **champion of change** may be appointed. This may be an external consultant or a senior manager.

[margin note: eg – e-Champions driving the push towards utilizing the web in Local Auth.]

(b) It is vital that all employees should know the purpose of the planned changes.

[annotation: → Provide ∆ Information + distribute]

(c) Having established the required mutual trust, the change agent may then proceed with a data-gathering and diagnostic exercise. Although it is possible to use questionnaires, it is usual to collect data by interviewing individuals.

- (i) Individuals should be encouraged to say what they think is wrong and how it should be put right.
- (ii) All the collected data should be cross-checked.
- (iii) Suggestions about the causes of problems and deficiencies should be raised for discussion. This may lead employees to discover for themselves what is at fault.

(d) The conclusions from the diagnostic exercise should be **fed back to higher management** in order that a **strategy for organisation development may be agreed**.

(e) Once the objective has been agreed, the support and knowledge of the employees concerned must be secured.

(f) Implementing the changes will generally necessitate teaching employees to change their attitudes.

(h) The implementation of any such change will require monitoring. The actual effects on the faults at work must be gauged to decide whether the aims of the programme have been achieved. It is also likely that new problems will emerge, and that these in turn will require diagnosis and educative, corrective action.

External consultants

4.6 Benefits of using external consultants

- They will use specialist analytical techniques and knowledge.
- They bring experience of similar problems in other organisations.
- They can resolve internal conflicts by acting as an independent referee.
- They are neutrals, outside departmental politics.
- They are not tied by status or rank, and can discuss problems freely at all levels within the organisation.
- They can look at problems objectively and don't have to worry about the consequences of their recommendations for their career prospects.

4.7 Disadvantages of using consultants

- They might be seen as mere agents of top management.
- They might try to impose a standard solution on a unique problem.
- They might to be too academic.

- They will need time to learn about an organisation themselves. The client organisation will have to pay consultancy fees for this learning process.

Marketing at Work

Ericsson, the Swedish electronics firm has two main divisions, public telecommunications, growing at 11% in a one-year period before December 1995, and mobile phones, which grew 42% (*Financial Times*, 15 December 1995). The company indicated plans to shift resources between divisions.

(a) 80,000 staff and several factories are affected: 'Ericsson is moving thousands of staff and at least three factories from its public telecoms unit ... to ... its mobile phone business'.

(b) 'We could not have expanded mobile phones as rapidly as we have done if we had not had the opportunity to reduce the public telecoms side'.

(c) 'There is a massive change in competence requirement ... manufacturing and hardware, are decreasing in size, while the emphasis on product development, software and systems is increasing'.

5 THE IMPACT OF CHANGE ON INDIVIDUALS

5.1 Perhaps the trickiest problem with managing organisational change is the fact **that people dislike it.** Because change is likely to be ever present, successful managers must be able to manage the process of change implementation. To do this effectively they must have an appreciation of the problems change causes the individual. People frequently resist change to their jobs.

(a) **It makes them feel insecure and uncertain**; they misunderstand the reasons for change and fear a threat to their competence or success in their jobs

(b) It **disrupts the social structure** and relationships they are used to, for example, by relocation, reshuffles and redundancies.

Changes in response to crises are often resisted less than routine changes, however, because people understand that there is a **need** for change and that change is even in their own interests.

5.2 **A marketing approach may be used**. Managers must put themselves into employees' shoes and look at change from their perspective. Changes which appear relatively minor from a strategic vantage point can have considerable implications at the operational level.

5.3 As we will see later in this chapter when we consider developing internal marketing plans to help sell change, there is a price to change. Individuals must perceive they will benefit to an extent which outweighs the cost. Once managers have stood in the employees' shoes they will have a greater appreciation of the cost of change to them and so be able to present plans and strategies in a way which emphasises relevant benefits.

> **Action Programme 3**
>
> Think about the following situations and how might you feel as the employee. What is the possible cost to you?
>
> (a) As manager of a retail branch you are faced with a change of opening times to take advantage of Sunday trading.
>
> (b) You have been assistant manager in the marketing department for four years. The existing manager is retiring in three months.
>
> - You have been offered her job
> - A new younger manager has been appointed from outside the company.
>
> (c) A reorganisation of sales territories means that you are now only looking after 20% of your old customers - 80% of your territory is new.

5.4 Managers need to think about how individuals in their teams will respond to change. Reaction may vary widely.

- **Acceptance**, whether enthusiastic espousal, co-operation, grudging co-operation or resignation

- **Indifference**, usually where the change does not directly affect the individual: apathy, lack of interest and inaction

- **Passive resistance** including refusal to learn, working to rule, pleas of ignorance and delayed judgement

- **Active resistance** such as go-slows, deliberate errors, sabotage, absenteeism or strikes (the *Royal Mail* strikes in 1996 related to the introduction of teamworking).

5.5 **Adaptability** is a trait which can be considered in the selection process, and perhaps developed through training and encouraged by the culture and organisational systems. Perhaps change should become the routine, as teams without exposure to change will be resentful when inevitable change occurs. **Job rotation** can give individuals experience of change. Managers could encourage some change for its own sake to get people used to it.

5.6 When change is significant or particularly distressing, managers need to take account of the fact that it will affect individuals in the team differently. Monitoring individuals for evidence of stress caused by change should be a routine part of the feedback and control process.

5.7 Where stress is apparent, counselling and coping strategies should be provided. Individuals should **not** be made to feel they have failed but given every support to help them through. It will be a lot cheaper to work with valued staff members than to replace them.

Change and the manager

5.8 Managers often suffer from a degree of divided loyalty when implementing change. Like the team, the manager may resent or be scared of the implications of change, but is forced to implement it. It is hard to sell something you have no confidence in, so a manager should try to talk through concerns about the change with his or her own line managers.

6 THE ROLE OF THE MANAGER IN FACILITATING CHANGE

A systematic approach to change

6.1 For an organisation to be innovative and continually responsive to the need for change, a systematic approach can be established for planning and implementing changes.

6.2 A step-by-step model for change is shown below.

Step 1. **Determine** need or desire for change *in a particular area.*
Step 2. **Brainstorm possible** strategies.
Step 3. **Analyse probable** reactions *to the change.*
Step 4. **Select a plan** *from the range of options, possibly by group problem solving.*
Step 5. **Establish a timetable** *for change*

- Coerced changes can probably be implemented faster and without need for discussions.
- Speed of implementation that is achievable will depend on the likely reactions of the people affected.
- Identify those in favour of change, and perhaps set up a pilot programme involving them.

Step 6. **Communicate** *the plan for change.*
Step 7. **Implement** *the change.* Review the change with continuous evaluation and modifications.

NB: No point change 4 change's sake eg Education.

6.3 The change should be worth undertaking. The major tests of whether a change is worthwhile is a cost-benefit analysis. The benefits from the change, which might be non-money benefits as well as money benefits, must justify the costs of making the change. The costs of change include the time and effort it takes, as well as the money cost. Also, management should have the resources to make the change. This includes money, to buy the new equipment or premises or other assets they will need, and staff, properly **trained in advance**, to deal with the new situation.

6.4 The manager may have a difficult role especially if not involved in the decision making which has resulted in the change. However, it is worth noting that marketers are often spearheading change, certainly in terms of developing new products and markets, and so perhaps quite excited by it.

6.5 The manager has two possibly conflicting responsibilities during the process of change.

- To look after the interests and welfare of the team
- To ensure change is carried through efficiently

Marketing at work

The magazine *People Management* recently reported how Butlins, faced with increased competition in the holiday market, tried to adapt their operations without alienating staff and without alienating their core loyal customer base. The company has chosen to make two of its five sites action parks, and three focused on family entertainment. The three family entertainment sites will provide identical products at identical standards and prices. This implies a significant increase in central control where previously there had been a large degree of autonomy at each site.

Butlins' tried to overcome resistance to change by a communications campaign which had a number of elements. These included site visits by managers from head office and videos presented by the managing and operations directors. Site managers were also asked to carry out a self assessment exercise, to assess customer views of Butlins and suggest improvements in work processes.

Part C: Managing people

The main results of the review exercise will be to change the emphasis of the role of site directors. Greater priority will be given to a general management role. Personnel and training executives will have a more broadly based human resources role. The latter reflects the fact that Butlins sites are likely to stay open in future for 48 weeks a year with a resulting increase in the percentage of staff on permanent contracts. Training will also reflect the emphasis on greater consistency between sites and will include secondments and work experience. Specific opportunities are planned for certain staff; the company is currently discussing the possibility that redcoat work will lead to an equity card.

Early indications are that the staff are impressed by the new opportunities that will be created. The staff have seen the communications process as being of prime importance since they in turn will have to explain the changes to the campers.

Looking after the team

6.6 During any discussions and planning for change, the **manager is responsible** for identifying the **implications for the team**, and where necessary negotiating for adjustments to the plan. The manager should also recognise the implications of change on **individuals** and identify coping strategies which will help smooth the process of change.

6.7 The manager must consider the most effective time, place and manner to present the change to the team. This should emphasise the positive aspects of change, whilst acknowledging the costs. By involving the team in the decision making about how best to implement the change, the manager can make the change feel less threatening and such participation can be a positive motivator in the acceptance of change.

Looking after the organisation

6.8 Try the exercise below.

Action Programme 4

Think about what actions the manager must take from the organisation's point of view, when introducing change. You will find many of them coincide with those outlined above.

Exam Tip

There was a question on the management of change in the December 2000 exam. The setting was a catering company. You were required to produce a report for the MD, describing the problems associated with change, including the effects on employees, and how they may be overcome.

As always, the examiner wants you to work in a practical, marketing context, so the setting makes it clear that the changes taking place in the company are concerned with encouraging a more customer focussed approach. This is an absolutely typical environment for change and one you should be able to relate to very closely. When tackling a question like this, use the theory but nail it firmly to the question setting.

7 THE INTERNAL MARKETING OF PLANS AND CHANGE

7.1 Managers have come to recognise a number of things about change.

- It is inevitable.
- It is easy to plan to change.
- It is difficult to implement change as people resist.

7.2 Recognising that success of a plan depends on its implementation, increasing attention and support is being given to those managers charged with implementation. Amongst the tools and techniques available is **internal marketing**. In this context, we mean the use of a **marketing approach to help in the presentation of change to those it affects**.

7.3 The following, as a recipe for change management, suggests a marketing approach.

Suggested approach	Comment
Tell	The **people**: clearly, realistically, openly
Sell	The **pressures** which make change necessary and desirable
	The **vision of** successful, realistically attainable change
Evolve	The people's **attitudes, ideas, capacity** to learn new ways
Involve	The **people** where possible in planning implementation

Marketing can play an important part in the **telling and selling** activity.

7.4 **Principles of internal marketing**

(a) A plan's implementation itself needs planning.

(b) Staff needs must be identified and the benefits of the plan must be presented to them.

(c) Those who influence the organisation must be identified and targeted. They represent the equivalent of **innovators** in the adoption, and must be sold the plan first.

(d) Plans need **packaging and promoting**. Resources may be needed to achieve this.

(e) Managers must make use of **informal networks of communication** within the organisation. It is not sufficient to rely wholly on the formal networks which are the result of the prevailing organisation structure.

Internal marketing plans should be based on research to identify the relevant decision making unit and their needs and concerns.

7.5 The **internal marketing mix** can be described in terms of the 4Ps.

(a) **Product**: this is the plan or change which management wants to implement.

(b) **Price**: there will be a perceived price tag. The costs and benefits to staff must be clearly assessed. As with any product, there may need to be negotiation, but managers must be clear what the costs and benefits are. For example, a move to a new office block may entail a longer journey to work, but it may offer improved working conditions. A change in the sales commission package may depress potential earnings in exchange for a higher average salary overall; employees must feel that the change is to their benefit.

(c) **Place**: in marketing, place represents when and where the product is available. The method and timing of the announcement of plans can have a dramatic effect on the way they are received.

(d) **Promotion**: poor communication is probably the biggest single internal company problem. The grapevine tends to work quickly and not always very accurately. Therefore, when plans are announced they are often met by hostility and antagonism. Improving the communication of plans is an essential step to ensuring that they are owned and supported by those who have to implement them. Communication should be two way and meetings and discussions to take account of staff's views and thoughts at an early stage will help implementation later.

Part C: Managing people

7.6 **Internal marketing** is about the **manner** in which plans and change are presented to those they affect. The right manner is important in creating a motivated and successful team at whatever level the plan is being implemented.

The internal marketing plan

7.7 Just as the normal processes of marketing outside the organisation are determined by a marketing plan, so to should the process of internal marketing be the subject of an **internal marketing plan**. Clearly, you must be familiar with marketing plans generally (the BPP Study Text *Marketing Operations* will help you here), but for convenience we will outline the essentials of an internal marketing plan.

7.8 We commence by considering where we are now and where we would like to be; that is, what we consider to be our **objectives**. These must be stated as clearly as possible For example, if we are embarking on a change programme, our overall objective might be to achieve a culture change which will support a new commitment to customer service.

7.9 When we are sure of our aims we may consider our **strategy**. This may be assisted by establishing a number of subordinate aims, given in terms of outcomes. For instance, we might set a specific objective of explaining the board's analysis of our current problems to every employee by a given date. This might indicate that a mass marketing strategy such as the distribution of videotapes is required.

7.10 The determination of the targets for our communication effort will be assisted by **segmenting the market**, just as in external marketing. When *British Aerospace* embarked on its major culture change strategy, it identified senior managers who had to be convinced of the need for the new approach. This approach will also make it easier to prescribe the most effective communication techniques.

7.11 In the context of organisational change, **training** will be of particular importance. Training policy is properly a Human Resources responsibility, but if the Marketing Department is in overall charge of change management, they will have to work closely with the HR specialists.

7.12 The final element of the internal marketing plan is **control**. The progress of the various activities must be monitored and action taken to push them along as necessary. A **double loop** approach may be necessary. This means that feedback in the control system is not just used to control outcomes; it may indicate that the **plan itself** is unrealistic and needs amendment

Evaluating change management

7.13 The effectiveness of change management can be evaluated in a number of ways.

(a) The impact of the change on organisational goals: **has the change contributed to the overall objectives of the organisation** as defined by the corporate plan?

(b) The success of the change in meeting its specified objective (and short-term targets set measure progress): **has the change solved the problem?**

(c) The behaviour of people in the organisation: **has the change programme resulted in the behavioural changes planned** (for example higher output, better teamwork, more attention to customer care)?

(d) The **reaction of the people** in the organisation: has the change programme been implemented without arousing hostility or fear with their symptoms of absenteeism, labour turnover and conflict?

7.14 **Problems in change management**

(a) Failure to identify the **need** to change (typically a failure to pay attention to change in the environment).

(b) Failure to identify the **objectives** of change, so that the wrong areas are addressed.

(c) Failure to identify correctly the **strategy** required to achieve the objectives. The result is that change takes place, but not in the relevant direction. New technology, for example, is sometimes regarded as a universal solution to organisational problems, but it will not necessarily improve productivity or profitability if the product/market strategy or the workforce is the real problem.

(d) Failure to commit **sufficient resources** to the strategy.

(e) Failure to identify the **appropriate method** of implementing change, for the situation and the people involved (typically, failing to anticipate resistance to change).

(f) Failure to implement the change in a way that **secures acceptance**, because of the **leadership style** of the person managing the change (typically, **failure to consult** and involve employees).

7.15 The first four of the above reasons for failure are to do with **strategic planning** generally: they are potential shortcomings in any planning exercise. The peculiar difficulties of introducing change, however, are human factors. When implementing plans or changes, managers must never lose sight of the fact that their success depends on people.

Chapter roundup

- Change is a constant challenge and requirement for business and its managers. Those who fail to respond to change will fail to survive.

- Change, in the context of organisation and management, could involve any of the following.

    The **environment**. These could be changes in what competitors are doing, what customers are buying, how they spend their money, changes in the law, changes in social behaviour and attitudes, economic changes, and so on.

    The **products** the organisation makes, or the services it provides. These are made in response to changes in customer demands, competitors' actions, new technology, and so on.

    Management, working relationships and **corporate culture**. These include changes in leadership style, and in the way that employees are encouraged to work together. Changes in training and staff development are also relevant here.

    Organisation structure or size. These might involve creating new departments and divisions, greater delegation of authority or more centralisation, changes in the way that plans are made, management information is provided and control is exercised, and so on. Organisation re-structuring will be made in response to changes in environment, products, working methods or corporate culture.

- Change can be gradual or dramatic. Managers need to consider the appropriate time frame for change. They should balance the need to retain momentum for change with the need to give staff time to organise for it.

- Innovation is an essential element in the organisational culture and can be stimulated and encouraged by management in a number of ways.

- It is not always growth and expansion which has to be managed - it can be contraction. Management has to be prepared to meet every eventuality and implement whatever strategic plans are decided on.

- The main problem with change is the impact it has on people - the manager therefore must take great care when presenting change to teams. A great deal can be done to prepare staff for change by creating a culture which rewards and values change.

- The use of marketing techniques and involving the staff in the process of change can also help ensure change is implemented with the minimum of pain to both individuals and the organisation.

- The **culture** of the organisation can **either promote or stifle** change and organisations which recognise the need for change will take positive steps to 'change' their culture to one which stimulates it. Throughout it all good managers and organisations recognise the cost of change for the individual and take positive steps to reward and support those required to change.

9: Managing change

Quick Quiz

1. Distinguish between change and transformation (see para 2.3)
2. How can innovation and creativity be encouraged? (3.4 - 3.5)
3. Does an organisation have to innovate in stable conditions? (3.9)
4. Why might organisations want to grow? (3.14)
5. What are the stages of an organisation development programme? (4.5)
6. What are the advantages of involving external consultants in the process of organisational development? (4.6)
7. Why might an individual resist change? (5.1)
8. Why might the manager find it particularly difficult to implement change? (5.8)
9. What is the seven point plan for implementing change? (6.2)
10. What is the dual responsibility of the manager in the process of change? (6.5)
11. What should managers consider under the headings of the internal marketing mix, when preparing a plan for change? (7.5)

Action Programme Review

1. You could have simply ignored the product, on the grounds that a glue which does not stick things together is not a glue that is worth making or selling. This is one response.

    Another response would be to discuss with the employee, and other employees, the possible use for such a glue. In this case, you might come up with a revolutionary idea - the 'Post-It' note. Then you reward the employee.

3. (a) There may be staff (possibly including yourself) who object to this change. You will certainly have to be present on at least some Sundays, assuming you have a deputy with whom you can share the work. You will also have the task of dealing with staff's objections and motivating them to accept the change, because that is part of your management role.

    (b) (i) Your responsibility, status, pay and prospects will all increase. You may have to work longer hours and deal with more demanding tasks. How do you feel about this?

    (ii) All the considerations above apply, but in reverse. Also, you may experience frustration and disappointment if you thought you were ready for the job.

    (c) You are faced with a major change in your work role and duties. Instead of building on existing successful relationships, you have to start from scratch. However, if your territory was a particularly difficult one, you may be better off.

4. Essentially, it is the people dimension which makes the implementation of change unpredictable. The manager's efforts to introduce change enthusiastically and sympathetically will greatly increase the likelihood of it being achieved.

    Managers will be the first to know if the change is not working. By being alert and monitoring feedback carefully they will be able to advise when modification is needed to achieve the desired objectives.

    By being enthusiastic, the manager can help reduce the negative dimensions of change in the organisation's culture.

Now try illustrative question 15 at the end of the Study Text

10 Managing Client Relations

Chapter Topic List	Syllabus reference
1 Setting the scene	
2 Managing the organisation/client interface	3.6
3 Activities to establish and build customer relationships	3.6
4 Relationship marketing	3.6
5 Total quality and marketing	3.6
6 Improving negotiation skills	3.6
7 Solving customers' problems	3.6

Learning Outcomes

- Students will be able to explain the theory underpinning effective management of self, other people, resources and client relationships

- Students will be able to explain the principles and techniques of successful negotiation with internal colleagues and external customers, suppliers and distributors with a view to mutually successful outcomes.

Key Concepts Introduced

- Consumerism
- Relationship marketing

Examples of Marketing at Work

- Ethics in advertising at Philip Morris
- Change of target at Coutts Bank
- Complaints
- Customer loyalty
- South West trains and customer goodwill

10: Managing client relations

1 SETTING THE SCENE

1.1 When we discussed the role of the marketing manager in Chapter 1, we identified that the marketer acts as a bridge between the firm and its customers. In this chapter we return to this external focus of marketing by concentrating on various issues involved in client and customer relations.

1.2 In Section 2 we briefly discuss the role of **social responsibility** of the marketing manager and the firm's accountability to the customer.

1.3 In Section 3 we see why, in economic terms, **client relations** need to be managed. Customers need to be converted from light usage to heavy usage. We also discuss how existing customers can be retained, by paying attention to customer care and service quality.

1.4 **Relationship marketing**, which we discuss in Section 4, takes the issue of customer relationships further. It is the opposite of transaction marketing (the 'one off' or 'quick' sale). It is an approach which aims to build up long-term relationships with customers.

1.5 All activities of the organisation should be orientated towards **satisfying customer needs** profitably, and this is where **total quality** comes in, as it introduces the needs of the customer into the heart of the process of production. This is dealt with in Section 5.

1.6 In Section 6 we consider negotiation from the marketing perspective, and in Section 7 we round off with various situations where the marketer has to deal with customer complaints.

1.7 Recent case studies in the exam have been built round the very common situation of implementing a programme of change that improves service to customers, but has other aspects as well, particularly developing and motivating staff. *Marketing Business* and other marketing trade publications often give examples of how companies have implemented a change in culture to become more customer focused, and you should understand what their objectives are, how they have tried to change, and the steps they have taken to change.

Links with other papers

1.8 Client relations underpin relationship marketing, covered in some depth in the **Marketing/Customer Interface**. The focus in this syllabus is **managing** these relationships.

2 MANAGING THE ORGANISATION/CLIENT INTERFACE

2.1 The role of the marketing manager involves managing external as well as internal relationships. This added external dimension means that the people skills of the marketing manager must be particularly strong, since he or she represents the organisation when communicating or negotiating with the organisation's external publics.

> ### Action Programme 1
> What external audiences might marketers be working with on behalf of the organisation? Identify the main ones for your organisation.

2.2 The marketing manager acts as a communications bridge between these stakeholder groups and the organisation, listening and reporting. To the customer, marketing and sales staff represent the organisation, and perhaps personify it. It is important therefore that those in the team **project an image and style** consistent with the positioning of the business.

2.3 At the same time, the marketing team represents the customers and stakeholders' needs and views within the decision-making process of the company. The team members must be good communicators, if the case from the customer's perspective is to be made convincing to managers and other departments.

2.4 The marketer is in essence responsible for bringing buyer and seller together and ensuring that a mutually profitable exchange takes place. This role as negotiator is a key responsibility.

Consumerism and marketing ethics

> **Key concept**
> **Consumerism** has been defined by *Mann and Thornton* as a 'social movement seeking to augment the rights and powers of buyers in relation to sellers up to the point where the consumer is able to defend his interests'.

2.5 **Ethical responsibilities** towards customers are mainly those of providing a product or service of a quality that customers expect, and of dealing honestly and fairly. To some extent these responsibilities coincide with the organisation's marketing objectives. The guidelines of United Biscuits plc provide a good example of how these responsibilities might be expressed.

> 'UB's reputation for integrity is the foundation on which the mutual trust between the company and its customers is based. That relationship is the key to our trading success.
>
> Both employees and customers need to know that products sold by any of our operating companies will always meet their highest expectations. The integrity of our products is sacrosanct and implicit in the commitment is an absolute and uncompromising dedication to quality. We will never compromise on recipes or specification of products in order to save costs. Quality improvement must always be our goal.
>
> No employee may give money or any gift of significant value to a customer if it could reasonably be viewed as being done to gain a business advantage. Winning an order by violating this policy or by providing free or extra services, or unauthorised contract terms, is contrary to our trading policy.'
>
> *United Biscuits plc*

2.6 Social responsibility, which is desirable in theory, is not easily achieved in practice, because managers are commonly judged by a different set of criteria - profits, sales growth, market share, earnings per share and so on, and not in terms of achievements for society. After all, why should company A incur high costs on improving the safety standards of its product when a competitor, company B, does not spend any money on such improvements, and would therefore be able to undercut company A's prices on the market? Enhanced safety may, in fact, be a source of competitive advantage as in, for instance, Volvo cars.

2.7 Managers are unlikely to act with proper responsibility unless they are made accountable for what they do. Social and ethical responsibilities are unlikely to be anything more than fine words and phrases unless managers are judged according to their achievements.

2.8 Social responsibility is to some extent forced on managers by the wishes of consumers. Consumer organisations have focussed attention on a number of issues.

- **Dangerous products** such as cigarettes and the content of car exhaust emissions.

- **Dishonest marketing or promotion**. In the UK there is legislation designed to deal with this kind of abuse.

- The **abuse of power** by organisations which are large enough to disregard external constraints and even government pressure.

- The **availability of information**. For example, consumers are anxious to be informed of any artificial additives in foodstuffs.

Marketing at Work

The US tobacco company Philip Morris took out a series of advertisements in which it claimed that certain scientific studies reveal that the dangers of passive smoking have been much exaggerated.

This campaign was very controversial. Allegedly, the tobacco industry funded the research, and as importantly, other research studies contradict these conclusions. The general public is probably imperfectly aware of scientific procedure and much of the literature on the topic.

The accountability of managers

2.9 Managers might only feel socially responsible, in the long run, if they are held accountable by their companies. However, by what means can managers be made accountable to the public? For private companies, we have seen that accountability can be achieved through the exercise of law, or adverse public reaction and the threat of lost customer demand. For public sector organisations, however, where social responsibility ought to be strong, management might choose to escape its responsibility by passing the blame on to someone else.

Action Programme 2

A company manufacturing baby food, in a very competitive market, has received in private a disturbing phone call. Some cartons of its product have been tampered with, and contain shards of broken glass. The affected cartons are already for sale in chemists and supermarkets. What would be the most ethical approach to deal with this problem? What do you think would be in the best interests of the company?

(a) Withdraw all goods from sale?

(b) Take out warning advertisements in newspapers?

(c) Assume a hoax, but offer substantial compensation to people whose children were affected, in return for their silence if the threats turn out to be true?

2.10 As issues of accountability in social and ethical terms are often concerned with consumer's **perception** of the organisation, the marketing manager is likely to be required to guide the organisation's responses to such issues.

- **Market views and feedback** should inform management decision making.

- **Policy and strategy** must be communicated to the market through public relations and other communication options.

- It will be necessary to direct the company towards satisfying **all** the customers' needs, including those driven by ethical or environmental concerns.

3 ACTIVITIES TO ESTABLISH AND BUILD CUSTOMER RELATIONSHIPS

The need for long-term relationships

3.1 The cost of attracting new customers is considerable and servicing a new account may not be profitable for a year or two. On the other hand it is usually relatively inexpensive to retain an existing customer, so marketing strategy favours increasing sales to existing customers and reducing the proportion of lost customers through the development of customer loyalty schemes.

3.2 **To turn a non-user into a light or infrequent customer is very expensive in promotional and marketing costs.** The non-user has to be taken through the whole decision-making process from unawareness to awareness, to interest, to desire and final action. In practical terms converting non-users to light users can involve several techniques such as general advertising, building mailing lists, and general mailshots which are expensive and the direct impact of which is uncertain.

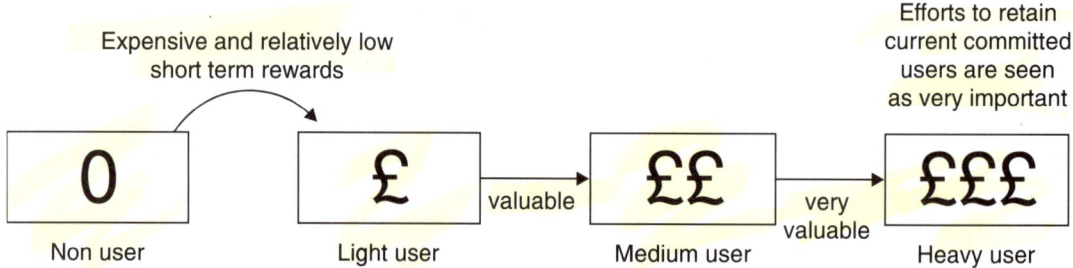

On the other hand, the loss of an established heavy user may require three or more new customers in the short term to replace the value of the business lost. In the long run, of course, you would hope new customers will become committed heavy users. James Crosby, chief executive of the Halifax, recently referred to the bank's strategy of **building up sales to existing customers**.

Marketing at Work

Coutts Bank has gradually changed its operations. Over 90% of its customers use it for simple account maintenance facilities, and are not terribly profitable. The bulk of its profits come from the 10% who are very wealthy and who use the bank's investment advice services. Coutts has decided to withdraw from the higher volume business to concentrate on the very wealthy and profitable 10%. The bank has also announced the closure of most of its counter service branches.

3.3 Losing customers is bad news for any business; not only are **today's** sales lost, but **future potential earnings** are also sacrificed.

(a) A woman in her mid 20's spends an estimated £100 a year on cosmetics. Dissatisfied by her current brand she switches to a competitor. She remains loyal for over 20 years to the new product. Cash revenue from the lost client is worth £2,000 before the time value of money is taken into account.

(b) The car manufacturer who estimates an average driver will buy seven cars in his or her lifetime is looking at perhaps £140,000 in lost custom if the salesperson fails to provide the service or approach needed to convert the buyer into a driver loyal to the brand.

3.4 Such an approach results in a **change in the salesperson's role** from selling more goods to solving the customer's problems. This is a shift from a product orientation to a marketing orientation. Such a change in positioning requires management support and commitment as well. Emphasis on short-term sales targets instead of long-term customer relationships is likely to produce a task orientated sales force.

3.5 Building customer loyalty has two aspects.

(a) Delivering **customer satisfaction,** that is providing a quality product which meets the customer's expectations

(b) Providing **customer care** to ensure that customers are valued and looked after effectively

3.6 We will be considering the impact of quality in more detail in the next section, but it is important to emphasise here that quality has to be defined from the customer's perspective. Quality does not mean 'best', or even 'fit for purpose', but '**satisfies the needs of the customers**'.

3.7 Marketers have to avoid falling into the trap of raising a customer's expectations through glamorous promotion and fancy packaging, because if the product fails to meet these expectations, a disappointed and dissatisfied customer may choose alternative suppliers.

Service quality

3.8 **Benefits of service quality**

- Improved customer retention rates and higher customer loyalty
- Word of mouth recommendation
- Higher market share
- Improved morale
- Some insulation from price competition
- Lower advertising and promotion costs
- Lower operating costs
- Increased productivity

3.9 **The two dimensions of service quality**

(a) **Technical quality** depends on the inherent technical characteristics of the product.

(b) The **functional quality** of the service encounter is **how** the service is provided. It relates to the psychological interaction between the buyer and seller and is perceived in a very subjective way. It depends on a number of factors.

(i) The **attitudes and behaviour of sales employees to the customer**. For instance are they positive about the company and its products? Do they appear competent, knowledgeable and aware? Do they seem to care about the customer?

(ii) **Relationships between employees**. For instance, do these relationships appear to be professional? Do they chat to each other whilst serving the customer? Do they appear to know their roles in the team and the function of their colleagues? Do they know who to refer the customer to in case of the need for more specialist advice?

(iii) **Appearance and personality of service personnel**. For instance, do they seem interested in the customer and the customer's needs? Are they smartly presented? Are they in uniform? Do they convey an attractive and positive image?

(iv) **Accessibility of the service to the customer**. For instance, do employees speak in language which the customer can understand? Are the sales aids easy to follow, sensibly written and not full of small print?

Part C: Managing people

Auditing fulfilment of customer needs

3.10 In their book *The Success Culture - how to build an organisation with vision and purpose,* Lesley and Malcolm Munro-Faure list the following ways in which organisations can tell whether customer needs are being identified and satisfied and whether the quality of service can be improved.

- Customer satisfaction surveys
- Mystery shopper surveys
- Work won and lost
- Changes in market share
- Monthly ratings from major customers
- Revenue from newly released products
- Sales backlog
- Quality control reviews
- Rework and warranties
- Assessment of needs of non-customers
- Time spent with prospective customers

3.11 In *Perfect Customer Care*, Johns argues that 'The majority of customer complaints will **not** directly relate to the quality of the service/product, but to the peripheral issues. Quality in the eyes of the customer is always supposedly much more than the quality of the product or basic service offered'.

Action Programme 3

Assume that you have ordered two fencing panels from a local DIY store. For a small extra charge, the panels will be delivered (as they are too big to fit into your car). On the appointed day, a delivery is made, but of only one of the panels you purchased, not two. You phone; delivery is promised the following day, but fails to arrive. You phone again and speak to a senior manager, who apologises for her staff. Delivery is made, and you are given a third extra panel to compensate for the inconvenience. The fencing panels themselves are fine. What customer care lessons can you learn from this example?

Achieving improvements in service quality

3.12 Service quality requires a **customer focus**, which has several aspects.

- Customer satisfaction
- Putting the customer first
- Anticipating customer needs or problems, tailoring products to customer needs
- Establishing lasting customer relationships

3.13 To achieve this customer focus, there is a need to ensure that service staff are trained to provide good service. This should apply the **right product** to the customer's **needs**; be **friendly, caring, polite quick and efficient** service; and should aspire to be a service which is **right first time**.

3.14 Any programme which aims to improve the level of customer care would need to achieve a range of important objectives.

(a) **Identify key aspects of service quality** both inside and outside the organisation. This process of identification may well involve market research to identify existing levels of satisfaction. The research could also be used to identify expectations of service quality and the gaps between expected and actual levels of service quality.

(b) **Set standards for service delivery.** These should be quantifiable and potentially attainable. For instance, a maximum queuing time (or length of queue) or a maximum time before a telephone is answered are targets that can be quantified.

(c) **Set up systems for service delivery.** It is pointless setting targets if there is no operating system in place which can enable service staff to meet the targets.

(d) **Analyse employee training needs.** Before setting up training programmes it is necessary to decide on the content of such programmes. Do employees know enough about the company products? Do they have sufficient interpersonal skills? The analysis should examine current practice and identify weaknesses.

(e) **Develop training programmes.**
- Business and product knowledge
- Customer awareness
- Interpersonal skills

as identified by the analysis of training needs.

(f) Set up systems to **measure and monitor success** in achievement of the targets. Market research may well be involved to examine customer perceptions of actual service quality.

(g) Set up **performance related pay and recognition systems** for employees. It is necessary to back organisational commitment to service quality by relating reward systems to good performance, thus motivating staff.

(h) If necessary, examine the possibility of restructuring of the organisation to achieve necessary **cultural change**.

Marketing at Work

Customers really are the last straw. That must have been the view of the gym owner who moved premises without leaving a forwarding address.

When a female customer finally caught up with him and demanded a refund, his reply was partly unprintable. 'Quite honestly, I'm sick of people like you constantly whinging and whining and generally getting on my nerves,' he wrote. He threatened to go to the police if she contacted him again.

'The British public has a ferocious battle every year in getting often legitimate complaints heard,' says David Lazenby, the BSI's director of standards. Reported complaints about products and services are rising by an average of 3-4 per cent a year, according to the Office of Fair Trading. About 850,000 complaints are now made to trading standards departments and service agencies. But studies show that more than half those dissatisfied with a product or service do not complain. They avoid the supplier in future and warn off others.

'Conversely, where a complaint can be made easily and is effectively dealt with, customer loyalty is frequently enhanced,' says the BSI.

BS860: 1999 is designed to take the pain out of complaining by encouraging best practice in managing customers' problems.

By treating a complaint as an opportunity for improvement rather than a problem, companies can retain customer loyalty and create an image of a responsible organisation. A systematic approach gathers feedback which can be used to increase competitiveness. To follow best practice, organisations must foster a culture of accountability rather than blame. Chief executives should be involved in complaints procedures. A manager should be designated to ensure the process works smoothly.

Financial Times, 13 May 1999

Action Programme 4

Do you have a programme or procedure for customer care in your company? Find out about it and identify any ways in which it could be improved. Try and find out about other customer care schemes or charters. Compare them with your own. How do those of the public sector compare with those of the private sector?

Part C: Managing people

Changing the culture

3.15 It is easy for the management of the organisation to pay lip service to the need for better customer care. In reality, higher service quality can only be achieved by careful planning and implementation of operating systems which can be monitored to ensure that they meet set performance standards. **Cultural change** may be required.

(a) **Internal communications** may be improved by adequately informing staff about their role in the organisation. Both vertical and horizontal communications often need to be improved.

(b) It may be necessary to overcome inflexible **attitudes and behaviour** on the part of staff who do not accept the need for change. Such staff resist change and often do not want to accept new concepts of development of responsibility and authority. Apathy and open resistance to change can be very difficult to overcome as we saw in Chapter 9.

3.16 Customer care has to be inspired by the culture of the business. It has to be supported by management actions which facilitate problem solving for the customer. It can only be implemented when staff are trained, so that they have the skills necessary to ensure they provide a quality service. This often means encouraging others in the business to see their role as supporting those spearheading the organisation. Sales and marketing are at the sharp end of the business and need help.

3.17 It is worth emphasising some key lessons underlying **customer care and customer retention**, as they directly affect relationship marketing and quality, which are discussed shortly.

- Putting things right is fine, but it would be better had they not gone wrong in the first place. Effectiveness in customer care 'happens before the product/service even reaches the customer'.

- Most customer complaints relate to peripheral issues: but the customer buys the package.

- The problems of the producer are not those of the consumer; in other words if things break down, this is not the customer's problem.

- It is the customer who decides ultimately, what quality is. Quality satisfies the needs of the customer.

- Market research is limited in that customers do not always know what they want.

- Quality information is often hidden from senior decision makers.

- Better customer service has to be driven from the top, and managers need training as well as customer service staff.

- Good customer service is not something that is achieved once only; it requires constant reinforcement.

4 RELATIONSHIP MARKETING

Key concept

The principles of customer care are applied most thoroughly in **relationship marketing.** This is defined by Cram as: 'The consistent application of up-to-date knowledge of individual customers to product and service design ... in order to develop a continuous and long term relationship.'

4.1 The marketing concept improved on the sales orientation to business by aiming to satisfy the customer's needs. In **practical terms** this meant a **mass marketing** approach in which products were aimed at the *average* customer. Relationship marketing aims to satisfy the needs of *individual* customers. It is the **ultimate form of market segmentation** in which each segment contains just one customer. It is made possible for large markets by IT and the development of detailed customer databases.

4.2 *Cram* says 'the customer receives ... consistent and appropriate behaviour from a knowledgeable partner'. The requirement for consistency means that all staff who come into contact with customers share the responsibility for customer care. For example, hotel cleaning staff may well interact personally with guests as well as servicing their rooms and thus contribute to the overall impression formed. This is **internal marketing** (introduced in Chapter 5) in the sense of a customer focus in the activities of all employees.

4.3 The greater multi-disciplinary perspective of relationship marketing is emphasised by *Christopher, Payne and Ballantyne* when they suggest that successful relationship marketing requires the integration of customer service, quality and marketing.

4.4 The notion of trust and keeping promises is also important. To have an on-going relationship, both parties need to trust each other and keep the promises they make. Marketing moves from potentially manipulative one-off exchanges towards co-operative relationships built on financial, social and structural benefits.

4.5 Another characteristic of relationship marketing that distinguishes it from traditional marketing is the idea of multiple parties, or a network of exchange partners. Customer relationships are important but so too are the relationships which organisations have with other parties such as suppliers, distributors, professional bodies, banks and trade associations.

4.6 **Distinguishing characteristics of relationship marketing**

- A focus on **customer retention** rather than attraction
- The development of an on-going relationship as opposed to a one-off transaction
- A **long timescale** rather than a short timescale
- Direct and **regular customer contact** rather than impersonal sales
- **Multiple employee/customer contacts,** hence the increased importance of part-time marketers and internal marketing
- Quality and customer satisfaction being the concern of all employees rather than just those who work in the marketing department
- Emphasis on key account relationship management, service quality and buyer (partner) behaviour rather than the marketing mix
- Importance of **trust** and keeping promises rather than making the sale
- Multiple exchanges with a number of parties and network relationships, rather than a single focus on customers

5 TOTAL QUALITY AND MARKETING

5.1 The increased emphasis on retention of customers and building the core business leads directly to the ideas behind **quality** and **relationship** marketing. Both concepts have already been overviewed in this chapter.

Part C: Managing people

5.2 Many marketers would say that the underlying concept of quality is a repackaged version of the marketing concept. Marketers have not been very successful at selling the marketing concept and value of a strategic marketing focus to others in the company. **Quality**, with its emphasis on **internal customers** and their role in delivering external customer satisfaction, has helped to ensure organisational integration.

5.3 What is quality? From a marketing point of view, quality is what customers say it is. However, this has to be translated into the operating mechanisms of the business. *Juran* noted two aspects to quality.

(a) **Quality of design**. This comprises the customer satisfactions built into the product.

(b) **Quality of conformance**. This relates to the conformance of a finished product to its design specification (in effect, that it does what it is supposed to do).

Total quality management (TQM)

5.4 *Holmes* defines TQM as 'a culture aimed at continually improving performance in meeting the requirements in all functions of a company'. In other words, it is a **way of managing a business, not just a technique**. Traditional approaches to quality implied that it was bolted on at the end rather than being integral to the product and designed in at the beginning. The basic principle of TQM is that the cost of preventing mistakes is less than the cost of correcting them once they occur and the cost of loss potential for future sales. The aim should therefore be to get things right first time consistently.

5.5 **Ideas of importance in TQM**

- **Zero defects**. No product made should ever be defective. In other words there is **never** an acceptable level of rejects. In a JIT environment zero defects takes on significant operational importance: no inspection would be necessary.

- A corollary of this is **right first time**: no product should need rectification once it is built.

- **Continuous improvement**. We examine this in more detail later.

Reducing wasteful activities

5.6 **Qualified Total Quality** (QTQ) is an example of an approach which requires a work group to analyse its activities and classify them into three groups.

- **Core activities** are the reason for the existence of the work group and add value to the business.

- **Support activities** support core activities but do not themselves add value.

- **Discretionary activities** such as checking, progress chasing and dealing with complaints are all symptoms of failure within the organisation.

5.7 **Poor quality might be caused by process failures**

- Poorly trained or inappropriate staff
- Unfriendly computers
- Poor or non-existent co-ordination between functions
- Poor organisation of work within the organisation
- Lack of resources

Notice how many of these are central to the management activities we have been discussing in this Study Text.

Statistical techniques: conformance quality

5.8 **Statistical process control** (SPC) is an aspect of TQM. Statistical quality control charts might be used to record and monitor the accuracy of the physical dimensions of products. **Representational samples** of an output manufacturing process may be taken daily or even every hour, and faults in the manufacturing process which are revealed may be fairly simple to correct by adjusting the appropriate machinery. If output exceeds the **control limits** consistently, more urgent management action would be called for, because this would indicate that the process is out of control. This may have many causes.

- Inefficiency in production
- Inadequacy in production methods
- Inadequate quality of raw materials and components
- Excessively tight tolerances in the first place

The ultimate goal of SPC is the reduction of variation.

Quality function deployment: design quality

5.9 SPC enables the review of the actual production process. However, many of the thinkers quoted earlier refer to the much wider role of quality in the organisation. **Quality function deployment** (QFD) is a quality technique used to cut across functional boundaries. QFD is aimed at getting design quality right, early in the process. This is achieved by assessing in detail the customer's needs and including them in a design specification, so that they are accurately translated into **relevant technical requirements**.

Continuous improvement

5.10 Quality management is not a one-off process, but is the continual examination and improvement of existing processes. The idea of continuous improvement might appear to go against the law of diminishing returns, in that it might be arguable that there is a limit beyond which there is no point in pursuing any further improvements.

5.11 Advocates of continuous improvement, however, believe that this can be over-emphasised. Remember, continuous improvement does not only apply to the finished product, but also to the processes which give rise to it.

- It is not easy to determine where diminishing returns set in.

- A philosophy of continuous improvement ensures that management is not **complacent**, which can be a cultural disaster.

- Customer needs change, so a philosophy of continuous improvement enables these changes to be taken into account **in the normal course of events**.

- New technologies or materials might be developed, enabling cost savings or design improvements.

- Rarely do businesses know every possible fact about the production process. Continuous improvement encourages experimentation and **a scientific approach** to production.

- It is a way of tapping **employees' knowledge**.

- Reducing **variability** is a key issue for quality. It often requires **improving the process** itself, rather than changing the machines or adjusting them.

Part C: Managing people

- Improvement on a continual, step by step basis **is more prudent** in some cases than changing things all at once.

Organisational implications

5.12 Quality seems such a desirable objective that you might wonder why it has not been implemented before now. As ever, quality inevitably encounters a variety of organisational problems. In practice all the techniques and approaches to TQM involve a significant shake up.

(a) Employees are consulted in the **quality survey** and encouraged to **suggest improvements**.

(b) **Greater discipline** is required in the process of production and the establishment of better linkages between the business functions.

(c) New relationships must be developed **with suppliers**, since they must improve their output quality so that less effort is spent rectifying poor **input**. Long-term relationships with a small number of suppliers might be preferable to choosing material and sub-components on price.

(d) Work standardisation and **employee commitment** are both necessary.

5.13 **Participation** is important in TQM, especially in the process of continuous improvement, where workforce views are valued. The management task is to encourage everybody to contribute. There are many barriers to participation.

- An **autocratic chief executive**, who believes he or she is the sole key to the process
- **Individualism**, in which people 'possess' ideas in order to take credit for them rather than share them for mutual benefit; Komatsu found that the British emphasis on individual development can be very destructive of team working
- Ideas of managers as leaders and directors rather than facilitators and supporters
- Middle managers who feel their **authority is threatened**

Quality circles

5.14 A policy of **continuous improvement** of quality could be implemented by **empowerment** of employees. Operational-level workers who know how processes are failing should be able to make improvements by being given some form of authority to do so. In turn, managers who have authority but who have less idea of what is going on should have access to their ideas. This necessity for involvement and participation are probably best fulfilled by the use of **quality circles**.

5.15 A **quality circle** consists of a group of employees, perhaps about eight in number, which meets regularly to discuss problems of quality and quality control in their area of work, and perhaps to suggest ways of improving quality. The quality circle has a leader or supervisor who directs discussions and possibly also helps to train other members of the circle. It is also a way to encourage innovation and motivate staff through participation.

5.16 Some **training** in methods of quality control such as quality testing methods, will be necessary for each member of the circle. Equally, it is important to ensure that good communications exist within the circle, perhaps by formal training in techniques of communication. Also a problem with quality circles in many Western companies arises from the separation of the functions of product design, quality design, work methods and operations

10: Managing client relations

- If a quality circle consists of production workers, their role may be restricted to controlling quality within pre-designed specifications.

- If the quality circle consists of design staff, quality decisions might be taken without any consultation with production staff.

- A quality circle that consists of both design and production staff might need a supervisor whose level of seniority is quite high.

5.17 **Quality circles are not random groups of employees**. To make the system work a number of factors must be considered when the circle is being formed.

(a) A quality circle is a **voluntary grouping**. There is no point in coercing employees to join because the whole point is to develop a spontaneous concern for quality amongst workers.

(b) Quality circles do not function automatically. Training may be needed in methods of quality control, problem-solving techniques and methods of communication.

(c) The right leader must be chosen. The person required is one who is capable of directing discussions and drawing out contributions from each member of the circle.

5.18 Ideally, quality circles should be given more responsibility than merely suggesting improvements. Shop-floor commitment may be increased if the members of quality circles also have responsibility for implementing their recommendations.

5.19 **Benefits claimed to arise from the use of quality circles**

- Greater motivation of employees
- Improved productivity
- Improved quality of output
- Greater awareness of problems by shop-floor staff

Relationship marketing and quality

5.20 If quality production and output is to be assured, then the quality of raw materials and components must also be reliable and consistent. The result of this need has been a further shift in how business organises its activities. The annual re-negotiation of contracts with suppliers is being replaced with the shift towards establishing longer term contractual relationships. In this way suppliers and companies work in partnership to solve problems together.

Action Programme 5

What are the benefits of the approach in paragraph 5.20 for:

(a) suppliers?
(b) manufacturers?

Just-in-time (JIT)

5.21 Just-in-time is a system of working which aims to eliminate waste by means of managing workflow. For this purpose, waste can be described as the use of resources which fail to add value to a product. There are four main aspects of JIT.

Part C: Managing people

(a) **JIT purchasing**. This seeks to match as closely as possible the usage of raw materials in production with the delivery of materials from suppliers. Stock is therefore kept at the near-zero level. This depends on the longer term partnership with suppliers referred to above.

(b) **JIT production**. Production only takes place when there is actual customer demand for the output. This means that work in progress and finished goods stock levels are at a minimum.

(c) **Quality** must be high at all stages as no stock of spares is carried.

(d) **Modern manufacturing technology** and **production organisation** are employed to cut down work-in-progress stocks and response time.

Quality assurance and standards: BS EN ISO 9000

5.22 The essentials of **quality assurance** are that the supplier guarantees the quality of goods supplied and allows the customers' inspectors access while the items are being manufactured. Usually, inspection procedures and quality control standards are agreed by the customer and supplier, and checks are made to ensure that they are being adhered to.

(a) The customer can almost eliminate goods inwards inspection and items can be directed straight to production. This can give large savings in cost and time in flow production, and can facilitate JIT production.

(b) The supplier produces to the customer's requirement, thereby reducing rejects and the cost of producing substitutes.

5.23 Quality assurance schemes are being used increasingly, particularly where extensive sub-contracting work is carried out. One such scheme is BS EN ISO 9000 certification. This is a nationally promoted standard, only awarded after audit and inspection of a company's operations. In order to gain registration, a company must obtain **independent** verification that its quality system meets standards. The British Standards Institution is the largest of the UK certification bodies.

5.24 Be aware that the award of BS EN ISO 9000 is based on **consistent** quality rather than **high** quality.

6 IMPROVING NEGOTIATION SKILLS   12/99, 6/00

6.1 The new approaches do not imply that organisations no longer negotiate. However the basis and nature of the negotiation has extended to a broader range of issues than simply price.

6.2 We have already considered negotiation as a key management skill in Chapter 5 of this Study Text. In this Section we are concerned with **negotiating in selling**.

6.3 Negotiation is the process of bringing the buyer and seller together. The objective is straightforward enough: to ensure that both parties are satisfied by the exchange.

6.4 The diagram below identifies possible outcomes of a negotiation.

	Buyer Win	Buyer Lose
Seller Win	1	2
Seller Lose	3	4

Box 1 This is the goal. Both parties benefit. Repeat business and satisfactory relationships should continue.

Box 2 The seller wins, but the buyer loses, possibly the result of an imbalance of power between the two or a lack of choice in the short term. The customer feels cheated or dissatisfied. In the long run, the customer will be looking for a new supplier.

Action Programme 6

What has happened in box 3?

6.5 Box 4 is the worst scenario: neither party is happy with the exchange. A low price perhaps is unsatisfactory to the seller and the resulting low quality of product or service fails to satisfy the customer. Without re-negotiation or open communication this relationship is doomed.

Negotiation of terms: the sales perspective

6.6 Even when a sale is almost certain, its close can often be determined by the detailed negotiation of the terms of business. The salesperson may use the flexibility of terms like price or delivery to help close the sale, or the added benefits and support which can be provided.

6.7 **The sales team must be well briefed as to the extent of their authority to negotiate terms.** The size of discounts acceptable and the ability to deliver service promises should all be known in advance of the sales interview. Confirming availability and delivery dates for products is an important part of the preparation stage of selling, and the sales team must be well briefed to ensure they do not offer what cannot be delivered.

6.8 The degree of autonomy the sales team has in such negotiations is clearly a matter of policy.

- Too much autonomy can have considerable impact on the profitability of new business. In other words sales might be won at **any** cost.

- Too little autonomy might result in sales opportunities being missed simply because of the salesperson's inability to be flexible on terms.

Part C: Managing people

Negotiations on price

6.9 It is the area of **price discounts** that causes the greatest concerns for managers. A sales team, with authority to offer discounts, is often suspected of giving these away, perhaps unnecessarily, certainly too easily. The fear is that it becomes too easy to offer inducements, and that the sales team will use discounts rather than persuasion to motivate a purchase.

6.10 Certainly selling on **price** is a minefield. Lower prices today tend to lead to an expectation of similarly low prices in the future. In consumer markets particularly, price is taken to be the guide to quality, and lowering price can directly impact on product image. Ideally it is preferable to sell added benefits rather than to **lower prices**. This is relevant when developing sales promotions, when agreeing policy on sales negotiations and when training the sales force.

Marketing at Work

A report in *Marketing Business* in March 1998 showed that although promotional activity accounts for the majority of marketing budgets, the expenditure may not be very effective. The glut of price promotions, loyalty cards and long-term low pricing strategies has disorientated customers, and not led to the desired results.

In the newspaper industry for example *The Times*, *Independent* and *Daily Telegraph* have all experimented with price-cutting strategies. However opinion in the industry is divided about the effectiveness of this strategy. It can be argued that many people buy the same paper for many years, and if they do change, having changed once they are more likely to change again.

Many stores now have loyalty cards. There are approximately 150 loyalty card schemes in operation. Research suggests that most consumers carry between five and ten loyalty cards, but only use one or two on a regular basis. Stores could be doing more to establish relationships with individual cardholders by for example reminding them of how they can use their loyalty card points.

There is also evidence that stores are not using the information on cardholders to the best effect. They should be trying to identify more precisely how consumers react to promotions. Research suggests some consumers are loyal to brands and not to stores, some are loyal to stores and not to brands, some get a thrill out of taking advantage of promotions, some will take advantage of promotions to hoard and stockpile, and some consumers are totally oblivious to promotions, remaining both brand and store loyal. Stores should be trying to identify what type of consumer predominates in their own customer base and target their promotional activity accordingly.

6.11 Negotiating and clarifying all the relevant terms of business are essential first stages in establishing a positive future relationship. Misunderstanding about payment terms, delivery dates or quality of product can all lead to dissatisfaction and lost future business.

Action Programme 7

You have been asked to advise a colleague who is about to embark on a negotiation with a key client about a continuation of contract. How should she prepare?

Action Programme 8

Think about a negotiation you have been involved in. How did it go, what could you have done differently?

Did it end in a win/win situation?

7 SOLVING CUSTOMERS' PROBLEMS

7.1 Central to the new more customer focused approach is **solving customers' problems**. The front line position of sales and marketing staff means they are likely to be the first point of contact if the customer has a problem or a complaint. How these situations are handled is important to maintaining and enhancing the long-term relationship.

7.2 The alert marketing person who **anticipates a problem** and is able to take corrective action early is likely to win approval from both employer and client. It may be easier to sort out a potential problem in advance than unravelling a situation once something has gone wrong. Prompt and consistent follow ups are also a key to effective trouble shooting.

7.3 Trouble shooting and problem solving can only be achieved by the marketing person if there is organisational support for such an approach. Production, finance, distribution and administration may all be required to demonstrate flexibility and a commitment to customer care in order to correct a mistake or help to solve a customer's problem.

Handling and reporting complaints

7.4 A problem which is undetected by the front line person and the organisation is likely to generate a complaint. Complaints must be handled in a way which limits the damage to the long-term business relationship.

7.5 Procedures should be established to **ensure managers know about complaints and how they have been resolved**. Otherwise it is too easy for complaints to be handled lower down the organisation with managers unaware there is a problem. This means staff have to be unafraid of reporting complaints; there must be a trusting and open environment in which problems can be handled openly. Complaints handled willingly and efficiently can actually enhance the customer's view of the organisation.

7.6 Complaints require action, but sales people have to take care.

(a) They must not to make the situation worse by arguing with the client.

(b) They must not accept liability either personally or on behalf of the company (product failures, or late deliveries can result in financial loss, and complaints can all too easily end up in court).

(c) They should not necessarily to try and solve the problem **alone**. They should see their role as facilitators of the solution.

7.7 **Six actions when faced with a complaint**

(a) **Listen**. Make sure you have understood the customer's view of the complaint. It is very easy to jump to conclusions and impose your own perception of a problem. People who are complaining can very easily get angry. If you constantly interrupt, or ask them to repeat details, they are likely to feel you are not taking them seriously.

(b) **Sympathise**. This is **not** the same as accepting responsibility. You are simply saying you are sorry there is a problem. Not many people enjoy complaining and so have already expended a considerable amount of emotional energy in worrying about the problem and building up the courage to complain. Sympathise, but do not accept the blame.

(c) **Do not justify**. It is a human response to try and defend yourself and your company against an attack in the form of a complaint. A client complaining of late delivery does not want to know about your broken down vans or sick drivers. These are your problems not the client's. Try to avoid justifications. They are likely to lead to an angry

exchange. The way to deal with this is to avoid looking back at what has happened and concentrate on the future - what is going to happen now?

(d) **Ask questions**. After giving the details of the problem and being sympathised with, the customer is likely to be much less emotional. It is the sales person's responsibility to make sure that all the relevant details of the complaint have been obtained. Open ended questions enable the customer to give more descriptive answers.

(e) **Agree a course of action**. This does not necessarily mean a final solution to the problem. It may require referral to senior management or negotiations with other colleagues. However, it is essential to draw up a course of action which includes a guaranteed time for coming back with a proposal, details of who is to be talked to and so forth. Any course of action agreed must be deliverable, acceptable to both parties and include a time frame.

(f) **Check the action is followed through**. The sales person is responsible for ensuring that agreed action is carried out and that the customer is eventually satisfied with the outcome.

7.8 It will be obvious that **it is sometimes necessary to report complaints upwards** in order to gain management support and assistance in devising an acceptable solution. Senior managers not only have more authority within the company to get speedy action, their personal involvement also expresses to the client how seriously you are treating the complaint and how valuable is the client's business.

7.9 There can be a concern about reporting complaints because it is seen as possibly **causing trouble for colleagues**. It is important that management creates an atmosphere where complaints can be openly reported without too much blame. Problem areas need to be known about. They may be recurring or just provide an opportunity for improved performance.

7.10 Customers who complain are giving the firm a second chance and are giving a clear indication of their needs. Complaints should be seen positively, as an opportunity for improving customer satisfaction.

> ### Action Programme 9
>
> As a customer you have almost certainly had cause to complain. How was your complaint handled? Were you satisfied with the outcome? Are you still a customer?
>
> Take time to find out about the complaints procedure in your organisation. Produce a brief report making recommendations on two things.
>
> (a) How to improve the complaints system
> (b) How to improve training to staff who handle complaints

7.11 A crisis can affect a business's ability to deliver customer satisfaction. In Action Programme 2 of this chapter, we saw an example of product tampering. The time spent building up strong customer relations will be invaluable in these cases. Customers can be informed using existing established communication channels, rather than through the media second-hand. Coping strategies and alternatives should be identified and suggested to these clients. This could involve helping them, however reluctantly, to source supplies from elsewhere. Perhaps your other clients could reduce stockholdings to help you through a temporary shortage. At such times it is important to remember that the manager's job is to help customers solve problems, and the manager's actions now will determine the quality of the long-term relationship.

10: Managing client relations

Marketing at Work

An example of how to lose customer goodwill through poor handling of complaints was South West Trains' actions in early 1997. Their redundancy programme meant that not enough drivers were available to run all timetabled trains with the result that a number of trains were cancelled regularly or suspended.

To compensate passengers, South West Trains offered a day's free travel on tickets obtained from stations through which the company's trains passed. However many regular passengers were not able to take advantage of the offer (because of the short notice), whilst enterprising travellers exploited the offer in ways not anticipated by South West Trains' management (such as obtaining free tickets to Paris).

Any goodwill effects of the gesture were quickly undermined. It took some weeks for services to be fully restored and there were newspaper stories of impending service cuts the next time the timetable was revised. Most serious were press reports of remarks allegedly made by Brian Souter of Stagecoach, the operating company running South West Trains, about passengers spending time at work writing letters complaining about the service. The company's experience demonstrates:

(i) how customer dissatisfaction can remain if organisations do not address the problems causing the dissatisfaction

(ii) how appearing to question customer complaints can undermine attempts to restore goodwill.

Exam Tip

The 40 mark case study in the June 1999 exam in the old syllabus was based on customer satisfaction but set in the context of the post-privatisation UK rail industry. The essence of the scenario was that the fragmentation of the once unitary business into separate companies impeded the wide co-ordination and co-operation necessary to achieve satisfactory levels of customer service.

To produce an acceptable answer it was necessary to apply basic principles in a marketing approach. Note that it was **not** necessary to have any specialist knowledge of rail transport or its management. It was, however, necessary to use ordinary business and marketing awareness to discern the important issues and how to deal with them.

When confronted with a case study that seems obscure or difficult to approach, it is a good idea to pause for thought, and try to look behind the setting to what the examiner is concerned with. Then to keep focussed, you **must** plan your answer, if only to avoid straying into irrelevancy.

In the new syllabus, there was a specific question about remedying the problems caused by poor customer perceptions in June 2001, in the context of building and maintaining long-term relationships. A similar question was asked in December 2000: the focus was on the underlying decision process in the company.

Part C: Managing people

Chapter Roundup

- Marketing managers have a direct responsibility for managing external as well as internal relations.
- These relationships with the organisation's stakeholders are vital and require the same type of interpersonal skills we have discussed in other chapters.
- The marketing manager is the bridge or link which brings together buyer and seller in a way which ensures the satisfaction of both parties. This means skills of communication, research and negotiation are critical.
- It is increasingly recognised that current customers are very valuable, they need to be looked after (customer care) and developed. They cost a lot to win and even more to replace.
- The key to retaining customers lies in providing a quality service or product which delivers what is promised and satisfies the customer's needs.
- Organisations in both public and private sectors are paying increasing attention to customer care - establishing standards of service and working through quality programmes to improve on these.
- Relationship marketing involves all the company's staff in the maintenance of a satisfactory long-term relationship with individual customers.
- **Negotiations** are important because they establish the basis on which the business relationship is established. Win/win situations are the only option for an organisation committed to long-term relationships.
- With the best efforts in the world, problems will arise. The quality of customer care will be judged by **how** problems are tackled and resolved.
- Systems for reporting complaints and their outcomes must enable complaints to be dealt with routinely.
- In one sense, marketing has done its job when everyone in the organisation really **cares** about the customer. Delivering satisfaction is an easier challenge if everyone is committed to it.

Quick Quiz

1. Why is social responsibility often difficult to deliver in practice? (see para 2.6)
2. What are the relative costs and values of winning more business from:
   - non-users?
   - medium users?
   - heavy users?   (3.2)
3. What is the danger of marketers raising customer expectations? (3.7)
4. List six benefits which can result from improved quality and customer care. (3.8)
5. Service quality has two dimensions - what are they? (3.9)
6. What three aspects would you include if you were developing a customer care training programme? (3.14)
7. What are the distinguishing characteristics of relationship marketing? (4.6)
8. Distinguish between design quality and conformance quality. (5.3)
9. What are the most likely process failures which reduce quality? (5.7)
10. Describe a quality circle. (5.15)
11. What are the benefits of using quality circles? (5.19)
12. What is the principle of JIT? And what are its characteristics? (5.21)
13. What is meant by a win/win position when negotiating? (6.4)
14. What are the possible dangers of selling on price? (6.10)
15. What are the six stages for handling a complaint? (7.7)

Action Programme Review

1. Some audiences

   - Customers and consumers
   - Intermediaries, eg distributors and advertising agencies
   - Political and industry influences
   - Shareholders and financial community

2. This is similar to a case in the USA. The affected company withdrew all its products for sale, and better security procedures were installed at the factory. An advertising campaign was instituted to reach people who had purchased the product. This draconian approach earned the company public goodwill.

3. Customer care lessons from this example

   - Offering delivery is good customer care, focused around the customer's needs.
   - The failure to deliver was a mistake, which should have been rectified immediately together with an apology. It should not have been compounded.
   - The extra fencing panel, whilst symbolic of the company's contrition, is not really appropriate if there is no use for it. Similarly, if a manager has to apologise for his staff, it means they are not properly trained.
   - It is far better to get things **right first time**, a key belief of the quality movement.

5.

Supplier	*Manufacturer*
1 No fear annually of losing the contract	1 Support and help in solving customer problems
2 Opportunity to plan longer term	2 Added value services, eg JIT delivery
3 More security in financial terms	3 No management time wasted in annual contract reviews
4 Lower costs from tendering or presenting to potential and past clients	4 Certain levels of supply quality

6. The seller has lost, and the buyer won. The abuse of buying power has enabled the buyer to dictate terms that the supplier is not happy with. In the long run, the supplier will seek more profitable business elsewhere.

7. Stage 1: **Fact find**

   Research to identify everything known about the company, its future plans, key personnel and record of business with you.

   Stage 2: **Establish authority**

   Find out how important this contract is to the business and what authority there is for negotiation and in what areas.

   Stage 3: **Think about the Golden Rule**

   The golden rule is to offer what is valuable to them, but relatively cheap to you. What options are available, eg a second delivery each week costs you little as your vans are passing, but cuts down the cost of their stock holdings and inventory.

   Stage 4: **Confirm the arrangements**

   Check out when and where the negotiations are taking place. Be ready in plenty of time.

Now try illustrative questions 16 and 17 at the end of Study Text

Part D
International influences on management style

11 International Influences on Management

Chapter Topic List	Syllabus reference
1 Setting the scene	
2 Globalisation	4.2
3 International environmental influences	4.1, 4.2
4 Social and cultural considerations	4.1
5 Culture and the organisation	4.2, 4.3
6 Managing across borders	4.3
7 Human resource management	4.2, 4.3

Learning Outcome

- Students will be able to describe international influences on management practice and their uses and abuses.

Key Concepts Introduced

- Global company
- Management culture

Examples of Marketing at Work

- Demographics
- Boots in Japan
- Cultural checklist
- Volvo
- Structures

Part D: International influences on management style

1 SETTING THE SCENE

1.1 The aim of this part of the syllabus is for you to acquire an appreciation of some of the problems of managing internationally and their implications for management practice.

1.2 Section 2 deals with the trade background to international management and the idea of the global company. This is not an entirely satisfactory theory, as the section discusses, but it helps to put the rest of the chapter in context.

1.3 Section 3 is introduces the international environment and its complexity compared with the much simpler business environment in a single country. The social and cultural aspects of international business are particularly relevant for management and so we devote section 4 to these topics.

1.4 Section 5 focuses our consideration of culture on the organisation and cultural influences on management style.

1.5 Section 6 considers a number of practical issues including structure and control systems, and Section 7 discusses the special features of human resource management in an international setting.

Links with other papers

1.6 Your reading of the relevant chapters in the BPP Study Text for *Marketing Operations* will help here.

> **Exam Tip**
> Questions on international activities as such have been comparatively rare — one set in June 2000 in fact. This asked in the most general terms about differences in international marketing management practice in overseas markets —you were directed to focus on PEST (Political, Economic, Social, Technological) and people factors.

2 GLOBALISATION

2.1 Since 1945, the volume of world trade has increased. This has meant a proliferation of suppliers exporting to, or trading in, a wider variety of places. However, the existence of global markets should not be taken for granted in terms of all products and services, or indeed in all territories.

(a) Some **services** are still subject to managed trade (for example, some countries prohibit firms from other countries from selling insurance). Trade in services has been liberalised under the auspices of the World Trade Organisation.

(b) **Immigration.** There is unlikely ever to be a global market for labour, given the disparity in skills between different countries, and restrictions on immigration.

(c) The market for some goods is much more globalised than for others.

　　(i) Upmarket luxury goods may not be required or afforded by people in developing nations.

　　(ii) Some goods can be sold almost anywhere, but to limited degrees. Television sets are consumer durables in some countries, but still luxury or relatively expensive items in other ones.

　　(iii) Other goods are needed almost everywhere. In oil a truly global industry exists in both production (e.g. North Sea, Venezuela, Russia, Azerbaijan, Gulf states)

and consumption (any country using cars and buses, not to mention those with chemical industries based on oil).

Global production

2.2 Global production implies that a firm's production planning is considered on a global scale.

(a) **Global manufacture**. A company can **manufacture** components for a product in a number of different countries. Japanese companies sometimes ship components for assembly to their factories overseas.

(b) **Global sourcing**. Sub-components may be purchased from countries overseas. As the case example below demonstrates, companies can exploit the comparative advantages of different countries.

2.3 The extreme form of global production has been referred to by *Kenichi Ohmae* as **insiderisation**. In other words, in each of your markets you build up a production and distribution organisation from scratch or in conjunction with local suppliers, even though there may be few variants to the product from market to market. (*Coca-Cola* has done this in Japan.)

> **KEY CONCEPT**
>
> A **global company** is 'an organisation that makes no distinction between domestic and international business' (Terpstra). Few such organisations genuinely exist.

2.4 While more and more companies are competing in the world market place, most of them tend to focus on the developed markets of North America, Europe and Japan. A vast majority (86%) of the world's population resides in countries where GDP is less than $10,000 per head. Such countries offer tremendous marketing opportunities if the offering is presented correctly.

2.5 Going international can add to the **value chain**. Integrating the supply chain across several countries can lead to considerable cost savings. Increased levels of customer service allied with these cost savings can lead to a dominant market position. This needs an organisational culture that is aware of the supply chain and customer service whatever the country (or countries) of operation.

2.6 **Other factors encouraging the globalisation of world trade**

(a) **Financial factors** such as Third world debt. Often the lenders require the initiation of economic reforms as a condition of the loan.

(b) **Country/continent** alliances, such as that between the UK and USA, which fosters trade and other phenomena such as tourism.

(c) **Legal factors** such as patents and trade marks, which encourage the development of technology and design.

(d) **Markets** trading in international commodities. Commodities are not physically exchanged, only the rights to ownership. A buyer can, thanks to efficient systems of trading and modern communications, buy a commodity in its country of origin for delivery to a specific port. There is also a market in **futures**, enabling buyers to avoid the effect of price changes by buying for future delivery at a set price. This smoothes the process of international trade and lowers risk.

Do global firms really exist?

2.7 Some writers believe that there is an increasing number of 'stateless corporations', whose activities transcend national boundaries, and whose personnel come from any country.

2.8 This theory looks attractive on the surface, particularly in a relatively open economy like that of the UK, which is host to a number of multinational corporations and has attracted a fair degree of inward investment.

2.9 Do these global or stateless corporations really exist? The following objections have been raised by *Yao-Su Hue* and *John Cantwell* of Reading University.

   (a) Most multinationals, other than those based in small nations, have **less than half of their employees abroad**.

   (b) **Ownership and control** of multinationals remain **restricted**. This is partly because of the way in which capital markets are structured. Few so-called global companies are quoted on more than two stock markets.

   (c) **Top management** is rarely as multinational as the firm's activities. This is particularly true of Japanese companies. A foreigner is rarely seen on the Tokyo-based board of a Japanese multinational. The *Financial Times* reported that the membership of the Board of Directors of UK firms is the most cosmopolitan.

   (d) **National residence and status** is important for tax reasons. Boundary-less corporations are not recognised as such by lawyers or tax officials.

   (e) The bulk of a multinational's **research and development** is generally done in the home country. Indeed Porter says that the home market is important for product development in the information it gives about consumers.

   (f) Where capital is limited, 'global' companies stick to the home market rather than developing overseas ones.

   (g) Finally, **profits** from a global company must be **remitted** somewhere.

2.10 However, it may be the case that firms will become more globally orientated if they are able to specialise and if it becomes easier to trade.

3 INTERNATIONAL ENVIRONMENTAL INFLUENCES

3.1 Managers responsible for international operations must be aware of the environmental differences they will encounter. In particular, the cultural aspect of the social environment is vitally important.

Law and politics

3.2 The **system of courts and the legal profession** may be unfamiliar. The very existence of the **rule of law** and an **independent judiciary** may be in doubt. Rules relating to corporate status, property, the regulation of business, and financial reporting may all be very different. There may be significant **political risk**. The government may be unstable; its ideology may be unsympathetic to Western business methods or it may have poor relations with the rest of the world. In many countries there is a need for political contacts and extensive lobbying before business can be done.

11: International influences on management

Economy

3.3 **Economic factors affecting international businesses**:

- Is there **growth** or is the economy stagnating?
- Is the **exchange rate** stable?
- How does the **interest rate** compare with other countries? Is it stable?
- What is the rate of **inflation**? What is the government's policy? Is it realistic?
- What are the existing **price structures** in the target markets?

3.4 Various forms of **protectionism** hamper international trade. Formal tariff barriers have been much reduced and are now policed by the World Trade Organisation, but non-tariff barriers are still a problem. These all protect the home producer and include licences, quotas, size and weight regulations, environmental protection standards and hidden domestic subsidies.

Regional trading groups

3.5 Currently, a number of **regional trading arrangements** exist, as well as global trading arrangements. These regional trading groups take three forms.

- Free trade areas
- Customs unions
- Common markets

Free trade areas

3.6 Members in these arrangements agree to lower barriers to trade amongst themselves. They enable free movement of **goods** and **services,** but not always the factors of production.

Customs unions

3.7 **Customs unions** provide the advantages of free trade areas and agree a common policy on tariff and non-tariff barriers to **external countries.** Internally they attempt to harmonise tariffs, taxes and duties amongst members.

Economic unions/common markets

3.8 In effect the members become one for economic purposes. There is free movement of the factors of production. The EU has economic union as an aim, although not all members, including the UK, necessarily see this goal as desirable. The EU has a 'rich' market of over 300 million people and could provide a counterweight to countries such as the USA and Japan.

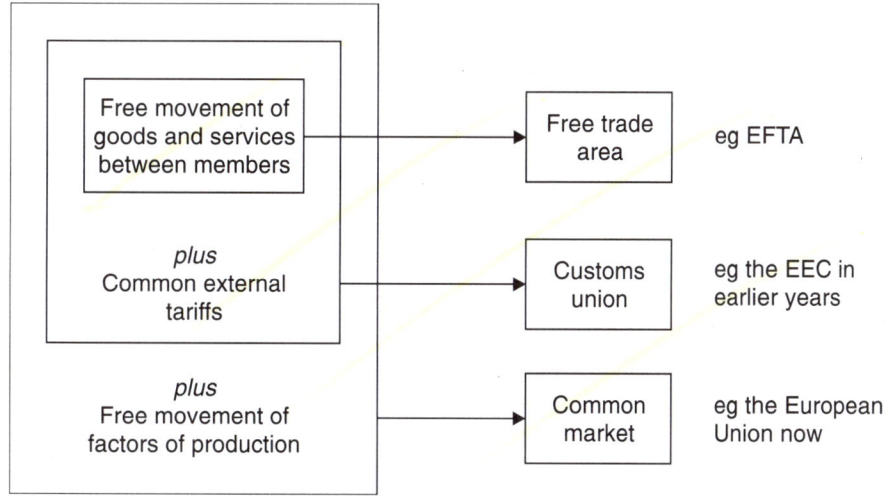

Part D: International influences on management style

3.9 The major regional trade organisations are as follows.

(a) North American Free Trade Agreement (NAFTA) - US, Canada and Mexico.

(b) European Free Trade Association (EFTA) - Norway, Switzerland, Iceland, Liechtenstein.

(c) European Union (EU) - Ireland, Britain, France, Germany, Italy, Spain, Portugal, Finland, Sweden, Denmark, Luxembourg, Belgium, the Netherlands, Austria, Greece. A number of other countries have applied to join.

Economic development

3.10 Economic factors affect both the demand and the ability to acquire goods and services. Even in lesser developed countries (see below) there often exists a wealthy elite who provide a significant demand for sophisticated consumer goods.

3.11 Countries generally have larger agricultural sectors in the earlier stages of economic development (for example India and Africa). As the economy develops, the manufacturing sector increases.

3.12 Commonly, economists and marketers categorise countries into five broad types. Each type then exhibits a fairly consistent pattern of demand for goods and services. Commonly used factors in classifying countries include the following.

- **Infrastructure** extent and quality
- **Education** and literacy
- Ownership of **consumer durables**
- **GDP per head**

3.13 All of the first three may be claimed to be dependent on GDP. GDP on a **per capita** basis, suitably adjusted for purchasing power, is probably the best single indicator of economic development. However, a danger in using GDP is that it considers only the **average**. The **distribution of wealth** is critical in poor countries, where a market may exist amongst above average sections of the population.

Classification of economic development

3.14 Generally each country can be classified under one of five headings.

(a) **Lesser developed country (LDC).** Relies heavily on primary industries (mining, agriculture, forestry, fishing) with low GDP per capita, and poorly developed infrastructure.

(b) **Early developed country (EDC).** Largely primary industry based, but with developing secondary (manufacturing) industrial sector. Low but growing GDP, developing infrastructure.

(c) **Semi-developed country (SDC).** Significant secondary sector still growing. Rising affluence and education with the emergence of a 'middle class'. Developed infrastructure.

(d) **Fully developed country (FDC).** Primary sector accounts for little of the economy. Secondary sector still dominates, but major growth in tertiary (service) sector. Sophisticated infrastructure.

(e) **Former Eastern Bloc country (EBC).** May be any of the above, but the 'command economy' under communism has left a legacy that defies straightforward classification. For example, Russia has most of the features of an SDC but lacks a developed infrastructure though, it has a well educated middle class.

Technology

3.15 Protection of **intellectual property** like patents, trademarks and copyright is particularly important in international operations. Can they be protected? Similarly, in manufacturing, can trade secrets be protected, perhaps by importing part-completed assemblies? Sometimes technology transfer to local businesses is required before permission can be obtained to do business. If advanced technology is involved, it will be necessary to consider local **standards of education and technical infrastructure**.

3.16 *Steven Yearley (Science, Technology and Social Change)* mentions the very uneven success that modern apparatus and technique have had in 'modernising' underdeveloped countries.

(a) The **environmental consequences** of introducing western technology to underdeveloped countries have been ill thought out.

(b) The **economic consequences** have not been as beneficial as might at first be supposed. 'The prestigious new production technologies have not worked optimally or even satisfactorily.' The problems are two-fold.

   (i) **Technological dependency** leading to a heavy foreign currency payments burdens. The country has to import **spare parts**, and even raw materials, to run machinery. It might have to pay for **expatriate technicians**. This is expensive, and so the costs of the technology might be greater than anticipated, thus reducing any economic benefit.

   (ii) The inappropriateness of Western technology. **Climatic** conditions can affect performance. **Infrastructural** deficiencies such as naturally poor roads affect, for example, the 'good design' of a car. The **labour/capital** mix means that in poor countries, with surplus labour, labour intensive industries rather than labour saving capital equipment might be a better use of resources.

4 SOCIAL AND CULTURAL CONSIDERATIONS   6/00

Demographic issues in overseas markets

4.1 **Demography** is the study of populations. It deals largely in statistics such as birth rates, death rates, incidence of disease and distribution densities.

4.2 The **purpose** of studying a country's population and trends within it is as follows.

(a) People create a demand for goods and services.

(b) If economic growth exceeds population growth you would expect to see enhanced **standards** of living. **Quality of life** measures would also include pollution measures, life expectancy rates, infant mortality and so on.

(c) Population is a source of labour, one of the **factors of production.**

(d) Population creates demands on the physical environment and its resources, a source of increased international political concern. (the Kyoto conference in Japan at the end of 1997 agreed reductions in carbon dioxide).

4.3 **Demographic factors** will affect both management in general and marketing in particular. A local workforce can only be recruited if the labour is available; **working practices** may have to conform to local norms. Demand for many categories of consumer goods is heavily influenced by social factors like **fashion and status**. The age structure, geographic distribution and class system of the target population will partly determine what can be achieved.

4.4 The higher rate of population growth in **less-developed countries** compared with developed countries has arisen due to a continuing high birth rate and a declining death rate although some populations are being threatened by the HIV virus (for example in South Africa). Social changes (eg attitudes to large families) have not accompanied medical advances imported from developed societies. People are living longer.

(a) **Growing populations**
- Require fast economic growth just to maintain living standards
- Result in overcrowding on land and/or cities and a decline in the quality of life
- Require more resources for capital investment
- Stimulate investment (as the market size is increasing)
- Lead to enhanced labour mobility

(b) **Falling populations**
- Require more productive techniques to maintain output
- Make some scale economies harder to achieve
- Put a greater burden on a decreasing number of young people
- Exhibit changing consumption patterns

Age structure and distribution

4.5 We should now discuss the **age structure** of the population.

(a) The effect of greater life expectancy is that a larger proportion of the population will be senior citizens and unlikely to be working. These offer significant opportunities to international marketers. The UK, Europe and Japan all face an ageing population.

(b) The proportion of old people is lower in developing countries. In Egypt and Iran, over half the population is below the age of 30.

Geographic distribution

4.6 Where we live is another important feature of demography. The above arguments have taken the individual country as a homogenous unit. In practice, however this is a vast oversimplification. A country may suffer the problems of overpopulation in some areas and underpopulation in others.

4.7 Demography also deals with the effect of concentration and dispersal of population in particular areas. Industrialisation has traditionally meant a shift from the countryside to the towns and can be seen in the explosive growth of **mega-cities** in Latin America (Mexico City, Sao Paolo in Brazil), and Asia (eg Bombay, Shanghai, Jakarta).

Sex

4.8 There is often an imbalance in the population between the numbers of men and the numbers of women. This has arisen for a number of reasons.

(a) Males tend to die younger.

(b) In some countries male children are more valued than female children, and female children are more likely to suffer infanticide.

4.9 The **work roles** played by males and females in different societies vary, even within the industrial world. In different societies, women and men have distinct purchasing and social powers. This is a key cultural issue.

Ethnicity

4.10 Only a few societies are homogenous, with populations of one culture and ethnic background. Japan is an example, although the population includes descendants of Koreans. On the other hand, societies like the USA and the UK have populations drawn from a variety of different areas.

Buying patterns

4.11 Buying behaviour is an important aspect of marketing. Many factors influence the buying decisions of individuals and households. Demography and the **class structure** (the distribution of wealth and power in a society) are relevant in that they can be both **behavioural determinants** and **inhibitors**.

   (a) **Behavioural determinants** encourage people to buy a product or service. The individual's personality, culture, social class, and the importance of the purchase decision (eg a necessity such as food or water, or a luxury) can predispose a person to purchase something.

   (b) **Inhibitors** are factors, such as the individual's income, which will make the person less likely to purchase something.

4.12 **Socio-economic status** can be related to buying patterns in a number of ways, both in the amount people have to spend and what they spend it on. It affects both the quantity of goods and services supplied, and the proportion of their income that households spend on goods and services.

Marketing at work

Demographics

(a) India has a large peasantry and an industrial proletariat, but its huge population size means that its wealthy middle class is bigger than the populations of many developed countries. With import liberalisation and economic deregulation, this should be an attractive segment for marketers.

(b) The level of inequality in society also influences its attractiveness to the marketer. Brazil has the greatest degree of inequality in the world. Japan, famously, has low inequality.

   (i) In societies of high inequality, wealth is concentrated, hence the buying power of the majority is limited. This might suggest more success in selling luxury goods.

   (ii) Where equality is higher, there may be a higher demand for mass market goods as more people will have access to them.

Family structure

4.13 The role of the family and family groupings varies from society to society.

   (a) In societies such as India, the **caste system** still exists and family structures can be part of this wider network.

   (b) **Extended families** are still strong in many countries, especially where the family is to assume most of the burden of looking after the elderly: many countries do not have a welfare state.

   (c) Family size varies.

4.14 Marketers have often used the model of the **family life cycle** model purchase and consumption patterns. You will have encountered it before.

Part D: International influences on management style

- Bachelor - single people
- Newly-weds - household and childcare products
- Full nest
- Empty-nest: children have left home
- Solitary survivor

4.15 This model may not hold.

(a) Quite often, households contain three generations (grand-parents, parents, children).

(b) People leave home later in life. In countries such as Italy and Spain it is common for adult children to live at home.

(c) Purchase and consumption decisions vary.

Culture

4.16 We discussed organisational culture in some detail earlier in this study text. We now need to look at the concept in the context of global business. Culture is inherent within the group and taken for granted. A national culture will be very difficult to change; if change occurs it will take place very slowly. National culture influences the perceptions and behaviour of consumers as well as employees and managers. We should beware of interpreting marketing research, in particular, according to our own cultural norms.

4.17 **Language** is an important aspect of culture. While English is more and more the international language of business, there are many areas where it is not commonly understood, sometimes as a matter of local pride. Mistaken use of a foreign language will undermine otherwise competent marketing operations.

4.18 The national way of doing things pervades society. **Business practice is part of the structure of society and therefore subject to cultural influences.** Contrast the USA: an individualistic and heterogeneous society with high job mobility, where decision making is brisk and authoritative and the specialist professional is highly valued. Japan: an ordered and hierarchical society which values long-term commitment and loyalty, where decisions are taken collectively and managers are expected to be generalists.

High context and low context cultures

4.19 *Hall* suggests that the content of all forms of communication, especially speech face to face, is influenced by the context or setting of the message. Consider the effect of a business letter laser-printed on high quality paper and contrast with the same text scribbled on the back of an envelope.

4.20 **Context has a number of aspects. Here are some examples.**

- Where the communication takes place
- The people involved and their age, sex and status
- The general subject area of the conversation, such as work, appraisal or leisure

4.21 In **low context** cultures, the context is of little importance to communication. The text means what it says. Examples are Germany, Scandinavia and North America.

4.22 In **high context** cultures, the message can only be understood by reference to its context and must not be taken at face value. Important topics like motivation, trustworthiness and co-operation are subject to much non-verbal communication. Examples are Latin America, Arabia and Japan.

11: International influences on management

4.23 The UK, France, Italy and Spain fall into an intermediate, **medium context** category.

Marketing at work

Boots in Japan

When Marks & Spencer twice sent a two-man team to have a look at Japan, they twice came back to its Baker Street headquarters shaking their heads. Japan may be another country, but Japanese retail is on another planet. The Boots ambassador to 'planet Japan' is Bill Spence, a Scotsman who has been in Tokyo since Boots sent him on an exploratory mission four years ago. His prize is clear: a £17 billion-a-year healthcare market four times larger than that of Britain. 'When I first came here', he jokes, 'I thought I knew a fair bit about the Japanese retail market. After a while here, I thought I knew a small bit. Now, I know nothing.'

The more you browse around Japanese health and beauty stores, the more you see his point. They sell medieval-style devices for stretching your neck or widening your smile. The bestselling drug is a medicinal-tasting caffeine and vitamin drink gulped down by exhausted businessmen. The next bestseller is a cream that makes skin look whiter. Boots itself sells condoms according to blood group (the Japanese believe this denotes spiritual compatibility), and even sells multi-packs covering blood types A, B and C. Next week Boots will start selling tea bags along the same demarcations.

Then come the health regulations. Of the 2,000 Boots lines sold in Japan, almost every one had to be reformulated to get around the country's strict rules banning substances common in everyday British medicine. At great expense, Boots has had every one of the offending products reformulated.

---

5 CULTURE AND THE ORGANISATION

5.1 We have discussed culture in a society and as a factor of a firm's environment and market for its products or services. The issue of **corporate culture** is quite important for multinational businesses. This is because many companies have their own culture.

(a) Culture embodies the common set of values: 'the way things are down around here.'

(b) Culture is embodied in rituals and behaviour.

(c) Culture is an important filter of information and an interpreter of it. For example, a firm might have a cultural predisposition against embarking on risky ventures. Finally existing behaviour patterns may make a proposed strategy incompatible with the culture and so impossible to implement.

5.2 An organisation's culture is influenced by many factors.

(a) The organisation's **founder**. A strong set of values and assumptions is set up by the organisation's founder, and even after he or she has retired, these values have their own momentum.

(b) The organisation's **history**. The effect of history can be determined by stories, rituals and symbolic behaviour. They legitimise behaviour and promote priorities. (In some organisations certain positions are regarded as intrinsically more 'heroic' than others.)

(c) **Leadership and management style.** An organisation with a strong culture recruits managers who naturally conform to it.

(d) **Structure and systems** affect culture as well as strategy.

(e) The industry (eg computer software firms in the 'silicon valley' had a reputation for being laid back on office dress).

(f) Location of head office - and its acquired culture

(g) Of most significance in this chapter, the wider **society**, discussed below.

Part D: International influences on management style

Management culture

5.3 A factor which has an impact on the culture of transnational organisations, or organisations competing in global markets, is **management culture**. This is the views about managing held by managers, their shared educational experiences, and the 'way business is done'. Obviously, this reflects wider cultural differences between countries, but national cultures can sometimes be subordinated to the corporate culture of the organisation (eg the efforts to ensure that staff of EuroDisney are as enthusiastic as their American counterparts).

> **Key concept**
> Culture in organisations was discussed in Chapter 2. **Management culture** is a part of overall organisational culture and relates to the prevailing view within the management about how they should do its job.

5.4 **Important aspects of management culture**

- The relative priorities accorded to such matters as technical excellence, customer service, workforce development and innovation.

- The relative value managers place on personal attributes such as people skills, creativity, leadership, drive and professional competence.

5.5 The way in which business practice can be affected by management culture can be indicated by an example.

(a) The Harvard Business Review reported (July-August 1991) that 'the successful development of executives depends on creating a distinctive shared identity, a sense of belonging to the French managerial class'. Further quotations are illuminating

> 'French managers see their work as an intellectual challenge, requiring the remorseless application of individual brainpower. They do not share the Anglo-Saxon view of management as an interpersonally demanding exercise, where plans have to be constantly "sold" upward and downward using personal skills. The bias is for intellect rather than for action. People who run big enterprises must above all else be clever - that is, they must be able to grasp complex issues, analyse problems, manipulate ideas and evaluate solutions. A revealing witticism contains this rejoinder, supposedly from one senior French civil servant to another: "That's fine in practice, but it will never work in theory"'.

(b) The 'world leadership survey' conducted by the *Harvard Business Review* asked a variety of questions to managers in different countries. Although the response to the survey (which appeared in business magazines) was self-selected, it could be concluded that managers in different countries do not have the same priorities when it came to business issues. When asked what they thought of as the three most important factors in organisation success, these were listed as follows, in order of priority.

> **Japan**: product development, management, product quality
> **Germany**: workforce skills, problem solving, management
> **USA**: customer service, product quality, technology

5.6 The existence of these different systems of priorities and ways of doing business affects the competitive environment, international marketing and the success of joint ventures. UK managers, who were described by the survey as among the least cosmopolitan, may have some adapting to do.

Marketing at work

Cultural checklist

In order to succeed when working across different cultures, keep in mind the following traits:

Americans value equality, independence, freedom, action and openness. They appreciate having all the cards on the table and discussing each idea on its own merits.

Arabs will be interested in your contacts, education and position in society. They value authority and personal relationships. They will base their decisions on intuition and religious beliefs.

Chinese value seniority and authority, usually achieved after hard work and recognition from peers and families. Managers' decisions are usually not questioned by subordinates.

Germans Do your homework before making a presentation. Openly challenge their views. Punctuality is highly valued, as are others' titles and degrees. They value their privacy and have an even larger personal space than Americans.

Japanese Make an extra effort to be properly introduced and establish long-term relationships. Always focus on achieving full agreement that will eventually lead to group achievement.

Malaysians and Indonesians Negotiating with Malaysians and Indonesians can be a long, drawn-out process. You have to identify and work with three important players: the person who introduces you, the person who will recommend your proposal and the person who will sign it off.

Farid Elashmawi, People Management, 30 March 2000

The Hofstede model of national cultures

5.7 A model was developed in 1980 by Professor *Geert Hofstede* in order to explain national differences by identifying 'key dimensions' which represent the essential 'programmes' forming a common culture in the value systems of all countries. Each country is represented on a scale for each dimension so as to explain and understand values, attitudes and behaviour.

5.8 In particular, Hofstede pointed out that countries differ on the following dimensions.

(a) **Power distance.** The extent to which unequal distribution of power is accepted. In a large power distance society, a strict hierarchy of power and inequality is maintained from the top down. Subordinates see this as inevitable.

(b) **Uncertainty avoidance.** Some cultures prefer security and order, whereas others are prepared to accept uncertainty. This affects the willingness of people to *change* rules, rather than simply obey them.

(c) **Individualism-collectivism.** In individualist cultures people look after themselves and their immediate families. In collectivist cultures, people expect their in-group (family, clan, organisations) to look after them and they are absolutely loyal to it in return.

(d) **'Masculinity'-'Femininity'.** 'Masculine' cultures place greater emphasis on ambition, achievement and independence, as opposed to the quality of life, the environment and so on.

Part D: International influences on management style

5.9 Hofstede grouped countries into eight groups.

Group		Power distance	Uncertainty avoidance	Individualism	'Masculinity'
I	'More developed Latin' (eg Belgium, France, Argentina, Brazil, Spain)	High	High	Medium to high	Medium
II	'Less developed Latin' (eg Portugal, Mexico, Peru)	High	High	Low	Whole range
III	'More developed Asian' (eg Japan)	Medium	High	Medium	High
IV	'Less developed Asian' (eg India, Taiwan, Thailand)	High	Low to medium	Low	Medium
V	Near Eastern (eg Greece, Iran, Turkey)	High	High	Low	Medium
VI	'Germanic' (eg Germany)	Low	Medium to high	Medium	Medium to high
VII	Anglo (eg UK, US, Australia)	Low to medium	Low to medium	High	High
VIII	Nordic (eg Scandinavia, the Netherlands)	Low	Low to medium	Medium to high	Low

5.10 Hofstede argues strongly that managerial methods may not transfer easily between cultural groups. One example he uses is Management by Objectives (MBO). MBO was developed in the US; it was successfully adopted in Germany, but with an enhanced emphasis on team as opposed to individual objectives. This reflects the lower individualism in Germany. MBO has been abandoned in France because French management culture has a very high power distance which precludes the negotiation necessary if MBO is to succeed.

5.11 There are dangers in using these models. In the management of individual businesses, other factors may be more important.

(a) **Type of industry**: people working in information technology from two countries might have more in common with each other than they might with people working in a different industry.

(b) **Size of company.** Some people may be accustomed to working in a **bureaucracy**.

Relevance to international marketing

5.12 What is the relevance of this issue for international marketers and managers? **Many argue that a corporate culture depends more on the industry sector than on the country.** That said, to ease communication between managers, many firms rely on corporate cultures to ensure a common value system throughout the organisation as a whole.

5.13 For example, performance related pay for individuals might be applied either in the UK or the USA, but it may have adverse consequences in cultures skewed towards collectivism such as Japan.

5.14 Some cultural problems can be solved if there is some **interchangeability of personnel**. Regular meetings, conferences, summaries, secondments etc can help instil a sense of corporate loyalty, and also give executives skills in dealing with different cultures. The senior managers of many large companies (eg ABB) need to be skilled in negotiating the many cultural minefields which exist in international businesses.

Marketing at work

Volvo

The following case is drawn from Corporate Culture: From Vicious to Virtuous Circles, by Charles Hampden-Turner.

The attitude of the staff of Volvo in France to the product they were selling was this.

'The Swedish people who make Volvo don't understand the French. We are hot-blooded Latins, with dash, romance and style. We like cars that perform and are in fashion. Volvos are too sober, too safe, too pedestrian, too cerebral and too practical, consisting of largely old models, which have not changed noticeably in years. Scandinavians have a temperament that dwells on accidents and upon keeping warm. The French have more joie de vivre. Despite heroic efforts to move these melancholy motors, we have not been very successful.'

A crucial aspect of changing a culture is to retell, reinterpret or transform a story which otherwise spells defeat. Goran Carstedt did that in Volvo France. By taking the dealers and their wives to Sweden and giving them the grand tour, the story of moody Scandinavians and dull cars was totally recast to read as follows.

'Volvos are made in Sweden by small, dedicated groups of craftsmen who make and sign each entire car and who manage themselves. Volvo symbolises for the world an individualism married to social concern, to which the virtues of safety and reliability are the key. There are enough French people of discernment and good sense to think of their families and future responsibilities. With the new support we are getting, the Volvo message is one we can deliver with pride and success.'

Exam Tip

The June 2000 exam included a question on the problems associated with international cultural differences. This was a very wide ranging question covering both behaviour in the workplace and environmental aspects. Marketing mix issues were specifically mentioned. As always, what the examiner calls a 'theory dump' would be useless. For instance, while a mention of the differences observed by Hofstede might be useful, a detailed description would not.

To answer this question well it would be necessary to review the information in this chapter through the lens of the question requirements, selecting and arranging to emphasise the **cultural** issues of greatest relevance to marketing management. Here are some examples.

Environmental issues

Language
Business practices eg credit and negotiation
Status of women
'Context'
Attitude to advertising
General educational level

Internal issues

Attitude to management and authority generally
View of appraisal systems
Status of women
Negotiating customs
Attitudes to customers

6 MANAGING ACROSS BORDERS

Management effectiveness

6.1 A problem is that there are often severe cultural differences as to what constitutes 'management' in the first place. Are **management** principles universally applicable? The

marketing function needs awareness of effective management approaches in different cultures.

6.2 Two American writers, *Gonzalez and McMillan*, suggested after a two-year study of management in Brazil that no general conclusions on management principles can be arrived at, and that different principles will apply in different cultures. It even opens up the possibility that general management principles may not be applicable throughout a large country such as the United States because of the variety of sub-cultures that may exist.

6.3 *Koontz, O'Donnell and Weihrich* on the other hand have argued that apparent differences between management **principles** in different countries are actually differences of **application**, and that this distinction has been blurred by careless use of terminology. Their idea is that certain universal **fundamentals** of management exist, which may be applied in different ways depending on the local culture.

6.4 *R N Farmer and B M Richman* emphasise the importance of the external environment in which an organisation operates. They developed a model to illustrate the distinction between the management process and the environment of managing.

The Farmer-Richman model

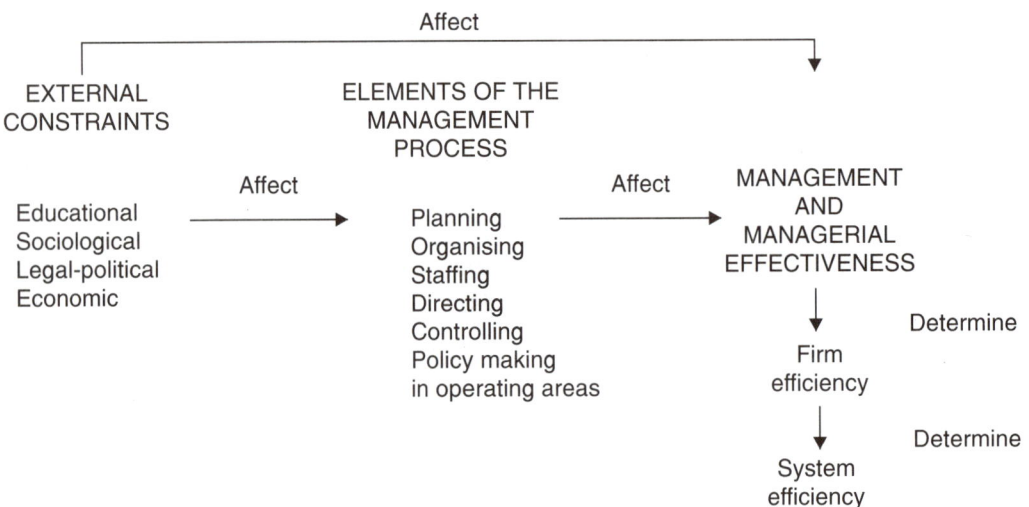

6.5 Farmer and Richman elaborate on the four categories of external constraints identified in the model.

(a) **Educational** constraints include the level of literacy in the environment (country) and the availability of secondary education, vocational training and higher education. Poor educational facilities will inevitably result in poor management.

(b) **Sociological** constraints are the most numerous category. For example, one country may have a tradition of antagonism between trade unions and management whereas another might have a history of mutual trust and co-operation.

(c) **Legal and political constraints.** It is much more difficult to reduce headcount in France than in the UK because of more restrictive French legislation, for example.

(d) **Economic constraints.** Some countries suffer from high rates of inflation and other symptoms of economic instability. The availability of capital is another important factor which varies from one environment to another.

Management structure

6.6 Local conditions and the scale of operations will influence the organisation structure of companies trading internationally. Structures vary from the inclusion of an export department into the usual pyramid, through variations on a combination of functional and geographic responsibility areas, to a matrix structure.

6.7 Conglomerates with widely differing product groups may organise globally by product, with each operating division having its own geographic structure suited to its own needs.

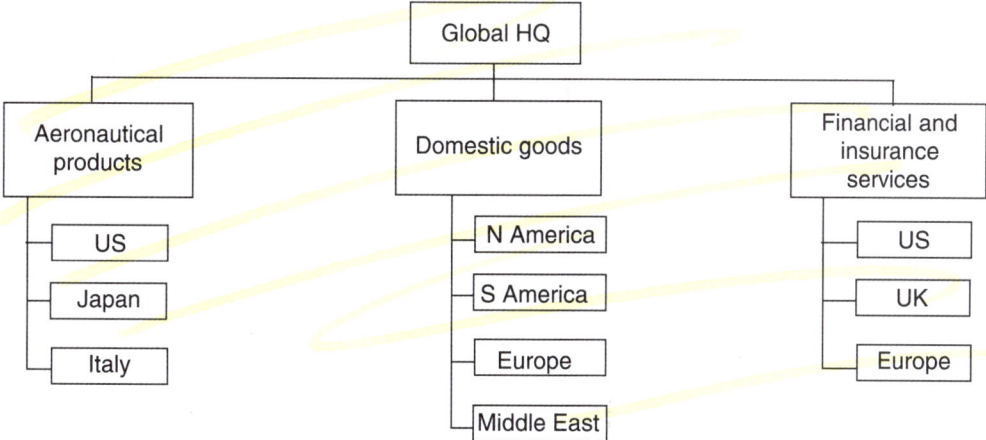

6.8 Companies with more integrated operations may prefer their top-level structure to be broken down geographically with product management conducted locally.

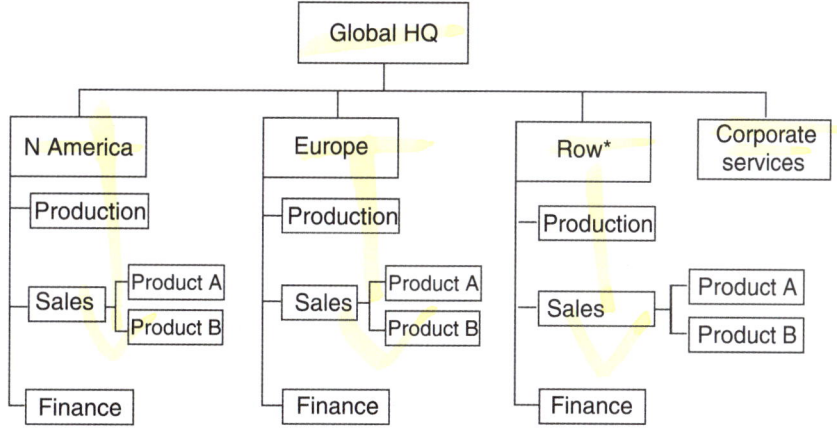

* Rest of the world

6.9 Very large and complex companies may be organised as a **hetarchy**. This is a rather organic structure with significant local control.

(a) **Some headquarters functions are diffused geographically**. For example, R&D might be in the UK, marketing in the US. Or again certain products will be made in one country, and others elsewhere. (Motor manufacturers do not make every model of car at each factory.) Some central functions might be split up: many firms are experimenting with having several centres for R&D.

(b) **Subsidiary managers have a strategic role for the corporation as a whole** (eg through bargaining and coalition forming).

(c) **Co-ordination is achieved through corporate culture and shared values** rather than a formal hierarchy. Employees with long experience might have worked in a number of different product divisions.

Part D: International influences on management style

(d) **Alliances** can be formed with other company parts and other firms, perhaps in joint ventures or consortia.

6.10 It has generally been assumed that a multinational or global company must be big, no matter how decentralised. This view is increasingly being challenged.

(a) In the past, big companies were the only ones able to surmount formidable **trade barriers** and the **legal and tax complications** of operating in more than one country. Open markets and common standards now make it easier for small firms to sell products worldwide, as these barriers are lower.

(b) **The use of technology**. When technology was expensive only big firms could afford it, so only they could benefit from the resulting scale economies. Cheap computers offer technological benefits to small firms and the scale at which economies are found is falling. The Internet, for example, is an inexpensive way of advertising.

(c) **Capital markets**. Previously, international capital markets could only be accessed by large companies. More efficient capital markets are now open to smaller companies.

Marketing at work

Structures

The two examples below suggest the varying pressures underlying the structure of a business on a worldwide scale.

Shell

In March 1995, Shell announced the end of its old matrix organisation. For historical reasons the firm had a complicated structure. Each country or region had its own operating companies.

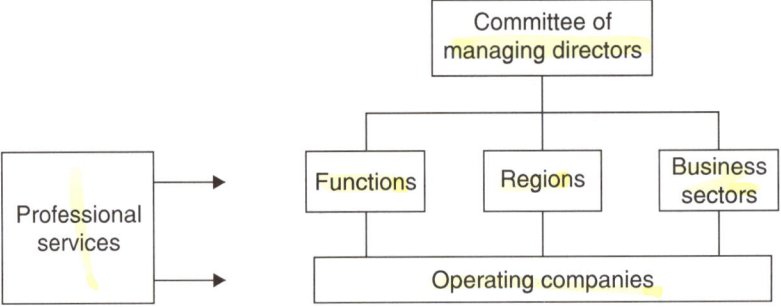

A given operating company could be defined by geography, or business sector for example. The structure was very elaborate and required the support of large groups of executives, representing national units, business divisions and functions such as finance. It was felt that cuts in the army of co-ordinators would speed decision making.

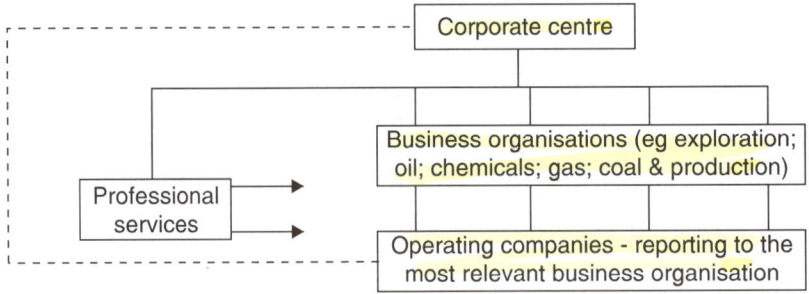

The operating companies are unchanged, so a local basis is maintained and the operating companies still have a link to the corporate centre.

11: International influences on management

Ford

However, whilst many firms, including BP, were trying to reduce their head offices and dismantling their matrix structures, Ford changed to a matrix structure in an effort to avoid duplication.

Ford had suffered for a long time from duplication: for example the North American and European Escorts were quite separate cars. However, the Mondeo was launched as a world car, and the lessons learned from that exercise were absorbed elsewhere.

- Formerly independent automative operations were integrated in order to reduce duplication, and a single worldwide product development organisation with five 'vehicle centres' for different ranges of car was set up.
- A matrix management system replaced the previous functional structure.
- Career development became a responsibility of the functional head, while performance evaluation became the responsibility of the vehicle programme team leader.'
- Individual loyalty is not to function, but to the car team.
- Ford wanted to make it virtually impossible for managers to 'micro manage' and thus achieve empowerment. 14 levels of management were reduced to 7.

Influences on structure and methods

6.11 A variety of factors influence management methods in the international setting; they pull in different directions and it may be that compromise is necessary. As always, a consideration of objectives is a good starting point. A company merely seeking to expand sales volume while concentrating on its home market will use very different methods from one seeking to operate in truly global markets such as energy and telecommunications.

6.12 **Central control** may be appropriate if the volume of international business or the company's experience in international operations is low. Centralisation is generally seen as promoting efficiency and prevents duplication of effort between regions. Even when operations are on a limited scale, when conformity with demanding technical standards is required, **functional representation** in international management may be necessary. Thus, a largely autonomous foreign subsidiary may have to accept supervision of its quality assurance or financial reporting functions.

6.13 If business is done globally, a form of **regional organisation** may be appropriate if there is some measure of social and economic integration within regions. The need for rapid response to local opportunities and threats may be served by a significant measure of **decentralisation**. National political and cultural sensitivities may reinforce this, but a shortage of local talent may limit it.

6.14 As far as **management processes and decision making** are concerned, typical problems include these.

(a) **Poor information systems and communications.** However, the rapidly falling costs of telecommunications in real terms, the development of e-mail and video-conferencing facilities make this less excusable than before.

(b) **Interpretation of information**. Culture filters information. It can also determine the priorities of the planners. By **failing to allow for diversity**, planners can make marketing on the ground more difficult.

   (i) Managing a local market in a large country with a low population density and whose main source of earnings is natural resources would be different from marketing to a small country with a high population density.

Part D: International influences on management style

(ii) High tech products may not be suitable to a country with a poorly developed educational and technological infrastructure as there might be no-one to service the equipment. So a high tech strategy at home would not work abroad.

(iii) Consumers in countries with very high rates of inflation will have different priorities to those who live in countries with low inflation. Managers' priorities will be to minimise any holdings of local currency, by converting it into a harder currency or into tangible assets. However, this makes financial reporting difficult.

Distance and implementation problems

6.15 The distance, as it were, between the corporate plan and its implementation 'on the ground' is greater than it is for a company which only deals with one market.

(a) **Physical**

(i) The degree of variation in environmental conditions is so much greater. Managers, in trying to get a global picture, may **aggregate data** from very dissimilar markets.

(ii) In order to compete effectively, local management must be able to respond to differing environmental conditions.

(b) **Psychological**. Corporate planners may not share the same assumptions as local managers.

6.16 As a consequence of the greater variety of factors involved in planning, any attempt at central control is likely to be much less certain.

(a) **Lack of experience**. The expertise and experience of head office planners might be limited by their careers in the 'head office' or by a gradual loss of a feel for their local roots.

(b) **Time horizons**. Corporate planners will be seeking to satisfy the firm's **investors**, whose desire for a return might be dominated by their local considerations. This is typically a problem when a long term investment is required in an overseas market.

Control systems

6.17 Meetings can become difficult and expensive when a company expands internationally. Air travel and hotel costs will be high and the stress on executives caused by extensive travel must be considered. Video-conferencing is emerging as an alternative to face-to-face meetings.

6.18 Culture can function as a control measure if resources are devoted to promoting shared values and principles. The importance of culture in operating a global heterarchy was discussed earlier.

6.19 In the specific area of **financial control**, international operations bring increased complexity.

(a) **Comparison** of national performance can be difficult because of widely different conditions. Only locally controllable cash flows should be considered and realistic expectations must be established.

(b) Different rates of interest may apply to **loan finance**; this will affect measures like return on investment, but may present an opportunity for reducing finance costs.

(c) **Financial** reporting rules vary across the world and considerable effort may be expended in converting financial statements.

(d) **Tax** is likely to be an issue, especially when remitting profits. **Transfer prices** are frequently examined by tax authorities as they can be used to move profits from one country to another.

(e) **Exchange rate risk** will have to be managed, which consumes time and money.

7 HUMAN RESOURCE MANAGEMENT

7.1 The balance between local and expatriate staff must be managed. There are a number of influences.

- The availability of technical skills such as financial management
- The need for control
- The importance of product and company experience
- The need to provide promotion opportunities
- Costs associated with expatriates such as travel and higher salaries
- Cultural factors

Expatriates or locals?

7.2 For an international company, which has to think globally as well as act locally, there are a number of problems.

- Do you employ mainly **expatriate staff** to control local operations?
- Do you employ **local managers**, with the possible loss of central control?
- Is there such a thing as the **global manager**, equally at home in different cultures?

7.3 Expatriate staff are sometimes favoured over local staff.

(a) Poor **educational opportunities** in the market may require the import of skilled technicians and managers. For example, expatriates have been needed in many western firms' operations in Russia and Eastern Europe, simply because they understand the meaning of profit.

(b) Some senior managers believe that a business run by expatriates is easier to **control** than one run by local staff.

(c) If the firm is a macropyramid, expatriates might be better able than locals to **communicate** with the corporate centre.

(d) The expatriate may **know more about the firm** overall, which is especially important if he or she is fronting a sales office.

7.4 The use of expatriates in overseas markets has certain disadvantages.

(a) They **cost** more (eg subsidised housing, school fees).

(b) **Culture shock**. The expatriate may fail to adjust to the culture (eg by associating only with other expatriates). This is likely to lead to poor management effectiveness, especially if the business requires personal contact.

(c) A substantial training programme might be needed.

(i) **Basic facts** about the country will be given with basic language training, and some briefings about cultural differences.

Part D: International influences on management style

(ii) **Immersion training** involves detailed language and cultural training and simulation of field social and business experiences. This is necessary to obtain an intellectual understanding and practical awareness of the culture.

7.5 Employing local managers raises the following issues.

(a) A **glass ceiling** might exist in some companies. Talented local managers may not make it to board levels if, as in many Japanese firms, most members of the board are drawn from one country.

(b) In some cases, it may be hard for locals to assimilate into the corporate culture, and this might led to communication problems.

(c) They will have greater local knowledge - but the difficulty of course is to get them to understand the wider corporate picture, but this is true of management at operational level generally.

7.6 Those firms which export sporadically might employ a home-based sales force. Their travel expenses will of course be high, and it might not always be easy to recruit people willing to cope with the pace.

7.7 **Relevant issues to keep in mind**

(a) **Recruitment and training.** In countries with low levels of literacy, more effort might need to be spent on basic training.

(b) **Career management.** Can overseas staff realistically expect promotion to the firm's highest levels if they do well?

(c) **Appraisal schemes.** These can be a minefield at the best of times, and the possibilities for communications failure are endless. For example, in some cultures, an appraisal is a two way discussion whereas in others arguing back might be considered a sign of insubordination.

(d) Problems associated with the status of women.

(e) **Communications.** HRM tries to mobilise employees' commitment to the goals of the organisation. In far-flung global firms, the normal panoply of staff newsletters and team briefings may be hard to institute but are vital. Time differences also make communication difficult.

(i) **E-mail** and satellite linkages between branch offices can be used for routine messages: e-mail is especially useful, as it allows swift access to a person's electronic mailbox.

(ii) Major conferences are also necessary.

(iii) Firms with many subsidiaries face additional problems of **language**. What language should be used for business communications? Some multinational firms have decreed English the language of official internal communications, even if they are not headquartered in the English speaking world.

Marketing at work

British Airways

An example of the role of communications in managing a business is provided by British Airways (as reported in the Guardian).

After privatisation, BA cut its staff by almost 20,000 to 35,000 although since that staff levels have increased as airline traffic has expanded.

BA attaches great important to internal corporate communications, as it wishes to make staff feel involved.

At a series of business seminars, costing £750,000, senior board members made detailed presentations to 4,500 junior and senior managers, and, as importantly, invited - and received - feedback and criticism. BA's senior managers 'say they benefit enormously from hearing how staff feel that BA can continue to improve its performance.'

Chapter Roundup

- The processes of globalism have massively expanded international trade, but there are still areas of protection. In particular, regional trading groups have emerged that are to some extent opposed to one another.
- The social, legal, economic, political and technical (SLEPT) business environment differs widely across the globe. **Demographic differences** are particularly important for business.
- Also, **cultural factors** influence both ways of doing business and management style and methods.
- In **high context** cultures, communication depends on far more than just the text of a message.
- **Management culture** drives management practice. The **Hofstede model** of national cultures indicates how far imported methods of management may be applicable in different countries.
- **Organisational structure** must suit both the global **need for control** and **local sensitivities**.
- **Control**, and especially **financial control**, is made more complicated by varying local conditions.
- **Human resource management** must accommodate the needs of both **indigenous** and **expatriate** staff.

Quick Quiz

1. What is the name of the body that regulates international trade? (see para 2.1)
2. What are the differences between a free trade area, a customs union and a common market? (3.6 – 3.8)
3. What is demography? (4.1)
4. Name two aspects of business culture which differ between Japan and the USA. (4.18)
5. What is the context of communication? (4.20 – 4.22)
6. What are the four dimensions of the Hofstede model of management cultures? (5.9)
7. Why is international financial control particularly complex? (6.19)
8. What are the advantages of employing expatriates? (7.3)

Now try illustrative question 24 at the end of the Study Text

Part E
Reviewing your progress

12: Reviewing Your Progress

Chapter Topic List

1. Setting the scene
2. Assessing personal progress
3. Reviewing the role of the manager in the marketing function
4. Revision of some key concepts in the context of the examination
5. Exam preparation

Part E: Reviewing your progress

1 SETTING THE SCENE

1.1 In this final chapter, we will be working towards your preparation for the examination, providing you with the frameworks which will help you to review your progress to date and telling you how to use them effectively in the examination.

2 ASSESSING PERSONAL PROGRESS

2.1 Throughout this Study Text we have been concentrating on various aspects of the management activity and the skills needed to be an effective manager. You should have started with a clear picture of your personal strengths and weaknesses and a set of development goals you have been working towards.

2.2 The Study Text contains ideas and exercises which should have helped you improve in the identified areas. You may have also taken the opportunities suggested for developing certain skills in other ways, such as formal courses and job shadowing.

2.3 As we have indicated, personal development is no longer concentrated in a year or two of training at the beginning of your career. It is an activity which must become routine.

2.4 Take time now to review your progress towards the goals you established earlier, and any you might have added during the course. Use the framework on the next page to help you. You also need to consider the process in general: was it difficult? Would you recommend it to others? Has the improvement been noticeable?

2.5 If you are committed to personal development you should take the time now to set goals for the next six months. Develop a plan for each dimension or objective and add review dates to your diary now.

2.6 Using this experience to help you in the examination will allow you to demonstrate your practical skills and experiences which will automatically add credibility to your work. Here is an example in the form of two possible elements in an examination answer.

> (a) I recommend that all managers in the section be encouraged to keep a detailed time log for a week.
>
> (b) Keeping a time log for a week will show the managers where time is being wasted. I identified 5 hours a week when I could study whilst travelling to clients, and I reduced the overtime I did by 10 hours a month by planning each day.

Item (b) would be more convincing to both the examiner and managers. Personal experience adds real credibility; however, take care not to become too anecdotal.

3 REVIEWING THE ROLE OF THE MANAGER IN THE MARKETING FUNCTION

3.1 Throughout this Study Text we have focused on the manager, not the marketer. However, the manager and the marketer are the same person. The management topics examined are common ground between managers of marketing and managers of finance or operations.

3.2 In the past, the management skills needed to do the marketing job have tended to be assumed. The toolbox of skills and techniques here are those which you will need to help you implement the plan. They fall essentially into two groups as indicated on the **Effective Management for Marketing Syllabus**.

- **Personal skills,** such as time management and communication.
- **People-based skills,** such as motivation and leadership.

12: Reviewing your progress

Area for development	Level of skill before (1 - 5)	Activities completed	Level of skill now	Comments on the process	New goals
1.					
2.					
3.					
4.					
5.					

Part E: Reviewing your progress

3.3 Organisations are changing in response to a changing environment. Increased competition and economic pressures have forced many organisations into a market situation where supply exceeds demand. Customers want to have a choice and companies have been forced to a more market oriented strategy in order to survive.

3.4 At the same time, information technology has enabled management to flatten hierarchies and reduce layers of middle management. This lowers costs and brings managers closer to the customer.

3.5 Both developments have important implications for the marketing manager.

(a) The greater degree of customer orientation means that marketing plays a more significant strategic role in the business. The representative of the customer becomes more important to any decision-making process.

(b) There is a greater appreciation throughout business of the activities of sales and marketing and there is thus more support and help, from other sections.

3.6 The **marketing job** in that sense is perhaps getting easier, as the contribution of marketing is recognised and the support of others can be obtained in delivering customer satisfaction. However, the management aspect of the job remains just as challenging. The old hierarchical structure enabled poor management or interpersonal skills to be overlooked, particularly in a functional expert. This is no longer the case.

3.7 Today the marketing manager will be judged not only on the quality of market analysis or the creativity of marketing strategy. Success is also assessed by the overall improvement achieved.

3.8 Achievement comes only when others can be motivated and the tasks necessary to the plan delegated, activities co-ordinated and the outcomes monitored and, where necessary, plans revised.

Action Programme 1

Look at the following list of skills which we have considered in this text. For each identify why it is important or relevant for the marketing manager:

Skill		Importance
1	Time Management	
2	Prioritisation	
3	Delegation	
4	Communication	
5	Negotiation	
6	Leadership	
7	Motivation	
8	Team Building	

4 REVISION OF SOME KEY CONCEPTS IN THE CONTEXT OF THE EXAMINATION

Action Programme 2

Look at the following short scenarios and identify what the basic problem appears to be.

(a) A sales manager who prefers not to visit staff in the field and holds a meeting of all the sales team once every two months at head office.

(b) A new staff member who is unwilling to participate in team meetings or integrate socially into the established group.

(c) A manager who is having problems disciplining the team. Complaints of lateness and poor work quality are increasingly being reported.

(d) A successful, well established team suddenly stops performing.

(e) A team with a new manager becomes bored and unco-operative.

(f) A member of the team returns from a management development programme and becomes disruptive, critical and a problem to others in the group.

(g) A sudden unexplained increase in the level of customer complaints coming to management's attention.

4.1 When tackling questions take the time to think about three things.

- The role you are in
- The characteristics of the business, such as size and sector
- The interpersonal implications of the situation

4.2 Consider for a moment a question on delegation.

Action Programme 3

You have been asked to prepare an outline for an interview in order to encourage delegation and better delegation practices. How would your answer vary for the following audiences?

(a) A subordinate
(b) A colleague
(c) Your manager

4.3 Think about the size of the problem or business indicated in the question; credibility and a sense of what is practical will be important. Introducing a customer care programme for a staff of ten is a very different prospect from what it would be for a staff of 1,000. Remember that a small company will have no human resources staff to help with recruitment and selection.

4.4 Try to take these points on board when you tackle questions 18 - 22 at the end of this Study Text. Do take time to compare your answers with ours and note any differences. After you have completed each one, take time to identify two or three points for improvement.

5 EXAM PREPARATION

Time management

5.1 How much time is there before the examination? Identify the study time available and allocate that between the projects and topics you need to prepare for.

Part E: Reviewing your progress

5.2 Create a plan, with clear objectives for completion of the various topics and outlining the activities you intend to undertake in preparation for the exam.

5.3 Do not make the mistake of avoiding revision on subjects you find easy or, alternatively, leaving difficult ones till last. Making time for a lot of shorter study periods is a better approach than undertaking only a few long sessions, and you will need to vary your activities within a study session to retain interest.

Motivation

5.4 What have you learnt about motivation? What schemes can you devise to help motivate yourself when the revision gets tough?

Prioritisation

5.5 Look at the syllabus and exam questions and prioritise your revision, allowing a longer and more detailed review of half a dozen topics which you think are most likely to be featured.

5.6 Importantly, this selection should be made after a general review of the whole course, as Section A questions are compulsory. Also remember to revise communication formats as these will be specified in each question.

5.7 If you are studying with colleagues, **plan group revision sessions to help you focus and create interest**. Small groups of four or five are best. Each person can then present an overview of a topic, set questions and scenarios for discussion and so on.

5.8 Plan your preparation right up to the exam day. Keep nerves to a minimum by arriving early and having all the writing equipment and resources which you need with you. You could need a calculator in this exam to analyse information.

> **Action Programme 4**
>
> Take some time to review Chapter 1 and our description of the exam paper and styles needed for the two sections. The advice in the following paragraphs may also help you plan how to tackle the paper.

The expectations of examiners

5.9 Examiners are experienced marketing managers. They know that mini-cases in Section A give only limited information and that candidates are working under a tight time constraint. They do not, therefore, require considered, fully rounded answers. There is insufficient data and time. The successful candidate learns to work with what is available, to make reasonable assumptions that help in the decision-making process, and to present an answer cogently and concisely.

5.10 **The examiner can only mark within the criteria that have been established.** The requirements are set out very clearly. It is not difficult to satisfy them. The well prepared candidate should not fail the mini-case. The information is limited, time is very constrained and any candidate who makes reasonable assumptions, takes clear and sensible decisions, and communicates these succinctly, must pass.

5.11 Also remember that mini-cases are set for all candidates. Some will know absolutely nothing about the industry, some will work in it and be expert. Candidates take the

12: Reviewing your progress

examinations in centres across the world. Therefore the examiner will not ask technical questions about the industry, nor any tied to a specific culture or economy. Questions have to be more general, more open and less specific. However, you will be expected to have acquired a level of business appreciation and marketing knowledge from your other studies. These should enable you to produce realistic recommendations which take into account the situation and the resources available.

5.12 **Summary.** The requirements are as follows.

Quality not *Quantity*
Insight not *Detail*
Report not *Essay*

Management reports in CIM mini-cases

5.13 A **management report** is a specialised form of communication. It is the language used in business. It is not difficult to learn to write in report style, but it does require practice to become fluent. Mini-cases **must always be answered in report style**, unless another format is specified. Management reports are **action planning documents** and are generally written in the third person. Their role is to make positive recommendations for action.

5.14 **Management reports: the basic rules**

- Always head a report with the name of the organisation concerned.
- State to whom it is addressed, from whom it comes, and give the date.
- Do not use your own name in the report.
- Title the report (for example 'Customer Care Plan').
- Number and sub-number paragraphs. Title them if appropriate.
- Present the contents in a logical order.
- Include diagrams, graphs and tables only if they have positive value.
- Include recommendations for action, perhaps with timescales and budgets.

5.15 Management reports are written in crisp, no-nonsense business English. There is no room for superlatives, flowery adjectives or flowing sentences. You are not trying to entertain, simply to present facts as clearly as possible. Think about the style you would adopt if writing a report to senior managers at work.

5.16 Presentation is of key importance in CIM examinations.

- Use a black or blue pen, never red.
- Start your first answer on the inside right-hand page of the answer book, never inside the cover.
- Make the first three pages as neat and well laid out as possible, to impress.
- Use plenty of space. Do not crowd your work (leave 25% white space per page).
- Number your questions above your answers. Never write in either margin.
- Leave space (four or five lines) between sections of your report.
- Start new questions on a new page.
- Charts and diagrams should be clearly labelled and cover between $1/3$ and $1/2$ a page.

5.17 Mini-cases and Section A questions are easy once you have mastered the basic techniques. The key to success lies in adopting a logical sequence of steps which with practice you will

Part E: Reviewing your progress

master. You must enter the exam room with the process as second nature, so that you can concentrate your attention on the management issues which face you.

5.18 Students who are at first apprehensive when faced with a mini-case often come to find them much more stimulating and rewarding than traditional examination questions. There is the added security of knowledge that there is no single correct answer to a case study. You will have to tackle mini-cases in all the Advanced Certificate and Diploma papers.

5.19 You will be assessed on your approach, style, creativity and commercial credibility, but you will not be judged against a single correct answer. Treat the mini-case as though it were happening in real life, at work or at a social meeting with a friend. Most of the mini-case is **narrative**: it tells a story or paints a picture. If a friend says over a drink 'I've got a problem at work' the most usual answer is 'Tell me about it'. The listener will need background information to establish a frame of reference and to understand the problem. That is what the case narrative is doing. Most of it is background, and it should be read to grasp the context and flavour of the situation. It is particularly important that you understand your position, what you are trying to achieve and the position and the requirements of those whom your recommendations will affect.

5.20 It helps to pretend to yourself that the examiner needs your advice. The questions posed indicate the advice which is being sought. Avoid rehearsing the details of how the situation arose. Concentrate on proposing a solution. Make clear recommendations for a course of action rather than offering a choice of options.

5.21 You will be faced with limited information, certainly much less than would be available to you in the real world. This is one of the limitations of case study examinations, but everyone is faced with the same constraint. You are able to make assumptions where it is necessary.

5.22 Reasonable assumptions are logically possible and factually credible. You may need to make and state two or three assumptions in order to tackle a case. Make assumptions which simplify your task rather than complicating it.

5.23 **Mini-case method**

		Time (minutes)
Step 1.	Read the mini-case very quickly	2
Step 2.	Read the questions and the case again, but carefully. Make brief notes of significant material. Determine key issues in relation to the questions.	5
Step 3.	Put the case on one side and turn to your notes. What do they contain? A clear picture of the situation? Go back if necessary and concentrate on getting a grip on the scenario outlined.	4
Step 4.	Prepare a timeplan for each part of the question, according to the marks allocated.	1
Step 5.	Prepare an answer structure plan for question (a) following exactly the structure suggested in the question, highlighting your decisions supported by case data and theory if appropriate. Follow the process outlined for question (b) and so on.	10
Step 6.	Write an answer.	35
Step 7.	**Read through** to correct errors and improve presentation.	7
		64

12: Reviewing your progress

A good answer will be a document on which a competent manager can take action.

Notes

(a) It is not seriously suggested that you can allocate your time so rigorously! The purpose of showing detailed timings is to demonstrate the need to move **with purpose and control** through each stage of the process.

(b) Take time to get the facts into your short-term memory. Making decisions is easier once the facts are in your head.

(c) Establish a clear plan and you will find that writing the report is straightforward.

(d) Some candidates will be writing answers within five minutes. **The better candidates will ignore them and concentrate on planning**. This is not easy to do, but management of your examination technique is the key to your personal success.

5.24 **Presentation is crucial**. You must take time to set the report out properly as a final draft that would go to typing. If the typist could understand every word and replicate the layout, then the examiner will be delighted and it will be marked highly.

5.25 However, do not provide logos for your consultancy/division/department. They take time and do not impress. Similarly do not waste time with an introductory letter. It will be taken for granted that your work would, in real life, be typed, bound and submitted under cover of an appropriate letter or memo.

5.26 A similar approach will help you with the more traditional section B questions. Plan your time allocation carefully and think about how you would respond, or recommend a friend responds, in the situation identified.

Chapter Roundup

- Management and marketing activities might be distinct in theory, but often they are carried out by the same people.
- Marketing is gaining a more significant role in the strategic orientation of the business.
- Skills of time management, prioritisation, delegation, communication, negotiation, leadership, motivation and team building are necessary for effective marketing managers.
- Examiners attitudes can be summarised in the following way.

Preferred	*As opposed to*
Quality	Quantity
Insight	Detail
Report	Essay

- You are often **required** to use report formats in your answer.

Quick Quiz

1. What do examiners want from your answers? (see para 5.12)
2. What presentation rules should you adopt? (5.16)
3. Draft a timetable for tackling a mini-case. (5.23)

Action Programme Review

1   1   **Time management.** Fewer managers means more responsibility for those in the business. Time management is essential to avoid stress and to get everything done.

Part E: Reviewing your progress

2   **Prioritisation** is an integral part of time management. In marketing, managers may have to prioritise markets or customers and need to understand the process and criteria by which priorities can be established.

3   **Delegation** is essential:

   (a) in ensuring that tactical details of marketing activities are attended to
   (b) to give younger marketers experience and a chance to develop their skills
   (c) to act as a motivator.

4   **Communication**. The essence of the marketer's job is communicating, both sending messages and listening to them. It must be done professionally both inside and outside the organisation.

5   **Negotiation** with clients and staff is a key aspect of bringing buyers and sellers, employees and the organisation together in a way which satisfies everyone's needs.

6   **Leadership**. The marketing manager is often a figurehead and must share the organisation's vision in order to communicate it effectively to others. Marketers are in the business of leading the business down the path of customer orientation.

7   **Motivation**. Marketing and sales roles can be very isolated and motivation has to be clear and effective to get the best out of those working at the customer interface.

8   **Team building**. Marketing is about co-ordination. Satisfying customers has to be a team effort. Marketers have to be able to build teams even when they have no line authority, for example, teams with advertising agencies and distributors as well as with operations and distribution.

2   (a) A number of possible causes can be suggested.

   - The manager is lazy and demotivated.
   - The manager has too much other work to undertake this important function.
   - The manager lacks confidence and is unclear of what his/her objectives in a field visit would be.

   (b) This can be the result of various problems

   - A lack of confidence
   - Poor induction into the group
   - A group which is inflexible and not making 'space' for this new colleague
   - Poor selection (the individual does not fit)
   - Poor briefing

   (c) This manager has perhaps been afraid to manage. He has positioned himself as a laissez faire leader. Alternatively he is not monitoring progress or setting targets through lack of time, interest or motivation, and the team is being left to get on with it.

   (d) Lack of stimulation or change might be a cause. Even success becomes dull if it is routine. A change which is being resisted such as new manager or working conditions might also be a reason.

   (e) Possible causes include the following.

   - A clash of management styles
   - Wrong person chosen for the job
   - Resentment because an alternative candidate was rejected
   - Resistance to change

   (f) The problem may be lack of recognition of the person's development. The person may not want to be kept in the same role. Resistance from old traditional team members to the changes suggested might be encountered.

   (g) Possible causes include the following

   - New member of staff dealing directly with customer
   - Introduction of new operations system
   - Introduction of a new system of management reporting so the manager is more aware of complaints made

3   The style and tone of your comments would clearly need to vary; in the first instance you might be training and telling, in the second advising or counselling and in the third selling.

The examiner will be looking for evidence that you are able to respond sympathetically in a variety of situations.

Now try questions 18 to 23 at the end of the Study Text

(If you wish to tackle these as a mock exam, answer question 18 and three from questions 19 to 23, in three hours without notes. Review your answers. Later, take time to tackle the questions you chose not to do.)

Illustrative questions and suggested answers

Illustrative questions

Questions with mark and time allocations are in the style of full examination questions.

1   STUDENT MEETING (20 MARKS)   *32 mins*

You have been invited to speak to a student meeting organised by the local CIM branch. You are to speak on the *Rationale and Approach for the Effective Management for Marketing paper.*

Outline the key points you would want to make to the students.

2   MIDDLE MANAGERS (20 MARKS)   *32 mins*

As a member of a Business Consultancy Team, you are working with a traditionally run, product orientated manufacturing firm. Faced with increased competition and declining profitability, the senior management team has broadly accepted the need for organisational and cultural change.

You have been asked to make notes that will form the basis of a report to middle managers to explain the benefits of a shift to a marketing orientation and to outline the process of doing so.

3   KATHY (20 MARKS)   *32 mins*

Kathy, the daughter of a friend, has just won a place as a management trainee for an international consumer goods manufacturer. She has been asked to produce a draft for a learning contract to be implemented over the two years of her traineeship. This draft will be the basis of a discussion with her manager and on the basis of its outcomes she will be allocated her projects and secondments.

She has a degree in Business Studies with Marketing and has already enrolled for her CIM Diploma exams next December.

She has approached you for advice on how to decide what to include in her learning contract. What advice would you give her? Justify your recommendations.

4   POOR DELEGATION SKILLS (20 MARKS)   *32 mins*

A small group of staff working in the new product development team has approached you as the Marketing Director. Their grievance is that their manager, who has been in post for six months, will not delegate. Whilst he is working late every night, others in the team are bored and de-motivated. They had much more autonomy and authority under the previous manager.

You have agreed to talk to the manager and try to resolve the problem.

(a)   What might be the reasons for this problem?
(b)   What actions can be taken to help encourage a manager to delegate?
(c)   In this situation, what actions will you now take?

5   COMMUNICATION PROBLEMS

The efficiency of your department is being impaired because two members of your staff seem to be unable to communicate properly with each other. What are the barriers to effective personal communication that you would investigate and the remedies you would seek to apply in an attempt to solve the problem?

6   LUDDITE BANKERS (20 MARKS)   *32 mins*

Gerry and Alan do not meet face to face very often, partly because they do not get on, partly because, although working on the same site, they are in different buildings. They find this a nuisance as their work really necessitates frequent contact. They get over the problem by talking to each other on the telephone when they have to.

Gerry is a young mathematics graduate who works in the data processing department of a commercial bank. He has been promoted quickly to supervisor level, having joined the bank a few years ago straight from university. He is single and lives close to the office, which means he can often work late.

Alan is in his mid-fifties and joined the bank at the age of sixteen, eventually becoming a supervisor. His long experience in his particular specialism means that his technical skill is high but he is not familiar with the latest developments in data processing. In fact, he deplores what he considers to be the overproduction of essentially useless information. He always claims he has all the information he wants at his finger tips. But his subordinates point out that he often ignores information which does not

Illustrative questions

coincide with his own opinions. He sticks to a strict routine, arriving and leaving work punctually to go home to his wife and family in the suburbs.

Gerry thinks the bank is a fairly 'fuddy duddy' institution that needs to be dragged into the twentieth century, a view he expresses frequently and fluently to anyone who will listen. He is very absorbed in his world of computers and talks its language perfectly. He has no time for people - 'Luddites' he says - 'who can't see the advantages of the information revolution'.

Alan, a taciturn man, listens, disapproves and does his work in the way he always has.

> *Tutorial note.* The word 'Luddites' used by Gerry could itself be a barrier to communication. Luddites is a name given to groups of people, who, during the British industrial revolution, feared the effects of machines on their jobs. This fear turned to anger and the Luddites smashed machinery in factories in the mistaken belief that it would prevent mechanisation. The use of the term in the case is to describe those people in the 20th century who mistakenly attempt to prevent or delay the information revolution.

(a) What do you think about these two bank staff?
(b) What actions would you take as a manager to help them improve their communication skills?

7 MANAGEMENT MEETINGS

Your manager has asked you to assist a newly appointed colleague. Although she has ample product and market knowledge, she has had little practice at managing the meetings with colleagues, clients and suppliers which her new role will involve.

Prepare some notes outlining the key factors for success in these factors.

8 EFFECTIVE TEAM

What are the characteristics of an effective work team? Describe briefly one training method by which an effective team can be developed.

9 PARTICIPATION (20 MARKS)   *32 mins*

What are the disadvantages of a participative style of management? How can these be minimised?

10 RECRUITMENT ISSUES

John Hoskins is a friend of yours. He runs a medium sized manufacturing and distribution business. In conversation you discover he has a very high staff turnover - much higher than average for the area.

Closer questions reveals that the bulk of the turnover is among young trainees recruited locally by John himself. 60% tend to leave in the first month of employment.

He recruits on the basis of ten minute interview because he believes you can sum anyone up in that time. He blames the turnover on local schools who fill kids' heads with ideas above their situation.

He is interested in your advice. What selection methods would you introduce to John Hoskins to help him to improve his selection? What would you suggest in terms of his attitude to local schools?

11 STAFF APPRAISAL SCHEMES (20 MARKS)   *32 mins*

As assistant to the marketing director, you have been asked to help with the implementation of staff appraisals in the marketing department.

(a) Describe the benefits of a well run appraisal scheme to individuals, managers and the organisation as a whole.   (12 marks)

(b) Outline the procedures necessary to put such a scheme into practice.   (8 marks)

Illustrative questions

12 APPRAISAL DREAD (20 MARKS) *32 mins*

Douglas Wentworth is a very capable manager, who gets good performance from his staff by setting them clear goals, by telling them how they are getting on and by giving them help and advice when they need it. His staff say they learn a tremendous amount from him and they are never afraid of going to see him when they need help. All of them, however, without exception, dread the annual appraisal interview, and so does he. He says that he is appraising staff all the time and that there is no need to do an annual interview. He feels uncomfortable sitting down formally to talk over issues which he discusses frequently with each of his subordinates. He thinks it is a ritual and a waste of time and aims to get through the interviews as quickly as possible.

His subordinates agree that, as at present conducted, the interviews are a waste of time. Douglas seems to have no clear goals, is obviously ill at ease, and so they become uneasy too. Most of them would like the opportunity for a longer-term assessment of what they have done and how they can develop, but it is never forthcoming.

How would you help Douglas to make the annual appraisal interview useful both to him and to his subordinates?

13 DIFFICULT JUNIOR (20 MARKS) *32 mins*

You are concerned about the attitude and performance of Ian Dalgleish, a member of your section. Since your appointment as supervisor a few months ago, you have been able to come to terms with the rest of the team. Performance was mediocre when you arrived but you have obtained improvements by discussing and agreeing new ideas, by establishing clear short-term goals for all your staff, and by giving them frequent feed-back. It has not worked with Ian.

His work is sloppy and untidy. He misses deadlines. He sometimes comes in late and goes early. He seems to resent you and to take perverse pleasure in thwarting your intentions. You know he has considerable potential. He is honorary treasurer of two local societies both of which are full of praise for him. He runs a football team very successfully and is popular with his colleagues.

What will you do now? If your proposed actions fail, what will be your next step?

14 MOTIVATION PRINCIPLES

Outline some principles for the motivation of staff. Using illustrations from your own observations, which of these principles seem to you to work in practice, and which do not? Give reasons for each of your answers.

15 CHANGE AGENT (20 MARKS) *32 mins*

Sandra Wilson became a supervisor three months ago at the age of 24. She is very able and well qualified (BA(Hons)). She was spotted very quickly as potential management material and this is her first managerial appointment. She wants to succeed and she believes that the best way to do so is to encourage performance by supporting her staff in every possible way. The staff are all older than she is and have all worked in the department for at least three years. Their previous supervisor has recently retired after managing the section for fifteen years.

On her own initiative Sandra has already made three innovations.

(a) She has rearranged the office to give a better workflow, at the same time having it redecorated and getting new office furniture.

(b) She was the first manager to welcome word processors and first to train her staff in their use.

(c) She arranged that the annual section outing should go to a different seaside resort and she planned a full programme of exciting events.

Much to Sandra's surprise each of these innovations has met considerable resistance and resentment, although they benefit the staff.

Required

(a) Describe the cause(s) of the difficulties that Sandra has encountered.

(b) How would you help Sandra to plan her three innovations and learn to manage her department more effectively?

Illustrative questions

16 QUALITY CIRCLE (20 MARKS) *32 mins*

The production director in a large manufacturing company wants to introduce quality circles into the company's factories, because he has heard of their success in several Japanese companies. He asks for your advice about introducing a system of quality circles, and he tells you: 'My objectives in wanting to introduce these circles are to arrive at decisions for change in product designs and production methods and to get a maximum degree of acceptance. Quality circles can improve quality, productivity, interdepartmental communication, teamwork and team spirit. They can reduce costs and absenteeism and create more job satisfaction. I want them.'

He asks you for your views about whether you can foresee any problems with introducing quality circles, and how you would set about implementing a programme for setting them up and using them. How would you respond?

17 CUSTOMER CARE (20 MARKS) *32 mins*

You are discussing the concept of customer care with some friends over a drink. One of them is very sceptical and points to the example of the banks, many of whom have instituted customer care schemes but several of which appear to have lost their energy or been a publicity exercise only. How would you justify the value of such schemes? How would you monitor such a scheme?

> *Tutorial note.* Questions 18 to 23 may be attempted singly, or you can use them as a mock examination, in which case you *must* do question 18, and you must choose 3 from questions 19 to 23. Having done that, it would be advisable to attempt the two questions you did not choose, considering why you did not choose them and whether you need more practice in the areas the two questions cover.

SPECIMEN PAPER

18 LONG CASE STUDY (50 MARKS) *80 mins*

> *Tutorial note.* From June 1996, the long case study has been worth 40 marks and 64 minutes of exam time.

The Garden Design and Landscape Company - Getting More Out Of Less ...

The early 1990s have been tough for businesses of all sizes. Markets have been increasingly competitive and demand sluggish. Survival has been the goal of many and the need to get the best out of all available resources has been paramount to that goal being successfully achieved.

The Garden Design and Landscape Company is one such organisation. It has survived for over 18 years and has a turnover of some £2.5 million, about £1 million from household contracts, new drives, patios and garden layouts. The balance is a mixture of public sector and corporate work, mainly maintenance contracts, but with some new project work. Sales revenue has fallen slightly over the last few years, but has declined in real terms by over 15% since 1989. Average order values have fallen and so has the operating profit.

Based in the South East of England, the company has three centres, each with a small sales office and showroom. There are currently some 120 full time staff, but a number of casual workers are employed as necessary to meet the seasonal shifts in workload. Staff numbers have fallen from 160 in 1988.

Having attended a recent seminar which examined the value of a strategic marketing approach to planning, the Managing Director approached you to act as a consultant and undertake an objective review of the current position of the business and to make recommendations for the changes which might be necessary if they are to be ready to meet the challenges of the rest of the 1990's and improve the overall financial performance of the business.

You have completed your initial audits and the following summarises some of your key findings.

- The business is operationally/product oriented.
- There is little use of available information and no real information system.
- Planning is ad hoc and its value not really understood.

- The organisation is hierarchical in structure with no real incentives for the individual work teams.

- Absenteeism is high, averaging over 1.5 days per month per manual worker.

- There is a small field sales team of a sales manager and four sales staff and six full time administrative support staff. There is also a marketing manager who is mainly responsible for sales literature and advertising and reports directly to the Managing Director.

- There is increased competition and the market is increasingly price competitive.

- There are no clear links between sales and marketing and little co-ordination of effort between the sales teams in the three centres.

- Enquiries generated are high, but the conversion from sales visits to orders are low, only 1 in 7. In the past they have been as high as 1 in 3.

- Only the most basic customer records are maintained.

(a) Bearing in mind that any available budget for change will be limited, what proposals would you make to help the firm change to a more market orientated cultures. Provide an indication of the timescales and likely costs for your recommendations. (25 marks)

(b) What actions would you recommend to improve the effectiveness of the marketing and sales team? (25 marks)

Specimen paper

Tutorial note. From June 1996, section B questions are each worth 20 marks and you have to do three of them.

---

19 TIME MANAGEMENT (25 MARKS) *40 minutes*

You have noticed that a recently promoted member of your marketing team seems to have been finding the new responsibilities and workload difficult. Although a reliable and thorough worker over the past three years, in the last few months several deadlines have been missed and a few silly errors have been made. You know he has been working late in order to try and keep up, and that he was planning to start his studies for a CIM qualification next month.

(a) Explain briefly how you would handle the situation and give your justification for adopting this approach. (10 marks)

(b) What advise would you give this staff member to help reduce the pressures and improve his time management? (15 marks)

Specimen paper

20 TRAINEES (25 MARKS) *40 mins*

As assistant to the Marketing Director in a large manufacturing company, you have been asked to help with the plans for recruitment, selection and induction of three graduate trainees.

(a) Produce a profile of the characteristics and competencies you would recommend be included as a basis for the job specification and explain briefly your justification for their inclusion.

(10 marks)

(b) Prepare a detailed plan, indicating the steps which should be undertaken to recruit successfully these three trainees. Include a timetable, and a budget expressed in terms of the management time required. (15 marks)

Specimen paper

21 DETERIORATION (25 MARKS) *40 minutes*

You have recently been appointed manager of a sales and marketing team of 25 people, having won the job over two internal candidates. Your initial review indicates that the department's performance has been deteriorating for some time, and there is a lack of motivation and enthusiasm evident across all areas and grades within the team.

Illustrative questions

(a) What options are available to you in tackling this problem? (15 marks)
(b) What steps would you take to help decide the best approach to adopt? (10 marks)

22 QUALITY PRESENTATION (25 MARKS) *40 mins*

As part of a company wide quality initiative, a programme of staff appraisals is to be introduced. The directors have asked for your suggestions as to how best to present this development to the staff. Prepare your proposals and a plan for their implementation for presentation at the next board meeting.

Specimen paper

23 RELATIONSHIP MARKETING (25 MARKS) *40 mins*

Relationship marketing is becoming a very important dimension in cementing client, supplier and customer relations. Explain briefly what is meant by relationship marketing and outline both its advantages and possible disadvantages to a firm operating in a rapidly changing marketing place.

Specimen paper

24 ORGANISATION STRUCTURES (20 MARKS) *32 mins*

What organisation structures can a multi-national enterprise (MNE) use? Examine the usefulness of two different structures.

Suggested answers

1 STUDENT MEETING

Presentation: key points

Opening

Objectives

1. To ensure students appreciate the relevance and value of management to their careers in marketing.
2. To demonstrate the distinction between knowledge and skills and show how to develop them.
3. To reinforce understanding of the examiner's requirements and the need for practice.

Rationale

1. Need for change. Marketing has matured and demands on professional marketers continue to develop.
2. Research undertaken amongst employers and past students has highlighted the need for more emphasis on practical management skills. Students in the past have been ill equipped to apply their knowledge in the work place.
3. The marketing manager is a manager first, and is responsible for the use of scarce resources.
4. This broader management role can be seen particularly when marketing personnel and techniques help to market culture change or plans to internal customers. They are actively involved in strategic issues related to the whole organisation.
5. Marketers, with their expertise in communication and understanding of human behaviour, are well equipped to develop management skills.

Approach

1. Management is a hands on activity, which needs more than an understanding of theory. Practical experience builds the skills which enable the manager to develop his or her role. In the past, managers learnt by their mistakes. There was little formal teaching or development of management skills. Today we recognise this is wrong.

    Knowledge + skills = competence

2. The CIM has sought to develop an examination which requires students to understand the theory, but will also go some way to test their practical skill. This will be done by asking them to describe the approach and steps a manager would take when faced with a variety of problems.
3. The examiner will be looking for evidence that students:

    (a) utilise logical and established frameworks for tackling these situations.

    (b) demonstrate their own experience by identifying the possible practical problems which they will be faced with.

    (c) show their interpersonal skills in the tone and style they adopt.

    (d) show communication skills in the way in which they present their ideas and views.

4. Success in this paper can only be ensured if students have the chance to practice and develop their own management skills as they progress through their studies.
5. Management development is not an activity which should be limited to this course. This paper should help establish a pattern whereby students take control of their own personal management development and constantly review and update their personal development objectives. This extended learning is a characteristic of the successful manager of the future. It is endorsed by the Institute's Continuing Professional Development Programme.
6. Besides practising the skills of management when learning about the theory, students must also practise examination technique. More students fail exams through their inability to apply what they know within the context of the examination than fail because of a lack of subject knowledge.
7. In this paper, in particular, the approach chosen will be to present direct evidence of the skills the examiner expects.

    (i) a failure to complete the paper indicates poor time management.
    (ii) poor presentation equals unprofessional communication skills.
    (iii) a failure to answer the question asked equals a failure to listen.

Suggested answers

Conclusion

This should be an interesting and directly relevant subject which will allow you to improve your own performance immediately. Have fun studying it.

2 MIDDLE MANAGERS

Objectives

1. To encourage the management team to recognise the changing environment and need for cultural change.

2. To encourage them to recognise the difference between product and customer oriented approaches.

3. To help them identify the essential steps needed to implement change.

Reasons and Tasks

1. *Why the need to change?*

    The environment is constantly changing:

    (a) new technology
    (b) increased competition.

    This has been evidenced by declining profits.

2. *What has happened?*

    Fundamentally, a change in the levels of demand and supply has changed the balance of power making it a buyer's market. Buyers have a choice and will go to the supplier most precisely matching their needs.

    To survive in such an environment, that firm has to be you. So before committing resources to production, customers' needs should be found out in advance.

    It might be faster delivery, special services or advice, rather than lower prices, which entice a buyer.

3. *What will a shift do for you?*

    A change towards a marketing culture will focus the business on the needs of its customers and will:

    (a) ensure flexible, responsive operations.
    (b) avoid wasting resources by producing goods no one wants.
    (c) help you identify ways of adding value and improving profitability.

4. *What has to be done?*

    Change is not an easy process. It takes time and requires commitment and resources from senior management.

    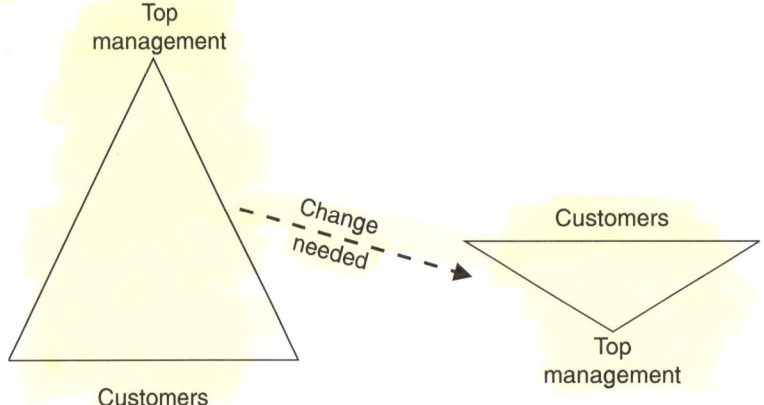

    The change needed will transform the company by bringing senior managers closer to the customers and placing the customers at the top, not the bottom, of business decision-making.

Suggested answers

The change is essentially a change of attitude - but the old attitude is ingrained in the very structure of the business. Objectives set in terms of products rather than customers and managers organised in specialist chimneys - very limited horizontal communication.

Reorganisation and training as well as motivation and team building will be critical to any change. Management will need to develop both communication and information systems as well as a marketing function.

3 KATHY

Advice on the process

1 Getting started

I would advise Kathy that she needs a logical framework to help her work through this process. It is clearly important to get it right because:

(a) her draft will, in itself, be a document which the company may consider indicates her capabilities, attitudes and style and may contribute towards her first appraisal

(b) what she indicates will form the basis of the experience and development she receives during the two years: this is a significant development opportunity which should not be wasted.

2 The framework

The framework I would recommend could be shown as follows.

(a) An audit: a current strengths and weaknesses assessment.

(b) Identifying the skills and experience most valuable in her targeted career and area of specialism.

(c) Identification of the gap between (a) and (b), showing important strengths to be developed, and weaknesses to be tackled.

(d) Developing a framework for presentation.

3 The Personal Audit

Undertake a strengths and weakness analysis of management characteristics against the following list.

	1	2	3	4	5
Decisiveness					
Leadership					
Vision					
Proactive					
Flexibility					
Quick thinking					
Self-starter					
Communicator					
Analytical					
Sensitive					
Persuasive					
Co-ordinator					

She should be encouraged to rate herself on a scale of 1-5 on these and any other relevant criteria she identifies. She can ask others, such as friends from college, family and work experience managers, for their views and assessment.

Suggested answers

4 *What is needed*

Kathy needs to then consider her ideal job in two years time. What is her ambition? For example, if she wants to be a brand manager, what skills are needed. These can then be superimposed on the same sort of framework.

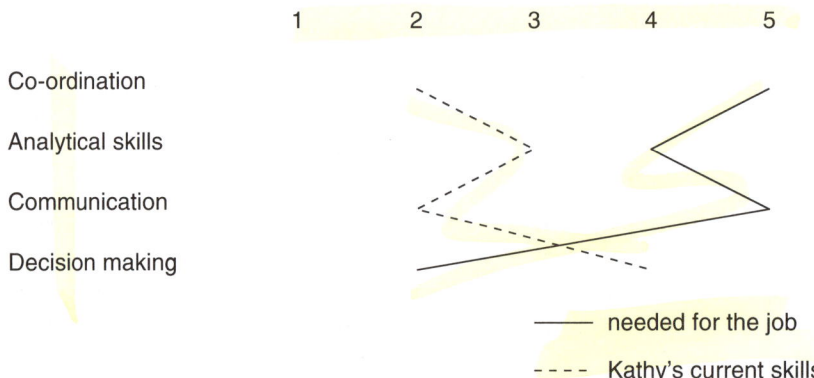

By comparing these across the profile and range of skills it is possible to demonstrate in visual terms the gap between what she can do and what she will need to do and identify areas of weakness that should be the focus of a personal development contract. This can also be used as a benchmark against which actual development is reviewed.

Notes

1   Care should be taken to ensure the level of skills is as accurate as possible (eg friends may say Kathy is a 'good' analyst, but this may not be at the level needed by the job of brand manager).

2   Kathy's perceptions of what are needed for the job should also be relevant and accurate.

This approach is thorough, adds some quantified objectives to the process, enlarging priorities to be established.

5 *Prioritisation of areas*

From this picture Kathy can draw up a short list prioritising areas for personal development.

Co-ordination and communication are clearly areas for attention and she may like to continue to strengthen her skills in decision making as this could be a particular personal strength and USP.

6 *Presentation*

(a)   Kathy should present her personal development goals as quantified objectives - either using her own scales or converting them into targets such as:

   (i)   producing x reports per period
   (ii) giving a specified number of presentations etc.

(b)   Her considerations should be supported by her strengths and weaknesses analysis (to demonstrate the approach she took and the rationale for her suggestions).

(c)   She may list a number of suggestions for her trainee placements justified in terms of her priorities, for example:

   (i)   Six months with New Product Development, to learn about co-ordination, analysis and presentation.

   (ii) Six months in the sales department to learn about communication, negotiation, self starting and self discipline etc.

4 POOR DELEGATION SKILLS

Tutorial note. Very similar questions to this one have appeared frequently in the exam.

Suggested answers

(a) There are a number of reasons why this manager will not delegate, which might be related to the fact that he has not been in the job for long.

 (i) Low confidence and trust in the abilities of the subordinates made worse by his being unsure of the skills of his team.

 (ii) The burden of responsibility and accountability for the mistakes of subordinates, aggravated by (i) above. This is particularly acute if he wants to make a good first impression on his superiors.

 (iii) A desire to stay in touch with the team and its work, especially if he does not feel at home in a management role, or misses aspects of the subordinate job such as camaraderie. Possibly this is his first management role.

 (iv) An unwillingness to admit that subordinates have developed to the extent that they could perform some of his duties. The manager might feel threatened by a sense of redundancy or in this case might be concerned he knows less than they do.

 (v) Poor control and communication systems in the organisation. The manager, perhaps, feels he has to do everything himself if he is to retain control and know what is going on. This may be a perception caused by his experiences in a previous job.

 (vi) Past experience of an organisational culture that has failed to reward effective delegation by superiors, so that he may not realise that delegation is positively regarded rather than seen as a shirking of responsibility.

 (vii) Lack of understanding that delegation does *not* mean giving subordinates total control and making himself redundant.

(b) What actions can be taken to encourage a manager to delegate? The action taken must be decided once the real reason for the unwillingness to delegate has been established, but it could include the following.

 (i) Encourage the manager to recognise the advantages and acceptability of delegating. These may be summarised as follows:

    (1) He will be freed from day-to-day decision-making so he can concentrate on strategic issues.

    (2) Better decisions will be made by people more involved in operations; this also means that decisions can be made quickly, so giving the organisation the chance to react quickly to local changes.

    (3) Work can be spread around, so avoiding overloads on individuals. He will need to work less overtime!

    (4) Subordinate staff are motivated by the trust placed in them and by the sense of participation. In addition, subordinates will have a sense of ownership of the tasks they perform.

    (5) The subordinates will develop skills and competences and they will learn to make increasingly complex decisions. In this sense, delegation is an important part of management development.

 (ii) Helping him to recognise the skills and experience of these subordinates who are capable of handling delegated authority in a responsible way. If subordinates are of the right quality, superiors should be prepared to trust them more.

 (iii) Helping him establish a system of open communications, in which he and subordinates freely interchange ideas and information. If the subordinate is given all the information he needs to do his job, and if the superior is aware of what the subordinate is doing:

    (1) the subordinate will make better-informed decisions;
    (2) the superior will not panic because he does not know what is going on.

    But although open lines of communication are important, they should not be used to command the subordinate in a matter where authority has been delegated; communication links must not be used as a means of reclaiming authority.

 (iv) A system of control. He might be reluctant to delegate authority because he retains absolute responsibility for the performance of the subordinates. If an efficient control system is in operation, responsibility and accountability will be monitored at all levels of the management hierarchy, and the dangers of relinquishing authority and control to subordinates are significantly lessened.

Suggested answers

(v) The rewarding of effective delegation and the efficient assumption of authority by subordinates. Rewards may be given in terms of pay, promotion, status, official approval and so on. Following your discussion about this issue, feedback on improvements can help reinforce a new style of working. Successes will build confidence in himself and the team.

(c) Actions now:

(i) Collect any further evidence and confirm where possible the grievance of the staff. Review the manager's experience from the job interview.

(ii) Arrange a meeting to counsel the manager. This must be in an undisturbed environment and in an informal friendly way - the manager must not feel this is a *disciplinary* interview!

(iii) Encourage the manger to discuss his views of how things are going. Discuss his assessment of the team and their capabilities, his worries about the job and reasons for working late so often.

(iv) Discuss broadly the issue of delegation, its advantages and the manager's experience.

(v) Try to identify the problem and discuss ways forward.

(vi) Encourage a meeting with the team to establish what their perceptions are and what is being considered as ways forward.

(vii) Follow up: monitor and review the situation every four weeks.

5 COMMUNICATION PROBLEMS

> *Tutorial note.* This question emphasises that there is more to improving communications than investing in a new Email system. Questions on improving communications often come up in the exam, and you should consider the barriers set out in (a) when deciding what action needs to be taken.

Barriers to effective personal communication.

(a) The employees might have different attitudes and perceptions arising out of the difference in their social and family background, education background, political opinions, or age. A university graduate might consider an older fellow employee stuffy, slow and pedantic, whereas the older employee might consider the graduate to be too full of himself for his own good and unable to get down to detail.

(b) Different backgrounds will tend to give individuals a different sense of values, and of what is important and what is irrelevant. The failure to communicate might be caused by completely different perspectives about priorities in the work, and job objectives.

(c) There might be inter-personal dislikes, rivalries or jealousies which prevent free and open communication between the two employees. The result might be that they tend to communicate with each other, incompletely and inefficiently, through a third person. This would be an inefficient and unsatisfactory system.

(d) Inter-personal rivalries might have broken out into conflict. This in turn will create poor communications between the employees.

(e) An employee might either try to communicate more information than the other can use, or transmit much irrelevant information. The recipient of the information might then be unable to see the wood for the trees.

(f) The employees might make important errors in information they provide, so that the recipient is unable to understand what he is being told.

(g) Again, the employee receiving the information might simply not understand what he is being told. The use of technical jargon might be one problem, but slang and poor English are equally likely to cause communication problems. There is a tendency for people receiving information to:

(i) hear what they want to hear
(ii) overlook or ignore what they don't want to hear.

Where two people have widely different backgrounds, the tendency towards incorrect interpretation of messages will be strong.

Suggested answers

(h) Where there is mistrust or dislike between two people, there is a tendency for:

  (i) the recipient of the message to evaluate the person giving the message rather than the content of the message itself

  (ii) the recipient to read between the lines, perhaps by misinterpreting non-verbal signs of the giver of the message

  (iii) the emotions of the recipient such as anger, frustration, and fear to interfere with the message.

  In the same way, evaluation of the recipient of the message, the use of non-verbal signs, and the emotions of the giver of the message might create serious barriers to communication.

Remedies to attempt to solve the problem

(a) The major problem might be the seemingly irreconcilable differences in background. Clearly, the differences must be overcome, and the department manager must discuss the problems with each individual.

  (i) One approach might be to encourage the person who feels inferior or aggrieved to lessen his sense of inferiority or grievance. Similarly, a person who feels superior or contemptuous of the other should be encouraged to treat the other person with more respect and regard.

  (ii) The two employees must be persuaded to recognise the problem and their own contribution towards it. When each individual in private discussion accepts his own personal failings in the matter, it might be possible to bring them into a joint discussion about their drawbacks to communication. Realisation of the other person's attitudes and difficulties should help towards a resolution of the problem.

  (iii) A mutual discussion of the problems should not be attempted prematurely, because it might anger each individual that he has been put to shame in front of the other by the department manager's rebukes. In the early stages of finding a remedy, it might be necessary to encourage each individual separately. This might be done by:

    (1) trying to get each individual to convey information to the other as unevaluated data rather than as evaluated information. In other words each person should try to give the other chance to make up his own mind.

    (2) try to discourage each individual from being cold or offhand in dealing with the other, and to instil some warmth into communications.

    (3) try to discourage any offhand attitude from an employee who implies to the other that he already knows all the answers.

    (4) try to encourage them to act spontaneously and normally towards each other instead of in a stylised and formalised way.

  The difficulties should be presented to the individual in such a way that he should want to try to resolve them, rather than to feel defensive about criticism from his superior, or fearful for his career development prospects.

(b) The department manager can also take a more procedural approach to some of the difficulties. He might institute a new set of guidelines or rules for the information system within the department, and justify the new guidelines on the grounds that there have been communication difficulties amongst employees, without naming names. The guidelines which he might issue are:

  (i) Communications between employees must be in simple English.

  (ii) The recipient of information should let the giver know what he has done or proposes to do about it, to check that he has understood the message correctly.

  (iii) The principle of redundancy should be used for certain types of communication - a message should be repeated, preferably in two or more different ways, so that if it is not properly understood the first time, it will become more clear on repetition.

(c) If these remedies fail to produce fairly rapid improvements in the situation the manager should take steps to have one (or both) of the employees transferred to another job.

Suggested answers

6 LUDDITE BANKERS

(a) Together these two would make a good team with complementary skills - one has technical excellence, the other understands the users' needs and the dangers of information overload. They need to be brought together to recognise the following facts.

Communication is both a *technical* and a *social* process. The meaning in a message is not simply a matter of selecting the right words - the meaning any message has also depends on the values and attitudes used in interpreting the message. Therefore, the meaning of any message is likely to be influenced by:

(i) the background and values of the people concerned

(ii) the social relationships between the people concerned, eg the degree of trust and sympathy which exists

(iii) the non-verbal signals such as facial expressions, hand movements and body language.

This problem concerns the lack of communication between two employees with different backgrounds, attitudes and values.

Barriers to communication

(i) The different ages and social backgrounds of Gerry and Alan mean they have different values and attitudes to life. Their perception of reality will be different in terms of what is important and unimportant.

(ii) There are problems of language between the two, since Gerry appears to use both technical jargon and words ('Luddites') which reflect his educational background.

(iii) Since they both work in different departments they 'do not meet face to face very often'. Therefore they cannot learn to interpret the other's non-verbal signals.

(iv) Both tend to ignore information they do not want to hear:

(1) Alan cannot accept anything which questions his perception of the need for traditional approaches based on his long experience.

(2) Gerry cannot accept anything that stands in the way of his vision of the need to change. His knowledge of computers means that change does not frighten him and his youthful enthusiasm has not been modified by experience.

(v) Each forms a stereotype (preconceived image) of the other.

(1) Gerry sees Alan as a 'Luddite' (resisting change).

(2) Alan sees Gerry a tearaway who has not seen enough of the world to understand the value of experience. Each regards information from the other as biased, distorted and prejudiced.

(vi) Both have different characters: Gerry is articulate and forceful; Alan is quiet and taciturn.

The way to remove the barriers

(i) Encourage more face-to-face communication as this usually stimulates more feedback, particularly non-verbal signals.

(ii) By individuals and joint counselling encourage them to give more feedback particularly Alan who appears not to express his views or the reasons for them.

(iii) Help Gerry to understand banking operations in more detail. Help Alan to grasp the ideas of information technology and particularly its role in the survival of banking business.

(iv) Encourage Gerry to understand that listening is an important part of the communication process.

(v) Get both to explain in everyday words the meaning of the technical terms they use.

(b) *Actions*

(i) Besides counselling the two, I would make every attempt to remove the physical barriers by bringing the two into the same work area, or at least encouraging a face to face weekly meeting.

(ii) Some training or development may help tackle specific problems.

(iii) Encourage them to job swap for a week to see what the other one does and needs from the systems.

Suggested answers

(iv) Monitor and control the situation to ensure improvements happen.

7   MANAGING MEETINGS

Often a considerable part of a manager's valuable *time* is taken up with *meetings*. It is therefore vital that managers make sure that meetings work in their favour. Although knowledge is important, the *ability to communicate* is often the key to success.

The different groups to be addressed in the course of this new job are numerous. Their *expectations* both of the individual manager and the organisation as a whole will be very different. Also the *knowledge* which they bring will vary. One must be sympathetic to this and wherever possible use it to mutual advantage. However, individuals within a meeting should not be allowed to hijack the proceedings to their individual benefit or for the purpose of exercising their own 'hobby-horse'.

Common pitfalls

Malcolm Peel (*How to Make Meetings Work*, 1988) exposes the most common reasons why meetings fail.

(a) *Unnecessary attendance*. Filling a board room with representatives from all levels and departments may look democratic. Taking senior executives to meet prospective customers may look impressive. However, if these people have nothing relevant to offer, one is simply wasting their time. If they are quite vociferous individuals, they may even inhibit significant contributions from less senior people.

(b) *Lack of preparation*. Failure to have the necessary information, or to remember the points which one wishes examined mean that the meeting will have to be repeated. The overall impression created is poor.

(c) *Bad tactics*. Failure to match the type of meeting or presentation to the interested parties, or meeting at the wrong time, or in the wrong place will limit the chances of success.

(d) *Personality problems*. Often a cause of interdepartmental difficulties, different personalities can hinder meetings, especially when a conflict of interests is also involved. Sales people might have to meet people in credit control for example.

(e) *Procedural problems*. Failure to follow the best procedures for meetings can mar an otherwise successful meeting. For example, not taking notes or minutes and failing to summarise decisions can leave delegates as uncertain about the action required as they were before they arrived.

Correct procedure

In the event that most of the above pitfalls can be avoided, there are some key elements of efficient and productive meetings.

(a) *Purpose known and shared by all*. This minimises misunderstandings, and the difficulties caused by conflicting objectives.

(b) *Agenda set and followed*. An agenda ensures that topics are not forgotten or given more attention than they warrant, and delegates are not side tracked by issues of lower priority.

(c) *Timetable set and agreed*. Even if the meeting is relatively informal, it is useful to have a clear timetable. This ensures that sufficient time is available for all matters and the meeting can finish on time.

(d) *Notes and minutes recorded*. It is always useful to have an accurate record of any meeting, for reference, to settle any disagreements and as to be a starting point for the next session.

(e) *Input and involvement*. A good chairperson will ensure that there is input and involvement by all attending. Forceful personalities should not be allowed to dominate at the expense of other people's relevant contributions. If individuals have nothing significant to offer, it must be asked whether their presence is really required.

(f) *Outcomes discussed and decided*. Meetings should not be a monologue by one particular manager. Topics should be discussed and a consensus achieved.

(g) *Action points summarised*. This is perhaps the most important part of the meeting. There is little use in discussion and agreement if people are unclear as to what they have to do once the meeting has finished.

Suggested answers

Benefits of meetings

Well run meetings offer several benefits to their participants.

Cross fertilisation of ideas can generate new perspectives. Alternative suggestions for dealing with problems can be developed. The arrival at an agreed and shared set of objectives is most valuable for any organisation or department. Meetings can help overcome the 'them and us' mentality which can prevail where there is little contact between departments. Finally, a team spirit can develop and improve motivation.

8 EFFECTIVE TEAM

> *Tutorial note.* This answer makes use of Handy's Model. You could also have used Belbin's typology as a basis for your answer to the first part of the question.

C B Handy in his book 'Understanding Organisations' describes a contingency approach to analysing group effectiveness. The factors involved are the 'givens', which are the group, the group's task and the group's environment, the 'intervening variables', which are group motivation, the style of leadership and processes and procedures, and the 'outcomes', which are the group's productivity and the satisfaction of group members.

Characteristics of an effective work team

Characteristics of an effective work team can be identified in each of the variables.

(a) The group itself should contain a suitable *blend* of the individual skills and abilities of its members, so that the group not only has enough personnel to do its job, and people with sufficient experience and skill, but also it should blend the individual members in an effective way. A project team, for example, probably needs a man of ideas, a man of drive and energy, a logical evaluator of suggestions, a man who can do the detailed, routine work and a 'conciliator' who can bring individuals to negotiate and settle their differences.

(b) The group's task must be *clearly defined*, otherwise it cannot be effective in carrying it out. The group should also be given the resources to do its job properly and if necessary, it should have the authority to carry out certain actions which it considers necessary as part of its task.

(c) If the task is a temporary one, the work group should be a temporary project team which will be disbanded when its job is done. If the task is a continuing one, the work group should be given a defined place and role in the formal organisation structure.

(d) The group's environment refers to conditions of work. The characteristics of an effective work group in this respect are that members of the group should have *ready contact* with each other. An open plan office for the group might achieve this purpose. The group must also have easy and good contacts with other groups with which they work; inter-group conflicts will reduce the efficiency of every group involved.

(e) The *motivation* of the group as a whole develops as a group norm. If motivation is good and positive, the group will try to be efficient and effective. Poor motivation will result in an ineffective group. It would not be true to say that participation by group members in decision-making is necessarily a characteristic of an effective group; however, participation, when it promotes a positive group motivation, will be a means toward group effectiveness.

(f) The style of a group's leader also plays an influential role in determining group effectiveness. This style might be autocratic, democratic or laissez-faire. Likert distinguished between exploitive authoritative, benevolent authoritative, consultative authoritative and participative group management, and suggested that the latter type will promote a more effective group.

(g) An effective work group will use well-designed processes and procedures. Characteristics of these might be a formally designed management information system, or the use of modelling and operational research techniques, a management by objectives system, up-to-date technology, or scientific management techniques etc. A formal group structure should not necessarily be rigid, but each member of the group should be aware of his own individual responsibilities and tasks.

The characteristics so far described should create outcomes which prove the group's effectiveness. The effective group will be efficient in its work, if the work is continuous, or it will achieve its task, as

Suggested answers

defined in its terms of reference. At the same time, it should be expected that in a group which works well and accomplishes its tasks, the individual members will show a marked amount of job satisfaction.

Training method

Training can help to create an effective work group both by building up a group identity and also by showing other members how each individual thinks and reacts in various situation. Although group learning is not common in industry, it is used by various non-industrial organisations. 'T groups' is one name given to group training, in which a series of exercises are carried out. Each exercise will involve certain members of the group, and at the end of the exercise, other group members will be asked to comment on how the exercise was performed. These exercises and discussions enable individuals to understand how they react in a given situation and how these reactions appear to other people. This helps to develop an understanding of how members of a group inter-act and to suggest ways in which these interactions can be made to work more constructively.

9 PARTICIPATION

Disadvantages of participative style

There are a number of potential disadvantages of a participative style.

(a) The degree of participation can vary. A consultative style of leadership allows some participation, and so too does a democratic style. A potential disadvantage of the participative style is that a manager might intend to allow participation to a limited extent, whereas subordinates expect to have an increasingly greater say in decisions that are taken.

(b) A long time might be required to reach decisions, and the decision reached might be an unsuitable compromise.

(c) Employees might be motivated to consider the interests of their own group, without having any loyalty for the organisation as a whole. A junior employee in one small section might participate in the decisions of his section, but will have little influence over decisions by his department or division.

(d) The superior might be able to adopt a participative style, but be unable to reward subordinates for their work. If there is no progress from more effort to more rewards, subordinates might quickly lose interest and motivation.

(e) Some work does not lend itself to a participative style. Highly programmed, routine work is a case in point. Unless subordinates are allowed to re-structure the jobs in their section so as to remove the monotony from jobs, participation in decision-making will be futile because decisions will be programmed or automatic.

(f) Not all employees necessarily want to participate in decision-making. Some might be content to accept orders.

(g) There might be disagreements between subordinates so that some decisions cannot be reached by common agreement. In such cases, the people losing the argument might resent the decision which is taken against them and might try to sabotage subsequent activities in order to prove themselves right.

Minimisation of disadvantages

The disadvantages of a participative style of management might be overcome as follows.

(a) The extent of participation should be established clearly for everyone to understand. In other words, the leadership style should be consistent.

(b) Authority should be delegated sufficiently to enable small groups to take decisions about matters which are of some interest to them. One way of doing this in a large organisation might be to split the organisation up into many semi-independent divisions, and to encourage decentralisation within each division.

(c) Jobs should be re-structured so as to provide challenging work for work groups.

(d) The participative style should be promoted by senior management and implemented throughout the organisation, provided that the circumstances allow this to be one without adverse consequences.

Suggested answers

(e) Managers should be given powers to reward or punish subordinates, so that subordinates will believe that by making more contributions to group discussions they will eventually receive fair reward.

(f) Senior managers must pay careful attention to co-ordination of the goals and activities of sub-units within the organisation.

  (i) The goals of the organisation should be made clear to all employees. Decisions by groups should be taken after giving full consideration to the needs of the organisation.

  (ii) A procedure for resolving inter-group differences should be provided. Likert suggested the idea of a linking pin in which the leader of one group is a participating member of a more senior gap, so that there is a continual overlap throughout organisation. The ultimate task of co-ordination would be carried out at board level.

10 RECRUITMENT ISSUES

> *Tutorial note.* In answering this question, it is not enough just to list selection procedures. The solutions have to be relevant to the given circumstances, and you also need to consider *why* problems have arisen. The second part of the question demands imaginative solutions.

Background. High staff turnover is a problem. It should not be accepted as normal and John needs to see the cost and waste that constantly re-interviewing for staff involves. The impact on staff morale and motivation must also be a problem.

Selection methods

(a) There should be a labour turnover target within the framework of a personnel plan (eg reducing turnover from the current level to 30% within 12 months?)

(b) Job descriptions, but more importantly personnel specifications, should be prepared and studied by the interviewer (Mr Hoskins).

(c) The jobs should be advertised in such a way that the short-term as well as long-term career prospects of employees should be explained, together with the nature of the work recruits will be expected to do.

(d) Applicants for a job should be asked to fill in an application form. The questions asked should:

  (i) help the selector to decide whether the applicant is possibly suitable for the job
  (ii) provide the interviewer with a basis for asking questions at the interview.

(e) The interviews should be planned, and should last longer than 10 minutes. They should enable not only the interviewer to assess the candidate, but the candidate to find out more about the job and assess the organisation. Candidates should be encouraged to talk at interviews and to answer questions.

(f) Candidates need to be judged against the requirements for the job and the personnel specification.

Before going on to consider Mr. Hoskins's relations with local schools, it is worth considering his failure to recruit applicants who stay in the job. New recruits tend to leave quickly which suggests that the job they have taken is nothing like what they were led to expect. Clearly, the problem could be due to a combination of two factors:

(a) failure of applicants to understand what the job entails
(b) failure of Mr Hoskins to select the right sort of applicant.

Misunderstanding by applicants can be put right in the following ways.

(a) Provide more information about jobs and career prospects in advertisements and brochures.

(b) Asking applicants to explain why they are seeking a career in manufacturing and distribution when they fill in an application form. Obvious misunderstandings can be identified from what the applicant writes.

(c) Making sure that the job is explained again at the interview.

Suggested answers

(d) Inviting candidates at interviews to put questions about the job, career prospects and the company as an employer.

(e) Better liaison with schools.

Failure of the interviewer to do his job properly can be put right in the following ways.

(a) Mr Hoskins's should show willingness to adopt the selection methods recommended above. If his judgement of people is suspect (which is quite possible) it might be suggested in particular that he gives candidates a score or rating out of a maximum number of points for each quality in the personnel specification. A scoring or rating system might help to clarify the interviewer's judgement by putting figures to opinions.

(b) If he considers himself unable to change his methods or opinions, he should be advised to delegate the job of interviewing and selection to a subordinate.

(c) He should try to find out more about potential applicants, by having a better liaison with local schools.

His *attitude to local schools* might be partially justified, but mere criticism is not constructive, and he should do something about the problem. Better careers literature about jobs in manufacturing should be made available to schools careers offices and other people enquiring about jobs, and he should discuss his recruitment problems with these schools. However, he could promote a better liaison and communication with school teachers and school children by implementing any of a number of possible schemes, eg:

(a) inviting teachers and children to open evenings at the company

(b) sending staff (or going himself) to talk to schools, with the aid of films (if schools are agreeable to such visits).

Mr Hoskins should be set a target of reducing the rate of staff turnover to 30%, comparable with those of other firms in the area.

Conclusion

The aim of recruitment and selection is to provide the quantity and quality of human resources needed to fulfil the organisation's objectives.

(a) *Recruitment* is concerned with finding applicants.
(b) *Selection* is concerned with choosing between applicants.

Getting the wrong people or people who do not stay long is a waste of money and effort - John should be advised that the situation can be changed with some careful planning and a more serious approach to the process.

11 STAFF APPRAISAL SCHEMES

(a) There are several benefits both to staff and their employers of well run appraisal schemes, which is why they are now a normal part of management in many established and successful businesses. Since the mid 1980s, it has been widely recognised that the training and development of staff should be a priority for any organisation.

(i) *Benefits to the individual*

An individual taking part in an effective appraisal scheme gains an opportunity to discuss his or her work objectively. Performance can be evaluated and constructive criticism and encouragement can be offered. Future career progression, including training and development needs, can be considered.

The employees should feel able to contribute in a structured way to company policy by offering insights based on their own experience. There may not be time to discuss matters of a possibly personal nature under normal circumstances, and the chance to do so in an organised way will lead to improved relations with the individual's manager.

(ii) *Benefits to the manager*

Appraisal schemes provide the manager with objective guidelines for staff assessment. The actual process of the appraisal allows the manager to gain a better understanding of staff needs. The formal opportunity for discussion and a commitment to agreed action on both sides will lead to improved relationships.

Suggested answers

(iii) *Benefits to the organisation*

The use of an appraisal scheme offers an organisation standardised information about its employees. Individual performance can then be improved, encouraged and developed, based on the information provided. The organisation will be able to plan its use of human resources more accurately.

(iv) *Implications for marketing*

Appraisal schemes are designed to maximise individual performance, and improve communications. This is an advantage for any department but is particularly important for marketing. As marketing is the interface between the company and its customers, disgruntled and/or ineffective employees can have an immediate impact on revenue. Also, there is usually considerable competition for capable marketers and sales people. A company which fails to offer adequate understanding of career opportunities is likely to lose its most successful people. Continuous staff development is essential for successful implementation of Total Quality Management or other such schemes.

(b) *Implementation*

To implement the scheme successfully would involve the following.

(i) The concerns of all those involved must be identified and any objections overcome. Staff may see the appraisal as threatening and as a form of disciplinary action. The developmental aspects of the scheme and benefits to the individual must be stressed. The scheme has a better chance of acceptance if the atmosphere is generally open, and if the company is seen to be reasonably profitable. This will reassure staff that funds are available for the promised training, and that candidates are not being selected for redundancy.

(ii) *Management skills*

Managers who are to appraise people need to be briefed on the skills required. They particularly need to understand the need for two-way discussion, an ultimate agreement on action necessary, and the objectivity required on the part of the appraiser.

(iii) *Adequate resources*

Resources of time and money must exist to support training and development. Without this, staff commitment will be short lived and they will be unlikely to 'buy' any future schemes.

(iv) *Preparation*

Actual appraisals themselves should take place within a planned time scale - say three months. The interviews should cover a predetermined range of questions, dealing with a range of topics. Some of these will be standard to all interviews and others will be job specific. Interviews should be conducted in private and be free from interruptions. Wherever possible, management should distance pay increases from appraisal interviews and thereby concentrate on the developmental aspects of the exercise. Management must be prepared to act positively and quickly to any problems or opportunities which come to light as a result of the appraisal process.

(v) *Review the process*

After appraisals have been done and results communicated, managers should review the process. Refinements can then be made to improve future appraisal rounds. In order to be successful and achieve the stated aims, appraisals need to be repeated on a regular basis. A year is the most common period, as this gives all parties the opportunity to undertake the agreed action. Results can then be reviewed in respect of goals set at the first appraisal.

(vi) *Organisational growth*

Appraisals are more likely to succeed as mechanisms for staff development and career planning in organisations committed to sustained growth. Only if this is the case are the necessary openings for promotion and career progression available.

12 APPRAISAL DREAD

> *Tutorial note.* This question is a good illustration of the importance of appraisals. Although Douglas is an excellent manager in other respects, his failure to give good appraisals is undermining his performance as a manager since staff are not receiving the long-term feedback they need.

(a) The possible causes of the problem are as follows.

   (i) Douglas gets nothing out of his own appraisal interviews with superiors and so assumes that the exercise cannot succeed.

   (ii) He has received no formal training in the conduct of such interviews.

   (iii) He is insensitive to the desire of his staff to have a longer-term assessment of their performance and potential.

   (iv) He is unable to distinguish between the short and long-term (he considers that his short-term guidance and counselling is sufficient for his employee's needs).

   (v) He prefers to manage staff on an informal basis and dislikes the idea of the formal interview and the accompanying paperwork.

   (vi) He is too close to his staff and does not want to have to make formal assessments of them which may affect their future.

(b) Fact finding would include the following.

   (i) A review of Douglas Wentworth's personnel records to discover his background, character, strengths and weaknesses.

   (ii) An investigation of how far his unsatisfactory appraisal interviews have hindered his staff's development and promotion.

   (iii) A review of his own appraisal interviews to see if they have been similarly unsatisfactory.

   (iv) Discussions with his staff to see what it is they require from the appraisal interview that they are not recovering at the moment, and why they think Douglas dislikes them.

(c) Help for Douglas Wentworth could consist of the following.

   (i) Counselling him:

   (1) to understand the role and importance of 'feedback' for human behaviour

   (2) to make sure he adequately prepares for each interview by isolating the points for praise and areas of performance which need improvement

   (3) to ensure he has the 'facts' or evidence to support his reasons for a low rating against some areas of performance

   (4) to plan the advice he intends to give on methods of improvement (are they feasible? are they practical?)

   (5) to explain that it is important not to end up with a set of 'woolly generalisations' as methods of improvement but specific targets

   (6) to understand that his employees need and desire a longer-term assessment of their performance and future

   (7) to appreciate that his loyalty to and friendship with his staff must be balanced with his duty to the company to develop its labour resources in the best possible manner

   (8) to understand that appraisal requires an overview which cannot be achieved through a series of short-term assessments.

   (ii) Training courses which:

   (1) give teaching in the social skills required in handling such interviews

   (2) provide an understanding of the social processes involved in interviewing, such as bias, supportive non-verbal signals

   (3) provide practical experience in guiding and directing an interview to achieve its purpose.

   (iii) Improving his own appraisal interviews with his superior.

Suggested answers

The situation would have to be reviewed in a few months' time to see if it had improved. If it had not, further counselling and training would be necessary. A short-term solution would be for another supervisor to conduct the annual appraisals until Douglas feels that he can conduct them for the benefit of his staff and the firm.

13 DIFFICULT JUNIOR

(a) The problem is Ian Dalgleish's failure to use his obvious talents in making a real contribution to the departmental goals and the objectives of the organisation. The problem is complicated by an attempt to challenge your leadership of the section. Many of his failures (timekeeping) are public failures which can be observed by other members of the department, and are a flouting of your authority.

(b) Possible reasons for his behaviour are as follows.

   (i) He wanted, or it was widely assumed (by the section) that he would be given a promotion to supervisor. Therefore he is personally frustrated and publicly embarrassed by your appointment and his behaviour is a typical 'fight syndrome' to compensate his frustration.

   (ii) His outside activities give him more challenge and responsibility and therefore provide more satisfaction of his 'need to achieve'; therefore 'work' does not command a high priority on his enthusiasm and efforts.

   (iii) He does not respond to your chosen leadership style. Possibly he prefers an authoritarian to a participative approach.

   (iv) He has personal problems which are affecting his attitude to work.

(c) Fact finding would include:

   (i) a discussion with the previous supervisor as to Ian's work before you came, his ambitions and objectives, and attitude towards your predecessor's leadership

   (ii) an examination of Ian's personal file to discover his background, appraisal ratings and any factors which may be influencing his behaviour, such as problems at home, family bereavement

   (iii) perhaps informal discussions with other members of the group, although care must be taken to ensure that this does not appear as gossiping behind Ian's back.

(d) Possible courses of action are as follows.

   Any course of action can only be selected after a full counselling interview with Ian to establish the cause rather than the symptom. This would be a difficult interview since Ian is unlikely to volunteer easily that his frustration at not being appointed is behind his behaviour, if this is the case. You should examine if you have the necessary social skills and consider obtaining specialist advice from a personnel manager, if there is one.

   The following courses of action could be undertaken depending on the cause identified for Ian's behaviour.

   (i) Consider the areas of your authority you can delegate to Ian. This will depend on the extent to which you can win back his trust and build a cooperative relationship.

   (ii) Attempt to provide more challenging work (see (a) above) and also try to accommodate his pressures by providing facilities to help his treasurer's work: calculators, paper, photocopier etc. Demonstrate your admiration for his outside work in front of his colleagues.

   (iii) Explain the benefits to Ian of a participative style of management, and point out that managers of the future would be expected to display their skills with people just as much as their ability to complete tasks.

   (iv) Give him advice and sympathy, and possibly time off to let him sort out his personal problems.

(e) Follow-up

   If these actions fail then transfer to another section might be the answer, particularly if it has promotion prospects. Organisations depend on the talent of their human resources and attempts to keep Ian and channel his abilities are a necessary aspect of organisational adaptation.

Suggested answers

14 MOTIVATION PRINCIPLES

Background

Motivation is essential if you are to get the 'best' performance from any team. Motivation affects both what individuals do but more importantly their attitude to doing it. In particular front line staff in direct contact with customers have to be motivated to deliver a quality service and 'care' about customers.

Theories of motivation

Because motivation is so important to the effectiveness of a team, it has attracted a lot of attention from management writers. Herzberg identified a range of factors which whilst not acting as positive motivators can and do act as disincentives to work. These are called hygiene factors, and include working conditions, like lighting and heating.

Managers must first ensure that the hygiene factors are in place and can then consider positive motivators, such as job satisfaction. Another theory is Maslow's hierarchy of needs.

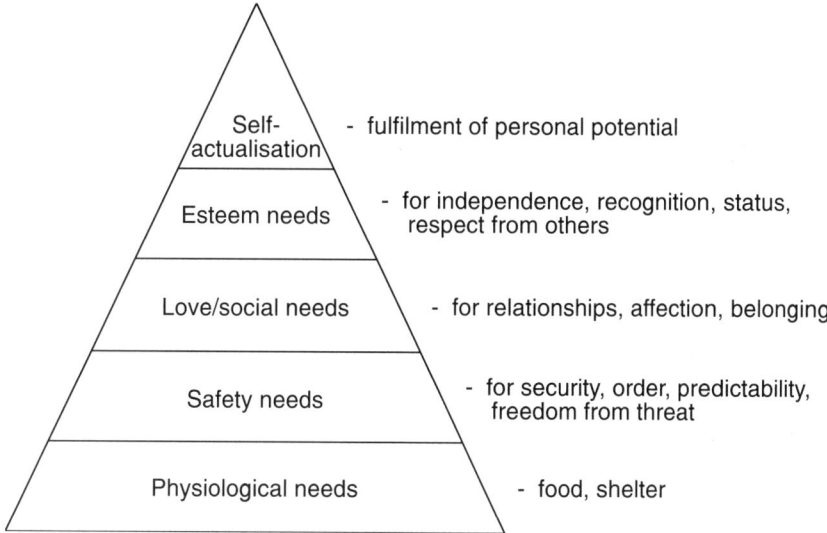

Maslow identified a hierarchy which indicates that people have levels through which they progress normally satisfying the most basic needs before moving up through the hierarchy. Although this does not always hold true for many people, the hierarchy does indicate that managers have to think about changing the motivators used, as staff move through the hierarchy, ie at low levels staff may be motivated by money, but at higher levels status and recognition of peers, time off or other rewards like job security may be more effective.

What works?

What actually works as a motivator will depend on the individual and his or her needs at that time. A poor student working in catering can be effectively motivated by financial rewards (tips) to offer high levels of customer care!

In sales teams, motivational schemes are often fairly sophisticated, with awards on the 'best' sales person, incentive gifts, prizes and competitions. This is necessary to get over the particular problems of staff working in isolation, often away from direct support.

In other cases individuals are motivated by the possibility of promotion and status, like those motivated to study for CIM examinations. Participation and involvement in work or a project can also act as a powerful motivator. Teams which are involved and committed to an objective or vision are often highly successful.

It is the job of the manager to find out what motivates staff in any particular environment or situation, and to take action to devise positive schemes to motivate them.

15 CHANGE AGENT

(a) The causes of Sandra's difficulties

Suggested answers

(i) She is a newcomer to the group. Newcomers often experience hostility at first because existing group members fear that they will not accept group norms. This is particularly the case when the newcomer arrives as the head of the group, because a group leader will have the authority to impose new, possibly unwelcome, group norms.

(ii) All the other group members are older than Sandra and have been in the department for three years or more. There may be resentment that a younger person has been brought in over the heads of more experienced staff.

(iii) Sandra's educational qualifications have contributed towards her rapid advancement in the organisation. Staff with less academic backgrounds may feel that exam results count for too much, while too little attention is paid to experience and non-academic talents.

(iv) Resistance to Sandra's innovations could also be caused by a feeling of frustrated ambition amongst some of her subordinates. During the long tenure of her predecessor one or more of the group members may have aspired to the position of department head after his retirement.

(v) The innovations themselves may be the cause of the resentment. Re-arranging and re-decorating the office may have disrupted familiar work arrangements. Resistance to new technology such as word processors is a common occurrence, perhaps arising from people's fears that they will be unable to cope with new techniques or from their fear of redundancies.

(vi) Sandra seems to have brought in changes on her own initiative. Her subordinates may resent the fact that they have not been consulted.

(b) Suggestions for improvement

(i) Sandra needs to discuss with each of the group what objectives she is setting herself in running the department. She should emphasise that she is anxious not to disrupt established procedures unnecessarily. She should explain how her philosophy for the department differs from that of her predecessor and how it fits in with the overall goals of the organisation. This may help her staff to understand her actions better and to co-operate in achieving her aims.

(ii) Her subordinates will be anxious about how they themselves fit into her plans for the department. She should reassure them that she wishes to work co-operatively with them. She should explain the benefits she intended by her innovations and in particular put to rest any fears they may have about the effects of the new technology on their jobs.

(iii) In general, she should try to understand the adverse effects on her staff of changes in their patterns of working. Where innovation is necessary to should be preceded by an effective programme of communication and consultation so that employees understand the reasons for it and the effects of it. Co-operative participation in new ideas will be more likely if subordinates are themselves encouraged to think about work procedures and suggest improvements.

(iv) Sandra has risen quickly to a managerial position and may be short of experience in handling subordinates. The initial difficulties might be reduced by appropriate counselling from her own superiors and perhaps formal training in management techniques.

(v) She needs to win the *respect* of her subordinates, to overcome resistance they might have to her ideas for change. This comes with time, and being a good boss!

16 QUALITY CIRCLE

Quality circles are a method of trying to encourage innovative ideas in production, and by involving employees they are likely to improve the prospects for acceptance of changes in products and working methods.

Limits of quality circles

The production director should be advised that the nature of the changes recommended by the quality circle will depend on the range of skills and experience of the circle members. The wider their skills are, and the broader their experience, the more significant and far-reaching will be the changes they might suggest. Groups of workers with similar skills are more likely to make suggestions for limited changes, within the sphere of their own work experience. What range of skills should the circles have?

The 'terms of reference' of the circles should be made clear. Are they to *recommend* changes to senior management, or will they have the authority to *decide* changes, and make them?

Suggested answers

Need for co-operation

Since the purpose of quality circles is to encourage innovation, the co-operation of employees will be crucial. The plans for setting up quality circles should therefore be discussed with the employees who will provide membership of the circles.

Problems with quality circles

Possible problems with the introduction of quality circles might be:

(a) not enough support from top management
(b) no co-operation from middle management
(c) discouragement because of unrealistic expectations of what the circles can do
(d) lack of support from trade unions
(e) poor choice of circle leaders
(f) insignificant training of circle members
(g) interference from non-circle members to deter the circle's operations
(h) unwillingness to participate among employees
(i) individual egos won't join in the circle 'team' spirit
(j) individual talkers dominate the circle
(k) poor communication
(l) lack of enthusiasm due to inadequate publicity.

Successful introduction of quality circles

The keys to a successful programme are:

(i) creating a proper atmosphere in which to launch them - a positive approach and good publicity

(ii) giving circle members adequate training in quality circle techniques

(iii) introducing circles slowly, one or two at a time, instead of setting up too many all at once; learning from experience; getting employees to accept the value of circles from their experience and observations over time

(iv) full support from top management

(v) an enthusiastic 'facilitator' - a manager in charge of making the circles a success

(vi) setting up a good system for following up and evaluating proposals for change

(vii) giving recognition to circle members - for instance, rewards for successful changes.

17 CUSTOMER CARE

Customer care is the application of marketing principles at the customer interface. It requires a change in culture and style which in large traditional organisations like banks has not been easy. Because banking is a service, the frontline staff are not essentially sales people but operational staff - banking experts.

Nonetheless the concept of customer care is a good one, and attempts to introduce such schemes should be applauded as they indicate evidence of a more marketing orientated culture.

Scope of customer care schemes

A typical bank customer care scheme will cover the following areas.

(a) A high level of customer service should be provided by professional and efficient staff.

(b) Staff should be fully trained to deal with the bank's main products and services.

(c) Premises and the staff in them should be well presented. This may include uniforms for certain key customer care staff.

Standards of service

Certain standards of service would be laid down.

(a) Customer queuing times at the counter should be kept to a certain number of minutes or a certain number of customers.

(b) Each telephone call should be answered within say three rings.

(c) Response to correspondence within, say, 48 hours and telephone enquiries within, say, 24 hours.

Suggested answers

  (d) Each member of staff should complete any customer care training programme within a specified timespan and if marks are given for the answers to any 'tests' set, at least 80% of answers should be correct.

  (e) Minimise complaints to the extent that none reach the Head Office or Area Office. Where a complaint is received, it is to be dealt with as swiftly as possible and by a member of management.

Monitoring

The success or failure of such a scheme depends on the level of *managerial monitoring*, action, recognition and reward following the initial flurry of activity when the scheme commences. The scheme may lose direction and impetus with changes in *personnel*. Regular enhancements and enforcement's so that the scheme remains relevant and in the forefront of customer service will result in its continued success. If staff enthusiasm at all levels can be maintained, this will be of significant benefit to the bank, its staff and its customers.

The standard of customer service should be regularly monitored by both the branch management and the area office and can take the following forms.

  (a) Undertaking customer surveys by requesting customers to complete, anonymously, an enquiry form as to the service received from staff and their perception of the banking hall during their visit.

  (b) The Area Office staff may also complete a more detailed survey form on visits to the branch. Their visits will be either announced or unannounced depending upon policy.

  (c) Certain members of staff might be responsible for certain areas of the branch, so that these can be checked regularly for tidiness, and to ensure that all posters and literature are neatly set out and up to date.

  (d) Telephone monitoring will usually be conducted by the Area Office to ascertain the service received in terms of the initial response (eg the manner of answering, the name of the member of staff offered, whether the query raised was dealt with quickly and efficiently).

One company's success at customer care will ensure it retains customers. Others will be forced to follow suit. It would be important to point out to the cynical friend that:

  (a) culture change takes time
  (b) some companies will fail to change and so fail to survive.

18 LONG CASE STUDY

> *Tutorial note.* A number of questions in both Sections A and B of recent papers have dealt with businesses changing from a product to a customer orientation.

(a) Report

A CONSULTANT AND CO

To: Managing Director, Garden Design and Landscape Company
From: A Consultant
Date: DD/MM/YY

MARKET ORIENTATION

Contents

1 Background
2 Changing to market orientation
3 Recommendations
4 Budgets and schedules for change

1 *Background*

  1.1 *Consultancy brief.* A Consultant and Co has been asked to review the current business position of the Garden Design and Landscape Company (GDLC) with a view to recommending changes for improved business and financial performance.

  1.2 The overall business strengths are:

Suggested answers

(a) its mix of customers, so that it does not rely only on domestic customers and so is partly insulated from fluctuations in the residential market

(b) its established maintenance contracts, providing a secure source of revenue (acting perhaps as a cash cow)

(c) a reasonable geographical spread

(d) existing profitability, and some success in controlling costs.

1.3 Weaknesses include the following.

(a) A lack of new business, partly induced by the recession, leading to declines in sales revenue and profit.

(b) A lack of a market orientation, in particular demonstrated by the lack of anything approaching a marketing information system.

(c) Decreasing sales force effectiveness in converting visits to orders suggesting that the company's marketing mix has become less attractive to customers over time.

(d) An organisation structure which underpins the lack of marketing orientation, being:
  (i) no link between sales teams
  (ii) poor communication between sales and marketing.

(e) Management problems include:
  (i) poor planning
  (ii) evidently, a poorly motivated staff.

1.4 The problems can be summed up in that the firm lacks a marketing orientation or culture.

(a) Customers are obviously not the centre of the decision making process.

(b) Customers needs are not identified, and so services cannot be designed to satisfy these needs.

2 *Changing to market orientation*

2.1 Currently, the firm has a product or at best a sales orientation. The long term cost of this approach is shown by the increasing order turnover rate, the declining profitability and the lack of new business.

2.2 Marketing, which is the identification and satisfaction of customer needs profitably, should be introduced to the organisation.

2.3 Introducing a marketing orientation will involve:

(a) changes to organisation structure, perhaps altering the responsibilities of various members of staff, including senior managers and board members

(b) developing a policy for human resources which supports the sales effort, reduces staff turnover (thereby retaining product and market knowledge *within* the company)

(c) improving or building the organisation's systems for conveying market and customer information to the company's decision making processes.

2.4 Finally, managers and staff must be trained in the new culture, so that the front-line staff are supported and coached by managers rather than controlled by them.

2.5 Changing a culture is a difficult process, as it involves challenging many of the established assumptions and ways of doing business. It will be particularly difficult given the firm's existing management style, where there is always a temptation to go back to old ways.

2.6 A culture change can only be introduced with senior management support. Senior managers are the company's senior decision makers, and they have to be the driving force for change.

3 *Recommendations*

3.1 Organisation structure. A number of proposals can be made.

(a) The sales and marketing function should be integrated, so that a coherent approach to all the company's promotional activities is developed.

(b) The new marketing function can be organised on a market basis to target effort effectively.

Suggested answers

3.2 To generate better business and reduced staff turnover, the sales force can be organised on a team basis, given incentives and targets. A certain degree of autonomy should be granted to these teams.

3.3 Together with the organisation structure, a new marketing information system should be developed. This may involve some market research, but obviously the needs of existing customers can be addressed in-house.

3.4 To introduce the marketing culture:

(a) managers will need management training, if possible, to introduce them to the new 'supportive culture'

(b) staff need to be trained in customer care.

3.5 The recruitment and remuneration policies should be redesigned to reduce staff turnover. The company might consider alternative sources of recruitment.

3.6 It might be worthwhile considering BS5750 for quality assurance, provided that:

(a) it can be considered relevant to the firm's business
(b) customers will appreciate it
(c) it can be afforded.

This is perhaps a long term objective.

4 Budgets and schedules

4.1 (*Tutorial note.* The budgets and schedules below have been reproduced from the answer guidelines written by the Senior Examiner.)

Activity	Time	Budget
Review current organisation structure	2 months	
Propose and agree changes with all staff	4 months	
Implementation of changes	3 months Consultancy time - 10 days assuming no redundancies	£8,000
Customer care training	Management time starting immediately with managers - 30 days	
	1 day course for each work team of 10 spread over 12 months	£7,200 (trainer costs)
Review of internal data	3 months - 20 staff days, 5 consultancy days	£4,000
Development of improved database and MIS	24 months	to be tendered
BS 5750	18 months from year 2	
Appointment of a Marketing Director	Year 2 - 8 staff days	£40,000 salary £5,000 selection costs

(b) *Improving the effectiveness of the sales and marketing team*

> *Tutorial note.* We have chosen to write in report format for this as well, and directed it to the managing director. We have reproduced below the senior examiner's answer guidelines for this question, it is intended to signpost the sort of things which the examiners would be looking for. 'There are no uniquely correct answers, but a number of alternative ways of tackling many of these questions which is supported and justified would be accepted.'

Suggested answers

Senior examiner's guidelines

Improving the effectiveness of sales and marketing team.

(i) Redirect organisation structure away from *area* sales offices towards customer segments.

(ii) Evaluate current customers to identify target segments.

(iii) Use ratio analysis to identify strengths and weakness of current sales and marketing effort.

(iv) Establish clear, realistic sales targets for each sector.

(v) Provide support to ensure the maximum benefit of sales effort (eg telesales and direct mail, to generate qualified customer leads and follow up on enquiries).

(vi) Establish a basis for monitoring performance of sales and marketing effort.)

REPORT

To: Managing Director, Garden Landscape and design company
From: A Consultant
Date: DD/MM/YY
Subject: Improving the sales and marketing team's effectiveness

Contents

1 Background

2 Recommendations

1 *Background*

1.1 A Consultant and Co has been requested to suggest ways of improving the effectiveness of the sales and marketing teams in the company.

1.2 This is in the light of the firm's overall change to a marketing orientation.

2 *Recommendation*

2.1 At present the sales teams are organised on an area basis. However, it has to be asked whether this is the most appropriate means of segmenting.

2.2 If the company's customers do not naturally segment geographically, it would seem logical that some other segmentation variable should be used, and the firm's marketing effect adjusted accordingly.

2.3 This can be achieved by:

(a) completely re-organising the sales team into teams based on customer segments

(b) operating a type of matrix structure whereby both area and customer segments are used.

2.4 The precise arrangements of the segments will depend on the circumstances. However, they will probably include the following.

(a) Key accounts (public sector). Each key account will be the responsibility of a designated member of staff. Relationship marketing techniques might be relevant here.

(b) A sales team for the corporate sector.

(c) A sales team for the domestic sector.

2.5 To improve effectiveness, the sales and marketing teams should be integrated, so that all the elements of the marketing mix are managed effectively.

Suggested answers

2.6 A further aspect of analysing 'where we are now?' is to analyse current performance in each of these segments, once they have been identified. This will take a considerable amount of time, as the information will need to be collected and analysed.

2.7 Once this analysis has been done, efforts can be made to compare competitors' performance in these key areas. This will give an idea as to the size of the mountain to be climbed. It will also have a motivational impact: the firm can aim to do at least as well as its competitors. This will also give some idea as to standards of performance.

2.8 Suggested performance measures include:

   (a) number of leads generated
   (b) conversion rates (leads into sales)
   (c) degree of repeat business
   (d) customer satisfaction, as surveyed
   (e) selling cost per sale
   (f) analysis of sales people's time (time spent travelling, or time spent with customers)
   (g) qualitatively, an assessment of further selling opportunities per customer.

2.9 To improve productivity, other marketing effort should be directed to support the sales team. Leads can be generated by telesales and direct mail.

2.10 A suitable marketing information system can be set up to analyse existing and potential customers.

2.11 The effectiveness of the sales effect needs monitoring:

   (a) set objectives for some of the key ratios established
   (b) monitor their achievement.

19 TIME MANAGEMENT

(a) *Handling the situation*

   (i) It is important to review the context of the problem. The team member has been recently promoted. It is likely that he is learning the ropes of the new job, and that he is still climbing a learning curve in both the technical content of the job and in any new managerial skills.

   (ii) The team member is clearly committed to the job, hence the overtime, and to the profession, hence his ambitions to study for the CIM examination. The fact he is working overtime indicates that he is aware of the new pressures, and he will already be feeling embarrassed or guilty about the missed deadlines.

   (iii) That said, we should clarify that his working habits are not the result of poor job design, involving too much work. This should be investigated.

   (iv) Also, we must be sure that he has been properly briefed and given suitable training in the new position. The silly errors for example might be easily rectified by new procedures or training.

   The approach taken must be sensitive to this situation. There is absolutely no need for any disciplinary proceedings to take place. These will almost certainly cause even greater stress than warranted, and it is unlikely that they will be effective as a first step at improving performance. A counselling approach is needed. He was promoted because it was felt he was up to the job, and so the management task must be to help him realise his potential, not penalise him for silly errors and missed deadlines, even though these must be cured.

(b) *Improving time management skills*

   If the situation arises because the new team member is not up to speed with the new job and is still on a learning curve, he needs to be supervised more closely, and perhaps some of his tasks can, for a short period, be given to someone with more experience. If, however, he has not adjusted his self-management habits, a different approach should be taken, as suggested in below.

(i) The manager should discern how the team member approaches his work, to see if he tries to plan. Any obvious inefficiencies should be pointed out to him.

(ii) He might need specific training in time management skills and he can be instructed in various techniques to manage his time.

(iii) He should be encouraged to assess which of his tasks are urgent and which are merely important for the time being, so as to reduce the number of urgent tasks which become critical and then which fail to be done on time.

(iv) He should be encouraged to draw up a timetable for each month, and an activity schedule (a 'to do' list) for each day.

(v) Certain project management techniques can be useful. He could learn how to plan and analyse a task into its distinct components: he would then know what had to be done, and in what order. He could set himself intermediate deadlines as to when the subcomponents of each task should be achieved. He would then be aware at an early stage of any problems, and so he could ask for help.

(vi) It may be the case that he has not got used to the idea of delegating work to others, and so he might be taking on too much work instead. He can be encouraged to delegate, and perhaps can be offered specific advice on how to do so. This also requires time management skills, because it involves reviewing and controlling the time of others.

(vii) Any skills gaps should be rectified by sending him a training course.

(viii) Although this will disappoint him, he should be requested to defer for a few months the beginnings of his CIM studies, until he is on top of the job, and until he does not need to work so late.

20 TRAINEES

> *Tutorial note.* The specification has been prepared on the assumption that the trainees will become marketing managers, reporting to the managing director.

(a) Job characteristics and competences for graduate trainee as the basis of a job specification.

Sometimes these would be included in a personnel specification.

PERSONNEL SPECIFICATION: Trainee Marketing Manager

	Essential	*Desirable*	*Contra-indicated*
Physical attributes	Clear speech Well-groomed Good health	Age 21-25	Age over 25 Chronic ill-health
Attainments	2 'A' levels	Degree (any discipline) Marketing training 2 years' experience in supervisory post	No work experience
Intelligence	High verbal intelligence		
Aptitudes	Good with people Attention to detail Creativity Analytical abilities (problem solving) Able to learn		No mathematical ability Low tolerance of technology
Interests		Social: team activity	Time-consuming hobbies
Disposition	Team player Persuasive Tolerance of pressure and change	Initiative	Anti-social Low tolerance of responsibility
Circumstances		Located in area of office	

These can be justified as follows.

Suggested answers

Physical attributes: marketers are communicators, and issues of spoken and body language are relevant to clients.

Attainments. Basic numeracy and literacy are essential for a manager. A driving license might also be essential, if the trainees will be visiting clients, or if, during their period of training, they are expected to be involved with field sales or client visits.

Intelligence: a high verbal intelligence is needed in order to communicate marketing messages effectively and to understand feedback. This does not mean that the marketing trainee should be a walking thesaurus. However an ability to use language effectively, in communication with management and customers, is essential. Clearly, as the company is a manufacturing firm, the trainee should be able to explain the company's products and justify them in terms of the benefits they will bring to customers.

Aptitudes. Learning ability is essential in any good trainee. They have not been recruited for skills they have already, but their ability to learn new ones, both professionally and socially. They must be able to learn the job and to get on with clients. Creativity and analytical problem solving abilities are necessary to understand problems and to offer solutions to them, and also to bring a broader and wider understanding to any particular issues: lateral thinking skills can be helpful.

Personal interests can be a minefield. Some sports for example can indicate teamworking abilities and interests, as can playing a musical instrument (in a band or orchestra). Similarly, scholastic pursuits may indicate enjoyment of ideas or debates with other people. Hobbies should not be so time consuming that they impede the real functions of the job.

Disposition. The graduates are being groomed for management positions, so they have to be able to show initiative, anticipate and manage change, and be prepared to be responsible and accountable.

Circumstances. Being located near the office means that the trainees do not tire themselves out through commuting, and are not too vulnerable to traffic jams or strikes.

(b) The indicative timetable below is reproduced from the answer guidelines supplied by the senior examiner.

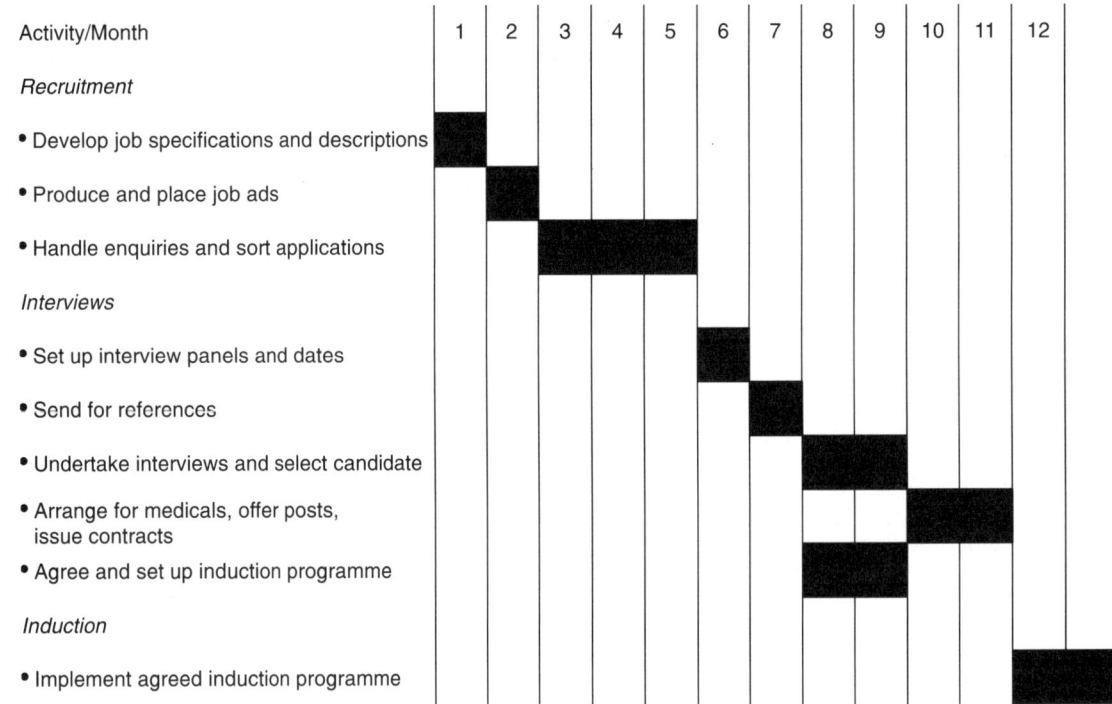

The guideline indicates both the steps that should be taken and also the timetable over which they will be taken. Note that the outline schedule indicates the timetable over which the activities will be conducted, not necessarily their duration in terms of manager hours. For example, the job will be advertised for a month, but it should not take a month's worth of manager hours to draft the advertisement. On the other hand, the firm might obtain many applications, and may interview large numbers of candidates to whittle down to a short list from which to select the final three.

A budget for the process might include the following.

Suggested answers

- Job specifications and descriptions: 1 person week (35-40 hours)
- Advertisement design and placement: 3 person days (21-24 hours)
- Enquiries, sorting applications, and planning interviews: perhaps 1 person week (35-40 hours)
- Interviewing: this depends on how many candidates are interviewed. If we assume that 20 are interviewed for two hours each, a further six are selected for a second interview of, say, three hours each and say that the final choice takes 7 hours for managers to make up their mind, this implies that the process takes 40 + 18 + 7 = 65 hours.
- References and arranging medicals: 2 person days (14-16 hours).
- The induction program will depend on how much training and management involvement is required. Let us say that of managers' time, 70-80 hours are needed.

The total therefore is between 240 and 265 hours. At, say, £40 per hour, the cost works out at £10,600 in management time alone, to which can be added say £3,000 on other expenses such as advertising, rail fares, hotel bills etc.

21 DETERIORATION

(a) *Options to tackle problems*

The two issues outlined are:

(i) poor performance
(ii) poor motivation.

We cannot simply assume that if people are poorly motivated that they will perform badly or that standards will fail. It may just be the case that they are prepared to work adequately, but that they are not bothered that their performance should get better.

The options the new manager believes to be available are perhaps determined by the his or her basic view of human nature.

(i) If the new manager holds a Theory X view of human nature, that people (apart from managers, of course) are naturally workshy, childish shirkers, then the team will be subject to detailed control over its performance, and there will be strict hierarchies. Dissent will not be tolerated. The danger of this approach is that, if the manager takes detailed control, he or she will have to take responsibility for everything that goes wrong, and will probably be overloaded. Morale certainly will not improve; most adults prefer to be treated as such.

(ii) If the new manager holds a Theory Y attitude, that people can find work satisfying in some way and welcome responsibility, he or she will probably be more concerned to deal with the overall welfare of the team. Measures might include:

(1) informal chats with all team members, especially the failed internal candidates, about their concerns, although it will take a while for the new manager to be trusted

(2) team meetings to set objectives and plans, and to have ideas discussed (eg brainstorming sessions)

(3) motivation schemes (eg some form of celebration if targets are exceeded)

(4) group team activities if this is what people would like to do

(5) regular meetings

(6) accession to reasonable requests.

It is quite possible that these very measures of participation will increase people's motivation if they are felt valued, appreciated and that their views matter.

(b) *Deciding the best approach*

The manager should take care to identify which factors leading to the deterioration are under the team's control, and which are not. It may be the case that an external factor is causing both the poor morale and the poor performance. Examples could be:

(i) a lack of resources

(ii) poor management. This latter point would be supported by the fact that there has been uncertainty as to whom is to run the team, and the team may not be mature enough, as it

Suggested answers

were, to run itself. On the other hand, the management style and practices of the previous boss may have been the cause of the poor performance.

In any case the situation must be investigated, in a non-confrontational way, to see if there any obvious matters which can be sorted out.

Once this has been done, the manager should have detailed discussions with team members, to discuss work programmes, their views as to possible improvements, and their ideas for enhancing performance.

Finally, the manager needs to set up feedback systems to monitor improved performance against new targets and to take corrective action.

22 QUALITY PRESENTATION

Tutorial note. Below we reproduce the senior examiner's answer guidelines. Although very thorough, it is not necessarily a full answer, but it indicates the kind of issues and views the examiners might expect to be covered.

Background: the appraisal scheme

(a) The Board has agreed to implement a company wide programme of appraisals as part of our ongoing drive for quality.

(b) We need to recognise that this is a change and is likely to be resisted by some or all staff unless the benefits to them are clearly presented. Appraisals can appear to be a threat.

Objective

To have successfully introduced the appraisal scheme within 18 months.

Strategy

(a) We need to take care how we present or position this scheme to the staff

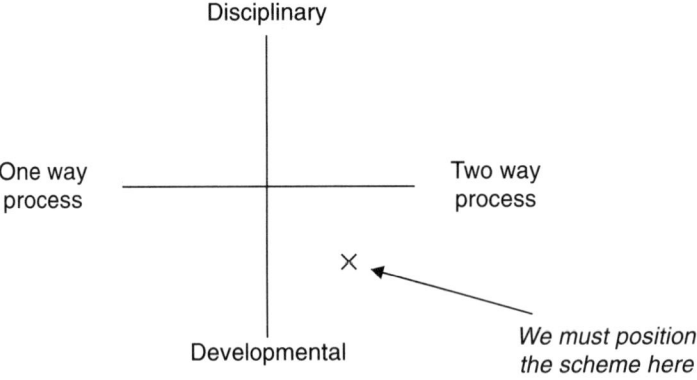

(b) It is important that is not seen as confrontational/disciplinary or 'one way'.

(c) We need to identify the various segments within our workforce, who may have similar worries or interests regarding the scheme:

    (i)   managers
    (ii)   production staff
    (iii) customer contact staff.

(d) It is possible that different age groups of staff will respond differently and so they should be targeted on this basis. Those involved in influencing or advising staff need to be identified and targeted including trade union representatives, staff committee members and so on. Identifying and using informal as well as formal communication networks will be important.

The plan

(a) The product is our appraisal scheme, so the features and benefits it offers must be clearly identified for the staff. Benefits to them include:

    (i)   personal development
    (ii) two way communication

Suggested answers

      (iii)   the opportunity to influence corporate/departmental policy
      (iv)   quantified objective feedback on performance in a structured way
      (v)   an agreed set of procedures.

(b) *Promotion.* Successful implementation depends on our communications being co-ordinated and effective.

    (i)   Staff briefings could be co-ordinated so the scheme is launched simultaneously with them.

    (ii)   Advance information and discussions with the unions should ensure their endorsement and support.

    (iii)   Written details can be circulated to all staff, enclosed in their pay advice notification.

    (iv)   Notice boards can be used for poster selling scheme benefits.

    (v)   Members of the personnel team should operate an enquiry hotline, handling personal enquiries for the first weeks following announcement of when the first appraisals are conducted.

(c) *Price.* There is a price staff are being asked to pay, and we need to recognise they are giving their time, support and trust if they buy this scheme.

(d) Value for money has to be evident. We should ensure adequate resources for staff development exist to support development in areas of agreed need.

(e) Training to ensure all participants get the maximum out of the process must be in place before the beginning of the scheme.

(f) Place. When and where will information and training about the scheme be available? They must be coordinated across the company to avoid rumour and misinformation.

Control

Research, either informal or formal can be undertaken to assess and monitor staff attitudes before and after appraisals have been conducted.

Monitoring of some key indicators over time would also be helpful:

(a) changes in the number of training days
(b) proportion of internal promotions
(c) improved measures of efficiency.

A budget training and staff time to prepare for and undertake appraisals will be needed. Quantification of this would depend on staff numbers. An allowance of about £4 per head should provide for internal promotion of the scheme.

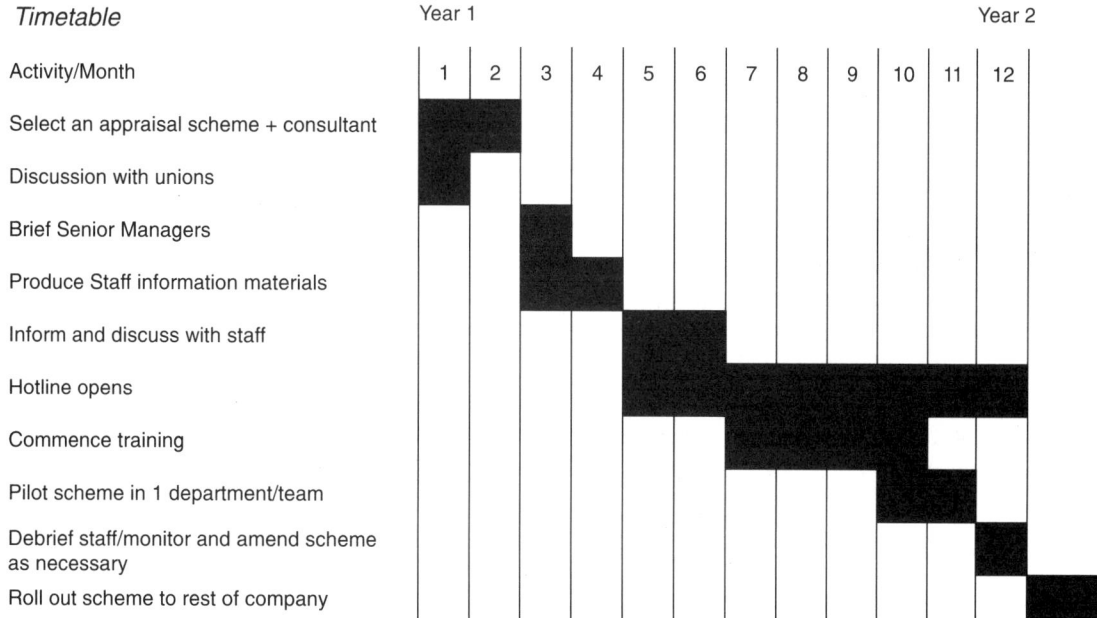

Suggested answers

23 RELATIONSHIP MARKETING

Relationship marketing is a broad term covering newer approaches to a firm's dealings with its customers. It is sometimes distinguished from transactions-orientated marketing. The difference between them perhaps can be stated that transactions-based marketing is about winning a sale whereas relationship marketing is more about building a relationship in which the customer becomes a client.

Uses of relationship marketing

The underlying justification of relationship marketing is that it is assumed that repeat business from existing customers is generally cheaper than winning new business. For example, a hotel with a regular visiting clientele needs advertise less frequently and less expensively for guests than a hotel with no such loyalty from customers.

Furthermore, relationship marketing might be entertained as an approach to get more business from existing customers. Banks have expanded their product ranges from current account to include mortgages, pensions and insurance. These are sold to existing customers (perhaps on the basis that customers are in a relationship with the bank, whether they like it or not).

The implications for relationship marketing are significant for customer service issues: a customer complaint dealt with effectively can improve the customer's view of the firm.

Relationship marketing can also be employed in an industrial context, and arguably might be regarded as essential in an environment where customers are demanding higher quality source components, and where just in time deliveries are expected. All this indicates that suppliers have to attune their processes and products more precisely to customer needs, in the hope that the relationship will become hard to break. Relationship marketing and TQM are not identical, as TQM has important implications for the organisation of the production process not related to marketing activities or customers, but they are relevant to each other.

A long term relationship can be better for both parties in that they can help solve each other's problems, or suggest improvements to products or processes of mutual benefit. The greater security of the long term approach enables a sharing of information.

Advantages and disadvantages for customer

The main advantages for the customer is that there is less need to search for new suppliers, and this can save on administration. Supply is likely to be secure, and the customer has more control over certain aspects of the supplier's marketing mix (particularly with regard to product specification and distribution). Furthermore, some of the advantages of in-house production can be provided by an external supplier, thereby saving costs. At the same time, if the supplier has the inconvenience of having to source for JIT production, it means that there is security as compensation.

The disadvantages can be both behavioural and financial.

(a) It is possible that long term business relationships can develop into long term personal relationships, and clan loyalties can develop. In itself this is not bad thing, if it means better trust and communication, but any hard decisions, such as to sever the relationship, can be personally stressing.

(b) Furthermore, there are security problems, as information might seep from the supplier firm for the benefit of other customers.

(c) The customer might end up paying more, in price terms, than under the old arrangement. Again there might be compensations (lower warehousing costs, in case of JIT, lower waste in the case of TQM and quality assurance), and they might not always be quantifiable. There are however circumstances where the best business decision is to buy on price.

The relationships can become complacent. In other words the relationship may not be flexible enough to respond to environmental change.

24 ORGANISATION STRUCTURES

No universally accepted definition of a multinational enterprise exists but for this purpose we may assume that it sells a range of products in a significant number of different countries.

A multinational enterprise (MNE) can use a wide variety of organisational structures. Classification of them tends to suggest that there are a predefined number of alternatives, of which the MNE can

Suggested answers

choose one. In fact, there is an infinite spectrum of alternatives and each MNE adopts the structure which its senior management believe will best serve its corporate objectives.

The following, or variations of them, tend to be the most common organisational structures for MNE's.

(a) *By function*

Employees in each subsidiary or branch report to their superior in the same function (such as marketing, finance, production and so forth). The senior manager in each function for each subsidiary then reports to the MNE's head office.

(b) *By area*

All functions for each geographic area of the MNE's activities report to a manager who is in overall charge for his or her own area. He in turn is likely to report to a head office manager responsible for a number of different areas.

(c) *By product line*

The MNE's structure in this case puts managers in charge of particular products, or groups of related products. The responsibilities of such managers may transcend both geographic area and function.

(d) *Matrix structure*

Managers report along more than one line of authority. If, for example, they are marketing specialists, they may report along function lines to other marketing specialist, but they may also report to managers of other disciplines along, say, geographical or product lines.

(e) *By project team*

Personnel are grouped together to meet the particular needs of a specific project. The project teams are assembled and disbanded whenever projects start and finish.

The usefulness of organisation by geographic and matrix structures

Organisations along geographic lines has been popular among MNEs for most of the twentieth century. There are two principal business situations in which this type of structure is preferred. Firstly, it tends to be used by MNEs with closely related product lines sold in similar end user markets around the world. For example oil companies and car manufacturers often use this type of structure. Secondly, at the opposite end of the spectrum, it is used when geographic units are the best way of meeting the needs of local markets. For products that are very culturally sensitive, such as foods or clothes, it can be an effective organisational structure.

A disadvantage of the geographic structure is that it does not cope well with the needs of true multinational conglomerates with very diverse product lines, since there is then little rationale for treating particular geographic areas as separate markets. The matrix structure was developed to handle the needs of very complex business operations. Neither national organisations nor product groups are treated as the single most important factor in organising the business. In theory it is a highly effective organisational structure since it brings to bear all the skills of the MNE around the world in any location where they are needed. In practice, however, it can result in organisational paralysis as managers report to two or more superiors and try to meet the sometimes conflicting demands of each. Potential for management conflict is inherent in the matrix structure. It can be minimised and harnessed in very well run companies that invest heavily in control systems. Otherwise it can create more problems than it solves by turning managers attention inwards to resolve intra-organisational problems rather than outwards to identify and meet the needs of customers.

List of key concepts and index

List of key concepts

Change management, 225
Communication, 89
Consumerism, 242
Control, 27
Culture, 21

Data warehouse, 122
Datamining, 122
Delegation, 74
Dualism, 49

Early developed country (EDC), 270
Expert system, 121

Formal organisation, 18
Former eastern bloc country (EBC), 270
Fully developed country (FDC), 270

Global company, 267
Group dynamics, 138
Groupware, 121

Intranet, 121

Leadership style, 151
Learning contract, 54
Learning styles, 58
Lesser developed country (LDC), 270

Management culture, 276
Motivation, 187

Negotiation, 128

Personal development plans, 53
Personality, 49
Prioritisation, 73

Relationship marketing, 248

Semi-developed country (SDC), 270

The functions of the manager, 18
Theory X and Theory Y, 154
Time management, 68

Index

360 degree appraisal, 206

ABB, 278
ACAS Code of Practice, 214
ACIB method of in-tray management, 70
Action plan, 29
Action planning documents, 297
Activist, 58
Adair, 140
Advertising medium, 170
Advising, 212
Africa, 270
Age structure of the population, 272
Allied Domecq, 48
Analysers, 24
Apollo, 22
Application forms, 172
Appraisal schemes, 286
Appraisal techniques, 203
Aptitude tests, 177
Asda, 108
Ashridge, 152
Ashridge studies, 151
Asia, 272
Assistant to positions, 62
Athena, 23
Autocratic style, 151

Barriers to communication, 95
Becker, 49
Behaviour, 24
Behavioural determinants, 273
Belbin, 124
Beliefs, 21
Blake and Mouton, 152
Blake's grid, 152
Body language, 103
Braddick, 60
Brainstorming, 29, 105, 140
Brand managers, 20
Brazil, 280
British Airways, 286
Budget, 27
Bureaucracy, 22
Butlins, 233
Buying behaviour, 273

Career management, 286
Champion of change, 230
Champy, 34

Change agent, 230
Checklist, 78
CIM minicases, 297
Class structure, 273
Classical school, 17
Closed question, 102
Club culture, 22
Coca-Cola, 267
Commanding, 19
Commando leader's dilemma, 47
Common markets, 269
Communication process., 93
Communications, 286
Complaints, 257
Complex man, 193
Connock, Stephen, 168
Consultative style, 151
Consumerism, 242
Contagious bias, 176
Content theories, 189
Contingency approach, 17
Continuous improvement, 250, 251
Contraction, 228
Control, 27
Controlling, 19
Co-ordinating, 19
Co-ordinator, 125
Core activities, 250
Corporate culture, 275
Cost/benefit analysis of training, 211
Counselling, 212
Countryside, 272
Creativity, 226
Crisis, 258
Crisis situations, 231
Critical path analysis, 83
Culture, 21, 275
Culture shock, 285
Culture, the environment and strategy, 23
Customer behaviour, 187
Customer care, 244
Customer relationships, 243
Customs unions, 269

Daily Telegraph, 256
Dale and Kennedy, 25
Decision sequence, 29
Decisional roles, 20
Decision-making, 28
Defenders, 24
Definition, 113

Index

Delegation, 74
Democratic style, 151
Development, 60
Dictatorial style., 151
Differences in background, 96
Dilemma of the cultures, 47
Dilemma of time horizons, 47
Dionysus, 23
Discipline, 213
Discretionary activities, 250
Distance, 284
Divestment, 228
Drucker, 36

E factors, 192
Early developed country (EDC), 270
Economic constraints, 280
Economic unions, 269
Education, 60
Educational, 280
Effectiveness of communications, 95
Egypt, 272
Elite, 270
Email, 107, 286
Employee development programmes, 54
Employee satisfaction, 194
Employment agencies, 171
Empowerment, 37, 197, 199, 252
Ethnicity, 272
Europe, 272
European Free Trade Association (EFTA), 269
European Union (EU), 269
Examination technique, 4
Excellence, 21
Existential culture, 23
Exit interviews, 216
Expatriate, 285
Experiential learning cycle, 59
Experts, 23
External consultants, 230
External environment, 31

Face to face communication, 98
Falling populations, 272
Family life cycle, 273
Family structure, 273
Faxes, 106
Fayol, 17
Feedback, 94, 202
Finisher, 125

Five point pattern of personality, 166
FMCG, 38
Followership, 150
Ford, 283
Forecast, 27
Formal groups, 139
Former Eastern Bloc Country (EBC), 270
Founder, 22
Free trade areas, 269
Freeling, anthony, 141
Fully developed country (FDC), 270

Gantt charts, 82
Geographic distribution, 272
Givens, 144
Global company, 267
Gonzalez and McMillan, 280
Grading, 203
Grapevine, 91
Grievance, 213
Grievance interview, 216
Group, 138
Group decision-making, 76
Group development, 143
Group norms, 213
Growing populations, 272
Growth, 228

Half open door, 71
Halo effect, 175
Handy, Charles, 20, 46
Harvester restaurants, 199
Herzberg, 17, 190
Hierarchy of needs, 189
Hofstede, 277
Honey and Mumford, 58, 60
Horizontal communication, 91
Human relations, 17
Human resources, 162
Huneryager and Heckman, 151
Hygiene factors, 190

Immigration, 266
Implementer (or company worker), 125
Incentive schemes, 200
Independent, 256
India, 270, 273
Induction, 182
Industrialisation, 272
Informal groups, 139

Index

Information overload, 110
Informational roles, 19
Inhibitors, 273
Innovation, 225
Insiderisation, 267
Intelligence tests, 177
Internal communication, 108
Internal marketing, 234, 235
Internal recruitment, 169
Interpersonal roles, 19
Interpersonal skills, 99
Interviewing, 101
Iran, 272

Japan, 272
Job
   analysis, 164
   centres, 171
   description, 166
   design, 195
   enlargement, 191, 196
   enrichment, 191, 195
   management, 68
   rotation, 191
   specification, 165
Johns, 68
Joining instructions, 182
Just-in-time, 253

Kanter, 36, 227
Key results, 73
Key tasks, 73
Knowledge management, 119
Knowledge workers, 33
Kolb, David, 59
Koontz, O'Donnell and Weihrich (KOW), 280

Labour, 266
Laissez-faire style, 151
Language, 286
Latin America, 272
Leadership, 22, 150
   styles, 151
   traits, 150
Learning
   contracts, 54
   cycle, 59
   organisation, 56
   styles, 58

Legal and political constraints, 280
Lesser developed country (LDC), 270, 271
Letter, 106
Local managers, 285, 286
Logica, 169
Luxury goods, 266

Macropyramid, 285
Management by exception, 110
Management by walking around, 110
Management culture, 276
Management grid, 152
Management principles, 279
Management report, 297
Managerial dilemmas, 47
Manager-subordinate relationship, 214
Market research, 247
Marketing and sales managers, 37
Marketing director, 20
Masculinity/femininity, 277
Maslow, 189
Matrix style approaches, 35
Mayo, 17
Mayo, Elton, 145
McClelland, 191
McGregor, Douglas, 154
Means of allocating resources, 27
Meetings, 103
Mega-cities, 272
Memorandum, 106
Mental models, 57
Miles and Snow, 24
Mintzberg, Henry, 19
Mission, 22
Model for change, 233
Monitor-evaluator, 125
Motivation, 187
Motivation calculus, 192
Motivator factors, 190
Motivators, 188
Multinationals, 268
Multi-skilling, 163
Munro Fraser, 166
Munro-Faure, Lesley and Malcolm, 245
Mythology, 22

National residence, 268
Negotiation skills, 254
New technology, 33
Non-verbal communication, 118

Index

North American Free Trade Agreement (NAFTA), 269
Norwich Union, 107

OJT, 61
Open questions, 102
Opportunity costs, 70
Organisation development, 230
Organisation's culture, 275
Organising, 19
Outcomes, 144
Overall assessment, 203

Participation, 197
Payment by results, 200
Pedler, Burgoyne and Boydell, 51
Peer rating, 206
Person specification, 166
Personal development logs, 54
Personal development plan, 52, 53
Personal log book, 4
Personality, 49
Peters and Waterman, 21, 49
Peters, Tom, 163
Philip Morris, 243
Planning, 19, 78
Plant, 125
Population, 271
Power culture, 22
Power-distance, 277
Pragmatist, 59
Presentation skills, 112
Prioritisation, 73
Process theories,, 189
Product life cycle, 165
Proficiency tests, 177
Project life cycle, 81
Project teams, 23
Prospectors, 24
Psychological contract, 193
Psychological tests, 177

Qualified total quality (QTQ), 250
Quality, 249, 252
Quality assurance, 254
Quality circles, 140
Quality control, 252
Quality function deployment (QFD), 251
Questions, 102

Rational-economic man, 193
Reaction decisions, 28
Reactors, 24
Recession, 33
Recruitment and selection, 162
Recruitment and training, 286
Recruitment consultant, 171
References, 179
Reflector, 58
Regional Electricity Companies (RECS), 24
Regional trading groups, 269
Relationship marketing, 248, 253
Reports, 106
Representational samples, 251
Research and development, 268
Resource-investigator, 125
Responsibility, 194
Results-orientated schemes, 203
Risks, 25
Rodger, 166
Role culture, 22

Schein, 192
Scientific decision-making, 28
Scientific management, 17
Selection testing, 177
Self-actualisation, 189, 193
Sells style, 151
Semi-developed country (SDC), 270
Service quality, 245
Services, 266
Seven point plan, 166
Sex, 272
Shaper, 125
Shell, 282
Social man, 193
Social responsibility, 242
Socio-economic status, 273
South West Trains, 259
Specialist, 125
Stakeholders, 17
Starbuck, 228
Statistical process control, 251
Stereotype, 175
Stress, 232
Structure, 22
Styles of leadership, 151
Suppliers' quality assurance schemes, 254
Support activities, 250
Sweden, 279
Systems approach, 17

Index

Target, 28
Task culture, 23
Taylor, FW, 17
Team briefings, 91, 105
Team development, 143
Team meetings, 91
Team roles, 124
Team worker, 125
Teams, 138
Technological dependency, 271
Teleconferencing, 103
Telephone, 103
Tells style, 151
Test battery, 177
The assessment report, 203
The experiential learning cycle, 59
The selection interview, 174
Theorist, 58
Theory X, 154
Theory Y, 154
Time management, 68, 78
Total quality management (TQM), 38, 250, 252
Trade, technical or professional journals, 170
Training, 60, 207
   needs, 202, 209
      programme, 285

Trust-control dilemma, 47
Tuckman, 143

Uncertainty-avoidance., 277
Unfair dismissal, 213
USA, 272

Valence, 192
Value chain, 267
Values, 21
Visible artefacts, 22
Volvo, 279
Vroom, 192

Welfare officer, 213
Whitbread, 209
Wnek, Nicky, 142
Written communication, 114
Wrongful dismissal, 213

Yardstick, 28

Zero defects, 250
Zeus, 22

CIM Order

To BPP Publishing Ltd, Aldine Place, London W12 8AA
Tel: 020 8740 2211. Fax: 020 8740 1184
email: publishing@bpp.com
online: www.bpp.com

Mr/Mrs/Ms (Full name) _____

Daytime delivery address _____

_____ Postcode _____

Daytime Tel _____ Date of exam (month/year) _____

		7/01 Texts	9/01 Kit	Success Tapes
CERTIFICATE				
1	Marketing Environment	£18.95 ☐	£9.95 ☐	£12.95 ☐
2	Customer Communications in Marketing	£18.95 ☐	£9.95 ☐	£12.95 ☐
3	Marketing in Practice	£18.95 ☐	£9.95 ☐	£12.95 ☐
4	Marketing Fundamentals	£18.95 ☐	£9.95 ☐	£12.95 ☐
ADVANCED CERTIFICATE				
5	The Marketing Customer Interface	£18.95 ☐	£9.95 ☐	£12.95 ☐
6	Management Information for Marketing Decisions	£18.95 ☐	£9.95 ☐	£12.95 ☐
7	Effective Management for Marketing	£18.95 ☐	£9.95 ☐	£12.95 ☐
8	Marketing Operations	£18.95 ☐	£9.95 ☐	£12.95 ☐
DIPLOMA				
9	Integrated Marketing Communications	£18.95 ☐	£9.95 ☐	£12.95 ☐
10	International Marketing Strategy	£18.95 ☐	£9.95 ☐	£12.95 ☐
11	Strategic Marketing Management: Planning and Control	£18.95 ☐	£9.95 ☐	£12.95 ☐
12	Strategic Marketing Management: Analysis and Decision (9/01)	£25.95 ☐	N/A	£12.95 ☐

SUBTOTAL £ _____

POSTAGE & PACKING

Study Texts

	First	Each extra	
UK	£3.00	£2.00	£
Europe*	£5.00	£4.00	£
Rest of world	£20.00	£10.00	£

Kits/Success Tapes

	First	Each extra	
UK	£2.00	£1.00	£
Europe*	£2.50	£1.00	£
Rest of world	£15.00	£8.00	£

Grand Total (Cheques to *BPP Publishing*) I enclose a cheque for (incl. Postage) £ _____

Or charge to Access/Visa/Switch

Card Number _____

Expiry date _____ Start Date _____

Issue Number (Switch Only) _____

Signature _____

We aim to deliver to all UK addresses inside 5 working days. A signature will be required. Orders to all EU addresses should be delivered within 6 working days.

All other orders to overseas addresses should be delivered within 8 working days.

* Europe includes the Republic of Ireland and the Channel Islands.

CIM – Advanced Certificate: Effective Management for Marketing (7/01)

REVIEW FORM & FREE PRIZE DRAW

All original review forms from the entire BPP range, completed with genuine comments, will be entered into one of two draws on 31 January 2002 and 30 July 2002. The names on the first four forms picked out on each occasion will be sent a cheque for £50.

Name: _____   Address: _____

_____

How have you used this Kit?
(Tick one box only)
☐ Self study (book only)
☐ On a course: college_____
☐ With BPP Home Study package
☐ Other _____

Why did you decide to purchase this Kit?
(Tick one box only)
☐ Have used companion Kit
☐ Have used BPP Texts in the past
☐ Recommendation by friend/colleague
☐ Recommendation by a lecturer at college
☐ Saw advertising in journals
☐ Saw website
☐ Other _____

During the past six months do you recall seeing/receiving any of the following?
(Tick as many boxes as are relevant)
☐ Our advertisement in the *Marketing Success*
☐ Our advertisement in *Marketing Business*
☐ Our brochure with a letter through the post
☐ Our brochure with *Marketing Business*
☐ Saw website

Which (if any) aspects of our advertising do you find useful?
(Tick as many boxes as are relevant)
☐ Prices and publication dates of new editions
☐ Information on product content
☐ Facility to order books off-the-page
☐ None of the above

Have you used the companion Practice & Revision Kit for this subject?   ☐ Yes   ☐ No
Have you used the companion Success Tapes for this subject?   ☐ Yes   ☐ No

Your ratings, comments and suggestions would be appreciated on the following areas.

	Very useful	Useful	Not useful
Introductory section (How to use this text, study checklist, etc)	☐	☐	☐
Setting the Scene	☐	☐	☐
Syllabus coverage	☐	☐	☐
Action Programmes and Marketing at Work examples	☐	☐	☐
Chapter roundups	☐	☐	☐
Quick quizzes	☐	☐	☐
Illustrative questions	☐	☐	☐
Content of suggested answers	☐	☐	☐
Index	☐	☐	☐
Structure and presentation			

	Excellent	Good	Adequate	Poor
Overall opinion of this Text	☐	☐	☐	☐

Do you intend to continue using BPP Study Texts/Kits/Success Tapes?   ☐ Yes   ☐ No

Please note any further comments and suggestions/errors on the reverse of this page.

  Please return to: Kate Machattie, BPP Publishing Ltd, FREEPOST, London, W12 8BR

REVIEW FORM & FREE PRIZE DRAW (continued)

Please note any further comments and suggestions/errors below.

FREE PRIZE DRAW RULES

1. Closing date for 31 January 2002 draw is 31 December 2001. Closing date for 31 July 2002 draw is 30 June 2002.

2. Restricted to entries with UK and Eire addresses only. BPP employees, their families and business associates are excluded.

3. No purchase necessary. Entry forms are available upon request from BPP Publishing. No more than one entry per title, per person. Draw restricted to persons aged 16 and over.

4. Winners will be notified by post and receive their cheques not later than 6 weeks after the relevant draw date. List of winners will be supplied on request.

5. The decision of the promoter in all matters is final and binding. No correspondence will be entered into.